104

6

Dick Francis

Also by Graham Lord

NOVELS

Marshmallow Pie
A Roof Under Your Feet
The Spider and the Fly
God and All His Angels
The Nostradamus Horoscope
Time Out of Mind
A Party to Die For
Sorry, We're Going to Have to Let You Go

AUTOBIOGRAPHY

Ghosts of King Solomon's Mines

BIOGRAPHY

Just the One: The Wives and Times of Jeffrey Bernard
James Herriot: The Life of a Country Vet

Dick Francis

A Racing Life

GRAHAM LORD

LITTLE, BROWN AND COMPANY

A *Little, Brown* Book

First published in Great Britain in 1999
by Little, Brown and Company

Copyright © 1999 by Graham Lord

PICTURE CREDITS
4: Ray Studios Ltd; 7: Margaret Clark;
9: Margaret Lindsay; 10: Panora Ltd; 11: Christopher Bond;
13, 15: Jane Owen; 14, 20, 22, 23, 29, 30: Express Newspapers;
16, 18, 19, 21: Alpha; 17, 26, 32: Topham Picturepoint;
24, 25, 27, 28, 31: Solo Syndication Ltd;
33, 34, 35: Graham Lord

A CIP catalogue record for this book
is available from the British Library.

ISBN
HARDBACK: 0 316 64855 8
C-FORMAT: 0 316 85148 5

Typeset in Palatino by
Palimpsest Book Production Limited,
Polmont, Stirlingshire
Printed and bound in Great Britain by
Clays Ltd, St Ives plc

Little, Brown and Company (UK)
Brettenham House
Lancaster Place
London WC2E 7EN

For the other Jules Lewis,
Julian,
copain and cupid,
with affection and gratitude

CONTENTS

Dick Francis

Weighed Out

Dick Francis always wanted his wife Mary's name to appear as co-author on the covers of the Dick Francis racing thrillers because she played a much greater part in writing them than has ever been acknowledged, but she would never allow it. 'I want you to have the credit,' he told her in front of me at their home in Berkshire in 1973 – 'you will give people the wrong impression,' she said – and in the acknowledgements in his autobiography, *The Sport of Queens*, he thanked her 'for more than she will allow me to say.'

Dick always said he was a horseman rather than a writer, had left school at fifteen after a decidedly racketty education, and had never shown much interest in books, reading or writing, whereas the shrewd, highly intelligent Mary had always been an avid reader and writer, had had an excellent education, had won a degree in French and English at the age of nineteen after just two years' study instead of three, and had worked for a publisher.

Dick's oldest surviving friend, Vernon Heaver, who has known him ever since they went to school together at the age of six, told me when I asked whether Dick had ever been good at English or writing stories at school: 'No no no – not at all. I think his wife Mary was the main one behind him writing books.' At a racing dinner in the 1980s a journalist friend of mine asked

Dick's brother Doug whether he had read Dick's latest thriller. Doug looked at him as if he were an idiot. 'Why would I want to do that?' he said. 'He couldn't write at school and he can't write now.'

Kath Walwyn, the widow of the royal racehorse trainer Fulke Walwyn and a close friend of the Francises for more than forty years, told me:

> Mary's very brainy. I would think that he would do the racing research and she would do the actual writing. That's probably it: he gets the ideas and she would do the writing, because I can't quite see Dick doing the writing, actually.

So did Mary really write the books, not Dick? Several employees of Michael Joseph, the British publishers of the Dick Francis books, wondered if she did, and Olivia Kahn, who was for thirty years a publisher's reader for the New York firm of Harper and Row, which published seventeen of the Dick Francis novels in the USA, all edited by her sister, Joan Kahn, told me:

> Joan got letters from Dick, and the person who wrote those letters could not in my view have been the person who wrote the books. I can't think of any other situation in which this – *deception* is the wrong word – in which this kind of *collaboration* was kept under cover.

Many authors also doubted whether Dick could have written the books. 'I wondered, I must confess,' the Francises' novelist friend Gavin Lyall told me. Tim Heald, a former chairman of the Crime Writers' Association, told me: 'When I interviewed Dick once he was frightfully nice but it was impossible to get much out of him even about his own books.'

'Everybody's heard the rumours,' I was told by the crime novelist and Francises' friend Margaret Yorke. 'I think we all knew,' said another crime writer friend, Gwen Butler. 'Of course his was the selling name at the beginning but we all did know it. Yes. We did know. I knew she was the power behind the books.' She added with a laugh: 'I didn't talk writing to Dick: he wouldn't have responded very much, bless him!'

The distinguished crime novelist and critic H. R. F. Keating, who wrote for many years for *The Times*, told me: 'Mary has a considerable share in writing the books. She said so to me once years ago under a terrible oath of secrecy. I think it would be great for her to get the recognition at last.'

Karen Geary, who was the Publicity Director at Michael Joseph in the early 1980s, said: 'I always got the feeling that Mary was the one holding the reins.' Euan Cameron, an MJ Publicity Manager in the mid-1960s, remembered that whenever Dick came into the office

> Mary came too and you had to pay as much attention to her as you did to her husband. Peter Hebdon, the Managing Director, would make sure that everyone paid a lot of attention to Mary. I do remember feeling that she would get very difficult if you paid too much attention to Dick and lionised him. She took a back seat as far as the outer world was concerned but not inside Michael Joseph.

When I interviewed the Francises in 1980 Dick was so fulsome in praise of Mary's literary talents that I said that he made it sound as if it were she, not he, who actually wrote the books. There was a long, embarrassed pause. 'I'm just his researcher and adviser,' said Mary. But late that evening, Wednesday 30 July, she telephoned me at home to beg me to be discreet when I wrote the interview. I promised I would and then asked if she did in fact write the books under Dick's name. She said:

> That's an impossible question to answer. Yes, Dick would like me to have all the credit for them but believe me, Graham, it's much better for everyone, including the readers, to think that he writes them because they're taut, masculine books that might otherwise lose their credibility. *Please* don't mention it in your article.

I did not, of course, though I made an immediate note of the conversation and in the article itself I went as far as I could in praising her huge contribution to the books. But that was twenty years ago, when the success of any future books might still have been damaged. Now that Dick has announced that the 1999 novel, *Second Wind*, will be the final one, the time has come for Mary's part in their incredible success to be fully acknowledged at last, which is why a biography of Dick Francis must tell his wife's life story as well. It is surely time that Mary Francis emerged from her husband's shadow to be given full credit at last for her part in writing all those beautifully crafted bestsellers that were published under his name.

Many people refuse to believe the rumours. 'Don't fall into that trap,' the trainer Tim Fitzgeorge-Parker warned me:

> It's a complete joint effort. Dick thinks up the plot, they then mull it over between them, they then go off on location for maybe six months, and then they rough out something. Mary will write so much, Dick will go away into his ivory tower – he used to sit in a boat at one time – and he'll go right through it and change it here and change it there and change it there, then it goes back to Mary, then it goes back to Dick, and eventually on April 1st they have a book.

It sounds a novel way to write a novel.

Elaine Mellor, the wife of ex-champion jockey Stan Mellor and a friend of the Francises for many years, told me:

> It's strange, this myth. I know that Mary was and still is a tremendous help, a great sounding board and researcher, but it's Dick's inspirations and it's he who actually struggles to put the words on the paper. She plays a major part but she isn't actually the one who writes it.

'There's no doubt whatsoever that Mary had a great deal to do with the books but I don't think she could have written them,' I was told by Sheila Murphy, who was Publicity Manager at Michael Joseph from 1984 to 1987. 'Dick is such an honourable, transparent man that he wouldn't have carried off all the interviews and publicity, signings and everything, unless he felt that he had a right to it.'

And the racing journalist Tom Forrest, who worked with Dick for sixteen years at the *Sunday Express*, told me:

> Dick has always said that there was a lot of teamwork. He's never done anything other than acknowledge that Mary's a part of it. She's a very bright lady indeed, but there's a difference between acknowledging Mary's partnership and in any way weakening Dick's position.

In any case, even if Mary was in fact 'Dick Francis' and Dick himself was just a 'ringer' – does it really matter? If that were so then their double bluff was a magnificent and hilarious hoax, a wonderfully funny practical joke. If all those macho, horsey novels were not in fact written by a scarred, gnarled male jockey but by a beautiful woman who was actually nervous of horses, it is difficult to resist a chuckle at our own expense – let alone a guffaw at the expense of all those literary critics who kept insisting knowingly over the years that the Dick Francis books were so beautifully paced because their author had once had to pace his races so perfectly. If Dick did indeed have his tongue in his cheek throughout all of those scores of interviews he gave and all those speeches he made – and if Mary was secretly grinning as she watched him – theirs was the most amusing literary camouflage since Marian Evans pretended to be George Eliot. And if it is indeed all true then it also seems wonderfully appropriate that, just at the very time that modern feminism was blossoming in Britain, the most popular British adventure writer of the second half of the twentieth century, 'Dick Francis', should in fact have been a woman disguised as a man.

None of which should detract at all from the books themselves or from any account of Dick and Mary's lives, for it is a wonderfully warm, inspiring love story of more than half a century of partnership and devotion. The truth about how the books were written, whatever it is, should not in any way tarnish the huge pleasure that the 'Dick Francis' novels have given to millions of readers all over the world.

CHAPTER 1

Starter's Orders

(1920–24)

D ick Francis was destined by his genes to become a champion
jockey. Born in 1920 into the rural Welsh gentry in a beautiful old farmhouse in a remote corner of south-western Wales,
in the wilds of Pembrokeshire, he came from a line of Welsh
gentlemen horsemen. His father, Vince, was a distinguished
show rider, jockey, horse dealer and manager of several hunting
stables, and had himself as a young man ridden over the daunting
Grand National steeplechase course at Aintree. His grandfather,
Willie Francis, a farmer, had also been an amateur jockey and
had won numerous point-to-points and steeplechase races. His
great-uncle Robert Harries was also a jockey and Master of the
Carmarthenshire Hounds. On the other side of the family Dick's
maternal grandfather, Willie Thomas, was a fine rider who bred
hunters and rode to hounds at least twice a week, and Dick's
maternal great-uncle, George Phelps, had been a Master of the
South Pembrokeshire Foxhounds. So how could Dick himself
have become anything but a horseman?

He was born on 31 October 1920 in the middle bedroom of three
on the first floor of his mother's childhood home, Coedcanlas,
one of the oldest farmhouses in south-west Wales, a house

without electricity or gas that was lit by candles, oil lamps and flickering log fires. Coedcanlas was his grandfather Willie Thomas's impressive but isolated old stone-and-slate country house high on a hillside looking south-west across the benign winding estuary of the Cleddau River where it meanders down through silent wooded hills towards the sunset and the Atlantic Ocean. It was an idyllic place to be born, an enchanted land of wood and water, oak and ash, orchids and bluebells, of herons, kingfishers and woodpeckers, of badgers and otters. It is a place that Merlin would recognise – a place with a whiff of magic.

Dick's tall, slim, elegant thirty-year-old mother, Catherine, who was always known as Molly – her second name was Mary – had been married to Dick's father for five years and already had a four-year-old son, Douglas. It was five weeks before anyone bothered to register Dick's birth, when he was given the names Richard Stanley. Considering that Doug and Dick were both to live far longer than three-score-years-and-ten, both boys were surprisingly sickly infants. Dick, who was small for his age until he reached his teens, nearly died of pneumonia when he was six months old and later seemed to catch almost every infection available, while Doug's childhood was haunted by such constant threats of tuberculosis that he had to avoid urban areas and spent much of his youth with his grandparents in Wales.

Their thirty-one-year-old father, Vince – who had himself been born a few miles from Coedcanlas in the deliciously named hamlet of Wedlock – had begun his riding career at the age of sixteen by working in the swish National Hunt stables of the rich local squire and racehorse trainer Lieut.-Colonel John Lort-Phillips, who lived in the castle at the village of Lawrenny, two miles from Coedcanlas, where he had trained the 1905 Grand National winner Kirkland. Vince became one of Lort-Phillips's stable jockeys and rode several winners in the early years of the century but in 1914, at the age of twenty-five, he volunteered to fight in France. Somehow he survived more than four years of the most terrible and lethal war of them all, and when he returned home in 1918 with the rank of Captain he decided that he would never make the big time as a jockey and went into horse dealing instead. By the time Dick was born, Vince – a short, skinny man with the narrow, equine face typical of a Celtic horseman – was working miles away in England as the manager of a small fifteen-box hunting stables in Berkshire in a quiet, elegant, tree-lined area of Maidenhead down by the Thames, in Chauntry Road, owned by the riding teacher Horace Smith. Smith already owned the fashionable Horace Smith's Riding School in Little Cadogan Place, London, just off Sloane Street, in Belgravia, which was in those days the biggest supplier of carriage horses, hacks and hunters in Britain and where many of the rich and famous learned to ride, including several members of the Royal Family. Vince Francis was so successful at assessing, buying and training hunters that soon after Dick was born Smith bought a much bigger yard a few miles away at Holyport, near Bray, with sixty boxes and the biggest indoor riding school in England – the same size as the indoor arena at Olympia – and there he installed Vince as the manager of W. J. Smith's Hunting Stables, named after his father, who had started the original business in the 1870s.

Even though their parents were living in Maidenhead, Dick and Doug spent much of their childhoods at Coedcanlas with their grandparents, and Dick's happiest early childhood memories were of this glorious, distant corner of rural Wales, near Beggar's Reach, on the eastern bank of the Cleddau River (pronounced *Cleth-aye*). He loved the big, whitewashed farmhouse covered with ivy and wisteria and steeped in the warm family atmosphere cultivated by his grandmother, who filled the house with her children, in-laws and grandchildren and fed them from their own farm: hams, fruit and vegetables, butter and cheese from their own dairy, homemade bread. And he loved the fields that sprawled across the nearby hills and beckoned him and

Doug out to exploration and adventure. His grandfather, who was always known as W. G., was a strict, old-fashioned Victorian but the boys loved him dearly and adored going out with him as he rode around the farm in his cart. Above all, Dick – who grew into a good-looking, jolly, open-faced little boy with wide-set eyes and a broad forehead – loved his grandfather's stables, where he played with the foals and gazed in awe at the huge hunters and dreamed of riding them one day.

Coedcanlas farmhouse was a sad grey ruin when I discovered it in the summer of 1998. Discovered is right: it is difficult to find and seems to be miles from anywhere, lost like a whispered secret deep in a lush corner of the Pembrokeshire Coast National Park, a mysterious world of forgotten forest paths, of bridleways and narrow lanes winding between high banks, of thick woods, little meadows, sudden glimpses of little streams and creeks. This part of Wales is a land of ancient ruined castles, silent mudflats, the cawing of rooks, of narrow stone bridges, sudden hidden driveways, dark tunnels of trees, sly corners, a hint of unheard whispering, the sort of place where each mile feels like ten. Coedcanlas is only four miles from the main A40 road from Haverfordwest to Carmarthen but it might as well be forty miles and 100 years away. Few of the winding lanes were properly signposted and I was lost several times in a spookily tranquil world that seemed sinister even on a sunny summer afternoon. Here there must be ghosts.

Coedcanlas farmhouse itself is surely haunted today by the spirits of Dick's grandparents, W. G. and Annie Thomas, who lie buried together two miles away in Lawrenny churchyard beneath a tall, shiny red cross. For in 1998 their warm, cosy home was sad, cold and derelict. The walls of Coedcanlas were damp and discoloured, the windows broken, ceilings collapsed, beams rotting, rubble strewn across the floors, a fireplace falling to pieces, the staircase crumbling, outbuildings ruined, the grounds overgrown. Plants were growing out of the old stone walls. The aged building cowered in the shadow of a huge tree, unloved and neglected, uninhabited since 1989 when a family of local farmers, the Merrimans, moved out and sold it to some property developers. An estate agent's board announced that the house was for sale. The asking price was 'in the region of £150,000' and you would need to spend at least another £100,000 to make it habitable again. The locals told me that they hoped that Dick might buy it himself and save it, but fortunately there was to be no need for that: in the summer of 1998 a couple from London, John and Elizabeth Gossage, bought it as a second home and started the long, expensive task of gutting and renovating it while keeping some of its special old features.

Despite the neglect of so many years it was easy to imagine how impressive Coedcanlas had once been with its three storeys, five-feet-thick stone walls, seventeenth-century beams, Georgian staircase, six bedrooms, dining room with black engraved marble surround, walled gardens, orchard, one-acre paddock, stone barn, four stone outbuildings and acres of land. Even in 1998 it was still a Grade II listed house, 'an historic Pembrokeshire house of special interest', and from the upstairs windows the magnificent view swept across fields of sheep bleating at the pretty estuary of the Cleddau and the wooded hills on the other side of the river. In its day, according to the 1997 catalogue of *Welsh Historic Monuments*, Coedcanlas had been 'a major Pembrokeshire seat' and 'a very high status building', 'a stone-built gentry house' that had been owned by the Percivals in the fourteenth century, the Butler family in the fifteenth and sixteenth and in the eighteenth by the Owens, who rebuilt it in 1718 so successfully that it was described in the nineteenth century as 'a delightful situation for a great man's residence as any in this country.'

'Oh, it was a beautiful, *beautiful* house,' I was told by eighty-year-old Mrs Edie Owen, who lived as a child just up the lane, went with Doug and Dick to the village school in Lawrenny, and still lived in a cottage about a mile away. 'The Thomases were gentry. They used to entertain people and all that and W. G. was a fine man. People looked up to him.'

W. G. employed several men on the farm, among them Mrs Owen's father, Thomas Hughes, and W. G. and Annie raised five children in the house: Griff, Stanley, Jack and Janet as well as Dick's mother, Molly. Gentry they may have been but Doug and Dick played happily with the Hughes children even though Tom Hughes was their grandfather's farmhand. 'They were better off than us and they had a nice house and furniture and lovely gardens, and a huge farm with sheep, cows and crops, but they were not snooty at all,' I was told by another of Thomas Hughes' twelve children, seventy-seven-year-old Mrs Phyllis Grace, who was eleven days younger than Dick, often played with him as a child and sat in the same class:

> I shouldn't think they were short of money but they were lovely: very nice, ordinary people. Dick and Doug would come over to play every weekend at our little three-room cottage, Sunny Hill, just up the hill. There wasn't anywhere else to go and we didn't have bicycles so we'd just play around: hide-and-seek, rounders, hopscotch.

Doug was the same age as Phyllis's elder brother Norman and 'naturally they got up to mischief,' said Edie Owen:

> Dick's mother used to shout to them from down below at Coedcanlas to come home to go to bed, but d'you think they'd go? They wouldn't move. Their poor old mother had to chase them across the fields and by the time she'd come back they'd come back up the road.

Mrs Owen remembered that Dick was

smashing looking. They were two nice boys. There was more devilment in Douglas than in Dick. When he and my brother Norman got together you didn't know what they were going to do. Mammy used to give them a smacking. Once she smacked them both because they'd caught the cat, hung it up on the line and used it as a punch ball.

Dick was only three when he was sent off for the first time to Lawrenny School, a little two-room building on the edge of the village where three teachers – two men and a woman – tried to instil the basics of English, arithmetic, geography, history and handcraft into the heads of about fifty children aged between three and fourteen, after which most would go to work on the farms or into domestic service. They did not teach the children Welsh because no one in the area spoke it: this was such an anglicised part of Wales, dominated by the English since Norman times, that it is still known as Little England Beyond Wales. It was here in Pembrokeshire that the great English royal dynasty of the Tudors was founded when King Henry VII, then plain Henry Tudor, was born just down the road behind the grim grey walls of Pembroke Castle in 1457. Even the war memorial in front of the castle lauds the greatness of England rather than that of Wales.

Lawrenny today is a quiet hamlet of small stone houses, slate roofs and a whiff of cattle dung and distinguished only by its towering twelfth-century Norman church of St Caradog and its tranquil yachting centre three-quarters of a mile down the hill at Lawrenny Quay. In the 1920s it was still dominated by the Lort-Phillipses' Lawrenny Castle, which was to be demolished after the Second World War, but it was no longer the bustling village it had once been with its huge oyster beds dating from Tudor times, its coal mines, limestone quarries, a boatyard that had built more than sixty ships in Victorian times, and a busy harbour that had seen all sorts of ships carrying all manner of goods, from timber to anthracite. By the 1920s there was little left but yet another castle on the far bank of the Cleddau river, Benton Castle, whither old Tom the ferryman would row you and his pet spaniel across in his boat.

Starting school at three may explain why Dick spent the next twelve years doing everything he could to avoid an education. He had to walk to school and back, two miles each way along lanes and across fields, even in rain, snow or when the river was flooded, which must have been an exhausting daily journey for a child so young. It is still a testing walk even for an adult. Leaving the farmhouse at Coedcanlas, you turn right along a narrow winding lane, past fields of sheep, then down a very steep hill, past a little ruined stone chapel, across a little stone bridge, up another steep hill, past a farm and fields of cattle, through some woods, turn right at the crossroads, down another hill for half a mile, across another little bridge that spans the stream and muddy creek at Garan, which is liable to flooding, and then up yet another steep hill for the final third of a mile to the school. Perhaps all that early exercise explains how Dick became so fit that in later life his battered body was able to absorb all the accidents and broken bones that he was to suffer as a jump jockey.

He started his chaotic school career on 28 June 1924, shepherded along the country lanes and across the river by the Hughes children and by Doug, who was now nearly eight and had been going to the school since he had been just three years and two months old. Doug's school career was equally erratic: the Lawrenny National School Attendance Register shows that although he started there in September 1919 he left soon after, was readmitted in September 1922, left again in December 1924, returned, and left again in July 1926.

Dick probably started playing truant right from the start: on his third day at school it poured with rain and attendance fell noticeably; it rained all the next two weeks, too, right into July;

and the week after that the school log book records lugubriously that 'weather and a little haymaking have been the cause of rather low attendance.' July 21 was 'a terrible day of weather. Violent wind and heavy rain. At 10 a.m. 22 children only present. Registration cancelled.' Ten days later the school was closed for five weeks for the summer holidays, but even after it reopened on 8 September the headmaster, Thomas Williams, was bewailing in the log book the continual bad weather and the low attendance record. Little Dick must soon have picked up the message that school was somewhere you went only if there were nothing better to do.

Yet Lawrenny School, which is now part village hall and part youth hostel, was not some dismal institution. In May 1925 a Board of Education Inspector, Mr J. Owen, wrote in his report:

> This little school of 55 children, though isolated, is pleasantly situated on the edge of a park and an arm of the sea, and it is the proud boast of the school that it has as a playground 120 acres of parkland in which the pupils are privileged to spend their recreational periods . . . In the classroom the little children are taught by a teacher of experience and resource under whose supervision the pupils make satisfactory progress. They are frank and responsive. They also write neatly and read clearly and distinctly. Their classroom has of late too been brightened considerably and made more congenial by the addition of suitable wall illustrations . . . In the main room the boys and girls receive a sound training in the fundamental subjects and their work on the whole is thoroughly done. Particularly is this so in the case of their handwriting which is exceptionally neat in appearance. A distinct improvement is noticeable too in their power of expression and their Composition exercises are becoming freer and more natural in form.

He concluded:

> A pleasant tone pervades the school and the relations existing between pupils and teachers are most happy and cordial.

The children themselves remembered their days at Lawrenny with affection. 'It was a nice school,' I was told by seventy-four-year-old Kitty Cole, who was three years younger than Dick but later used to walk to school with him, spent forty years working at Coedcanlas as a domestic and milkmaid, and in 1999 still lived nearby in the little house where she was born. 'It was a very strict school but I was happy there,' said eighty-year-old Mrs Ruth Williams, who was nearly three years older than Dick and whose aunt, Elizabeth John, was one of the teachers.

The headmaster was an utterly dedicated man who had nurtured the little school for forty-three years, sacrificing even his evenings by running evening classes. For more than fifty years he played the organ in the church a hundred yards away and later persuaded young Dick to sing in the choir, and for seventeen years he was also churchwarden there. The atmosphere of his school can be gauged from some of his entries in the school log book at the end of 1925:

> Dec 26. Held our annual School Concert. Every child in school took some part in the programme . . . The Concert was a great success and every item was most cordially received. The audience crowded the room and marked their approval of the various items with loud applause. Col Lort Phillips complimented teachers and scholars and old scholars on the success achieved.
>
> Dec 29. Hon Mrs Lort Phillips, Manager, entertained all the children and their mothers to tea, and gave the children a Christmas tree from which every child received a

nice and useful present. The children repeated the various items which formed their part of the Christmas Concert so that Hon Mrs Lort Phillips, who was unable to be present, might hear them. Mrs Lort Phillips thanked children and teachers for this and complimented all on the nice way it was carried out. A very pleasant afternoon and evening was spent. The Head Teacher thanked Mrs Lort Phillips on behalf of all and the children gave her three ringing cheers.

Six weeks later 'Mrs Pickerell, of the South Wales Band of Hope Union, visited school at 2 p.m. and gave a very interesting and instructive address on Temperance and Hygiene.' It was not by any means Mrs Pickerell's only visit to the school. Over the next few years she returned time and again to browbeat the children of Lawrenny into a life of cleanliness and sobriety, and judging by the bright-eyed rectitude of those who are still alive her harangues worked.

But Dick's first spell at Lawrenny School was about to come to an end. In February 1926 Doug left to join their parents in Maidenhead and, although he returned briefly in June, both boys left for Maidenhead again in July, when Dick was not yet six. He was still in Class 0. Both boys returned to Lawrenny School yet again at the end of the summer holidays but they left after ten days to go back to Maidenhead, where Dick was to live for the next five years, though he and Doug were both to return often to Coedcanlas.

Before they went, however, Dick reached a major milestone in his life. He was five years old and he had his first ride – on a donkey. The donkey was called Jessie and belonged to the Hughes family. 'Dick learned to ride on Jessie,' Edie Owen told me. 'She'd come to our bedroom in the mornings and start to call for us kids to get up and come out, see. She was a rare old donkey. And then she used to run with the Coedcanlas cows in the field, like. When you put the halter over her head she'd run off.'

Not with Dick, she didn't. He rode her without a saddle, partly because he had heard his father say that you learned to balance best on horseback if you rode bareback and partly because Jessie's back was too high and bony for a saddle, and soon he was persuading Jessie to jump over a low rail fence, which encouraged nine-year-old Doug to bet him sixpence that he couldn't jump the fence backwards. Dick was hoping to save enough of his pocket money to buy a toy farm and accepted the bet, pointed Jessie towards the fence, sat on her facing backwards, kicked her in the ribs, and shot straight over her rump as she took off. Refusing to be beaten, he remounted the donkey, tried again, fell off again, doggedly climbed back on again, and after falling off six times he eventually jumped the fence and won his sixpence. 'We never thought Dick would be a jockey,' said Edie Owen, but the five-year-old boy himself knew straight away. Fifty years later he wrote in his autobiography, *The Sport of Queens*, that it was in that moment that he had known for sure that he was going to be a professional horseman.

Eleven days before little Dick toddled off to Lawrenny School for the first time, the baby girl who was destined to become his wife, Mary Brenchley, was born – on 17 June 1924 – two hundred miles to the east of Coedcanlas in a quiet suburban street in New Malden, two miles east of Kingston-upon-Thames, a district of Surrey that was fast becoming just another part of the huge south-western sprawl of suburban London.

Her father, William Walter Brenchley, the son of a south-east London tobacconist from Camberwell, was nearly thirty-five and the Works Manager and director of a cigarette paper printing company. Her mother, Janet, a bride of just twelve months, was a twenty-nine-year-old Scotswoman from Glasgow, the daughter of a Congregational minister, John Mathieson Forson, who had moved south to London and was now in charge of the 500-seat Congregational Church in Malden Road, New Malden, where he lived in the Manse with his wife, Maggie. It was John Forson who christened his daughter's first baby Mary Margaret.

Dick and Mary Francis could hardly have been born in much more different places. New Malden was still lit by gas, like Coedcanlas, but it was no longer the rural spot it had been only five or six years earlier, at the end of the First World War, when it had still been a village of leafy lanes, fields, farm animals and a few hundred inhabitants. By 1924 the population was rocketting and a turmoil of new development was swiftly turning it into yet another of London's many faceless new dormitory suburbs. New housing estates were springing up everywhere: long streets and avenues with names like Acacia Grove, Poplar Gardens, Woodside Road, Meadow Hill, Knightwood Crescent; each lined with rows of identical, huddled houses with tiny gardens and pebble-dashed frontages or black-and-white mock-Tudor timbers. And the clattering trains of the Southern Railway were herding thousands of new residents into New Malden from London's Waterloo station nine miles away, most of them daily city commuters, the sort of middle-class office workers who still wore bowler hats and stiff collars to the office, would never dream of allowing their wives to go out to work, and could still afford to employ at least one live-in servant. They were people with aspirations and pretensions, and when William Brenchley bought his first house just down the road at Worcester Park he named it Crofton, after his father, Frederick Elisha Crofton Brenchley, as though his new suburban home were some great old aristocratic family mansion.

It seems odd that Mary's father did not yet have his own house when she was born, considering that he was nearly thirty-five, a company director and had waited prudently until he was nearly thirty-four before getting married. He and Janet, who was known as Netta, were still living in his father's house, Thetford Lodge, at 16 Thetford Road, and there they stayed for nearly two more years until Netta became pregnant with her second daughter, Jean, and they finally moved out into their own home at 17 Kingsmead Avenue, Cuddington, Worcester Park, three miles down the road towards Cheam. It was a large, two-storey house with a big garden in one of the many newly developed areas and the Brenchleys were to live there for twenty-two years except for those of the Second World War.

The house where Mary was born, in Selwyn Road, is no longer there and the road is a run-down little street of oddly stunted buildings, the usual pebble-dash and fake Tudor, many with discoloured paint, broken fences and overgrown gardens. But Thetford Lodge, where she spent the first two years of her life, still stands genteel on the corner of Thetford Road and Westbury Road. Half red-brick, half greyish-blue plaster, it is set in a lushly leafy garden and still looks very much like a comfortable family home. It is now a 'Rest Home for the Elderly'.

Coedcanlas and Thetford Lodge: two childhoods that were utterly unlike each other, the one remote and rural, the other deeply suburban. Yet Dick and Mary were born into families with similar standards of behaviour, respectability, gentility and expectations. Both were firmly middle-class and proud of it, both sufficiently well-off not to have to worry too much about money. Despite the huge differences between them, that was going to be enough to help give them a perfect marriage.

CHAPTER 2

Maidenhead and Worcester Park

(1925–37)

M aidenhead, on the banks of the Thames five miles from Windsor, had begun to boom as a pleasure resort in Edwardian times and by the mid-1920s was a favourite spot for crowds of day-trippers from London, twenty-six miles away. The summer countryside around the town was England at her serene best, with the Thames winding tranquil from Cookham Lock to Boulters Lock between lush meadows and the gentle wooded hills of Berkshire and Buckinghamshire. Otherwise nothing much had happened there in a thousand years – even the English Civil War had ignored it – and the most interesting thing about it was its bizarre name, which no one can properly explain. The highlight of the 1920s was the opening of a second cinema, the Rialto in Bridge Street, as a rival to the Picture Theatre in Bridge Avenue. Ten years earlier the main attraction had been the presence of Edward VII's mistress Lily Langtry, who had lived in a huge old Tudor mansion, Bray Lodge, a mile away in the village of Bray, where equally little had happened in the three centuries since its turncoat vicar had kept changing sides during the Civil War so as to suck up to whichever side seemed to be winning.

Maidenhead in the 1920s was, however, a positive metropolis compared with the spacious, bosky, stylish little hamlet of Holyport another mile south along the road to Windsor, where Dick's father ran his stables. Dick was seven when he joined his parents at Hendens Bungalow in Blind Lane, Holyport, beside W. J. Smith's Hunting Stables. Holyport had once been a thriving medieval market centre but now had only two hundred inhabitants and was so quiet that you could hear the swans think. It had a vast, eleven-acre village green with two ponds, a flock of aggressive geese, and several shops. There was a surprisingly large number of pubs for such a small village: the sixteenth-century George; the Queen; the Jolly Gardener at Moneyrow Green; and the Belgian Arms, which had until recently been called the Eagle but had had its name changed during the First World War because German prisoners-of-war had taken the pub's sign of an eagle to depict their national symbol and had saluted it whenever they marched past. Holyport was a salubrious, elegant settlement, the home of the Royal County of Berkshire Real Tennis Club, with more than a dozen lovely big houses, one of them on the site of an old mansion, Philberds House, that had once been the home of Charles II's mistress Nell Gwynne. It seems appropriate that an area called Maidenhead (and so handy for Windsor Castle) should have sheltered at least two famous royal mistresses, and it was soon to have a third: the Marquis of Milford Haven was about to buy Lynden Manor in Holyport and, according to his brother, Lord Mountbatten, it was there in 1931 that the Prince of Wales, later Edward VIII, first met his mistress, Wallis Simpson. Holyport also boasted two other titled residents, Sir Roland and Lady Adams, who lived at Plashers Mead, and a Fellow of the Royal Society, Alfred Basset, who lived at Fledborough Hall. There was a little police station (manned by Sergeant George Harris), a little post office (sub-postmaster Archibald Bennett, who was also the butcher), an elementary school for 149 boys and infants and a private prep school, Sunnyside, run by Miss Gladys Sexton. There was a district nurse, a blacksmith, a couple of grocers, a cricket club, a Wesleyan chapel and a Working Men's Institute. At the southern edge of the village, at Redstone Farm, there was even a racecourse where two three-day meetings were held in spring and autumn every year. And there were horses all over the village, scores of them, and the boy Dick fell in love with them all. There could hardly have been a better place for a future champion jockey to learn to ride.

One of the village girls, Mabel Knight, the daughter of a poor scaffolder/poacher and just seven weeks younger than Dick, published in 1983 a vivid portrait of Holyport in those days under her married name, Mabel Coppins. Judging by her account it was in the 1920s a timeless place that had changed very little in 100 years. Some of the characters she describes could have stepped out of a novel by Dickens: the lanky old grocer John Norgrove in his long white apron and untidy 'Aladdin's cave' of a shop, with its large sacks of tea and sugar and its window full of sticky sweets buzzing with wasps and bluebottles; Bob Ranger, the Pickwickian butcher with his red face, grey hair, knee-length polished gaiters and huge, nagging wife; Mr Good the Milkman, from Moneyrow Green, trundling his trolley of milk around the village to ladle it out into customers' jugs; the fishmonger who pushed his wares round in an old pram; the two weird men who slept in the pig sties; old saucer-eyed Jacey Flitter, from the Maidenhead workhouse, who wandered the village selling shoelaces and matches and frightened the children by threatening that when he died he would come back as a dog and bite them; the summer tramp with the long black hair, known locally as the Wild Man of Borneo; the two tiny old village washerwomen, the Misses Sharp, who always wore black and collected laundry in a pram; Mr Rivers, who rode around the village on an old tricycle selling sausage rolls, pork pies and cakes. Above all, says Mrs Coppins, nothing was ever hurried in

Holyport in the 1920s: 'time was not very important; everything happened in its own good time.'

She makes no mention of Dick in her book, even though she saw him around the village. Unlike the Francises, her family was extremely poor. Her boozy father was often on the dole, her mother forced to scrub floors in the big houses for a few pence, so the social gulf between Mabel and Dick was huge. While she and her poor village friends were wandering the fields collecting wild flowers, chasing rabbits or bird nesting at Spratts Hill or Blackbird Lane or near Skippets Copse, Dick was out riding. Nor did he go to the village school: his parents sent him instead to Miss Whitmore's private school in Maidenhead, perhaps realising that something needed to be done to improve his haphazard education.

'I first saw him as a small boy on a Shetland pony,' Mrs Coppins, who was still living in Holyport, told me in 1998. 'He had a round, rosy face and he was always smart, but he looked down on us. He was a bit snooty and never spoke to us. He was very smart and we were probably in rags and tatters. It was class distinction.' Other contemporaries disagreed. 'He wasn't cocky at all,' I was told by another one-time neighbour, Mrs Frankie Arkle. 'He was always very smart and very nice.' Mrs Joan Hearne, now eighty-one, a farmer's daughter, agreed. 'The Francis family was very smart,' she said. 'Dick's mother didn't ride much but otherwise they were just an ordinary, horsey, hunting family. They didn't give dinner parties or anything like that but they were popular and sociable.'

The Francises occupied an uncertain niche in the class-conscious world of English rural society in the 1920s and 1930s. All of the family, including Dick, spoke with Welsh accents and although they mixed with some very wealthy people and had a car (an Austin 7, then a Riley) and could afford to take two weeks' holiday every year, they were not in the same class as most of their rich customers. 'I wasn't accepted into high society,' Dick told Geraldine Bedell of the *Times Saturday Review* in 1991, 'but I was received into households, and people were polite enough. I was never conscious of inferiority.' Perhaps he simply never noticed any condescension. 'I was not an introspective or even particularly thoughtful child,' he told Ms Bedell.

His world was very different from that of Mabel Knight, and the only time the two made much contact was when both went hunting, Dick regularly on horseback from the age of seven and Mabel following on foot. She wrote in her book:

> Fox hunting was great fun for the children of the village, and we ourselves would run miles on foot, taking all the short cuts once we knew which way the crafty old fox was heading. Opening gates for the mounted gentry would sometimes bring in a few coppers but more often than not we'd just get a cursory 'Thank You'. The cheekiest of us would then say, 'My thank-you bag's full, sir,' and probably get something for his cheek.

The local Garth hunt would meet for the 'stirrup cup' outside the Jolly Gardener. Mrs Coppins wrote:

> How nice it was to see the meet on Holyport Green, the huntsmen in their red tunics, the nobility astride their magnificent horses and of course the hounds who led the whole array off the green, tails quivering bolt upright with excitement. Then came the unforgettable sound of the English hunting horn. Following behind came half the village on a motley collection of old bikes, intent on following the hunt over hill and dale, partly for the fun of it but mostly to try to raise a few coppers to supplement the meagre dole money, for it was the time of much unemployment.

In later years Mrs Coppins had second thoughts about the beauty of hunting, especially of stag hunting, in Holyport.

> The poor unfortunate stag . . . was brought to the Long Meadow in a funny little black van pulled by a horse. After being let out the stag was chased by a man on horseback who made sure the poor frightened creature was well on its way before the hounds and huntsmen set out after it. I don't think the stag was ever killed – at least dad said it never was. It just ran and ran until it was utterly exhausted, put back in the cart, rested, and hunted again another day. Looking back over the years it all seems so terribly cruel, but as very young children we didn't realise.

Mrs Hearne remembered the stag hunt somewhat differently. 'The tame stag that we chased time and again used to find a lake and it would sit in the middle to disguise its scent,' she laughed.

Otherwise excitements were few, traditional and decidedly rustic. In winter the village children would slide in their boots across the frozen ponds or play ice hockey with an old tin and sticks pulled from a hedge. There were regular Saturday night hops and winter film shows in the Working Men's Institute. In May there was always the crowning of the May Queen on the 1st and on the 24th the annual Empire Day celebrations. In the summer the open-air mobile cinema would turn up, park on the village green and rig up a screen beside the war memorial. There were the annual Holyport Flower Show and funfair, and Sunday School coach outings to Burnham Beeches, Wokingham or even as far as Bognor Regis, and every year the villagers would sit on sawn-off tree trunks at The Lodge to watch cricket matches at Major Martineau's private cricket ground, the Warren, where touring Australian and West Indian Test cricketers as well as

English cricket stars tramped up and down the steps of the red pavilion during the major's annual cricket week. Every year there was also a village party at the Hotel de Paris in Bray and one day a huge silver airship drifted over the village, and on 8 June 1929 there was a brief flurry of excitement in Holyport when a new airfield, Maidenhead Aerodrome, opened at the junction of Holyport and Windsor Roads. Eight-year-old Dick would almost certainly have been there that summer Saturday afternoon to watch the 'Grand Opening Display of Flying' at the airfield, perhaps even to enjoy a scary passenger flight with Captain Geoffrey de Havilland, the designer of the Moth aeroplane and head of the de Havilland Aircraft Company, by odd coincidence the very man for whom Mary Francis would work during the Second World War. Time and again the edges of Dick and Mary's lives flirted with each other even before they had met. The airfield was not a success and closed four months later, but the Prince of Wales continued to use it whenever he flew from London to see Mrs Simpson at her home in Bray. 'The Prince of Wales used to fly over the village,' I was told by Frank Clark, who spent his childhood in Holyport and occasionally cycled to school with Dick, 'and Jack West, who ran a garage in the village, would go to the field and pick him up in a taxi and take him to Mrs Simpson's place at Ferry End, down by the river.'

In the 1920s Horace Smith was kept busy in London teaching Society people how to ride, among them Lady Docker, the actresses Gladys Cooper, Evelyn Laye and Fay Compton, the artist Sir Alfred Munnings, and Edward Hulton, the owner of *Picture Post*. 'By 1925 80% of the horses in Rotten Row came from our stables,' Smith wrote in his autobiography, 'and we employed 12 riding masters and gave between 100 and 120 lessons a day. [*It was*] the leading establishment of its kind in the country.' Because Smith was so busy and planning to open several other stables around the country, he came down to Holyport only once or twice a week, so Dick's father was able to run the stables as he liked. He hired a riding master, Jack Grayston, and several nagsmen to help him train the hunters, and he encouraged his two small sons to ride whenever they wished. Starting with the smallest ponies in the yard, Dick learned to ride in the best way possible, by trial and error, and his interest in horses swiftly became a passion. Neither he nor Doug ever had a proper riding lesson, though they would eavesdrop when Jack Grayston was teaching other children and Vince would often yell instructions. 'Keep your elbows *in*!' he would bellow at Dick. 'Sit up, boy! Sit up!'

Vince was not, however, a bullying father, even though many of the Dick Francis novels were later to describe numerous terrible relationships between fathers and sons. In Dick's autobiography he always referred to Vince forbiddingly as 'Father', which the narrator of the 1997 Dick Francis novel *10-lb Penalty* admits is more formal and less affectionate than 'Dad', but when John C. Carr – who was writing a book called *The Craft of Crime* – asked him in 1982 about Vince, Dick replied: 'Yes, he was stern. But he didn't knock you about or anything, although he did give me a good hiding once and I never forgot it. But he wasn't one for giving credit . . . People used to come up to me and say, "Oh, well done, Dick, you did great things," and Father would say, "Oh, you've got another one to do tomorrow."' The fact that Dick was one of the best boy riders in Britain 'was never allowed to go to my head,' he told Geraldine Bedell. 'My father never let me be satisfied: he always pushed me to greater efforts. If I won, I was expected to assume the pony had done well. If I won riding classes, my father would criticise me as I came out of the ring.'

Yet in a foreword to the paperback edition of *Bonecrack* Dick said that Vince had been funny and affectionate. Vince certainly sounds as if he could be fun: when he went bald and young Dick asked him how he had lost his hair Vince grinned: 'It was all shot off during the war.' Dick's best friend during those years,

Vernon Heaver, told me that Dick had loved both his parents and that the Francises had been a very close family. 'His father was a very strict disciplinarian but not unkindly so,' said Mr Heaver, a retired civil servant, 'and his mother was a charming woman: a very tall, slim, Welsh woman. He adored her.'

Dick and Vernon became close friends at the end of 1927 when they were seven and joined Miss Whitmore's old fashioned little one-woman Dame school in Maidenhead on the same day: Cromer School in High Town Road, a private, fee-paying school for twenty-five boys and girls between the ages of five and ten which was run by a middle-aged spinster, Emily Whitmore, who taught all the pupils of all ages together in one room in her house. From her, for a fee of 2/6d a week, they learned reading, writing, arithmetic, history and geography. 'She was one of those grand old ladies, very old fashioned,' recalled Mr Heaver. 'She spoke perfect English and was an excellent teacher, strict but in a very kind manner, not abusive. The worst you'd ever get was a slap behind the ears – Dick often had one for being silly or larking about in class – but whenever she gave us a clip around the ear it was justified.'

Another of Dick's contemporaries at Cromer, Peggy Munday, told me:

> Miss Whitmore looked very Victorian, with high-necked blouses with little frills and thin glasses and her hair just so in a bun, and those high boots that old people wore years ago. She was marvellous, a very good, strict teacher, and if you showed any interest she really pushed you, and if you were really good she gave you these crystallized fruits. Even the boys were called by their Christian names and we even had a religious lesson in the morning: she had a funny little wireless set and we had to sing hymns and say prayers. And she had a piano so that anyone who was interested in music could play it. And I remember

her two dinner ladies, Mrs Cole and Mrs Peacock, who were very good cooks. They were two nice old ladies and they really did cook lovely dinners for us. I used to stay to lunch and they used to give us old-fashioned puddings like roly-poly and Spotted Dick. The house is still there – it's still a private house – but now they've got double-glazing and a porch.

The school had no uniform and the children wore their own clothes, 'but we envied Dick,' said Miss Munday, 'because he always came to school in riding breeches and we thought how lucky he was being involved with horses. Otherwise he was just a quiet lad. All he wanted to talk about was horses.' Cromer School had no playing field and did not provide any games or other extra-mural activities, but this hardly bothered Dick. Mr Heaver said:

> He wasn't ever involved in any sports at all, it was nothing but riding. He had no other interests, though we did go to the local cinema in Maidenhead every Saturday evening as a special treat with the Francis family's house-keeper, Irene Winnie. He didn't even collect stamps, like me. We were very close together as children – joining the same school on the same day automatically threw us together and it stuck for the rest of our lives – but I don't think he had any other friends apart from me.

Riding became such a passion for Dick that he begged his parents not to make him go to school. He hated it, could never see the point of arithmetic or history, and considered that anything that kept him away from horses was a terrible waste of time. His father would have been quite happy for him to play truant every day but his mother insisted that he went to school at least some of the time. Even so, Dick was crafty enough to dodge out of going for a couple of days each week and his average attendance was no more than three days a week. He would pretend that he was developing a temperature or that if he went to school he would pick up somebody's terrible cold, so it is no wonder that he was never to pass any exams. Nor did he show any aptitude for English or for writing stories. 'No no no, not at all,' Mr Heaver told me. 'He was not academically clever. Horses were all his life and he spent most of his time riding. He was absent from school for roughly a third of the school year and there wasn't much Miss Whitmore could do to interfere with it.'

By the time he was seven Dick was already helping to train the ponies himself, murmuring quietly and patting the nervous ones, so that soon his father started asking him whether a particular new pony was any good, or what sort of a mouth it had. Before long Jack Grayston was asking Doug and Dick to show his pupils how some particular aspect of riding should be done, and Dick became so skilful at training the ponies that Horace Smith would take the best ones back to his riding school in London, some of which were used in later years to teach the future Queen, young Princess Elizabeth, and her sister, Princess Margaret, when they started to learn to ride in the 1930s. Yet despite the boys' growing skills, Vince never allowed them to become arrogant and constantly reminded them of how much they *didn't* know and of how much better they could be if they tried. And every now and then one would fall off and be reminded not to become complacent.

Doug was sent back often to Coedcanlas because of his ill-health and his need for sea air, and Dick would join him there for the Easter and summer holidays and for Christmas, travelling alone by train from Maidenhead to Kilgetty in the care of the guard. But even in Wales they could still make a fuss of their grandfather's horses and ride poor old Jessie the donkey across the fields or harness her between the shafts of a cart to pull them around the farm.

Dick was six when he first announced that he wanted to be a jockey, and seven when he decided that he was going to win the Grand National. On the afternoon of 30 March 1928 he was playing cricket in the garden at Coedcanlas but listened with mounting excitement to the radio commentary of the National as a 100-1 outsider, Tipperary Tim, stunned the racing world by winning the race. It was only a mediocre ten-year-old gelding with a tube in its throat and ridden by a young amateur jockey, a Chester solicitor called Billy Dutton, and its unlikely victory came after thirty-five of the forty-two runners fell at the Canal Turn after being brought down by one horse, Easter Hero. It was the most catastrophic pile-up ever seen on a racetrack. Only two horses actually finished the race and even the second, Billy Barton, fell at the last fence and had to be remounted by its jockey before crossing the line. The excitement was such that little Dick swore that one day he too would take part in such a thrilling race. After that, whenever he crouched on his rocking horse, he closed his eyes and imagined that he was soaring over Becher's and the Chair and his dream of winning the National stayed with him until the end of his life. From then on, whenever anyone asked him what he wanted to be, he would always reply: 'a jockey'.

He was eight when he won his first race – apple-bobbing at a local gymkhana – and soon he was riding in the show ring to exhibit ponies that his father wanted to sell. For the next decade he spent most of every summer riding in horse shows, winning numerous red rosettes for being the Best Boy Rider and trying hard not to show off since his father was always there with a brusque criticism about the way he held his head or used his heels – which is probably why Dick grew up to be so incredibly modest.

For all his success in the summer horse shows, the great love of Dick's young life was going out hunting on a brisk winter morning. For more than ten years, until the outbreak of the

Second World War in 1939, when he was eighteen, he spent every possible day of every summer riding in horse shows and every possible day of every winter out hunting. He was seven when he experienced his first day's hunting and was 'blooded' by the huntsman smearing his cheek with the fox's blood and giving him the fox's brush, and from then on he went out regularly with the hunt, usually riding a bolshie pony called Mickey, which was renowned for being a bolter. 'He took a bit of stopping and we used to run him into the back of the horse in front!' Dick told Sally Patience of *Woman and Home* in 1975. From an early age he was never squeamish or sentimental about the killing of the fox, and he revelled in the wild freedom of racing across fields and recklessly jumping fences and hedges. What better training could there possibly have been for a future jump-jockey? When Doug and Dick went hunting with the Garth they rode so fast after the fox that sometimes they overtook the hounds, which was simply Not Done. 'This isn't a bloody race,' bellowed the Huntsman. 'I suppose those young devils think they look like jockeys.'

When Dick was ten, in March 1931, his grandfather Willie Thomas – W. G. – died aged sixty-seven and Dick was sent to live with his grandmother at Coedcanlas for nine months to try to relieve her loneliness because her own children had all married and moved away, and Doug no longer lived with her since his health had improved and he was now living back in Holyport. The return to Wales was not a happy time for Dick. Not only was the big old house hollow with sadness, it was also obvious that the farm where they had all spent such happy days would have to be sold and the workers laid off – including the Hughes children's father, Tom – because farming was in the doldrums and none of W. G.'s three sons wanted to take it on. Equally depressing, Dick found himself walking again unwillingly every day to Lawrenny School, where he was readmitted on 20 April. His attendance was as erratic as ever: just two weeks later he left again (the school register says 'left District'), though he was readmitted ten days later, on 18 May, and stayed on the roll until 14 October, when he was once again recorded as having 'left District'. Highlights of this return to school included an inevitable lecture on the evils of alcohol by the doughty Mrs Pickerell of the Band of Hope Union and the annual school sports and garden party that Mrs Lort-Phillips gave every year for the village children in the grounds of Lawrenny Castle, during the summer holidays in August. 'It was always a wonderful day out,' Phyllis Grace told me, and that year the weather was glorious for the party. Dick's attendance that summer was in fact better than usual because if he did play truant and stayed at home on the farm he had to clear the corn dust from under the threshing machine, a job he loathed: even going to school was better than that.

Although stern old Thomas Williams had retired as head-master in 1927 and been replaced by his son Bertie, Miss John was still teaching there and Dick's old schoolmates were delighted to have him back. 'He was a nice young feller,' Kitty Cole told me, and Ruth Williams agreed. 'I remember him being a very nice looking boy,' she said, 'and we all thought it was wonderful that he came to Lawrenny School, I suppose because we thought that he was much better off than we were. He was always very smart, very polite and dressed better than us.'

Phyllis Grace helped him with his homework:

> He used to come up to our cottage and we'd compare our work and we always had the same answers! There were six or seven of us in the same class and we were taught every subject by Mr Williams. School was one small room and one big one divided into two, so you could hear what was going on in the other class. Dick was polite but no different from anybody else: he was just ordinary and I didn't think he was going to be famous.

Edie Owen had a signed copy of one of Dick's novels but confessed that she had not read it. 'We'd never have thought he'd be a writer,' she said. 'He didn't do a lot in Lawrenny School.'

There was not much for Dick to do at Coedcanlas, though there were plenty of pretty places to visit in the area. The magnificent ruins of twelfth-century Carew Castle were just down the road, complete with its ancient Celtic cross and two ghosts. Nineteenth-century Carew Mill was still grinding corn in the 1930s, powered by flood waters. Local beauty spots included Lawrenny Quay and Cresswell Quay, the haunt of herons and kingfishers, and ten miles away was Tenby, a genteel Victorian seaside holiday resort with wide, sandy beaches, an ancient castle, thick thirteenth-century walls, narrow cobbled streets, striking panoramic views high across the harbour and the sweep of the bay, and dozens of little hotels and bed-and-breakfast guest houses. Tenby turned out to be Dick's salvation during those long months at Coedcanlas, for it was there that his other grandfather, the pop-eyed, luxuriantly moustachioed ex-jockey Willie Francis, lived – in Picton Road, near South Beach – and his maternal uncle and aunt Griff and Daisy Thomas were nearby in Begelly House. Dick visited them all often and it was the Tenby racehorse trainer Brychan Rees, who lived next door to Willie Francis, who gave the eleven-year-old Dick his first ride on racehorses, letting him take them out on the beach at morning exercise.

At the end of the summer it was time to return to the real world and on Dick's last day at Coedcanlas he rode the old donkey on a final nostalgic journey around the farm, fields and estuary to say goodbye to his childhood, knowing that nothing would ever be the same again. Back in Holyport he nagged his parents endlessly to let him leave school to become apprenticed as a Flat jockey – twelve was the usual age for apprentices to start – but although he was small enough (he still weighed little more than four stone) he was only eleven and his mother put her foot down. He was, however, too old to return to Cromer School, where the upper age limit was ten, and he and Vernon Heaver were sent together to another little private academy in Maidenhead, Ruskin School in St Luke's Road, which catered for boys and girls up to sixteen and where once again one teacher, Thomas Evans, taught all thirty pupils every subject simultaneously in one room. 'Mr Evans was fairly strict but in a nice, pleasant, firm manner, and an excellent teacher,' Mr Heaver told me.

But Ruskin had no facilities for sports or extra-mural activities either and Molly Francis, by now seriously worried about Dick's lack of education, persuaded Vince to send him to one of the best fee-paying schools in the area, Maidenhead County Boys' School, where Doug had been a pupil until the end of 1930 before leaving to help his father in the Holyport stables. It was generous of the school to accept Dick in January 1932 since only a few months earlier the governors had been pursuing Vince to make him pay a term's fees in lieu of notice for Doug, who had suddenly left without any warning. Perhaps it helped that the school thought that Dick was ten, not eleven: his date of birth appears in the school register as 31/9/21 instead of 31/10/20. He turned up for school at 8.55 a.m. on Monday 11 January, perhaps in his new school uniform of primrose and lilac cap and tie, perhaps not. 'My cousin Harold Dovey was at Maidenhead Boys' with Dick,' said Miss Munday with a chuckle, 'and he told me that Dick always wore riding breeches there, too! I don't know how he got away with it there.' The school – which is now called Desborough School – was in Shoppenhanger's Road, near Maidenhead railway station, and it is the only one of the four schools Dick attended that is mentioned in his entry in *Who's Who* – and even in *Who's Who* it has been called Maidenhead Grammar School. Yet he was there for only a year and two weeks and it occupied less than a tenth of his schooldays. In the school photograph taken a month after he joined he looks chubbily cheerful, but beneath the smile he disliked the place even more than his other schools and made little effort to live up to its Latin motto, *Strenuis Ardua Cedunt* ('Difficulties yield to those who make an effort'). Two of the teachers there in 1998 told me that as the school's most famous Old Boy he had been invited to several functions but had always declined, making it plain that he had been unhappy there.

Yet the school, which had 174 boys aged from eight to eighteen and charged £20 a year for those whose parents could afford it, was a good one: in the year that Dick was there fourteen boys obtained their School Certificates, winning twelve distinctions, two more than any other school. Latin and French were on the curriculum and many pupils went on to Oxford and Cambridge, a remarkable number with scholarships. There were physics and chemistry laboratories, six acres of playing fields with three soccer fields and a cricket pitch, and the boys put on regular plays, concerts and Gilbert and Sullivan operas. There was also a school cadet corps attached to the Royal Berkshire Regiment. Such a variety of extra-mural activities was remarkable because the school had only nine full-time teachers and the headmaster, Arthur Brooks, an Oxford MA, fought a constant battle against the lack of interest of most of the boys and their parents as well as the financial constraints set by the governors. In June 1929 Brooks had reported to the governors with a sigh that it was difficult to ensure full attendance, especially in the summer, since Maidenhead was 'a district whose only industry is that of amusing summer visitors' and consequently pupils were often absent in the summer helping their parents run their business. Dick was obviously not the only pupil playing truant.

Dick's year at the school was undistinguished, his only achievement being to win the first heat of the Under-12 220-Yards Handicap in the school sports on Saturday 25 June 1932, even though the handicapper had given him just a one-yard handicap against rivals with an advantage of four and five yards. Otherwise he left no mark at all. This was hardly the fault of the teachers since many other Old Maidonians of Dick's vintage told David

Evans for his official school history *One Hundred Not Out* how grateful they were for the quality of the staff. The senior English master, for instance, Dickie Richards, had captained Maidenhead United football team in 1922–23. Mathematics was taught by Joe Leggett, who had been a pilot during the First World War. A. B. Targett, the history and geography master who was nicknamed Skelley because of his skeletal face, was an ex-boxing champion. Peter Wrench, the popular Latin master, whose gammy leg had been wounded during the war, had been an international hockey player. They were nostalgic even about Nick Nicholls despite his regular habit of clouting every boy as he left the classroom, and they chuckled at the memory of the part-time Latin master, E. J. Brooks, a Fellow of St John's College, Cambridge, who alarmed the boys by warning them: 'You must learn Latin or you'll have to teach it.'

The headmaster himself, however, did not appeal to everybody. One ex-pupil, George Allan, described Arthur Brooks in the 1956 issue of the school magazine *The Maidonian* as a man driven by dynamic, aggressive enthusiasm:

> He was positive, decisive, inspiring and uncompromising. He never suffered fools gladly. He never tolerated apathy. He had firm ideas on what was best for 'his boys' and told them and their parents in no uncertain terms. It follows that Mr Brooks did not always make friends, but it also follows that he influenced people.

It is easy to see that a man like Brooks and a boy like Dick might well have taken against each other right from the start, though Brooks was a keen sportsman who would surely have appreciated Dick's skill as a horseman. Brooks was renowned for announcing that 'every boy should have at least one good sweat each week' but he also believed that each boy should aim for the highest possible academic standards, a belief that Dick did not share. Nor was Dick the sort of boy to take kindly to strict discipline and he may well have objected to the regimented prefect system at the school. Another major objection may well have been that the headmaster was obsessed with the cadet corps (he called himself Major Brooks) and forced the entire school to parade after prayers every morning and to drill with carbines and wooden dummy rifles. If you did not want to join the cadet corps – and spend every Thursday afternoon marching around being drilled and yelled at by the old First World War Sergeant A. Glass – you were forced to go off instead on a five-mile cross-country run. Some Old Maidonians told Evans that

> on the Field Days held twice a year, they marched behind Major Brooks mounted on a white horse and leading his troops into Maidenhead Thicket for manoeuvres, while the NCOs busied themselves in the rear rounding up those who felt inclined to desert the column and take advantage of the thick cover . . . There were also the endless 'drills', which were 15-minute punishments done after school on Thursdays. These were under the control of Sergeant Glass and are remembered by Mr Les Lowrie. 'He used to start us off marching and if he was not satisfied with the standard we would be sent off to get a rifle. If he was still not satisfied we had to double with the rifle at sloped position, sometimes on each shoulder.'

It is easy to see that such a regime would have had little appeal for Dick, but all his pleading was still in vain: his mother insisted that he was still too young to leave school and that he needed to learn something other than horsemanship. He had no friends at all apart from Vernon Heaver and no interest in any sports or hobbies, let alone in anything remotely academic. I was told by Frank Clark:

I would never have thought that he'd turn out to be what he is now. He was horse-mad. I only went to the pictures with him once and it was one of those animal forest films and he couldn't take the sight of a reptile! It struck me later that a fellow who could ride in the Grand National would have been a bit tougher than a fellow who would close his eyes when the snakes came on the screen!

Dick finally escaped Maidenhead Boys' School after he had been there little more than a year and had a bad accident one afternoon when he was riding a nervous pony called Tulip in the indoor riding school at Holyport: the horse fell on top of him and the pommel of his saddle smashed into his face, breaking his teeth, jaw, palate and nose. When he woke up in hospital he was not a pretty sight but to his joy the doctors said that he would have to miss the entire summer term and that from the autumn he would be better off going to a smaller, quieter private school where there were no rough games – in other words back to Ruskin School again.

Dick left Maidenhead County Boys' on 28 February 1933, five weeks before the end of term, to go on (according to the school minutes) to 'Private Tuition (delicate)'. Delicate? Dick Francis? His teachers would have been astonished to know that twenty years later he would become champion jump jockey after breaking numerous bones in one of the most dangerous sports in the world. The school was still under the impression that he was a year younger than he was, just eleven years and eight months. In fact he was twelve-and-a-half.

His face healed quickly and he was soon back in the saddle to enjoy a blissful summer of riding and going to horse shows thanks to Vince's sixty-year-old friend and riding rival Bertram Mills, the circus owner. Mills lived twelve miles from Holyport at Chalfont St Giles, owned many horses and entered them in shows all over England, and when he heard that Dick would not be going to school for several months he engaged him to ride his ponies at horse shows all over the country. Dick could hardly believe his luck: it was going to be an unforgettable summer.

Bertram Wagstaff Mills was an ebullient, cheery, ex-undertaker and coachbuilder from Paddington who had in 1905 had the honour of supervising the funeral of the actor Sir Henry Irving, whose corpse he had ushered down Piccadilly in a hearse drawn by black horses. Mills, as bald as a billiard ball and energetic as a jack-in-the-box, had made a fortune at the end of the First World War by selling British Government surplus rubber boots to the Canadian Government, which had allowed him to start his hugely popular Christmas circus at Olympia in 1920 despite having no circus experience at all. By the time he asked Dick to ride his ponies he was also running a touring circus, working as an elected member of London County Council and prospective Conservative candidate for Parliament, riding to hounds, keenly attending meetings of the Coaching Club that met regularly in Hyde Park, driving a coach-and-four in horse shows, and running stage coaches from London to Brighton, Oxford and Box Hill as a hobby, sometimes driving them himself. One of his more exuberant wheezes was to offer £20,000 in 1934 – the equivalent of £642,000 in 1999 – to anyone who could bring him, dead or alive, the Loch Ness Monster. Always immaculately dressed, with a cornflower in his buttonhole whatever the season, Mills was described by the circus ringmaster Frank Foster in his memoirs *Pink Coat, Spangles and Sawdust* as 'the greatest English showman since the days of Lord George Sanger.'

He certainly vitalised young Dick Francis, of whom Mills's circus horsemaster Tom Masson remarked at the time: 'A better pair of hands on a pony I have yet to see.' Dick spent that summer happily travelling all over England by train with Mills's horses, caring for them, grooming them, riding them, and sleeping beside them on a bunk in railway horse-boxes if necessary. It was a very different England then, when parents could let a twelve-year-old boy travel long distances alone without worrying about his safety. Mills had several worries of his own that summer: when his circus was performing in Devonport, Plymouth, three tigers escaped from their cage and one attacked a woman spectator, and in Gloucester a wooden grandstand caught fire. Yet towards Dick he remained as genial as ever. One day that summer Dick had to ask Mills for half a crown to pay for his three bus fares home, and Mills jovially gave the boy a big old white £5 note, telling him to keep the change. Dick did not merely keep the change, he kept the entire £5, the equivalent of £160 in 1999, because not surprisingly none of the three bus conductors on the route back to Holyport had enough change for £5 so he travelled free the whole way. A modern English bus conductor, offered a £160 note for a ticket, would undoubtedly become violent.

Mills was for many years a famous sight at Richmond Horse Show, where he would drive into the ring in a grey top hat to compete in the four-in-hand class, and it was at Richmond that Dick won a riding class in the summer of 1933 and met the future Queen Elizabeth II for the first time: Princess Elizabeth, six years old and deeply solemn. She presented him with his prize, a hunting crop. He bowed and thanked her and she smiled at him, neither suspecting that their paths would cross many times in later years.

In the autumn of 1933 Dick, now thirteen, rejoined Vernon Heaver at Ruskin School, where they discovered together the joys of drinking beer and where Dick found to his delight that it was easier than ever to play truant since the school had no inspector to check on his attendance. At Christmas Mills gave all the Francises tickets for the circus and Dick was so impressed by the horses and their acrobats that afterwards he tried to train himself to stand on a pony's rump while it cantered around the indoor training school, but soon decided that he was cut out to be a jockey rather than a spangled, sparkly artiste of the Big Top.

In May his grandmother Annie Thomas died at Coedcanlas, aged sixty-nine, just three years after her beloved W. G., and Coedcanlas Farm was sold to James Merriman and the last lingering memories of Dick's Welsh childhood faded like old photographs. By now he had become not only an accomplished, prizewinning horseman but also a fastidious one. Photographs show a boy determined to look his very best on horseback and even at the age of thirteen he would ride in shows wearing a bowler hat, smart hacking jacket, immaculate jodhpurs and gleaming boots. He looked exactly what his old Welsh school friends had always thought he was: a sprig of the gentry; a little toff. Doug came home by motorbike late one night that summer after a party, climbed quietly through the window of the bedroom he shared with Dick, and dropped some muck from his shoes onto Dick's beautifully washed and ironed hunting clothes which he had laid out ready for an early start. Dick was furious when he found his soiled clothes the next morning and they had a huge row about it.

His skill was such that he was only fourteen when he started to ride in hunter classes at horse shows. In 1935 Vince was due to ride a large, high-spirited horse called Ballymonis in the lightweight hunter class at the Islington Royal Agricultural Show but was felled by a sudden attack of sciatica at the last minute and suggested to the horse's owner, Bernard Selby, that Dick should ride it instead. Selby was dubious. Dick still weighed no more than five stone, just 70lbs, and the horse could be wild and unpredictable. But Dick had ridden Ballymonis at home, did so again and won his class. Selby was so delighted that he bought him a new suit and coat, and from then on Dick rode regularly in hunter classes and stood in for Vince whenever necessary.

As soon as Dick reached his fourteenth birthday, which was when the law allowed children to leave school, he was nagging his mother yet again to let him leave Ruskin, but she fought a valiant rearguard action and refused to think of it for another year. By the time he was fifteen, however, it had become obvious even to Molly that his future lay with horses and that it was useless to go on trying to stuff him with English Literature, Latin and mathematics. With a sigh she agreed at last and Dick went to work full-time as his father's assistant at the yard in Holyport, helping to train the horses and riding hunters in the show ring all summer and hunting all winter, sometimes five days a week, with the Garth and the Berks and Bucks Farmers' Staghounds. One of his favourite jobs was to take a couple of possible hunters to prospective purchasers across country by horse-box and ride out to hounds with them to let them try them out. These trips allowed him to ride out with numerous hunts, from the Duke of Beaufort's and the Belvoir to the Pytcheley and the Whaddon Chase.

For many years it had seemed possible that Dick might become a Flat-racing jockey because he was so tiny. Vince's friend Bert Rich suggested that Dick should drink gin to stop him growing, but when he was fifteen he suddenly shot up and became tall, gangly and much heavier. In just over three years he grew a foot and a half so that by the time he was sixteen he was quite the wrong shape and weight for the Flat. Still, his love of hunting, jumping and steeplechasing meant that his real dream had always been to become a National Hunt rather than a Flat jockey, and he persuaded Vince to help him find a job as a junior assistant in a National Hunt stable in the hope that this would lead to his being able to ride as a jockey. Vince introduced him to an old Welsh boyhood friend, Gwynne Evans, who was so impressed by Dick's enthusiasm that he promised to take him on at his stables as soon as he turned seventeen. For more than six months Dick wished the weeks away, dreaming of the day that he would turn seventeen and be able to start to work in a National Hunt yard, but then Gwynne Evans died in a car crash.

Vince approached several other contacts but none had a vacancy. And then he made a decision that could well have crushed Dick's hopes for ever: he decided to leave Horace Smith and open a hunting stables of his own, which meant that Dick would be needed to help at home even more than before.

Vince had worked hard and with great success for Horace Smith. 'In the period between the two wars, from 1920 until 1939, our hunting business thrived exceedingly,' wrote Smith in his autobiography, 'and some of the finest show hunters in the country, as well as a large number of their workaday cousins, were produced from our stables.' In the 1930s his riding school pupils included the Princesses Elizabeth and Margaret and later he also taught Princess Alexandra, the Duke of Kent, Prince Michael of Kent, Prince Charles and Princess Anne. It was to Horace Smith that Princess Elizabeth once made her famous remark, 'I would like to be a lady living in the country, with lots of dogs and horses,' and towards the end of the Second World War she often had lessons at the Holyport stables when she was staying at Windsor.

Vince, however, felt that Smith did not pay him well enough and that he could be financially more successful on his own, so early in 1938 he gave up his secure job and moved to Wokingham, nine miles away, where he sank his savings into setting up a hunting stables business at Embrook House, a large Victorian property with twenty-five horse boxes. It was out of the question now for Dick even to think of going to work for anyone else. His father needed him. His dream of becoming a jockey seemed less likely than ever.

W. J. Smith's Hunting Stables in Holyport have long been demolished and the only memory of them today is in the name of the cul-de-sac of modern houses that has been built on the site: it is called Cadogan Close after Little Cadogan Place in London where Horace Smith's original stables stood. Nor has the Francises' bungalow survived. In its place is a row of modern cottages – and none carries even the smallest plaque to record that here once lived a world-famous writer and jockey who learned to ride on this very spot. Dick himself, of course, would completely understand the omission: he never could see the point of history, either.

Mary Brenchley's childhood was very different. She told me many years later:

> My father had a printing factory. He printed cigarette papers, and one of the first things I learned was how machines work and my first playground was in the factory with the machines thundering. One of my first memories, when I was about four, was of my father showing me a tin of peaches and asking me how many colours were printed on the label.

The ground floor of the factory, which was in south London at Clapham Common, six miles north of Mary's home at Worcester Park, was filled with vast presses that were so noisy that it was impossible to hear anyone speak but also so powerful and intriguing that she fell in love with them. Her passion in later life for finding out how things work came, she said later, from that early fascination for 'the huge, roaring monsters of the presses.' On the first floor there were smaller machines and on the top floor several comparatively silent sorting, cutting, gluing and counting machines. The machines on the upper floors were powered by heavy belts that ran along the ceilings and were driven by an engine on the ground floor. All those huge, thundering, moving belts, spindles, pulleys and rollers were not only exciting for a little girl, they were also dangerous: one of her father's print workers was dragged one day into a heavy belt and crushed to death. Mary was never to forget the horror of that terrible accident. More than forty years later it was to inspire a similarly grisly accident in the Dick Francis novel *High Stakes* in which a villain is whirled screaming to his death.

Mary's schooling was much more conventional, stable and academic than Dick's. Whereas he was a horseman from a very early age, Mary was much more cerebral even as a little girl. When she was six years and three months old, on 18 September 1930, her parents sent her to Sutton Girls' High School just two suburban South London miles away from her home at 17 Kingsmead Avenue, and she studied there without interruption for seven years. Sutton Girls' was a highly reputable private school whose privileged, genteel, middle-class pupils often stayed on until they were seventeen or eighteen and went on to university, several winning places at Oxford and Cambridge and some even taking Oxbridge scholarships. Its curriculum included not only French, Latin and Science but also Greek and German, a rarity in girls' schools then. When Mary joined the school there were over five hundred pupils and a year later there were six hundred, but no class had more than thirty girls and the form she started in had just twenty-three. The school's facilities were admirably varied and ranged from the Classical Music Club and Historical Society to the Literary and Debating Society, the Photography Club, the Cadet-Rangers Company, the Girl Guides and the Brownies. The girls performed French plays as well as Milton's *Comus*, played cricket as well as hockey and netball, and were able to have lessons in the piano, violin and cello.

Four months before Mary joined the school it was examined for four consecutive days by seven Board of Education inspectors who reported that the general standard of teaching was satisfactory and particularly strong in history, French and English, and they commended especially the good reference library and the 'excellent' school orchestra. They were also highly impressed by the standards in the junior school, which Mary was about to join. 'The Mistress in charge of the Junior School is singularly well fitted for her post,' they reported.

The school – at 55 Cheam Road, Sutton – was a direct grant establishment which was partly subsidised by the government but which also charged fees ranging from £15-15s a year for pupils under six to £28-10s a year for girls aged over ten. Mary's fees in her first two years were £19-10s a year.

The headmistress, Miss Edith Lees, was a deeply religious and committed perfectionist who was loved by many of her pupils. Tributes from Old Girls in the school archives bear warm witness to her qualities. 'When we worked or played she insisted that we should do so with the utmost concentration on the job in hand,' reported one. 'She was *fierce* about our manners and consideration for other people's feelings. She was often stern about weaknesses, but quick to praise if she could find a single thing worth praising.' Another Old Girl wrote: 'Though aristocratic by nature and consumed by a passion for the best that never allowed her to relax into triviality, she had great generosity of heart . . . she was also deeply kind to individuals . . . To a child she was a completely satisfying headmistress.' One of Mary's classmates, Sheila Read (*née* White), told me: 'Miss Lees could quell us with a glance. She was however very fond of exhorting us "if a job is worth doing, it's worth doing well". This, and the discipline instilled in us, has I think made us able to cope with what life throws at us.' It was certainly a philosophy that Mary herself adopted and that enabled her to overcome the numerous setbacks and obstacles that were to beset her throughout her life.

You would think that a bright little girl like Mary would have shone at a school like Sutton Girls but the records suggest otherwise. Prizes were given in every class every year but Mary never won anything. The school magazine was brighter than most, containing several creative contributions written by the girls, but none was written by Mary except possibly one: a brief report of Girl Guide activities, including the annual camp in the New Forest in the summer of 1935, written by 'MB' in collaboration with two others. During all the years that Mary was at Sutton Girls, numerous plays were performed and concerts given, but nowhere does her name appear. Her only distinction was as a swimmer: inspired perhaps by regular summer seaside holidays in Cornwall and Sussex, she was swimming captain of her class at the age of eleven and at thirteen she was selected for the school swimming team along with girls who were much older. Otherwise 'I don't remember Mary standing out in any particular,' Sheila Read told me. 'There was nothing special about her, and although girls of that age tend to have a close friend or two, Mary didn't.' Perhaps she was simply a late developer.

Another classmate, Mary Harding, later Mary Youll, told me that she did not remember Mary at all in class at Sutton High, 'but I used to get invited to the Brenchleys' birthday parties, which I thoroughly enjoyed. Mary's mother used to have a great big box which she used to keep old clothes in and we played charades practically the entire time in their big garden.' The charades and dressing up ignited in Mary a lifelong passion for the theatre.

Life at Sutton Girls' High was a warm and very English ritual as comforting as the seasons: the daily two-mile bus journey from Kingsmead Avenue to Sutton via leafy Malden Road, Cheam High Street and Cheam Road; the regular timetable of lessons and clubs and games; the spring fete in May to raise money to pay for the new hard tennis courts; the summer sports and swimming day; the autumn Armistice Day service; the Brownies' motor-coach outing to Windsor Castle to see the Queen's Dolls' House; the annual prizegiving in November. At the Junior School prizegiving in the Public Hall at Sutton on 17 November 1931 the girls gave a drill display, a Brownie display, and sang songs and performed scenes adapted from Longfellow's *Hiawatha*, for which they had themselves made all the Indian costumes and props, an early excitement that must have stirred yet again little Mary's interest in the theatre. Her class band also played a tune called *The Little Wanderer*.

In September her sister Jean joined her at Sutton Girls' High, going into the kindergarten class, even though she was only five years and two months old, and in January 1931 their baby brother

Ewen was born at home in Kingsmead Avenue, but despite the responsibility of being now the eldest of three children, Mary was still a little young for her age: when she was eight she wept when Sir Alan Cobham's circus came to town but her mother refused to let her go up on one of the five-shilling pleasure flights; Mary had to be taken home in tears. Mrs Read told me:

> She had very fair hair and wore golden pigtails, and I have always remembered one conversation. We were not particular friends but there was an occasion when Mary was waiting in Cheam Road to get the bus home and had obviously been instructed not to go without the younger Jean, who was also very fair. I don't remember my question but have always remembered her answer, which was that she did love Jean because she was her sister but that she didn't really like her!

The contrast between Mary's education and Dick's lack of education could not have been more striking. Each year she worked hard enough to be promoted to the next class up and there were plenty of extra-mural activities to feed her mind. A Science Club was formed, then a Middle School Dramatic Society to stir her theatrical instincts yet again. There was folk dancing and the foundation of a fourth Brownie pack that celebrated with a rice-pudding feast and a Baby Show during which they showed all their dolls to Brown Owl, chanting as they did:

> *We're the Brownies,*
> *Here's our aim –*
> *Lend a hand*
> *And play the game.*

In 1934 the school marked its Golden Jubilee with a week of afternoon celebrations at the end of May and beginning of June:

a garden party for parents; a demonstration of physical training; a Beethoven recital followed by rounders; a series of plays and songs in French, German and Latin; a demonstration by the Rangers, Girl Guides and Brownies; a cricket match at Cheam; a thanksgiving service at Christ Church in Sutton. In 1935 they celebrated King George V's Jubilee with a Thanksgiving Service in Cheam Park. A new school hall was built and in May the Senior School gave four performances of the Greek play *Medea*. The Middle School Dramatic Society put on lots of short playlets during the year, too, and after the Middle School prizegiving in Sutton Public Hall the girls sang and performed ballad plays in English and German, and a Latin play called *The Gorgon's Head*. Although five form prizes were awarded to Mary's class, in which there were thirty girls, she won none of them. But her moments of glory in the swimming pool were at hand. Class Upper III[1] elected her Form Swimming Captain in the summer term of 1936 and her team duly came second in both the Junior File and Junior Relay races. A year later she was elected swimming captain of Lower IV[1], which went on to win the Junior Form Relay. And the peak of her career at Sutton Girls came in July 1937, a month after her thirteenth birthday and a week before she was due to leave, when she was selected for the school swimming team and took part in the Inter-Schools Swimming Gala at Hampstead Baths as a member of Sutton's diving and medley relay teams, both of which came third in their races. Mary also won a Royal Life Saving Society Intermediate Certificate in her last year.

She left Sutton Girls' High on 28 July 1937 to go on to her mother's old boarding school, Milton Mount College, at Worth Park, near Crawley in Sussex, which catered especially for the daughters and granddaughters of Congregational ministers. Netta Brenchley had loved her own schooldays at Milton Mount, had kept up almost obsessively with her old schoolfriends, and was now the assistant secretary of the Old Girls' society, the

Miltonian Guild, so it was natural that she wanted her daughters to follow her.

Mary embarked on her new life at Milton Mount at the end of 1937, a few weeks before Dick was also about to start a new life by moving from Holyport to Wokingham. Both were moving south, towards new horizons, she just entering adolescence, he just leaving it. Once again the patterns of their lives were nudging each other. Just seven years to go now and then they would meet and change each other's lives.

CHAPTER 3

Wokingham and Worth Park

(1938–40)

W hen Vince, Molly, Doug and Dick moved to Wokingham early in 1938 it was a pleasant little country town, once famous for its bustling poultry market but now a quiet backwater with narrow, higgledy-piggledy streets, a central market place with a tall, chiming clocktower, and a population of fewer than eight thousand. It was only one year since the Ritz cinema had opened and thirteen since the arrival of electricity. Had you glanced down some timeless alleyway you would have glimpsed the Middle Ages. Eight 'deserving' paupers still lived in almshouses founded in 1451 and were given weekly handouts of meat, groceries and coal. Each year 'poor maidens' and apprentices of the parish shared a £43-a-year bequest that had been left to the town by Charles I's Archbishop of Canterbury, Archbishop Laud, when he was beheaded in 1645. Another bequest, dating back to 1661, provided the burghers with enough funds each year for 'the purchase of a bull, to be baited at Christmas.' Until 1939 there was still a workhouse for the poor in Barkham Road, and the town's main claim to fame was that one day in the early eighteenth century John Arbuthnot, John Gay, Alexander Pope and Dean Swift had stayed at the Rose Inn and had written a poem about the landlord's beautiful daughter.

Embrook House, where the Francises established their stables, was a large, red-brick dwelling with six bedrooms, three acres of land, a driveway, a lodge and twenty-five horse boxes at 100 Reading Road, a mile out of town along a leafy, rural avenue. Here Vince set up his livery and horse-dealing business with an Irish groom, Paddy Gallagher, who lived in the lodge at the end of the drive, and Dick and Doug – by now a tall, gangly twenty-one-year-old – set to work as his assistants. Doug had given up his ambition to be a competitive rider after a motorcycle accident nearly cost him his leg when he was eighteen, and Dick worked so hard to help his father make a go of the new business that his own ambition to become a jockey all but evaporated. For several months he simply had no time for serious riding, though he did win the Champion Hunter rosette on Sir Roger at the Richmond Royal Horse Show that year, and he had to give up competing in point-to-points because Vince's horses never stayed in the yard long enough to qualify.

Just after they moved to Wokingham the family was saddened by the death of Bertram Mills in April at the age of sixty-five, but they quickly settled into their new home and Dick's mother took a great delight in having plenty of room at last. She filled the numerous rooms with antiques that she hunted down at auctions – she had always had a passion for old furniture – and took in and mothered a string of paying pupils who came to Vince to learn how to manage stables.

Dick consoled himself by getting engaged to his first real girlfriend, Beryl Bonner, the daughter of Vince's friend Harry Bonner. 'Dick wasn't one for taking girls out to the cinema or parties,' Vernon Heaver told me. 'Beryl was about the only one that got really serious until he met Mary and she was quite a good choice from Dick's point of view.' But eventually she broke the engagement off when Dick was sent abroad during the Second World War. A glimmer of hope flickered on the horizon when

Oliver Dixon, a horse-dealer friend of Vince's, asked Dick to ride his horses in point-to-points the following year, but before that could happen Dixon died. First Gwynne Evans had died, now Oliver Dixon. It seemed as if Dick was jinxed. And then his hopes were dashed completely, for six years, by the outbreak of the Second World War just before his nineteenth birthday in 1939.

The war also had a devastating effect on Vince's business. Who now could afford the money or the time to keep horses and go hunting or riding at point-to-points? With desperate bad luck he had chosen just the wrong time to go it alone. Had he stayed with Horace Smith at Holyport he would still have had a regular income throughout the war, since Smith was well enough established to ride out the recession, but Vince had to stand and watch his own business dwindle and die. In a final blaze of glory he won the hunter championship on Mount Royal that year at the last Olympia International Horse Show ever held, at the age of fifty, and Dick was reserve champion, but otherwise 'Vince Francis went downhill after he left Horry Smith,' Joan Hearne told me. 'Nobody could afford to keep horses during the war and there wasn't the feed for them.' Vince's bad luck inspired little compassion in his old boss's heart. Seventeen years after Vince left Holyport, Horace Smith wrote without pity in his autobiography in 1955: 'Vincent Francis left me, and he took several horses with him. Several of my employees have left me and taken my clients with them, but they have none of them had a great deal of success.'

To make ends meet Vince rented Embrook House to an Indian prince, the Maharajah of Bundi, who was rich enough to have an enormous car and his own doctor, secretary, chauffeur and bodyguard, and to present a Spitfire to the RAF. The Maharajah, who dressed in traditional Indian fashion and could not speak English, moved in with a retinue of six, and a twenty-year-old girl, Elizabeth Ellett, who spoke Hindustani after living in India, where her father had been in the army, was hired to wait at table and to play draughts with the Indians. 'Dick and the family were still there,' Miss Ellett told me, 'and Dick would come in for tea or coffee, but otherwise they kept away and didn't join in. I never saw Dick in anything else but his jodhpurs and boots. He was always in the stables with his horses.'

Since Dick had little work to do now in his father's stables he volunteered for the cavalry early in 1940, hoping to join some friends who were with the Royal Scots Greys in Edinburgh, whose Commander-in-Chief was Vince's friend Colonel Joe Dudgeon. But Dick was told by the Reading recruiting office that the only job open to him was as an assistant cook in the infantry. He tried again, this time applying to become an RAF pilot, but was told that they had plenty of pilots already. But he could be an air-gunner, or a member of ground staff: an erk. No, he wanted to be a pilot, he insisted. And then he fell for the oldest trick in the recruiting officer's book: he was told that if he signed on as a tradesman he could easily become a pilot later. Dick believed the lie, signed on as an airframe fitter, and joined the Royal Air Force as a second class aircraftman, 922385 AC2 Francis R – the lowest form of human life in the RAF. It was one of the unhappiest decisions he ever made.

Mary Brenchley's new school, Milton Mount College, which she joined in September 1937 at the age of thirteen, was positively palatial by comparison with Sutton Girls' High. It was housed in a sumptuous, four-storey country mansion set in eighty acres of parkland at Worth Park, near Crawley in Sussex, and surrounded by imposing woods, lawns, formal gardens, a fountain, a Camellia Walk, a swimming pool, stables and six tennis courts. It had two laboratories, a music block, a gymnasium and an art studio and its rooms were astonishingly spacious and luxurious for a school. The walls of the assembly hall were covered with gold silk hangings, its ceiling intricately carved, and the interiors of each room were unbelievably ornate, with high marble pillars and archways, painted ceilings, tall windows, an impossibly elegant mahogany staircase. Here each girl was allocated to one of six houses named after British heroes – Gordon, Livingstone, Raleigh, Scott, Shackleton, Shaftesbury – that took each other on not only at lacrosse, netball, rounders, tennis and swimming, but also at flower arranging, punctuality, carefulness, tidiness and country dancing. There was even an inter-House cup for Deportment. Milton Mount College made Maidenhead County Boys' School look like an oiks' institute. No wonder Dick was so proud of Mary when he boasted in later years that while he was barely educated at all, she had been to Milton Mount.

The school had been founded for the daughters of Congregationalist ministers, reported Mary's senior English teacher Miss Hilda Harwood in her book *The History of Milton Mount College*, 'not only to give ministers' daughters a good education at a low fee . ... but to train many of them to become teachers,' so there were numerous clubs and societies in the school: music, art, literary, photographic and natural history as well as a League of Nations Union Study Circle, two companies of Girl Guides and a company of Rangers.

As for Milton Mount's academic standard, five girls on average went on to universities each year, usually at least one of them to Oxford or Cambridge. The headmistress was a Cambridge MA whose husband had died during the First World War, Mrs D. M. Henman, and all the senior teachers (except those teaching French and German) had degrees from Cambridge or London universities. Four years before Mary's arrival a Board of Education inspection had given the school a very satisfactory report and in the year before Mary arrived twenty out of the twenty-four candidates passed their School Certificates and several Old Girls had gone on to university. The school was also renowned for its art and music departments and in that year twenty-seven girls passed their public Associated Board music exams, two of them with distinction. Mary's first term was graced by a visit by the Russian cellist Mischel Cherniavsky, who played selections from Boccarini, Beethoven, Paderewsky and Chopin, and in May each year the school mounted a highly regarded concert and sometimes performed operas. Plays were regularly performed by groups within the school, not only by the Dramatic Society – which put on Sheridan's *The School for Scandal* during Mary's second term – and by individual houses, forms and clubs. For all of this the poorest ministers' daughters were charged only £20 a year (£585 in 1999) although wealthy parents paid £110-7s-6d a year (£3,230).

Mary's mother, Netta – a fair-haired, broad-browed, good-looking, soft-spoken woman – had herself been at Milton Mount from 1906 to 1912 and had been the school tennis champion and a notable singer. After school she had started to train as a doctor but found the work too hard, fell ill, and gave it up, marrying Mary's father instead, so that in later years she looked back on her schooldays with that special nostalgia that is common among those who feel that they never fulfilled their potential. Netta Brenchley became one of those eternal Old Girls who never cut the umbilical cord with their old school. Consequently Mary's own schooldays at Milton Mount were lived in the constant shadow of her mother, who kept popping up at the school, became secretary to the Miltonian Guild, was elected to the Board of Management, and became the school's representative on its favourite London charity, the Canning Town Committee, which helped poor girls from the East End of London. As children Mary and Jean spent many tedious hours addressing thousands of envelopes to Old Miltonians for their mother and sticking on thousands of stamps, and there must have been times when they wished that their mother's presence at the school were not quite so constant.

Mary started her first term at Milton Mount at the same time as her Sutton classmate Mary Harding, who told me: 'at that stage most girls went to boarding school and right from the very beginning we were in the same house, Livingstone House, quartered in the quadrangle, a beautiful old place.' There were 158 girls at the school: 133 of them boarders and twenty-five of them 'day-bugs'. A vivid portrait of everyday life at Milton Mount in the thirties was given by Prime Minister Harold Wilson's wife, Mary, who had been a pupil there from 1929 to 1933 under her maiden name Gladys Baldwin, in an interview with Lynda Black of the *Crawley Observer* in May 1988. Even after fifty-five years Lady Wilson still dreamed of the leafy drive at Worth Park, 'the heady perfumed air of the flower garden, the magnificent and overpowering great hall,' she told Lynda Black. 'My memories of the school are extremely happy ones. It was such a beautiful place.' Deportment and discipline were considered vitally important and girls were punished with black marks if they did not sit up straight or ran in the corridors. Sweets were allowed only twice a week and contact with boys forbidden. There were no radios and books had to be vetted by the headmistress. Letters were read by the staff before they were posted: 'I suppose it was to stop us from writing to boyfriends,' said Lady Wilson, although 'you could always give them to a day girl. We were not allowed to read newspapers, either. The headmistress used to read us extracts from *The Times* in assembly.'

Visits to Crawley were rare. 'We only used to go there once a month to attend the local Congregational church,' said Lady Wilson. 'We used to walk there in a crocodile chain.' In fact the girls walked everywhere in a crocodile chain except for the sixth formers, who were allowed to walk out independently but only if there were at least six of them. 'We even had to have a chaperone when we had our hair cut by the local barber,' said Lady Wilson. 'Being at Milton Mount had more of a spiritual quality. It did not really teach you about real life. I must admit that I did have the wrong idea about men when I left school. I thought they were all great romantics like Byron and Charles II . . . The upbringing we received at Milton Mount was based very much upon plain living and high thinking.'

'It was a very strict schooling when you compare it with today's,' Mary Youll (*née* Harding) told me. A few weeks after they became Miltonians they were given an inkling of what might be expected of them when the Speech Day prizes were handed out by one of the school's most distinguished Old Girls, Mrs Evelyn Lowe, one of the first female Justices of the Peace and the first woman Chairman of London County Council, who made a speech telling the girls how lucky they were to have so many more opportunities than previous generations of women and urging them to reach their full potential. Afterwards the guests watched a demonstration of Keep Fit exercises in the gym, of which *The Miltonian* later reported: 'The audience was much amused at seeing Form VI demonstrating gentle exercises suitable for staid matrons of forty!' It was that sort of school, terribly English, terribly proper, the kind of place where lantern lectures were often on the programme and the piano was always called the pianoforte.

The other highlight of Mary's first term – during which the school was swept by crazes for permed hair and model animals – was the fete in December, when her taste for the theatre was tickled by a Fancy Dress Dance, Form IVa's production of a play called *Oliver's Island*, and Form Va's presentation of a series of gruesome tableaux that ended with Macbeth spattering the crowd with 'blood'.

Among Mary's new friends one of the closest was Nesta Evans, a girl who had won a couple of years previously a Royal Academy of Music singing scholarship and who was to be hugely significant for Mary's future since it was to be at her wedding that Mary was at last to meet Dick Francis. The standard of music at Milton Mount was always notably high and the annual concert in May during Mary's third term was as accomplished as ever, consisting as it did of vocal and instrumental music by individuals as well as the school orchestra. There was also an operetta performed by the two most junior forms, *The Charcoal Burner's Son* by L. Du Garde Peach and V. Hely-Hutchinson, for which the scenery and props were outstanding. *The Miltonian* later praised 'the enchanted castle with its gleaming red roofs and flights of steps leading through open portals to the black magic of the ogre's den; . . . the well-drilled army, red-coated and busbied in the true English fashion . . . the ogre with the thunderous voice; . . . the silver-mailed dragon . . .' Mary's taste for the theatre, already nurtured at Sutton Girls', was now being well fertilised at Milton Mount.

So too was her interest in the Girl Guides. At the end of July 1938 she spent a week under canvas on a farm in Surrey a few miles north of Crawley with Guides from Paddington and Canning Town as well as Milton Mount, where the girls pitched tents, made fires, cooked, explored, patrolled, hiked and played tracking games, cricket and rounders – and in the process Mary won her First Class Hike badge for leading one of the two groups of hikers. On the Saturday night they sang songs and played pipes around a blazing camp fire, and afterwards Mary wrote a report of the week for the school magazine *The Miltonian* which shows that at the age of fourteen her style was already laced with that humorous tongue-in-cheek deftness that was later to become such a feature of the Dick Francis novels, when she reported that the girls had spent an entire morning tidying the camp and then the whole afternoon messing it up again.

Of all her teenage interests and hobbies there was only one into which she did not throw herself with enthusiasm: horse riding. Considering she was to spend most of her life with a horseman who was to become famous as the author of horsey thrillers, there is a splendid irony in the fact that Mary was never very keen on horses herself. She did learn to ride for a couple of years in her early teens but she was never especially keen on it, gave up when she was fifteen and rode again only twice.

By the autumn of 1938 the threat of war was darkening even the green fields of southern England and since Milton Mount was right beneath the flightpath of any German bombers that might head towards London, Mrs Henman had an air raid shelter built in the cellars and made plans for all the windows to be darkened, for extra food supplies to be laid down and for every girl to be issued with a gas mask. But she was never to guide the school through the war because she had to resign as headmistress, after a heart operation, in the summer of 1939.

The weather during that last year of peace was almost as dismal as the news from Germany. The spring and summer terms were remarkably wet and many of the girls were victims of a mumps epidemic. Rain spoilt the concert day in May – where Nesta Evans was one of the Junior Verse-Speakers – as well as the Whole Day Holiday outing to Leith Hill and Ashdown Forest in June. But Mary herself was at last beginning to shine. By now a very fair-haired, pale-skinned, blue-eyed beauty, she won the Biology and Scripture Recitation Prizes in July as well as qualifying for a Royal Life Saving Society Bronze Medallion and passing her Piano Grade III exam. One of her brilliantly clever contemporaries at Milton Mount, Alison Shrubsole, who was ten months younger than she and went on to take degrees at London and Cambridge universities, to become Principal of Cambridge's Homerton College from 1971 to 1985 and to be awarded the CBE, recalled the schoolgirl Mary vividly sixty years later. 'I remember her as in the hymn we often sang – bright and beautiful,' she told me. 'We all envied her ash-blonde hair, blue eyes and freckles, which we considered glamorous. She had the good fortune to be gifted both at her academic work (though I suspect she never exerted herself) and at sport: she was an excellent tennis player.'

Mary Youll agreed:

We were both in the same lacrosse teams. She was good

at games and played a very good game of tennis and I was her partner with our tennis team against other schools. She gravitated towards any sort of sport. And certainly she was good at her book work. I used to get quite annoyed because she used to sit with a novel – I think one of them was *Anthony Adverse* – on her lap and read all the way through a class and then blow me down if she didn't top the class invariably. She had a very retentive brain and of course that helped her a great deal with helping Dick, and she had so many more interests than I did, she was so much more academic. I don't remember Mary having any of what we used to call 'pashes' on anybody. She was a fairly level-headed sort of person and didn't go in for that sort of thing. But I do remember what lovely fair hair she had – what a beautiful, thick, blonde plait – and how well she stood up among the other girls.

The Brenchleys retreated that nervous summer to their favourite seaside holiday spot at Bracklesham Bay in Sussex, and with war looming Netta had thirteen-year-old Jean 'temporarily withdrawn' from Sutton Girls' High School in July. In August Netta organised a Miltonian Bathing Party at Bracklesham Bay for Milton Mount Old Girls and laid on a picnic lunch, tea and supper which turned out in the event to be a poignant little farewell to peace just two weeks before the outbreak of the war. There is a touching photograph of Jean and fifteen-year-old Mary riding horses along the beach at Bracklesham during that last golden peacetime childhood summer. It was one of the last times that Mary rode a horse.

Mrs Henman's successor as headmistress was a teacher from Christ's Hospital, Miss M. L. Farrell, a Cambridge MA who took over at the end of August and immediately put the school on a war footing, ensuring that every door and window in the entire vast building could be blacked out swiftly if necessary. Miss Harwood reported in her history of the school:

> Domes and skylights were painted black, windows blocked with brown paper, cubicle curtains, dress curtains and dust sheets cut up to make window curtains! Bits of felt had to be attached to the shutters where rays of light penetrated. A large roll of black-out paper ordered by Mr Johnes arrived when the work was almost completed! Girls already in school were kept busy cutting up paper, sewing curtain rings, etc. Fortunately the weather was beautiful and they were able to be out in the grounds a great deal.

On the morning of Sunday 3 September, the day that Britain and France declared war on Germany, the staff and girls had gathered in the dining-hall for the Sunday service when they heard the first warning air-raid siren and they all marched down into the basement shelter until the sounding of the All Clear. For nine months, during the 'Phoney War', the school's routine continued much as before, though Mary's mother, nervous of German bombs, refused to return to London and was still staying at Bracklesham Bay even in the chilly unseaside-holiday month of October. Lessons continued as usual and were disrupted during the spring term more by an epidemic of German measles than by the German war, though throughout the early months of 1940 the girls endured regular gas-mask and air-raid drills and often scuttled down into the basement shelter when the siren sounded. As the Phoney War dragged on the girls produced a creditable performance of Verdi's opera *Il Trovatore*, raised £10 to buy wool (worth £248 in 1999) and, according to Miss Farrell's annual report that year, 'knitted vigorously for the Navy.'

On 2 June, as Germany was about to launch the first terrible air raids of the blitz, the school was hit by a dreadful scandal.

The German mistress, whom the girls nicknamed 'The Hun', was suspected of spying for the Nazis and was sacked with only two weeks' pay after a meeting of the school Board of Management's Emergency Committee. 'Though there was no definite proof of any unpatriotic actions Miss Michael's behaviour had created suspicions in the minds of members of the staff,' reported the committee's minutes. 'In the very grave circumstances which the Nation is having to face it was felt necessary to ask her to leave immediately.' Whatever she had done to arouse suspicion, she was certainly 'an odd person,' according to Mary Youll.

Miss Michael was not alone in being expelled. The entire school was about to be kicked out. On Saturday 22 June Worth Park was commandeered by the War Office and the school given just seven days to get out. The girls were sent home three days later even though twenty-nine of them were about to sit important external examinations – among them Mary, who was due to take her Cambridge School Certificate three weeks later – and 100 Canadian soldiers moved into the mansion to pack up the furniture and books. 'The next few days were rather like the worst kind of nightmare,' wrote Miss Harwood in her history, 'but by noon on Saturday, June 29th, the whole building was empty, the greater part of the furniture having been taken to the Quadrangle, while the music rooms were full of chairs and the Camellia walk of desks.'

Somehow time was found to award the annual prizes and Mary distinguished herself yet again, sharing the Form Vb Form Prize with B. Mason and A. Shrubsole and the English Prize with J. King and A. Shrubsole. To share two prizes with the brilliantly clever Alison Shrubsole was a remarkable achievement. And, despite the disruption, Mary and the other School Certificate examinees all managed to take their exams, some of them being billeted with neighbours near the school and sitting their papers in a nearby cottage. Remarkably, nineteen of the twenty-four candidates passed their exams, six (including Mary) with exemption from Matriculation, and all five Higher School Certificate candidates passed as well. It is also miraculous that Miss Farrell found time to invigilate the exams since her main priority as headmistress was urgently to find another building as far from the war as possible where the school might be reopened when the new term started on 5 September. For two weeks she hunted feverishly through Wales and the West Country for some suitable mansion to rent and in the second week of July discovered with amazing speed that the Imperial Hotel at Lynton in North Devon was available for hire. She rented it for the duration of the war and within a few short weeks – despite the fact that there were still guests staying in the hotel – she and a handful of helpers turned it into a girls' boarding school.

Hot on her heels came Mary's mother, who was so worried about the possibility of being bombed in London that she had abandoned the family home in Kingsmead Avenue early in 1940, determined not to return until the war was over. So disturbed was Netta by the dangers of the blitz that she had even given up her post on the Milton Mount Canning Town Committee and now, as the school moved down to North Devon, she moved to Lynton too and rented the cottage right next door.

CHAPTER 4

The Western Desert and Little Switzerland

(1940–42)

Just as sixteen-year-old Mary and her mother, sister and brother were moving down to Devon in September 1940 to escape the war, Dick, the nineteen-year-old RAF 'erk', was about to be propelled right into the middle of it. He was training as an airframe fitter at a camp near Coningsby in Lincolnshire and knee deep in aeroplane parts, and for the next two-and-a-half years he dismantled, greased, repaired and reassembled every bit of an aircraft except the engine itself. He hated every minute of it. Time and again he begged to be allowed to train instead as a pilot. Time and again his applications were ignored. Instead, towards the end of 1940, he was sent to join the war in the Middle East – a long sea journey around Africa, via Cape Town, that took ten weeks – and thence to Egypt, where he was to nurse the RAF's aircraft for two years during the long war against the Italians and Germans in the Western Desert that juddered to and fro across North Africa from September 1940 to May 1943 and included major battles at Sidi Barrani, Bardia, Tobruk, Benghazi and El Alamein.

The life of an RAF 'erk' – the RAF's nickname for the lowest rank in the air force – has been described vividly by several of Dick's contemporaries in Chaz Bowyer's two collections of wartime airforce reminiscences, *The Wellington Bomber* and *Wellington at War*. 'Not for them the rakishly-tilted, crumpled peaked cap, top tunic-button carefully left undone, glamour of a pair of "silver wings", or rows of bright medal ribbons offering public display of prowess,' wrote Bowyer in *The Wellington Bomber*. Or as he put it in *Wellington at War*: 'Steely-eyed fighter and bomber crews may well have cornered the "market" on glittering awards and lavish public acclaim, yet without [the] loyalty, stoic endurance and unceasing toils of the ground crews, all aircrew would be redundant.'

An erk was paid very little and his living quarters in the desert might consist of just a hurried hole in the sand. Dick spent much of 1941 and 1942 living in the ruins and rubble of bombed-out airfields and remote desert landing grounds as the Allied armies advanced, retreated, advanced, retreated and advanced again across the Western Desert. At other times he had to hole up in slit trenches as enemy bombs rained down on him night and day. And all the while he and his fellow erks worked feverishly to service and repair damaged aeroplanes so that they could return to the fray as soon as possible. 'A seven-days' working week was the norm, with a 36- or 48-hours' leave pass a rarity, and actual leave a luxury,' reported Chaz Bowyer:

> A bicycle, however ancient, was a prized possession for transportation – cars were luxuries for officers only – while off-duty entertainment often depended solely upon self-improvisation. Indeed, improvisation was the key to much of an Erk's existence, whether at work or at play; adhering to the book, particularly in technical matters, was too often impossible due to the lack of the proper tools or parts. Such omissions were never permitted to

delay essential maintenance; the ubiquitous Erk always managed to find a solution, however crude or temporary the available material might be. The universal motto was *Ubendum, Wemendum*.

One of Bowyer's witnesses, Selwyn Barrett, an erk who served in Egypt at the same time as Dick did, remembered how each man was restricted to one bottle of water a day and how his skin was constantly coated with sand:

> A truck would take parties to the beach a couple of times a week . . . The journey was terrible – over 20 miles of rough desert track when one didn't know whether to stand or sit; the bouncing was equally bad and painful. Swimming in the sea was a joy, and salt-water soap produced a reasonable lather to clean off the layers of sand. Ten minutes after starting back, however, we'd have a fresh fine coating of sand, and by the time we [*returned*] all we were fit for was sleep.

Now and then, however, there were moments of sheer bliss.

> To alleviate the strain of operating from a desert strip, where water was always short, beer not exactly plentiful, and the food pretty awful, crews were given five days leave in Tel Aviv occasionally. These were most enjoyable breaks with the added bonus of a few bags of oranges for the messes.

Another erk who served in Egypt in 1941 and 1942, G. F. Wilson, told Bowyer:

> For dinner we had what was to become staple desert fare – meat and vegetables, followed by rice pudding.

I asked another erk sitting opposite to me why he was picking currants out of his rice and putting them on the side of his plate. When he told me that they were flies, I felt distinctly queasy, having almost finished my rice, flies and all.

Like Barrett, Wilson was also haunted by the shortage of water and his memories of thirst in the desert:

Each tent held eight men, and occasionally a lorry would bring water in 50-gallon drums that had once contained oil. Each tent received five gallons of oily water, in which we were supposed to wash; needless to say there wasn't a lot of washing among the erks. Each day we received one pint of drinking water, and considerable self-control was needed to make it last until the next day's ration. I used to shampoo my hair in paraffin, and my clothes in petrol – the latter being a sure way of keeping free of body lice.

Jim 'Curly' Gardner remembered

the terrific camaraderie of all ranks; at least when you were at the operational sharp end . . . Everything boiled down to one priority, to keep the aircraft flying, no matter what it took. We were always suffering shortages – food, water, spares, etc – but improvisation was the order of the day . . . Accommodation was equally simple – a spade to dig a square hole in the desert, two planks of wood covered in a sack for your bed, and a pup tent rigged over the hole for a home . . . Food was monotonous, yet apparently adequate, because I cannot remember ever being really hungry – only perpetually thirsty. Working dress on a forward airstrip was a joke.

The variety of styles – worn by officers or erks – resembled a circus parade; ranging from issue KD (khaki drill) to lovingly-knitted weird pullovers and jackets provided by relatives in the UK or some comforts-for-the-troops fund or organisation. Basically, everything was some shade of brown – RAF blue uniform was a rarity, usually worn only by newcomers to the unit. A pair of faded shorts, stockings and boots/shoes were normal and sufficient dress during the day, but at night it could often get cold enough to necessitate some form of greatcoat or fur-lined jacket. The sun faded everything to a neutral sand-colour, even issue black boots after a while!

And the desert could have a strange effect on some men, said Gardner, recalling the 'sand-happy' corporal who kept a trained scorpion on a string leash and took it for early morning walks and the airman who kept a chameleon tied to his lapel with a bootlace.

Not surprisingly the usually natty Dick loathed his time in the desert. Those two years were the unhappiest of his life. He detested the dirt, drudgery and lack of privacy. Even so, he was promoted to the rank of LAC – Leading Aircraftman – which allowed him to wear the insignia of a propeller on the sleeve of his uniform. Nor were all his memories of North Africa miserable. He enjoyed short trips to Cairo and up the Nile and longer leaves when he hitch-hiked as far as Jersualem, Tel Aviv, Beirut and Damascus. Pictures of him taken in Tel Aviv in 1942 show him looking handsome and dapper in his RAF uniform and jaunty beret and smoking a chunky pipe. One day when he went to look at the pyramids he even managed to ride again for the first time in months: not a horse but a mangy hired camel. Perched atop its hump, he felt distinctly queasy as it loped along in ungainly fashion, and eventually he felt so sick that he had to dismount.

He kept badgering the authorities to let him train as a pilot and every six months or so he was given yet another hopeless interview, but each time he was turned down because erks were in short supply and pilots were not. Each time he had an interview he was asked what his hobbies were and at first, in desperation, he came up with every possible pastime that might persuade the authorities of his huge enthusiasm for the air. He told them that he loved bird watching, flying kites and astronomy, but eventually he ran out of ideas and when his next interviewer, an irascible Squadron Leader, asked what his hobbies were, Dick replied truthfully: 'Huntin', shootin' and fishin'.' He was chucked out for being cheeky. It was not until early in 1943 that Dick was eventually to escape the drudgery of his life in the North African desert.

For Mary, by contrast, 1940 to 1942 were vintage years when she blossomed academically, became head of her house, won a leaving scholarship and a place at London University and began to realise her full potential.

It helped that Milton Mount's new home in the Imperial Hotel at Lynton, perched high on a clifftop on the beautiful chocolate-box north coast of Devon, between Ilfracombe and Minehead, was far removed from the noise and brutality of the war. Thousands of injured and exhausted servicemen had been sent to the area to convalesce after the retreat from Dunkirk, and thousands of children had been evacuated from London to North Devon, especially to Ilfracombe, twelve miles away, but there were 'no sounds of war', reported the *Miltonian News Sheet* in December 1940. During 1941 the girls were able to see some of the heavy German bombing of Cardiff and Swansea on the coast of south Wales across the Bristol Channel – but Swansea was twenty-six miles away and Cardiff thirty. Later, from February 1942, many American troops were billeted in the village but they did not arrive in any great numbers until that summer, by which time Mary had left the school. As the headmistress, Miss Farrell, wrote in her annual report for 1940–41: 'We have been quite untroubled by air raids since our arrival, and though planes pass over us on their way to Wales and the North West, no bombs have been dropped or guns fired within twenty miles of Lynton.'

There was of course food rationing – of sugar, butter and meat but not sausages – and 'we did know there was a war on,' I was told in 1998 by seventy-four-year-old Joyce Greenslade, who was living in the cottage right beside the school, Tarr Cottage, that Mary's mother had rented from 1940 to 1944. Netta Brenchley was by no means the only refugee who had taken cover in Lynton. 'There were four schools here during the war and the Valley of Rocks Hotel and the Lynton Cottage Hotel were full of rich evacuees,' said Mrs Greenslade, who had lived in the village all her life and played hockey against Milton Mount as a girl. 'They were good girls,' she said, 'very friendly.' She recalled seeing several British ships sunk in the distance in the Bristol Channel – 'I remember seeing one ship blazing away before it went down' – and her husband Eddie was startled one day when he was home on leave and went for a stroll along the coastal cliff path, the North Walk, no more than three hundred feet above sea level, and saw a German bomber flying right beside him. 'I couldn't believe it was so low,' he said. 'It was level with me. I threw a stone at it.' The bomber was probably a Ju88, many of which were busy laying mines in the Bristol Channel from July 1940.

Lynton has hardly changed at all since the war, according to Mrs Greenslade, and is still a quaint, quiet, little old hilltop village tucked into a fold in the coast five hundred feet above sea level and the small seaside resort of Lynmouth, its twin village at the bottom of the cliffs on the banks of a sparkling, rocky little river. Even in 1998 it felt like a relic of the 1930s with its crooked little alleys, thirteenth-century church tower, old village stocks, three churches within three hundred yards of each other, sleepy little pubs and boarding houses, and the steep Victorian hydraulic cliff railway ('The Lift') that connects it to Lynmouth. The locals call the area 'Little Switzerland . . . where Exmoor meets the sea' and its reputation as a spectacular beauty spot is well deserved. Shelley, Wordsworth and Coleridge were all delighted by the charm and beauty of the place – Shelley came to live in Lynmouth in 1812 – and there is indeed a wild, breathtaking romanticism about the area. Lynton's high, clifftop, moorland setting is numbingly beautiful with its glorious views across the Bristol Channel towards Wales, its steep wooded hills plunging sheer and dramatic into the sea, its rugged eastern cliffs that turn a deep red in the sunset, its bracing sea breezes even in June, its magnificent walks, the names of which even *smell* so very English: the Valley of Rocks, Wringcliffe Bay, Woody Bay, Hunters' Inn, Heddon's Mouth, Summerhouse Hill, Watersmeet. At night the distant lights of South Wales sparkle across the horizon like fireflies. Lynton in 1940 did not have much in common with the Western Desert.

Into this idyllic, peaceful place Miss Farrell brought her pupils in September 1940 and soon there were 112 of them housed in the three-storey, twenty-nine-bedroom Imperial Hotel and two nearby buildings which the governors had rented furnished 'until three months after the resumption of normal postal services between England and Germany.' The hotel, which had a magnificent view towards Wales over Lynmouth Bay, was supplemented by an adjoining annexe in Castle Hill and a large flat 100 yards away in Church Hill House. The local Congregational minister, the Revd H. F. Sanders, agreed to let the school use his church hall as a classroom or gymnasium, and opposite the hotel, on Castle Hill, there was an unused field that Miss Farrell arranged to use as a playground for the younger girls, who would play 'houses and shops' there in the branches of a large elderberry tree. Nearby there was also a large public recreation ground with a cricket pitch and four tennis courts, and the school hired other halls for dancing and art.

There were still numerous problems. Church Hill House, which the school was soon calling Churchill House, was in bad repair and so crowded that Miss Farrell dubbed it 'The Rabbit Warren'. The corridor carpets in the hotel itself were badly worn. The drains were in a poor condition and Miss Farrell was so worried about the 'bacteriologically impure' water that she insisted it should be boiled or filtered until the system at the reservoir was improved. Conditions were also decidedly cramped: the girls were packed into the bedrooms like rush-hour commuters and could barely move in the dining room. There was no assembly hall and the hotel's games room had to do quintuple duty each day as assembly hall, classroom, music room, dining room and evening playroom. Later, when the Congregational church hall was requisitioned by the local education authority to provide a classroom for evacuated children, the hotel games room had to act as Milton Mount's gymnasium as well. There was no laboratory or music room and pianos were jammed into bedrooms, attics and the vestibule. But the achievement of Miss Farrell and her staff in finding a new home for the school and moving everything in just ten weeks was miraculous. They barely blenched even when the removal men delivered all the books before the bookcases and the mattresses before the beds.

Despite all the problems there were several compensations. Miss Harwood wrote in her history of Milton Mount:

> In the first place they were all living together and not in billets as was the fate of so many schools. Secondly, and most important of all, they were in the heart of some of the most beautiful country in England, and because it was real country they were able to have much more freedom than had been possible in the somewhat sophisticated surroundings of Worth Park. Thirdly, they were living

in a little town and as time went on were able to take a real share in its life. They gave performances in the Town Hall, some in aid of local charities; the Guides undertook the collection of waste paper. On Saturdays the girls were able to do their own shopping which privilege they much enjoyed. Except on Sundays, after Church, 'croc walks' were a thing of the past, and the girls went for walks in 'house parties' with senior girls in charge. Then there was bathing in the swimming pool in Lynmouth and returning by the cliff railway or climbing up the steep cliff path, and on special occasions bathing at Lee Bay.

Badminton School, from Bristol, had also taken refuge in the area – at the Tors Hotel down the cliff in Lynmouth – and the two schools played matches against each other, shared the costs of lectures and concerts, and provided an extra audience for each other's plays, the first of which was a Christmas mystery play, *The Holy Quest*, which the Upper School (including Mary) performed at the end of that first term at Lynton in the town hall in aid of Dr Barnardo's Homes. And, despite all the upheaval, the school managed to organise at the end of term the usual Christmas sale, carol service and speech day.

The school stayed open throughout the Christmas holidays to accommodate twenty girls who had no homes or parents to go to and they were given a jolly Christmas party at which one of the leading lights was Mary's mother. Netta Brenchley had rented Tarr Cottage, a poky, dingy little Victorian house that had a small lawn and a good view of the sea but was so close in the shadow of the Imperial Hotel that the hotel's eastern windows, balconies and fire escape looked straight down into the cottage's garden. 'It was a funny old house,' said Joyce Greenslade, and it must have been decidedly claustrophobic for Mary to have had her mother living just yards away from her school, popping in constantly as though she were an extra matron. But Netta's tireless efforts on behalf of the school were much appreciated by the staff, and Hilda Harwood wrote of her in her history that during these years she showed 'much kindness and hospitality to girls and Staff, particularly to Form VI.' In return the school allowed Mrs Brenchley to keep Mary's fourteen-year-old sister, Jean, at home and send her to school as a day girl at the greatly reduced fee of thirty guineas a year instead of the usual 100 guineas or more. Mary too became in effect a day girl, much to the envy of others. 'I remember thinking how wonderful it must be to go home each day, not just for non-institutional meals but to a quiet place to read,' Alison Shrubsole told me. Another contemporary, Ursula Walker, told me: 'Every Sunday afternoon Mary's mother would invite either Mary's friends or those of her younger sister Jean to tea, which was a great treat.'

Netta was greatly relieved to have escaped the dangers of the London blitz when New Malden was heavily bombed on 16 August 1940 in its worst air raid of the war: eighty people were killed, nearly five hundred injured, and eighty-four houses were completely destroyed, 1,300 damaged, the railway station badly smashed up, water mains burst and gas mains broken. In September Kingston was heavily bombed and then on the night of 7 November high- explosive bombs fell on the front and back gardens of a house on the corner of Kingsmead Avenue and London Road, Londesborough Lodge, the closest of them less than two hundred yards away from the Brenchleys' house at number 17. In fact the bombs merely disturbed a vegetable patch at the back of 12 Kingsmead Avenue – and the only other bomb to fall anywhere nearby during the war landed a third of a mile away at the far end of Kingsmead Avenue, in the rear garden of 24 Hobart Road – but New Malden itself suffered throughout the war no fewer than 570 high-explosive bombs, twenty-two flying bombs and hundreds of incendiary bombs. They caused 552 casualties, destroyed 330 houses and damaged almost every house in the area. More than four thousand mothers and children were evacuated from New Malden during the war and 1,400 people were made homeless.

The first term of 1941 at Milton Mount began with a bang of its own: one of the pupils, Mary Bills, was expelled in the first week of term 'for being a disruptive influence'. Then the school suffered a measles epidemic, though this did not stop the girls playing lacrosse, organising an Eisteddfod of music, elocution, art and sewing, and putting on a couple of shows for the Congregational and Methodist Societies, including a play by Sheridan, *St Patrick's Day or The Scheming Lieutenant*, which was produced by Mary and performed by the Sixth Form. The Guides were already back at their active best and the older girls continued to knit for the troops and to darn the socks of soldiers who were billeted nearby. Perhaps Mary knitted one of the 'weird pullovers' that 'Curly' Gardner reported were being sent out to RAF erks in the desert and – who knows? – perhaps it was worn by Dick Francis.

Mary blossomed during her last two years at Milton Mount, working hard, reading widely, swimming, representing the school at tennis, and becoming immersed in theatrical productions such as Laurence Housman's *Brother Sun*, which the senior girls performed on the evening of speech day in November 1941, and the three plays that the Dramatic Society put on in the spring term of 1942. 'With Mary's ability went enormous charm,' Alison Shrubsole told me. 'When we were in the Sixth Form we were allowed to walk down the cliff path after lessons to bathe in the sea at Lynmouth. One evening we were rather late returning. Mary had the idea of seeking a lift up from a rare passing motorist. We had no money on us, but Mary's charm prevailed. She rode up, whereas we ran all the way, terrified of being late back to school.'

Oddly enough Mary never won any prizes in her last year, not even one of the three French prizes that were awarded in 1942, but she was made a prefect, head of Raleigh House, and given a Privilege Badge for service to the school, a silver shield engraved with the letters MMC. More than forty years later she wrote to the Old Girls' *Miltonian News Sheet* to say how grateful she was for the standards she had learned at Milton Mount – and nine years later she wrote again to say the same thing. The contrast with Dick's schooldays could hardly have been greater. 'We had a wonderful time at Lynton,' Mary Youll told me.

'When one looks back on these years at Lynton,' wrote Hilda Harwood, 'one forgets the difficulties and discomforts and remembers glorious tramps over the moors or along the coast, with a rucksack on one's back containing a picnic tea; . . . Conduct holidays, too, when the senior girls went for long expeditions, one of them expert in tickling trout which they cooked on the banks of the stream . . .' Most remarkable of all, Miss Farrell and her staff somehow managed to keep the standard of teaching at Lynton as high as it had been at Worth Park and the exam results were extraordinarily good, not only in the academic subjects but even in music and science, despite the lack of proper facilities.

During Mary's last two years at Milton Mount her favourite subjects were English and French, which were taught by Miss Harwood and Miss Rabey, both of whom had BA Honours degrees from London University, which doubtless influenced Mary's decision to go there when she passed her Higher School Certificate exams in July 1942. Given the circumstances, her excellent results were a credit to both women and when she left Milton Mount at the age of eighteen in the summer of 1942 the school awarded her one of its Thornley Leaving Scholarships, which was worth £20 a year (£455 in 1999) for the next three years. Of the five girls who won a Thornley that year only Mary and one other were sufficiently polite as to write to the Board of Management to say 'thank you', and every term for the next two years, whenever another scholarship cheque arrived from Milton Mount, she wrote again to thank the Board. Netta Brenchley had brought her daughter up properly.

Mary's last term at Lynton was typical of her time at Milton Mount. She and her fellow sixth formers provided teas twice a week for the patients at the local hospital. They supervised the cultivation of a new allotment to grow vegetables for the school. In June they were involved in an exciting practice invasion of the district, taking part as messengers or casualties, and members of the senior school sang a cantata, *The Lady of Shalott*, at the speech-day concert. And on Mary's last weekend at the school, during the Old Girls' reunion on the first three days of August, she played for the Leaving Sixth in a cricket match against the Old Girls – the schoolgirls won by 57 runs to 33 – and then took part in a huge communal picnic on Hollerday Hill followed by supper and two plays performed by the Leaving Sixth. On the Monday she played in her final tennis tournament before leaving school on the Tuesday, 4 August. It was all so very *English*, and all so very Milton Mount.

Milton Mount College was eventually to return to Worth Park in 1946 and to survive there until July 1960, when it had to be closed due to a combination of financial crises and the constant threat of new building development around Crawley which encroached on the college and its grounds. The school was also increasingly threatened by the noise and disruption caused by the expansion of nearby Gatwick Airport. 'Where there were lovely woods, and fields covered with buttercups in the spring and a stream where wild daffodils grew, there are now busy roads and rows of houses,' wrote Hilda Harwood sadly. The main house was demolished to make way for a new housing estate, which included a tower block called Milton Towers – 'a horrible block of six-floored units,' Mary Youll told me, 'but the gardens are still there and so is the Camellia Walk, and the quadrangle where Mary and I spent our days.' Two years later Milton Mount was merged with Wentworth College in Bournemouth. As for the Imperial Hotel in Lynton, it reverted to being the Imperial Hotel after the war but has since been converted into seventeen luxury flats. But Tarr Cottage is still there, jammed between the old hotel and a restaurant. Today the little rockery to the left of the front door is guarded by five tiny garden gnomes. Netta Brenchley would have been appalled.

CHAPTER 5

Southern Rhodesia and Royal Holloway

(1943–44)

At the end of 1942 twenty-two-year-old Dick Francis was still in the Western Desert and still nagging the RAF to let him train as a pilot, and his dogged persistence finally paid off early in 1943. By then the war in North Africa was almost won, his services as an erk were now not nearly as vital as they had been, and he was sent south to train as a pilot in the British Central African colony of Southern Rhodesia. He left with a feeling of huge relief and sailed to Cape Town by troopship via the Mediterranean and the Atlantic, and then took a train north through the wild bushlands of the Transvaal to the Southern Rhodesian city of Bulawayo, which had been no more than fifty years previously the capital kraal of King Lobengula, the chief of the warlike Matabele tribe.

The RAF had set up ten flying training schools in Southern Rhodesia (and others in Canada and South Africa) as part of its Empire Air Training Scheme because such loyal overseas locations allowed young pilots to learn to fly in good weather and free from enemy attacks. Southern Rhodesia, with its millions of acres of empty bushveld, granite kopjes, stunning scenery, teeming wildlife and huge open skies, was a magnificent place for a young man to learn to fly. As Hugh Morgan wrote in his history of the scheme, *By the Seat of Your Pants*, 'the cadets arrived in a country free from bombing, where the bright lights, luxurious and plentiful food, and welcoming and often extraordinarily generous inhabitants, were in striking contrast to the drab and dreary blackout and rationing conditions the cadets had left behind in Britain.'

Dick was sent first to the Initial Training Wing at Hillside, a few miles south of Bulawayo, near Cecil Rhodes's impressive hilltop grave high amid the granite rocks of the Matopo Hills. Luckily the arrival of his group was fully expected, unlike that of a group of three hundred men who had arrived a few months earlier much to the dismay of the Rhodesian Air Training Group, which had asked the Air Ministry in London to send out three hundred airscrews, not three hundred aircrew. The arrival at Hillside was described in *By the Seat of Your Pants* by Alan Holloway, who was there eighteen months earlier than Dick:

A Tiger Moth stood on display near the parade ground, no doubt to keep our hopes up, but the camp, far from being an airfield, was Bulawayo's agricultural showground and market. Large numbers of us were quartered in converted cattle stalls and pig pens, the remainder in long lines of grass and canvas bandus or huts with open space where doors and windows would normally be. There seemed to be thousands of us and we were soon disabused of any ideas of getting to a flying station soon. The countryside outside Bulawayo seemed red and desert, penetrated only by strip roads, red earth and dust, with two parallel strips of tarmac in the centre the width of a car's track. The dormitory huts were quite a distance from the ablution blocks, so large urinal buckets were placed in the lines outside the doorways for use at night. At one camp dance several men brought visiting girls down the lines to show them the huts where they lived. One girl innocently enquired, 'What are those buckets?' The embarrassed airman with presence of mind replied, 'They're fire buckets.' 'But they're empty,' pursued the girl. 'Er . . . yes,' said the young man, 'but they get filled up later'.

After his initial training at Hillside, Dick was sent to the flying training school at Kumalo, a few miles north-east of Bulawayo, for a twelve-week elementary flying course that was later to be followed by a more advanced twenty-four-week course at Thornhill airfield near Gwelo, all of which required a total of 225 flying hours – including night flying and bad-weather training – before a pilot was awarded his wings.

Dick was to spend nearly a year in Rhodesia and soon began to regret all the truancies of his schooldays. Because he had never done much maths he had great difficulty learning how to navigate – he had to count on his fingers when he wanted to calculate latitude and longitude – and this time there was no escaping hour after hour in the classroom listening to lectures on the theory of flying, signals, meteorology and a dozen other subjects. But when it came to flying itself he was in his element. His first instructor was delighted to hear that in civilian life Dick was a horseman because good horsemen tended to learn to fly easily, probably because their light, sensitive hands were just as good at sensing the balance of an aeroplane and the subtleties of a control column as they were at communicating with a horse. And so it turned out, even though Dick was so short that he had to sit on cushions to reach the controls. One of his instructors, Flight Lieutenant Thomas Sheldon Kilpatrick, later rated him as an 'average' pilot, but for Dick flying turned out to be every bit as exhilarating and liberating as he had dreamed it would be. He revelled in the loneliness of the skies and especially in the aerobatics – rolling, spinning and side-slipping his nippy, manoeuvrable little single-engined aircraft – and cavorted gloriously through the Central African air like a man released, skipping over the clouds as though he were a horseman again, his aircraft a glossy hunter, the clouds no more than fluffy hedges in the sky. He shrugged off the dangers, just as he had always shrugged off the dangers of hunting and steeplechasing, even though learning to fly was obviously hazardous and fledgling pilots did get lost in the bush and sometimes killed themselves and their instructors in accidents.

Not that Dick's training was completely blissful. 'There was one particular instructor who was well known for shouting on the intercom when you were flying and that was enough to put anyone off,' I was told by Roy Palmer, who also trained as a pilot in Rhodesia that year and later became a lifelong friend of Dick's. 'The more he shouted the worse it got, and Dick was unfortunate enough to have this particular man in Thornhill.'

In his autobiography Dick dismissed his year in Rhodesia in less than a page and made no mention of the friends he had made there – other pilots such as John Stephen and Eric Ginger – but a vivid impression of RAF life there was given by the future British Cabinet Minister Anthony Wedgwood-Benn, who trained as a young pilot in Southern Rhodesia just after Dick left, in his diaries *Years of Hope*. Benn also trained at Gwelo and told of being awakened at 6.15 a.m. each day by an African yelling 'wakey wakey'; of being allowed no more than one airletter a week; of being paid £5-10s a week (£125 in 1999) but being able to buy ten strong Tom Tom cigarettes for a penny (9p in 1999); of regular visits to the cinema to see films starring Rita Hayworth; and of frequent evenings at the Services Club, where he danced and flirted with several local girls and a

Polish air force woman. Like Dick, Benn had trouble navigating accurately and described one 3.30 a.m. navigation hike through the bush thus:

> We were issued spats, maps and compasses and we boarded the lorry just as the dawn was lifting. The lorry moved off and the flight began to sing as we drove through Bulawayo, the old sentimental soldier songs which in these surroundings were very pleasant. The sky in the east was yellow and orange and above a bank of black cloud shone Venus, the morning star. We were dropped at a gate with a course of 168 degrees and fifteen miles of rough bundu ahead. I pushed on and gradually as the heat increased and the country grew more difficult I stumbled more often, and began to swear under my breath.

One night Noël Coward turned up at the camp and gave his one-man show, singing *Don't Put Your Daughter on the Stage, Mrs Worthington*, *Let's Fly Away* and of course *Don't Let's Be Beastly to the Germans*. Like almost every airman under training, Benn made a trip to the Victoria Falls to see baboons and crocodiles and to marvel at the surging power of one of the great wonders of the world, *Mosi-oa-tunya* in the local dialect, 'The Smoke That Thunders'. And there was also the occasional week or weekend leave in the Rhodesian capital, Salisbury. 'It was much nicer than being in England, certainly as far as food was concerned,' Roy Palmer told me. 'We could go into a hotel there and have a marvellous meal, which you certainly couldn't do in the UK at the time.'

Like Dick, Tony Benn revelled in the flying itself, even though three pupils and an instructor were killed within less than three weeks in two separate accidents, one when a plane hit a high-tension cable, the other when two Oxford aircraft collided in mid-air. For sheer enjoyment and devilment he would sometimes fly so low across the parched countryside that his plane was lower than the tallest trees and rocky *kopjes*. Africans would wave as he roared over their village huts – or would run away or cower in terror if he was very low – and sometimes he and his instructor, Crownshaw, would fly along above the Lundi River looking for crocodiles: 'We saw three hippos in the centre of the river and as we flew over them they submerged like U-boats.' On another occasion he flew deliberately over a large bush fire and was whisked like a lift to a height of 9,000 feet by its thermal.

He relished even the early shift that began at 5.20 a.m. 'Crownshaw took me up just as the sun was rising and it was wizzo,' wrote Benn. 'The ground lay below us clouded with purple-tinted mist and the fine blues, oranges, and yellows of a Rhodesian sunrise were giving way to the bright glare of the new sun. We flew to Senale and there practised take-offs, circuits and landings.' On another early morning, when Benn was doing an hour's solo aerobatics, he saw the sun rise twice: 'As I opened up above the ground I looked over to the east and there was the faint yellow of approaching dawn. I climbed up once more and as I reached a greater height the whole splendid scene was recreated and I flew again in lightness while below me the first glimmer of the new day was showing on the tops of the mountains. I continued my climb, intoxicated by the beauty of it all . . .'

No wonder Dick felt so exhilarated after so many months bogged down in the sand, heat and drudgery of the Western Desert. When Tony Benn finally left Rhodesia by train in March 1945 he wrote in his diary: 'I stood on the end of the railway carriage and saw the sun set for the last time on Rhodesia. It was most impressive and I felt the magic of Africa.'

Dick must have felt much the same when he completed his training early in 1944 and returned to Britain to rejoin the war and to meet the woman who was to turn out to be the great love of his life.

While Dick was learning to fly, a vivid short story about an RAF fighter pilot appeared in the 1943 edition of *Erinna*, the annual magazine that was written and published by the staff and students of the Royal Holloway College at London University. The story was called *The Airman* and was written by Mary Brenchley. It described with uncanny precision the exact feelings that Dick was experiencing as a trainee pilot – the exhilaration and emptiness, the joyful freedom of the lonely skies, the laughing clouds – and it showed powerfully that at the age of nineteen Mary had fallen deeply in love with words and had already developed strikingly the strong narrative drive and some of the literary tricks that were to surface twenty years later in the Dick Francis novels. In seven short paragraphs describing the tension of an aerial dogfight, the pain of loss, the disillusionment of victory, the hopeless dream of a better world, you can hear the authentic voice of every Dick Francis hero in all the books to come. *Erinna* magazine – which was named after the young Greek poetess whose white marble statue adorned the picture gallery and still stands in the chapel cloisters – was only one of Mary's many interests at Holloway. She became the magazine's secretary in 1944 and wrote another story for that issue, a tale entitled *The Fireman* that was set during the London blitz and written as tensely and graphically as any Dick Francis thriller.

Mary entered the women-only Royal Holloway College on 1 October 1942, three weeks before General Montgomery launched the attack in North Africa that led to the victory of El Alamein. Although Holloway was a part of London University it was eighteen miles west of London, at Englefield Green near Egham in Surrey and no more than twelve miles from Vince Francis's hunting stables at Wokingham. It was a huge, impressive, four-storey red-brick and stone building, set in ninety-four acres of woodland, that had been founded in 1886 by the Victorian millionaire philanthropist Thomas Holloway, who had made a vast fortune out of peddling purgative pills and ointments. Mary must have been overawed when she arrived, even though she had already experienced the architectural glories of Worth Park, because Holloway was even bigger and looked like a fairytale Ruritanian castle rather than a modern place of learning. It was a fantasy extravaganza with numerous towers, turrets, terraces and colonnades, a forty-metre-high clock tower, a huge gateway and massive grassy double quadrangles, large statues of Queen Victoria and Thomas Holloway and his wife Jane, sweeping steps, a boating lake, chapel, a famous picture gallery stuffed with priceless paintings by Constable, Gainsborough, Landseer, Millais and Turner. 'As a symbol . . . as an image, as a manifestation touristique, Royal Holloway College was unbeatable,' wrote the architectural historian Joe Mordaunt Crook. 'It shared all the magnificence – and inconvenience – of its principal prototype, the palatial Chambord . . . The result is sensational.'

Into this overwhelming cultural and academic hot-house came eighteen-year-old Mary Brenchley, by now looking like some fairytale princess with her fair hair, pale freckled porcelain skin and deep blue eyes. She was one of seventy-three new undergraduates that brought the total number of students up to 170, each of them paying £144 a year for tuition and a study/bedroom. Before the war each Holloway student had enjoyed a bedroom *and* a study, but the demands of the war meant that no undergraduate had more than one room and some girls were forced to share one, since the east wing had been taken over by the Auxiliary Territorial Service (the ATS) to house its Junior Officers' School. So Mary had to make do with a cramped third-floor room furnished with a divan bed, a desk, one chair, a wardrobe and an inside view over a quadrangle.

The length of her course was also cramped. Previously most

undergraduates had three years to achieve their degrees but Mary and twenty-two other Holloway girls had to complete their courses in just two years because of wartime labour regulations which laid down that women would have to do some sort of National Service from the age of twenty. This cruelly diminished Mary's university career, and to make matters worse, just as she was leaving Holloway in July 1944, the tide of the war had turned and the rules were relaxed to allow girls who came up in October 1943 to take a full three years over their degrees, as before.

The war had of course a huge impact on the undergraduates' social lives as well as their conditions for study. Every one of the college's huge number of massive windows had to be blacked out every night by some dark material so that not a glimmer of light might escape to attract the German bombers. Each girl was forbidden to bath in more than three inches of water, and although the maids laid coal fires in the rooms these were allowed to be lit only on alternate nights, so the undergraduates foraged in the countryside round about to look for wood for their fires and took to wearing their gowns all day to keep warm. Cunningly the only really warm room in the college in winter was the library. Food was rationed and the college's huge asparagus beds were dug up and planted instead with potatoes, though the college did have a vegetable garden, an orchard and a pig farm, so that breakfasts at least were hearty, with fat, meaty sausages. One of Mary's contemporaries, Philippa Moeller, told Caroline Bingham for her book *The History of Royal Holloway College*: 'There was always plenty of soup, so our normal procedure was to grab and wolf our first course, grab and wolf our pudding, and fill up on soup. This was deplored by the Principal.' The service tunnel beneath the college was turned into an air-raid shelter and because many of the college's domestic and outdoor staff had been called up for National Service, the undergraduates were paid 10d an hour to help with the housework, washing up, sweeping leaves and the upkeep of the grounds. Some even did farm work and most took up sewing and knitting for the troops or collecting books and waste paper to raise funds for the Red Cross. Yet some of the old pre-war standards were staunchly retained and on Saturday nights the girls still wore long evening dresses and marched into the hall – two by two in a crocodile that must have reminded Mary of Milton Mount – to be served by maids in uniform under the steely eye of the college butler, Frank Pyne.

Because the other London University colleges had been evacuated and the Union closed there was none of the pre-war cross-fertilisation between Holloway and its sister colleges in the dangerous capital. Inter-college lectures and sports matches were cancelled all together and the students were all but cut off from London's theatres, cinemas, exhibitions, art galleries and museums. Now and then cadets from nearby Sandhurst and Camberley were invited to Holloway for an occasional dance, but otherwise the girls' social lives were restricted to the little tea parties they gave in their rooms or a bicycle ride along the roads to Egham, Englefield Green or Runnymede along roads unsignposted because of the fear of invasion. Students who were reading French were sometimes despatched to London to serve as waitresses in the French officers' canteen in St James's Square, but these rare occasions were hardly sufficient to compensate for the social desert of the girls' lives. Even so, two girls in Mary's year did get married and another managed to become pregnant. The expectant mother was asked to leave the college because 'some of the maids are very young'.

A modern university student would never accept the restrictions and regulations of Holloway in those days, for the girls' lives were so regimented that they might as well have been still at school. They were wakened by a rising bell at 7 a.m., summoned to chapel by another bell at 7.50, and made to work from nine until one, when another bell called them to lunch. After tea at four it was back to work until seven, when two more bells would order the first and second sittings in to supper. After supper they were expected to work again from 8.30 until ten, except on Saturdays. At 10.25 there was the final bell of the day and at 10.30 all the lights were turned off in the public rooms. Students were required to attend morning chapel and lectures and on Sundays to attend the college chapel 'or some other place of worship.' Everyone addressed everyone else as Miss, and there seemed to be no end to the mountain of fussy, bossy rules:

'Students are expected to take daily exercise. They are requested not to walk or bicycle alone beyond the immediate neighbourhood and to be within the grounds by one hour after sunset, unless leave of absence has been given'; 'Students must be within doors by 10 p.m. when the House is locked up, unless late leave has been given'; 'No student may be absent from Hall dinner without leave from the Principal or the Principal's Assistant'; 'Except in the case of father, brother or guardians, men can only be entertained in students' studies by special permission, to be obtained from the Principal or her Assistant'.

Each new girl was given a printed sheet ordering her to turn back her bedclothes and open her window before leaving her bedroom at 8 a.m. for breakfast. No wines or spirits were allowed in the rooms. If a student wanted to go out after dinner she had to obtain permission before 7 p.m. from the Principal or her assistant. And so it went on and on. Even a visit to your tutor was carefully regulated, Caroline Bingham was told by Charmian Hollyoak (*née* Humphreys): if you were invited for tea you stayed for forty minutes, if for coffee you stayed for no more than twenty minutes. In 1943 a college committee that had been asked to determine the college's post-war policy confessed that Holloway did have 'the atmosphere of a boarding school' and admitted that the college was too isolated from the rest of London University, with the result that good potential students and staff did not apply to the college because of its lack of intellectual stimulus. In addition, said the committee, 'the lack of social contacts, more particularly with men, produces in the students either immaturity or a sense of frustration, so that many of those who leave the College are still not sufficiently adult to take a full share of their social responsibilities.' It is indicative of the cosy, claustrophobic atmosphere of Holloway then that the girls rarely mixed with students in other years or studying other subjects but generally restricted their social contacts to girls in what were known as their own 'families' or year-groups of exact contemporaries.

When Mary arrived at Holloway – which is now co-educational and called Royal Holloway and Bedford New College – she had to sit almost immediately an examination in Additional Latin, which she passed, and from then on she could concentrate on French and English. She started by studying Old French, French prose, philology, translation and Old as well as Modern French literature. The girls in Mary's class were keen and clever and their teachers delighted with them. The youngest teacher, Nancy Jones, had been scathing in her report on the previous year's students – 'as a class, has no brain' – but of Mary's year she wrote at the end of their first term that they were 'Excellent students . . . Always enter wholeheartedly into their work. Enthusiastic. Intelligent.' Another teacher, Miss McWilliam (known as 'Quilly') agreed: 'Very good set of students. First Years show vigour and individuality.'

For her English course Mary studied comparative grammar, literary criticism, phonology, phonetics, Old and Middle English grammar and texts, Renaissance literature, English drama from 1400 to 1700 (including set Shakespeare and Marlowe plays) and sixteenth-, seventeenth- and eighteenth-century literature. The contrast with Dick's semi-literate 'education' could hardly have been greater.

Mary was 'a pleasant, fresh-faced, friendly girl who usually wore her very fair hair in plaits round her head,' I was told by her contemporary Margaret Lindsay (*née* Spencer). 'She was popular and outgoing.' Another contemporary, Beryl Caink (*née* Whitehead), remembered her as 'a delightful personality . . . a slender girl with flaxen hair, worn in a plait wound round her head like a coronet, very blue eyes, fair complexion and a smile – in fact I can't picture her face without a smile, often a grin. I think Mary had a great sense of humour.' When Mrs Caink learned many years afterwards that in later life Mary had learned to fly 'I thought "of course – she *would* have done that without turning a hair and with great glee!"'

Among Mary's closest friends (all but one of them eighteen years old) were Barbara Crockett, an accountant's daughter from Peterborough; Gwendoline Fellows, a headmaster's daughter from Leicester; Patricia Fitzmaurice-Kelly, who came from Hove in Sussex; Margaret Griffiths, a bank manager's daughter from Esher; Margaret Hall, the daughter of a Yorkshire vicar, from Tadcaster; Margaret Ogden, a jeweller's daughter from Accrington; Joan Plater, a builder's daughter from Coulsdon; Honor Sewell, the daughter of a Norfolk prep school owner; and Jean Sinclair, an orphan from London.

'We were part of the same "family" – college idiom for the informal groups of seven or eight friends who tended to congregate in each others' rooms for late-night chats, hot drinks and so on,' I was told by Gwendoline Fellows (Mrs Morley-Mower). 'Drinks in Mary's room were made special by her set of cups and saucers in Devon pottery – simple round shapes in various plain colours – unusual, stylish and very much Mary.' Mrs Morley-Mower added:

Mary had style. She was striking-looking with long blonde hair plaited in a coronet round her head. With her unhurried poised manner she gave, I always thought, an impression of a Scandinavian or Russian princess, especially on the occasions when she wore a fur hat. But she was in no way remote or pompous – far from it. She had a great sense of humour and a talent for deflating pomposity in others – but kindly, not maliciously. I don't remember seeing her angry or depressed: she had an enviable ability to appear unconcerned if, for example, an essay was overdue, while others would panic about getting work in on time. She didn't seem swayed by student fads and fancies, but gave the impression of quietly going her own way with determination but without aggression. Looking back, I think she was more emotionally mature than some of us were at that age, more sure of herself. I wouldn't have been surprised if she herself had developed a successful literary career.

Honor Sewell (later Mrs Preston) remembered Mary as having been particularly lively. 'We had to work hard but managed to enjoy life despite the pressures of the war,' she told me. 'Mary used to attend weekly ambulance/first aid classes outside college, specialising in realistic wound make-up. She also had a lovely high soprano voice.'

In addition to writing for the college magazine, Mary blossomed in every direction at Holloway. Despite having to complete a three-year course in two years, she lived up to the college's motto, *Nil Desperandum*, and dived into university life with relish and astonishing energy. She joined the Students' Union, Debating Society, French Play Reading Society, Cadet Rangers, the committees of the Music Association, the musical Orpheus Society, and the dramatic society, CHARD (an anagram of the initial letters of the name Royal Holloway College Amateur

Dramatics). She produced two plays, *Victoria Regina* and *Little Ladyship*, and acted in several others. She sang in the choir, played a reed pipe in the orchestra, became a member of the college's air-raid stretcher party and a deputy corridor warden. In her first year she played tennis and won a place in the lacrosse team and the netball second team, and she enjoyed fencing, punting and sculling, becoming a committee member of the Boat Club and Secretary of the Fencing Club. Outside the college she even found time to help with the local Girl Guides, the Virginia Water Brownie pack and the Egham Casualties Club. As Holloway's Principal, Miss Fanny Street, was to say of her in the testimonial she wrote when Mary finally left the college in 1944: 'She was prominent in almost all the general activities of the college, notably in athletic, dramatic and social spheres.' Miss Street was obviously fond of Mary, but made it clear that her energy and vivacity could at times be wearying. 'Her personality is pleasing as well as versatile,' wrote Miss Street. 'Her very attractive appearance, cheerful temper and humourous [*sic*] interest in things in general made contacts with her always pleasant even if a certain appearance of irresponsibility some-times provoked impatience. With fuller development and more self-discipline she should, I think, make her mark in any work she undertakes.'

Mary's class continued to please its teachers throughout 1943. 'A very good class,' reported Nancy Jones. 'Should produce good results.' And indeed Mary sailed through her intermediate exams when she sat them at the end of her first year, in June. 'A friend of mine who shared Mary's sessions in French conversation remembers being impressed by the fluency and facility with which she spoke the language,' said Margaret Lindsay. It was a similar story when they returned to Holloway in October after the summer vacation. Mary studied the French Romantic writer Alfred de Vigny as a special subject and an Old French set text, *Tristan*, as well as morphology, syntax, sixteenth-century set texts, eighteenth-century literature and translation. 'A good class which works well and is a pleasure to teach,' wrote Nancy Jones in her report that term. The girls were keen, she added the following term, 'an interesting class to work with. Thinks for itself and is prepared to discuss.'

In her second and last year Mary became busier than ever. She was an officer of the Students' Union Society, a member of the committee of eight that ran *Erinna* magazine, and a member of the committee of the dramatic society, CHARD, which involved her in that last term of 1943 in several play-reading groups as well as the production of two plays, *Arms and the Man* and *Berkeley Square*. Later in the year CHARD put on several more plays – among them *Tobias and the Angel*, *Richard of Bordeaux* and *Thunder Rock* – and Mary played the Earl of Rutland in *Richard of Bordeaux* and distinguished herself as the producer of *Little Ladyship* by Ian Hay in the cramped Lecture Theatre, which had only a narrow stage and no passage behind the scenes. Her taste for the theatre had become a passion, and in a review of *Little Ladyship* in the November 1944 issue of the *College Letter* J. W. Peel praised her stage direction and wrote: 'The difficulties which beset the staging of any play in the Lecture Theatre are well known . . . To M. Brenchley must be attributed the production's smoothness and lightness of touch, for it was her effort which resulted in such apparent effortlessness.' Mary's skill as a stage manager was to lead her into a job in the theatre two years later. That term she also won a competition for the more advanced members of the fencing club, which now had a professional coach.

She sat her final Bachelor of Arts exams in French and English in the middle of June 1944, along with the twenty-two other young women who had also been forced to complete their degree courses in just two hothouse years. The second week of her Finals was badly disrupted by German flying-bomb attacks so that last-minute revision and sleep were difficult, and 'the exams were actually sat (under a glass roof!) during and in spite of flying bombs/doodle-bugs,' Honor Sewell told me. 'But we all managed to pass and met in London later to celebrate.' The bombing, together with the fact that Mary had had to rush through her studies in two years, probably explains why she managed to achieve only a third-class degree, though several of her two-year-course friends did better and passed with a 2:1 or 2:2. Even so, her teachers were content with her Third. 'The reports of her lecturers show that this result was creditable to her,' Miss Street wrote in Mary's testimonial. 'It evidently attests the power of producing her best work at the right moment.' And she wrote prophetically: 'Her normal work showed a quick but not deep intelligence and a certain taste for literature.'

How right she was.

CHAPTER 6

Wings and Propellers

(1944–45)

Early in 1944 Dick won his wings and returned to Britain just as Mary was taking her final degree exams, but by now the Allies had achieved almost complete superiority in the air over Europe so that there was a glut of RAF pilots with little to do.

It is widely believed that Dick flew into battle piloting a Spitfire, the ultimate glamour fighter of the Second World War – an aircraft he was later to describe as 'superb' and 'my first love' – but his fellow pilot and lifelong friend Roy Palmer, whom he met on the troopship as they returned to Britain from Cape Town, told me that although they had both flown Spitfires this had been 'just part of the training programme' and they had flown the legendary fighter only over Britain. Neither of them actually saw any action, he said, and he did not think that Dick had ever flown over Germany during the war. 'No, we spent quite a lot of time messing about at Harrogate,' said Mr Palmer, 'and then we were posted up to Perth in Scotland in May 1944 to keep our hand in flying just basically Tiger Moths again. We spent most of the war just training.' Dick was, however, a 'very good' pilot, he said, 'very steady. One felt quite safe if you were in a formation exercise with him. There were certain other people with whom you felt a bit edgy: they were too pushy, pushing themselves in too close.' As for Dick the man, 'he had a good sense of humour and a pretty turn of phrase for the various jokes he used to tell, but he wasn't physically a sportsman and didn't partake of any of that.'

After Scotland Dick was posted back to Harrogate, then to Turnhill in Shropshire, and over the next year to RAF stations all over Britain. Since he was not needed as a fighter pilot he was transferred to Bomber Command where, to his dismay, he was retrained to fly Wellington bombers instead. He was mortified: after skipping about the sky in Tiger Moths – rolling, spinning and looping the loop – he found the un-aerobatic Wellingtons so heavy and sluggish that his arms ached each time he landed one.

Some pilots became deeply fond of the chunky, snub-nosed Wellington – or Wimpy, as they called it affectionately, after the chubby, lazy wartime cartoon character J. Wellington Wimpy. The aircraft historian Martin Bowman called it 'one of the greatest bombers of World War II' and when Chaz Bowyer contacted several hundred ex-Wellington crewmen while researching his book *The Wellington Bomber* he wrote: 'With only *very* rare exception, all were unanimous in their praise and sincere affection for the "good old Wimpy".' The plane's admirers were particularly grateful for its amazingly strong, geodetic, cloth-covered, flexible metal airframe – an aluminium latticework construction covered with fabric – which allowed Wellingtons time and again to limp home safely even after they had been damaged by flak so extensively that any other type of bomber would have crashed. The aircraft's remarkable ability to survive saved the lives of hundreds of Wimpy crewmen.

On the other hand the plane could offer a pilot some decidedly hairy moments. 'On take-off one always had to throttle back sharply in order to work the accelerator pump, otherwise the engines were likely to cut out when opening up to full power,' one Wimpy pilot, Denys White, told Bowyer. 'On landing one had to engage a sort of automatic trim, which meant one had to push hard on the control column during the approach run. Then, on levelling out, one took great care otherwise the nose came well up. The automatic pilot was also a dicey affair, sometimes causing the Wimpy to dive steeply. For such emergencies a fire axe was kept handy to sever the hydraulics pipeline if the automatic pilot couldn't be disengaged smartly. One other disquieting habit was for the escape hatch over the pilot to fly off on occasion.' Bowman reported that the plane was so disconcertingly flexible that one harassed pilot remarked in the middle of a storm: 'If this fucking aircraft flaps her wings any further we won't need engines.'

In general, though, 'the Wellington was universally loved,' said Air Transport Auxiliary ferry pilot Hugh Bergel in his book *Flying Wartime Aircraft*. 'It was such a docile and friendly thing.' Because of its flexible frame, however, the plane 'had the habit – not in the least disconcerting – of twitching slightly from time to time as it rattled along; it was almost as if it was wagging its tail at you. It was very easy to fly (though a bit marginal if one engine failed), and the view from the cockpit was good enough to make it one of the better aeroplanes for bad weather flying. And it was exceptionally easy to land.' His view was supported by another Wimpy ferry pilot, H. A. Taylor, who wrote in his memoir *Test Pilot at War*: 'Once a pilot had become accustomed to its minor quirks of behaviour and its oddly assorted controls, he found it to be a delightfully easy and forgiving affair. However much the structure quaked in rough air – with the control column wandering erratically backwards and forwards as the elevator cables moved to match the flexings of the fuselage – no one ever had any doubt about the strength of geodetic construction. We knew, too, that it was *meant* to flex.'

Dick's first real job as a pilot involved flying Wellingtons on hoax air raids that were meant to fool the Germans as to where the main British bombing attacks were to be made, and in his autobiography he claimed that one of his night missions was to divert attention from the famous RAF Dambusters' attack on the Möhne and Eder dams, but that is impossible since the Dambusters' attack took place on the night of 16 May 1943, when he was still in Rhodesia.

At the end of 1944, to his dismay, he and Roy Palmer were sent to Shobdon in Herefordshire to learn how to fly the heavy troop-carrying gliders that were to help complete the invasion of Germany over the Rhine. These engineless aircraft were even more cumbersome than the Wellington, and to add to Dick's misery he and Palmer were sent to Larkhill on Salisbury Plain to undergo an army assault training course in the middle of the freezing winter which involved crawling through the snow on their stomachs while a sadistic sergeant-major bellowed at them. The plan was to toughen them up, because once they had landed their glider-loads of soldiers in Germany they would be expected to grab a rifle and join the battle as infantrymen. 'We were the only two commissioned officers on the course,' said Mr Palmer. 'It was pretty horrible and we were treated very badly. The winter of 1944 was very, very severe and crawling about Salisbury Plain on your belly with your rifle and so on, learning the tricks of the trade as far as infantrymen were concerned . . . well, if we'd wanted to be infantrymen we would have joined the army.'

It was all a long way from the glamour of Dick's original dream of winning his wings. In the event he was never needed to glide into Germany: towards the end of the war German resistance was weaker than expected and only twenty groups of trained glider pilots were called to complete the task; Dick's group was the twenty-second and was never sent into battle. He was so relieved that he returned almost happily to the dreaded Wellingtons, flying them out of the RAF station at Turnhouse in Scotland, and since the war in Europe was coming to an end and Bomber Command had less and less to do, Dick and his Wellington and crew were transferred to Coastal Command where they became the aerial equivalent of cowboys rounding up cattle, undertaking the slow, boring task of escorting German ships that had surrendered into ports in Britain. It was such a routine, undemanding job that Dick's crew teasingly called him 'the chauffeur' and he would lie back in the cockpit, gazing at the heavens and flying by auto-pilot, until the day he suddenly spotted to his horror another plane so close above him that he could almost touch it. He sat up at attention after that.

Once every enemy ship had been rounded up Dick was given yet another dreary job, this time to nanny newly qualified navigators who needed practice in the air. He would fly out over the North Sea every day with some nervous navigator who then had to plot the plane's route back to base. If the navigator got it wrong Dick had to find their way home and since he had never been much good at navigation – and had in any case learned it in the southern hemisphere, by way of the Southern Cross – he came close several times to being lost himself.

With the end of the war Dick itched to return to his beloved horses and applied for compassionate release on the grounds that his father needed him to help with his business, but the RAF's bureaucracy was not nearly as speedy as its Spitfires and it was to be several months before he was finally demobbed. In the meantime he was forced to learn to fly yet another lumbering bomber, the Lancaster, a chunky, four-engined, twin-tailed beast with a stubby snout and so many instruments, controls, gauges and buttons that Dick at first just gazed at them in horror. Yet many pilots regarded the Lancaster as 'the perfect Heavy'. The legendary airman Group Captain Leonard Cheshire, VC, DSO, DFC considered the plane to be much more robust and reliable than the Wellington and wrote in an introduction to *The Lancaster Bomber* by D. B. Tubbs that 'an analysis of the figures show that it contributed more to the destruction of military and industrial targets in Hitler's Germany than any other type of aircraft, whether British or American.' Air Chief Marshal Sir Arthur Harris ('Bomber' Harris), the Commander-in-Chief of Bomber Command, agreed and said that the Lancaster was the greatest single factor in winning the Second World War. In his book Tubbs quotes another pilot as saying: 'The Lanc was fantastically strong. If there was one-quarter of one left by the German defences, that quarter would fly home.'

Despite his initial appalled reaction to the Lancaster, Dick soon mastered it and he flew it right until the day he left the RAF. Sadly his RAF career had not turned out at all as he had hoped. 'I don't know that he *hated* it,' said Roy Palmer, 'but he wasn't over-enamoured with it. He left the air force fairly promptly after the war finished.'

With the end of the war in sight at last as well as the end of Mary's years of education, her mother returned from Devon in 1944 to live again in south London. The family home was still standing at 17 Kingsmead Avenue – though one house half a mile away, at 52 Donnington Road, was destroyed by a direct hit by one of the new-fangled German V1 flying bombs on the evening of 27 July 1944.

Mary's sister Jean had just left Milton Mount to train as an occupational therapist and that autumn their brother Ewen started his first term at Mill Hill school. Mary herself, now twenty and a graduate, was conscripted under the Direction of Labour regulations and began her National Service by taking a draughtsmanship course at a government factory training centre in Croydon. 'Under the Direction of Labour regulations you had to be a nurse, teacher, go into industry, work on the land or join the Forces,' she told me many years later. 'I didn't want to go into uniform, I would have been no good on the land, and I would rather have been a doctor than a nurse, so I became a draughtsman.'

In 1945 she went to work for six months for £5 a week (£112 today) in the propeller division of the giant De Havilland Aircraft Company's big factory complex at Stag Lane in north London, where she joined a dozen other draughtsmen whose job was to compile complex, detailed drawings of propellers for all types of aircraft, from Tiger Moths to Mosquitoes, and all sorts of other aircraft parts as well, from spinners and hydromatic hub assemblies to constant-speed units and the insides of de-icing equipment. A single meticulous drawing might have as many as eighty-nine parts carefully labelled to show every single component, from the blade-retaining nut and the locking plate to the rotating cam, piston, valves, preload shims and rear chafing ring. 'I was drawing blueprints of propellers,' Mary told me in 1980. 'It was crazy. It makes you shudder. I had no engineering background, just a quick course in engineering drawing. De Havilland had just invented a hydraulic braking propeller and wanted an operating manual for it, so they told me to write it! It was crazy!'

Mary was one of three draughtswomen who worked together: the others were a twenty-one-year-old from Hampstead, Maureen Bocar, and a Malaysian girl called Betty Tagima. 'When I look back I think we were really rather bright!' Maureen Bocar (now Maureen Bolden) told me. They worked in a little hut at the bottom of the factory – the very hut in which Geoffrey de Havilland had designed the Tiger Moth. 'It was known as the Home Guard Hut,' Mrs Bolden remembered. 'I imagine Dad's Army used to meet there at evenings and weekends and one felt rather thrilled to be there.'

Each day throughout the summer of 1945 Mary travelled across London from Worcester Park to Burnt Oak, entering the factory before nine o'clock, punching her card into the time-clock like any other manual worker, working in the hut until lunchtime – which was normally spent with her drawing-office colleagues in the Green Man pub at Kingsbury, where there was rabbit on the menu every day – and then it was back to the hut to draw again until five o'clock, when she would return to Worcester Park.

Mrs Bolden said:

One just had to have an aptitude for figures and drawing. We had all manner of people there and it was fascinating to see the people who got to grips with drawing, designing and so on that really hadn't done much before. And it was a wonderful firm to work for in every way. One was very lucky to be there. It was a wonderfully happy place to work. We did all sorts of different things. Propellers are the most difficult things to draw because they're slightly shaped and turned. It's no joke, actually. You kept having to do these sections all the way through. You look closely now at these beautiful drawings and think *'how the heck did I do that?'* And we weren't *closely* supervised. After the war I didn't want to fly for a long time because at De Havilland's somebody said *'if that split pin happened to move, the whole thing would go'* and every time I thought of flying I imagined that there'd be a split pin that would do something horrific. Also, because Mary and I were both rather hot stuff at maths, we used to do specifications for the RAF: assembly, dismantling, repair and so on. I *loved* that bit. You had to be good at art and maths and Mary was fine at the job, an intelligent, delightful person. She was rather a magic person, really, a lovely person: lovely to look at, lovely nature, rather special – and very clever.

Mary had already started to immerse herself in the professional literary world and was reviewing books in her spare time. 'She was reading books for a publisher,' said Mrs Bolden, 'and she had to say what she felt about each one in twenty-five words. She got a pittance, half a crown a book, but she had a great interest in English and books and read a lot every week. She was definitely a very bright girl and she was *great* fun – and she played the piano. I remember her coming home once and playing to us.'

Fun or not, Mary soon tired of the job, which was too repetitive and meticulous for her restless, creative spirit. 'I got very bored,' she told me, 'and since the only other thing I could do was teaching I became a school-mistress for a year. And then I met Dick.'

CHAPTER 7

Love at First Sight

(1945–47)

They met on a sunny autumn Sunday afternoon on 21 October 1945, Trafalgar Day, the 140th anniversary of Nelson's great naval victory in 1805, and Dick too was conquered by his first glimpse of Mary. He fell in love with her before they even spoke.

They met at his aunt Nancy Evans's hotel in Weston-super-Mare, Somerset, where he and Mary had both been invited to the wedding the next day of his thirty-year-old RAF chum Sam Coleman to Mary's twenty-year-old Milton Mount schoolfriend Nesta Evans, Dick's cousin. The war had been over for two months but Dick still looked dashing in his RAF uniform with his Wings and Africa Star campaign ribbon. It was 4 p.m. and the hall of the hotel was full of Francis, Thomas and Evans relatives, all chattering away, so it was some time before Dick spotted the shy, beautiful girl with the brown dress, pale skin, waist-length golden hair plaited around her head and laughing eyes, who was standing on a short flight of steps a little away from the hubbub. His aunt, Nesta's mother, introduced them. They smiled at each other and somehow Dick knew immediately that this was his future wife.

Mary too was overcome by their meeting. She told me thirty-five years later:

> If he'd said *'let's get married tomorrow'* I would have done.
> We were both immediately attracted to each other and I
> said to my mother *'I've met the only man I'd like to marry'*.
> I said to myself *'this is ridiculous, you don't fall in love like
> that'* and we didn't get married for eighteen months. I've
> often wondered what it was that was special about Dick,
> but I remember the instant I met him, standing in the
> hall. I still have a clear picture of it in my mind. It was
> so quick and we spent the whole evening sitting talking
> together.

Five years after that conversation she told Lynda Lee-Potter of
the *Daily Mail*:

> For weeks after that I didn't feel the pavement under my
> feet. It's absolutely true what people say about feeling
> they're walking on air.

Dick was almost twenty-five, Mary twenty-one. She had no
interest at all in horses and had never been to a race meeting,
nor had she had a proper boyfriend yet, but from then on they had
eyes for no one else for more than fifty years. For their first date he
took her for a night out in London and soon afterwards, after they
had been to a hunt ball, he drove her home, sat in the car holding
her hand, and asked her to marry him. She turned him down. It
was too soon, she said. They ought to wait. 'She didn't want to
be a wife, she wanted to be a theatre stage manager,' Dick told
Janet Menzies of the *Daily Express* in 1990. No, said Mary, 'I just
felt that I hadn't lived yet. I thought life ended with marriage.
If only I'd known then that in reality it only began when we
got married.' But over the months he kept proposing until she

said yes. They became engaged when he drove her home and proposed yet again in the garage after another hunt ball in the winter of 1946.

Soon after they met Dick was demobbed from the RAF and returned to Wokingham to help his father with his ailing horse business. Doug had left home to marry Julia Thelwell in 1942 and was working as estate manager and Master of the Horse to Victor Dyke Dennis in North Wales. Vince, now fifty-six, had somehow managed to keep going with the help of the Irish groom, Paddy Gallagher, but business was terrible. He had kept going only because he wanted Dick to have a job to come back to, but Dick was not at all enthusiastic about taking it on, although he set to with a will to ease his father's burdens and took on all the muckiest jobs.

Since Mary was teaching French and English at a school at Harrow, about twenty-five miles from Wokingham, she and Dick saw each other often and she would spend regular weekends with the Francises, later telling friends: 'My courtship was spent leaning over the bottom halves of stable doors while Dick mucked out an endless row of horses, and on Sunday afternoons we sat in the tack-room while he washed a mountain of dirty leather.' What made their relationship particularly odd was not only that Mary was literary and intellectual and Dick was decidedly not, but that she did not particularly like horses. 'When I was eight or nine I used to ride ponies at the seaside on the sands occasionally,' she told me many years later, 'but when I met Dick and he put me on a horse I was really an embarrassment to him even though it was the quietest horse in the yard. Dick would say "*do keep your elbows IN*" and I decided that his girlfriend had to be a very good rider or not ride at all. Horses are so beautiful and I love to look at them and I do see the fascination of seeing them as people. I love horses – but at a distance.'

So what did they have in common? Very little except some mysterious chemistry, and for a good Congregational girl to marry a jockey was unheard-of. When they became engaged no one dared to tell Mary's clergyman grandfather, John Forson, who was so puritannical that he would not allow even a pack of cards in his house, let alone anything to do with a world of gamblers and bookies.

'It always surprised me that she should fall for somebody who rode and she didn't,' Maureen Bolden told me. 'It seemed incredible. She didn't like horses at all and she was very much his intellectual superior. He was also rather serious, I felt, for her. I don't know what she saw in him.' Maybe the explanation lies in one of the oldest clichés: that opposites attract. 'Oh, he's attractive!' I was told by the crime novelist Gwen Butler, who became a friend of the Francises in the 1970s. 'He has enormous charm. I'm sure that's what it was. He's very sensitive, too – and sexy.'

Vince sold Embrook House to a Charles Kirby, who moved in with his wife, son and three daughters, one of whom, Kathleen, continued to run the business with the help of Paddy Gallagher. 'Vince was an excellent horseman and the stables were well looked after but they were just not profitable,' Kathleen Kirby (later Mrs Gale) told me. 'Vince was a very pleasant man: short, a little bit bandy; and his wife was a very nice person too. So was Dick, whom I knew very well. They still kept a lot of show horses and Dick and I used to go to shows together.' Eventually Embrook House was demolished and replaced by a modern housing estate.

Vince and Molly moved into a much smaller house nearby on the other side of leafy Reading Road, number 169, which still exists: a pebble-dash chalet bungalow with a huge chestnut tree at the front (which gave the house its name, Chestnut Cottage) and a vast back garden running down to the railway line. At the end of the garden there was a little summer house where Dick would sleep whenever he came home. Vince was obviously no better educated than Dick had been and was curiously casual about spelling even his wife's name: when he registered himself and Molly on the voters' register in 1945 he spelt her name 'Catherine', whereas before the war he had been spelling it 'Kathleen' and two years later, in 1947, he was to spell it 'Katherine'. Avril May, who was then a young girl living next door, told me that Molly Francis was 'a charming person, tall, grey-haired, very thin, very elegant and dignified. She always wore wonderful hand-knitted suits and she gave my mother the pattern.'

Dick soon realised that he could never be happy just settling back into his old pre-war life of hunting and showing and came positively to dislike the world of showing, deciding that it was shallow and riven by vanity, bitching and backbiting. He wanted more than ever to become a jockey, especially after Doug's father-in-law, Bob Thelwell, let him ride his horses in a couple of point-to-points up in Denbighshire. In the first, on 23 March 1946, Dick won the Farmers Division of the Winstay point-to-point on a horse called Red Poker. Three weeks later he rode Louis the Great in the Cheshire Farmers Bona Fide Meeting Hunt Maiden Chase, but fell. A fortnight after that he made his first appearance on a real racecourse when he rode Louis the Great again, this time in a Hunter Chase at Bangor-on-Dee in north-east Wales. He was unplaced but he had loved every minute of it and afterwards wrote to every racehorse trainer he or his father had ever met to beg for a job as an amateur jockey. In vain. National Hunt racing was only just starting up again after the war and trainers were cautious about taking on staff. Dick's parents also tried to dissuade him. They both wanted him to take on the family business, ailing though it was. Vince warned him that it would be terribly difficult to make a decent living as a jockey and Molly said that she would always be worrying about his safety and that the racing world was dreadfully ruthless. And time was passing: Dick was nearly twenty-six and he could look forward to little more than ten years as a jockey because it was so physically testing. He did, however, have one great advantage: he could if necessary bring his weight down to 9st 10lbs, which was just about right for a jump-jockey.

It was Doug who came galloping to the rescue after hearing that George Owen, an ex-jockey who had won the Cheltenham Gold Cup in 1939 and was now farming and training a few horses near Chester, needed someone to organise his shambolic office. Owen would pay him £4-10s a week (£100 today), let him live as one of the family, and let him ride his horses in some races. It was a wonderful piece of luck, for Owen was to turn out to have a golden touch at launching young jockeys. Dick was overjoyed. In October 1946 he took the train 150 miles north to Chester and into the future of which he had always dreamed.

Chester is a glorious ancient city with a rare elegance in its beautifully preserved old buildings. There seems to be something magical in the air, a sense that all England's history is encapsulated here in its broad, cobbled, enchanted and enchanting streets, from the 2,000-year-old walls that its Roman founders erected to protect themselves from the wild marauding Welsh to the magnificent, awesome cathedral that the Normans and Plantagenets built over two-and-a-half centuries; from the black-and-white timbered Tudor houses to the stone tower where Charles I is said to have watched the defeat of his Royalist army during the English Civil War. And yet there is nothing of the museum about Chester: it is surprisingly young and lively, a living city with a zing in the air yet mature and relaxed; a city that knows itself and is happy in its skin.

George Owen's Decoy Farm – named after a nearby duck-decoy lake that had been dug by one of Oliver Cromwell's generals – was three miles south-west of the city centre along Lache Lane and just two handy miles from Chester racecourse, and Dick was soon made welcome by Owen, his wife Margot and their three little daughters, who treated him as a member of the family and introduced him to their wide circle of friends and relatives so that Dick soon felt completely at home.

Every morning he would ride out with two strings of horses, exercising and schooling them over fences and hurdles, and every afternoon he would plunge into the jumble of Owen's business affairs, hacking his way through a jungle of unpaid bills, unsent invoices, unanswered letters and lost records. In six months Owen had not sent out one bill for training his clients' horses, which meant that he was making a huge loss training horses. Dick resorted to inventing an expense called 'Chemistry' which he added to the owners' bills – his first attempt at writing fiction.

Owen gave him his first ride in a professional race a week after his arrival in a novices steeplechase at Woore, a racetrack twenty-five miles away. His mount, Russian Hero, a big six-year-old bay gelding, had been raced a few times in point-to-points but never in a professional race. At the racecourse Dick felt oddly nervous, despite all his long experience as a horseman. He borrowed breeches and a helmet from a valet and walked the whole course to gauge the feel of it, methodically studying each jump. For the next couple of years he did this at every new course before he rode on it, carefully examining the ground in advance so that he would never be taken by surprise by an unexpected turn or an awkward fence. As a jockey he was always to do his homework much more carefully than he had ever done it at school.

He came in a creditable fourth on Russian Hero that day and was soon riding Owen's horses regularly in races, at first only horses that had no real hope of winning because owners of horses with a real chance obviously preferred them to be ridden by experienced jockeys. Dick found it galling to school new horses and ride them in their early races only to be 'jocked off' when they were entered for a race that they might win, but during these first few months with Owen he was laying secure foundations for his career as a jump jockey, learning how to judge the pace of a race, how to assess the other horses, how to snatch a sudden advantage by riding through a gap. And he listened all the time, soaking up advice. Jack Moloney, who had thrice come second in Grand Nationals before the war, told him that at the start of a race he should watch not the tape but the starter's arm so that he could take off a second or two before the other jockeys as soon as he saw the starter press the lever which released the tape.

It was now, too, that he first encountered the cheating and skulduggery that were later to fuel every Dick Francis thriller. Most jockeys were decent and friendly but one tried to unseat him during a race by jabbing a knee into his thigh as they galloped side by side, and another cut him up deliberately so that his horse was edged roughly off the course and out of the race.

Early in 1947 Owen sold Decoy Farm and rented the Marquess of Cholmondeley's (pronounced *Chumley's*) vast, elegant stables at Cholmondeley Castle, near Malpas, twenty miles south-east of Chester. The red-brick, ivy-covered stables, with its towers, turrets and massive wooden doors, stood amid the rolling, wooded acres of the grounds of Cholmondeley Castle in the heart of some stunningly beautiful countryside, but that winter was unforgettably cold and it was a nightmare to move all the horses along snowbound roads and narrow, icy lanes. Racing was cancelled from 23 January until 15 March and Owen and Dick hunkered down in their magnificent new home at Cholmondeley to wait for the thaw, Dick in a first-floor flat on the left of the huge main entrance archway. But racehorses cannot be left to look after themselves and every day, for eight bitter weeks, no matter how awful the weather, Dick and the stable lads exercised the horses out in the open on icy straw-strewn circles.

When racing re-started in the middle of March Dick rode yet again the new horses, old horses and no-hopers. For week after week he came nowhere in thirty-nine races, until he began to feel

1. Dick's maternal grandparents, Willie and Annie Thomas, in whose remote Welsh farmhouse he was born in 1920 and with whom he spent a great deal of his childhood.

2. Dick's parents, Molly and Vince Francis, at the end of the First World War.

3. Little Dick Francis (back row, third from right, in striped tie) with fellow pupils and teachers at Lawrenny village school in the 1920s.

4. Chubby, eleven-year-old Dick (front row, seventh from right) looking much more cheerful than he felt in his first term at Maidenhead Boys' School in 1932.

5. Mary Brenchley's palatial senior school, Milton Mount College, set amid eighty acres of land at Worth Park in Sussex, where she was a boarder from 1937 to 1940.

6. The entrance hall and reading room at Worth Park. The interior of the mansion was astonishingly spacious and ornate for an English boarding school of the 1930s.

7. Fair-haired, fourteen-year-old Mary (right) with fellow pupils Sheila Hearn (left) and Margaret Roderick beside the swimming pool at Milton Mount in 1938.

8. The brilliant Alison Shrubsole (back row, far left) and Mary (back row, third from left) and other Milton Mount Old Girls and staff at a school reunion in the Imperial Hotel at Lynton, Devon, in August 1942. On the far right of the back row is Mary's lifelong friend Mary Youll (*née* Harding); Janet ('Netta') Brenchley, Mary's mother, is seated third from the right in the third row from the front.

9. Mary (second from left) as the Earl of Rutland in a Royal Holloway College production of *Richard of Bordeaux*, 1942.

10. Strikingly pale, beautiful and not quite twenty: Mary at Royal Holloway College in May 1944.

11. Assistant stage manager Mary Brenchley (second from left) with fellow members of the Hereford Repertory Theatre company at a cricket match in 1947.

12. Ex-Sergeant Arthur Lowe, aged thirty-one and already bald, who was later to become famous as the pompous Captain Mainwaring in the TV series *Dad's Army*, at the start of his acting career with Hereford Repertory in 1947. Lowe was earning just £3 a week at Hereford, was renowned for forgetting his lines, and became a lifelong friend of Mary's.

13. Dick Francis at the start of his career as a jockey, in 1947, with one of his earliest winners, Lighthead, in the humble winner's enclosure at Bangor-on-Dee. The owner – with binoculars and ill-fitting jacket and trousers – was Charlie Read; the proud stable lad Frank Perks.

4. Mary and Dick Francis on their wedding day, Saturday, 21 June 1947, at Paddington ongregationalist Chapel in London. Dick's arm was in a sling because he had broken his •llarbone a week earlier in a fall at Newport races. Because of post-war shortages, Mary made •er own wedding dress for less than £1.

15. The bitter-sweet morning after Dick's first Grand National in 1949, in which he had been leading the field on Roimond into the last mile only to be overtaken by Russian Hero, a horse he had helped to train and whose life he had saved three months earlier. Dick (far right) swallowed his disappointment to congratulate the winning owner, as well as trainer George Owen (far left) and jockey Leo McMorrow (second from right).

16. The rising star: 29-year-old Dick Francis in February 1950, his second season as a professional jump-jockey. It was a wonderfully successful season for him, but his worried look is understandable: a few months earlier Mary had bee struck down by polio and confined to an iron lung; in March they wer due to make a vital career move from Cheshire to Berkshire; and in April Mary was due to give birth to their first son, Merrick.

depressed and disillusioned. Was this what he had dreamed of for so long? Was this what he slogged for every day, mucking out, feeding, watering, grooming, polishing, mucking out again, collapsing into bed each night exhausted? What was the point of it all? And then, on 2 May, he rode his first winner – and it felt wonderful.

The horse was Wrenbury Tiger, the course Bangor-on-Dee, and together they won a hunter chase by more than two hundred yards. Dick had been extremely lucky to be given the ride at all: Owen's first-choice jockey, Mickey Moseley, had had to withdraw a few days earlier because of injury, and his second choice, who lived in Berkshire, had decided that Cheshire was too far to travel for just one race, so by chance Dick had bagged the first of his 345 winners. To crown an unforgettable day he came second on Rompworthy in a handicap chase and clocked up his second winner on Blitz Boy in a novice chase. By the time the season ended six weeks later he had ridden nine winners, enough to put him half-way up the amateur jockeys' chart for the year.

In an early photograph of Dick with a horse called Lighthead in the winner's enclosure at Bangor-on-Dee he looks shy and almost embarrassed to be there. The hut in the background is hardly stylish; the horse's owner, Charlie Read, is standing to awkward attention with trousers three inches too short, a jacket buttoned far too tight and bulging pockets stuffed to bursting; and the stable lad holding the horse, Frank Perks, looks gawky and undernourished. Dick certainly looks nothing like the glamorous RAF pilot he had once been. Yet he had no regrets about his new career. It was what he had always wanted to do. It was his destiny.

Mary spent the first five months of 1947 working behind the scenes at the County Theatre in Hereford, a pretty little market town eighty miles south-west of Cholmondeley Castle. 'I wanted to find out how the theatre worked,' she told me. She had had enough of teaching French and English in Harrow, had always been fascinated by the theatre, and at the end of 1946 she landed a job as assistant stage manager for Derek Salberg's Hereford Repertory Theatre Company.

Hereford was a cosy little market town that had for a thousand years suffered countless sieges and battles throughout the Middle Ages and into the seventeenth century, but in 1946 it sat genteel astride the sparkling River Wye, renowned for its salmon, cider, regatta and horse racing. Like so many ancient English towns, its stones ached with history: the aged fragments of Saxon walls; the beautiful, soaring, eleventh-century cathedral with its chained library of 1,400 books and its six-hundred-year old map of the world, the Mappa Mundi; the fourteenth-century first-floor hall at 20 Church Street; the Old House, a black-and-white timbered Jacobean dwelling built in 1621. Here in Hereford Owen Tudor, grandfather of Henry VII, had been beheaded in 1461. Here Roundheads and Cavaliers had battled time and again for possession of the town during the Civil War as King Charles I and Oliver Cromwell wrestled for the soul of England. And Hereford had the theatre too in its bones. A year after Charles I was beheaded, his son's future doxy, the actress Nell Gwynne, is said to have been born here in a hovel in Gwynne Street (then Pipewell Lane) in 1650 – the same Nell Gwynne who is reputed to have lived years later near Dick's childhood home in Holyport. Here in Hereford David Garrick was born in 1717 and christened in All Saints church. Here Sir Edward Elgar lived at Plas Gwyn from 1904 to 1911. And here at the Palladium Theatre before the war Derek Salberg's repertory company had been a popular part of local life. On New Year's Day 1947 the Palladium was renamed the County Theatre and taken over by Salberg's company again.

Mary moved into a bedsitter in digs run by a Mrs Wall in Barton Road, next door to the Royal Oak pub. 'She was a golden-haired English rose, with a real English complexion, and a lovely person,' I was told by Mel Lucas, who was in 1947 the theatre's (rather than the cast's) stage manager. The repertory company was welcomed back to the town by the weekly *Hereford Citizen and Bulletin*, which topped its front page on 3 January with a four-column photograph of the company, including Mary. Standing behind her in the picture was the short figure of Arthur Lowe, already bald and bespectacled even though he was only thirty-one, who was to go on to become famous as the squat, pompous, blustering bank manager Captain Mainwaring in the TV comedy series *Dad's Army*. Lowe had been an actor for just a year – after coming out of the army as a sergeant – and he was still paid just £3 a week (£66 today), of which a third went on rent and a third on food. Because of his shortness, baldness and spectacles 'he was never going to be offered the male lead,' admitted his son Stephen in his biography *Arthur Lowe: A Life*, 'but he was the perfect all-purpose recipe for character parts.' Salberg told Stephen Lowe that Arthur never knew his lines, but during his year on the stage at Hereford he appeared in no fewer than forty-two plays, learned the basic tricks of his profession and laid the foundations for his massive fame. By some strange chance the last play in which Lowe appeared at Hereford, *The Ghost Train*, was written by Arnold Ridley, who was also to achieve immortality in *Dad's Army* as the bumbling old weak-bladdered Private Godfrey.

'Arthur became a good friend of Mary's,' I was told by John Hodges, who was in 1947 a sixteen-year-old semi-professional actor appearing in small parts with the Hereford company and helping Mary backstage:

> I knew her very well. She was a cracker, really good looking, and a nice girl. She was one of the crowd and into everything. She had a hell of a sense of humour and she worked very hard, was dedicated to the job and loved

the theatre. She was there all the time and was very good indeed at her job. If something wanted doing, some flats wanted painting, she'd be down there and getting it done. She'd get stuck in doing the set for the following week and you'd very often find her covered in paint and thoroughly enjoying it. She was great fun. She would always have a book that she was engrossed in, but otherwise she had no real interests outside the theatre. There wasn't an awful lot to do in Hereford.

As for Arthur Lowe, 'he was an absolutely wonderful character with a wicked sense of humour,' said Mr Hodges. Nancy Powell, an actress who joined the company in 1948, agreed. 'He was very thin and ginger in those days,' she told me, 'great fun, and very good in the various parts that he played, mostly character parts. He really stood out.' And Michael Morris, another semi-professional actor, remembered Lowe as 'a lovely man, quite slim, with ginger hair, a small little fellow, but he had a very good speaking voice: out of this very small frame came these lovely, mellifluous tones.'

Mary's superior, the company stage manager, was Lowe's young mistress Joan Gatehouse (*née* Cooper), whom he was to marry a year later. Joan was twenty-three, only a year older than Mary but already experienced both as an actress and as a stage manager. 'Joan was a dear,' Nancy Powell told me. 'She was not at all theatrical, just ordinary and very pleasant.'

The Hereford company's producer, Martin Benson, had recently come out of the army after building a theatre in Egypt during the war, in Alexandria, where Lowe had been his sergeant. The theatre manager was Anthony Rutter, the designer Michael Ellis, and apart from Lowe the other leading actors were Douglas Bell, Gerald Cuff, Marianne Deeming, Kenneth More's wife Beryl Johnstone, Richard Leech, the character actress Nancy Roberts, the stunningly beautiful twenty-year-old junior lead Marguerite

Stone, Helen Uttley, Peter Wilde, Audrey Winter and Leslie Yeo as well as several semi-professionals who came and went – some of whom went on to have distinguished careers, among them Nancy Roberts, who later became famous as Grandma Grove in the first BBC television soap, *The Grove Family*.

Several of the Hereford company became lifelong friends of Mary's. 'I made an enormous number of actor and actress friends,' she told me, 'and lots of them lasted for years.' In fact the company was an unusually happy one. 'Most of us were at the start of our careers, brimming with enthusiasm and burning to get the war behind us and start a new life,' I was told by Christopher Bond, who played juvenile parts with the company under his original name, Geoffrey Bond, and went on to become an award-winning scriptwriter, editor, producer and director of hundreds of films, plays and TV episodes. 'It says much for the spirit of the company that so many of us kept in touch down the years,' said Bond, 'and rough hewn though it was, the burgeoning talent of that company was remarkable.'

Percy Arrowsmith, who ran theatrical digs in Hereford in 1947 and met most of the cast, confirmed that it was a very happy company, as did John Hodges, who told me: 'It was one big happy family. We'd all go down to the pub as a whole, and after a show we'd get up into the small, intimate bar above the theatre and allow everyone to buy us drinks. Mary enjoyed a drink, and many of us kept in touch for years afterwards.'

The County Theatre – now the Gala bingo hall – was in Berrington Street, three hundred yards from the cathedral, and could hold an audience of 580 people. 'The audience in Hereford was upper-middle-class, very respectable, and liked having a theatre,' Martin Benson told me. They certainly turned out in force to see the first production on Monday 6 January 1947 when J. B. Priestley's play *How Are They at Home?* attracted several local civic dignitaries and the local Member of Parliament, A. E. Baldwin. 'Martin Benson, the producer, is to be congratulated on the team-work which was displayed by a cast that had met but a week previously,' reported the *Hereford Citizen and Bulletin*.

Mary's job as assistant stage manager involved everything behind the scenes for six evening performances and two matinées each week. She helped with rehearsals, scenery, lighting, effects and prompting, working with the stage hands, arranging furniture, liaising with the actors regarding their props and checking that they had them before each performance, keeping a record of rehearsals, and generally acting as Joan Cooper's right-hand woman and dogsbody – even making the tea and understudying some of the minor parts in case of a last-minute crisis. Stage management was particularly tricky because the stage was only 14ft deep, and in those postwar months they had to battle constantly against shortages of almost everything, even paint brushes. Often it was impossible to find the right props, and since the plays were changed every week a huge amount of work had to be done fast each weekend to prepare new sets and props for the first performance each Monday night.

The first night of the company's second production, Noël Coward's *Blithe Spirit*, was a little chaotic but the *Citizen and Bulletin* declared that the actors had 'excelled in their presentation of the play.' The third production, *Pink String and Sealing Wax* by Roland Pertwee, was 'even better . . . The performances are improving each week as the players begin to settle down', and *The Hereford Times* agreed: 'The parts of the Irish doctor and his barrister son were excellently done by Arthur Lowe and Richard Leech . . . It is evident that if this standard of production is maintained, the success of the new repertory venture must be assumed.' As for the fourth play, *While the Sun Shines* by Terence Rattigan, in which Lowe played a Free French officer, the *Citizen and Bulletin* chortled that 'the "hot passion" burning in the breast of Arthur Lowe . . . reduced us to a state of helpless laughter.'

Mary loved being a part of all this after so many years of appearing in and producing plays at school and university:

the congenial friendship of creative people, the shared tension and excitement of a new challenge every week, the cosy post-mortems late into the night. The camaraderie of the company was made even closer by the dreadful weather during January, February and March as England suffered its worst winter in decades. There were terrible blizzards and that February was the coldest since 1895, with an average temperature of 28.7 degrees Fahrenheit. While Dick was trying to keep warm and to exercise George Owen's freezing horses up at Cholmondeley Castle, Mary in Hereford was gripped by an Arctic winter of severe frosts and snowstorms. The days were dark and gloomy and the streets resembled the deep-frozen winter scenes of old-fashioned Christmas cards. Children and soldiers pelted each other with snowballs in the streets. Major roads were impassable, trains cancelled, and railway freight services so badly disrupted that coal was in short supply and there were numerous power cuts. At the start of February all Hereford's street lighting was switched off, so that after an evening at the theatre the audience had to slither home in the icy dark, which inevitably deterred many from coming. When the company bravely put on its first serious play, Ibsen's *Ghosts*, on 3 February, there were many empty seats – and they stayed empty for the rest of the week.

After *Ghosts* Martin Benson produced only one more play, *Worm's Eye View* by R. F. Delderfield, before leaving to work in London and going on to make eighty-three films, among them *Cleopatra*, *The King and I*, *Goldfinger* and *The Omen*. John Hodges remembered that production of *Worm's Eye View* with special amusement:

> Somebody pinched a mattress from behind a window that Arthur Lowe was going to dive out of and replaced it with a sheet of corrugated iron as a practical joke. Arthur took a dive out of the window, landed on this corrugated iron and made a hell of a racket, and Mary said to him 'tell

him it was a hot tin roof', and Arthur came back on with his usual aplomb and said 'that was a hot tin roof' very, very drily. It was little things like that which made Mary so good.

Benson was replaced by Vernon Fortescue, an Australian character actor who had once worked in Hollywood as C. Aubrey Smith's double, and started by producing *Flare Path* by Terence Rattigan and *The Corn is Green* by Emlyn Williams.

In those icy months there was nothing much for Mary to do outside the theatre except to try to keep warm and to read her books and the local papers, which reported in March that a heavy coping stone had fallen from its parapet in St Peter's Street and killed three pedestrians. After the snow and ice came the rain: March was the wettest month since 1929 and the thaw caused the worst floods for 155 years. Hundreds of houses were awash and Hereford races had to be abandoned, but nothing could staunch the relentless flow of play after new play at the County Theatre, and the end of that dreadful winter brought the audiences flocking back. On Easter Monday there was a full house for the first night of *Jane Steps Out* by Kenneth Horne and the local Press singled out Joan Cooper and Mary for praise when the company performed Agatha Christie's *Ten Little Niggers*, which was set on an island: 'Throughout the play the background music of waves, wind and seagulls is most effective,' wrote the *Citizen and Bulletin* reviewer, and when the company performed *The Importance of Being Earnest* he reported: 'An outstanding feature of the play is the excellence of the sets. A different set is used for each of the three scenes and they are among the best to be seen in any theatre.' In a profile of Joan Cooper on 18 April the paper mentioned Mary by name, praised her work, and added: 'without this loyalty behind the scenes no show would have a chance of success.'

April ended with *This Happy Breed* by Noël Coward and in

May the highlight was Bernard Shaw's *Candida*, but by now the weather was so much better that Mary was able to get out and about and Dick could come and see her more often. 'He used to come into the theatre on Saturday nights after the races,' said Mel Lucas, and Percy Arrowsmith told me: 'he used to give racing tips to some of the cast.' On Whit Monday Mary took several of the cast to Hereford racecourse to watch Dick ride and he delighted them by riding a winner which they had all backed.

But Mary's brief time in the theatre was coming to an end as she prepared to sacrifice her own career for his. 'I loved the theatre and I wanted to be a stage manager,' she told Cassandra Jardine of the *Daily Telegraph* in 1997, 'but I couldn't add that on to his day job as a jockey.' In June she went home to prepare for their wedding. A legendary partnership was about to be born.

CHAPTER 8

Joy and Terror

(1947–50)

A week before Dick and Mary were due to be married she saw him fall off his horse and break his collar-bone during a race at Newport, so when her father took them up to London to see the musical *Oklahoma!* Dick's arm was in a sling, and it was still there at their wedding in London the following Saturday, 21 June 1947, although the rest of him looked handsome in morning suit, waistcoat, top hat, white gloves and carnation. His broken collar-bone did not stop ribald wedding guests making lewd jokes about that night being the shortest of the year.

It was almost impossible to buy new clothes in 1947 so Mary made her own wedding gown out of a cheese-straining cloth with gold sequins sewn around the hem. It cost her less than £1 to make (£22 today), including the zip, but she still looked palely beautiful in the long, white dress with puffed sleeves, headdress and veil, and she carried a huge bouquet of fern and carnations that cascaded well below her knees. They were married at the Paddington Congregationalist Chapel in Marylebone Road by Dick's Methodist minister uncle Jonathan Evans and Mary's clergyman grandfather John Forson, whose stern anti-jockey principles had melted once he met Dick and who was later to become an avid reader of the racing pages.

Dick was twenty-six, Mary twenty-three, and Doug best man. Many of their friends and family were gloomy about the marriage because of Mary's lack of interest in horses. 'My parents tried to talk me out of it,' Mary told me more than thirty years later. 'It wasn't usual for a girl like me to marry a jockey. That was really adventurous. We had nowhere to live, no proper paid job, no prospects. Dick was being paid just £4-10s a week as George Owen's secretary, assistant trainer and dogsbody, which wasn't very much [*the equivalent of £100 in 1999*]. He did have a small RAF gratuity but he spent that launching himself as an amateur jockey.' As an amateur Dick was offered many more rides than he could have expected as a pro because many of Owen's owners were farmers who could not afford a professional jockey, but it was expensive to ride for nothing since he had to buy a lot of costly equipment – saddles, breeches, boots – as well as to pay valet's fees and travelling expenses.

Vince and Molly gave them a little green Wolseley car as a wedding present and they spent their honeymoon driving around Scotland with Mary at the wheel and Dick navigating because of his useless left arm – a foolish thing to do since Mary did not yet have a driving licence and Dick had intended to teach her how to drive during the honeymoon. They had their first row when she stalled the car on a hill and Dick said, 'What the bloody hell do you think you're doing?' She replied, 'Right! I've had enough. I'm getting out,' but luckily they were miles from any-where and she had to climb back into the car. It was one of the few arguments they ever had in more than fifty years of marriage.

That summer was gloriously hot and sunny and the young couple moved happily into their first home together, a rented room at Faddiley, four miles from Cholmondeley Castle. Mary told me:

It was just a bedroom in a house and we had no electricity,

but those digs cost us twenty-eight shillings a week [*£31 in 1999*]. We lived mostly on porridge, with fish and chips on Saturday night. It was very difficult to be married to a steeplechase jockey and to have a steady job, especially miles out in the country in Cheshire. Steeplechase jockeys do tend to get hurt and they really do need a wife around to drive them and nurse them, so I always went with him to the races.

'She used to read a book,' George Owen's daughter Jane told me, 'but she always went with him.' Mary was also his public relations officer. 'It was her job to stroll around at the races,' I was told by the novelist Gavin Lyall, who became a great friend of the Francises in later years, 'and people would say "oh, there's Mary Francis. Hey, that gives me an idea: why don't I ask Dick to ride my horse?"'

Mary told me:

> Once we were married I never worked. I felt much more inclined to support Dick. I never felt that I'd lost out in any way whatever and I very much enjoyed being part of Dick's life. We've had a joint life. I was never actually bogged down at home feeling I'd been cheated by not having a career of my own. I have led really a most full and satisfying life.

When friends asked if she didn't worry terribly while watching Dick ride she used to reply half-jokingly: 'Only when they start waving the white flag for the ambulance.' Privately she admitted that her heart was in her mouth every time she saw the starting tapes go up and the dread did not diminish even after watching Dick in hundreds of races. Whenever he returned to her with blood on his face she would ask him apprehensively, 'are your teeth still there?' and Stan Mellor, who later became a champion jump jockey himself, told me: 'When Dick rode out for a race Mary would look at him as though he was never going to come back.'

Dick claimed that he never worried about his own safety, even though he expected to fall about once in every fifteen races – he compared it to falling off the roof of a car at 30 m.p.h. – and even though about one out of five hundred jockeys was killed every year. He always broke at least one or two bones every season yet still reckoned that the odds against being really badly hurt for a long time were about the same – 500/1. Even when he fell badly at Sandown and his horse, Fighting Line, rolled right over him, he was barely bruised. 'You'd have thought I'd be dead, but I was lucky,' he told the *Mail on Sunday* fifty years later. 'I just got up and walked away.' At Towcester he had an equally nasty accident when he fell on his head, was knocked unconscious, and the horse lay on top of his head and shoulders, rocking backwards and forwards for several minutes: eventually the horse clambered to its feet and Dick came to, got up and drove home without even a headache. Usually, he said, a fall would leave him merely with a few big bruises, some stiffness and maybe some patches of missing skin here and there. Unlike most jockeys then, he always wore a crash helmet and he liked to point out that more window cleaners died doing their job than jump-jockeys did.

Mary told me:

Yes, I used to worry about him, but you can't worry all the time. Dick was a jockey for ten years and in that time he broke his bones twenty-one times – not including his ribs. He broke his collar-bone twelve times, his nose five times, his arm, shoulderblade, vertebrae and wrist, and later he cracked his skull, and after he dislocated his left shoulder the doctor showed me how to put it back for him and now I've done it a dozen times.

In fact Dick managed during his career to dislocate both shoulders. When his right shoulder came adrift in 1948 it hung so loose and fell out of its socket so easily that it came apart several times during races. The renowned sports-injury specialist Bill Tucker performed a painful operation to put it right and Dick had to spend four months recuperating. But when the left shoulder went as well in 1954 Dick could not bear the thought of another agonizing operation and even more time spent out of racing – especially since he was at the time that season's leading winner and looked as if he might become Champion Jockey – and so he decided to leave the shoulder unrepaired and for the rest of his life simply gritted his teeth when Mary had to put it back for him.

'It's terribly painful,' Dick told me. 'I have to ride with a strap on and when I go to bed the shoulder will go out if I roll over the wrong way.'

'It takes me ten minutes to put the dislocated shoulder back,' said Mary, 'and it's excruciatingly painful for him. It goes back with a very audible crunch.' The whole queasy process of pushing a dislocated shoulder back into place is described in sickeningly graphic detail in the 1974 Dick Francis novel *Knock Down*, in which the hero, Jonah Dereham, a famous ex-jockey, also has a shoulder that tends to dislocate and has to be kept buckled and strapped up with webbing, like Dick's, to stop him raising his arm. Like Dick he has to wear a softer version of the webbing in bed and Dereham's girlfriend Sophie is surprised to find that he does not remove the webbing even when making love because vigorous sex can dislocate a damaged shoulder. When Dereham's shoulder comes excruciatingly out of its socket, Sophie puts it back for him by putting her left hand under his elbow, holding his wrist with her right hand, and sliding the top of the bone back into its socket by straightening his arm out, pulling his elbow hard across his chest and folding his wrist and pushing his arm back up towards the shoulder. The whole process was surprisingly exhausting for Mary as well as agony for Dick.

Dick also broke his nose so often that his sense of smell was permanently damaged. When Mary asked him once what he thought of her perfume he replied: 'What perfume?'

Since being a jockey involved so much pain and discomfort – not to mention all the disappointments of days wasted because of fog or ice, of losing when you thought you would win, of making silly mistakes in full view of the public, of feeling you have let owners, trainers and punters down, of being 'jocked off' in favour of some other rider – one wonders why anyone would want to be a jump-jockey at all. Dick's explanation was that he loved the speed and challenge of racing and that winning gave him a glorious high. Had he been a millionaire, he said, he would still have been a jockey.

After a few weeks in the rented room at Faddiley, Mary and Dick moved to a converted hayloft over a nearby stables at Higginsfield, where 'the wind would whip the carpet up off the floor if we left the doors open,' Dick told me in 1980. 'But really we were extremely happy,' said Mary. 'And we had electricity! We used to go round switching the lights on and off.'

Their happiness was such that they were to have only four major rows throughout their marriage, three in the first couple of years. On the second occasion Mary was bending over to clean the grate and Dick playfully spanked her bottom. She was furious, threatened him with the poker and cried, 'Don't you *ever* do that again! And I am never going to clean the fire again.' Nor did she. On the third occasion they had planned a brief holiday in Paris but when Vince asked Dick to ride in a horse show instead he agreed, and Mary wailed, 'You think more of your father than you do of me.' Dick was bewildered. 'But he's done so much for me all my life,' he said. In the end Mary agreed to postpone the trip and Dick agreed that they could stay in Paris longer. As for the fourth row, it happened after about ten years of marriage and they did not speak to each other for two or three days, but a few years later neither could remember what it had been about. In 1988 Mary told Fionnuala McHugh of the *Daily Mail*: 'There's no better cement for a marriage than knowing that your husband might die that afternoon, because you can't afford to quarrel in the morning.'

They spent most of their spare time at first redecorating the flat, but in August the new National Hunt season started and they went off to spend a couple of weeks two hundred miles away, in Devon, shepherding several of Owen's horses around the half-dozen Devon racetracks that always hosted the start of each season, beginning with Newton Abbot. Dick always enjoyed this southern start to each season because it was still warm enough to enjoy the seaside and it gave him a chance to catch up with old friends after the two-month summer break. He and Mary came to love this part of Devon so much that before long they were returning every year.

It was not until 30 August that he had his first winner – an unsatisfying one because his horse was the only entry – but soon he was clocking up several wins, especially on Rompworthy and Russian Hero. Rompworthy, a small brown gelding, belonged to Doug's ebullient boss, Victor Dyke Dennis, and was one of Dick's favourite mounts over the next couple of years even though the horse looked decidedly untidy and shaggy because he hated being clipped. Together they won two races before the end of the year, five in 1947, and eventually thirteen races in all, coming second or third in eighteen more. In the process Dick and Mary became friendly with Victor and Wenfra Dennis and they often spent jolly weekends together when Dick was riding one of Dennis's horses far from home.

On Russian Hero Dick won twice before the end of the year, and by the time he went to the Cheltenham meeting in March he had ridden in over a hundred races, more than any other amateur rider and more than all but four of the top professionals. He had won ten races, the most astonishing of which was at Haydock on Salmon Renown, which almost crashed at the second open ditch, fell far behind the rest of the field, skidded at the water jump, and yet still somehow caught and passed the rest of the field to win by ten lengths.

One genial sidelight that season was the wet Saturday afternoon when Dick and several other jockeys were mostly naked in the long jockeys' changing room at Rothbury racecourse and an old woman suddenly appeared among them, apparently looking for the ladies' lavatory. After finding the jockeys' washroom she wandered back again, peering about her at the naked jockeys, and left the hut, only to return immediately and repeat the journey: she had left her umbrella behind, she leered, 'by mistake'.

Dick had become such a fixture on the racetracks that in March he was called in by the Stewards of the National Hunt committee and told that if he wanted to continue to ride in professional races he would have to turn pro himself. He had become too successful to continue riding for nothing, and was depriving too many professional jockeys of their livelihoods. Dick had already been accepting illegally surreptitious 'presents' from grateful owners – a fancy dinner, a bottle of wine, a framed photograph, a briar pipe – so he was quite prepared to turn pro, but as luck would have it he had a disastrous Cheltenham, winning nothing and breaking his collar-bone again, which put him out of action for his first three weeks as a pro. But once the collar-bone was mended he discovered happily that, even though he was now charging for his services, he was offered almost as many rides as before.

He won his first race as a pro on Resurgent in a novices chase at Ludlow on 14 April, and at the Whitsun meeting at Cartmel delighted his brother Doug, who had become a trainer, by winning on one of his horses, Coastal Command. But those early triumphs were stained by sadness when Mary's father died on 1 May 1948 aged only fifty-eight. He, Netta and Ewen had moved a few months previously from Kingsmead Avenue into the heart of London, where they bought a boarding house at 129 Sussex Gardens, an elegant five-storey building set well back from a wide, stylish, leafy avenue near Paddington Station. It was there that William Brenchley died of a heart attack with Netta at his bedside. Although he left her his entire estate of £5,510-13s-3d, it was the equivalent of only £114,000 in 1999 and it seems that in later years Netta struggled to make ends meet. After his death she continued to run the guesthouse, which had eight regular lodgers that year, for nine more years, but the Paddington rate books show that she was often months late when it came to paying her local taxes and was regularly summonsed by the local council to pay off arrears. During the 1950s she shared the Sussex Gardens house with her mother, Jean and Ewen, who returned after doing his national service in the army to live at home for five years and to train as a hotel manager before marrying and moving to the Isle of Wight, where eventually he was to become director of the Isle of Wight Tourist Board. By 1998 129 Sussex Gardens had become a cheap twenty-one room hotel, the Gower. As for Kingsmead Avenue, where the Brenchleys had lived for twenty-two years, it is today a long, stark, unattractive road with stunted trees and an atmosphere of nondescript suburban dreariness. The house at number 17, where Mary was brought up, has been demolished and replaced by a modern block of Housing Association flats for old people with a resident warden, an institutional noticeboard in the entrance hall, and the brutal name of Pollard House. By strange coincidence Mary's earliest two houses had both become old folks' homes.

Dick finished the 1947/48 season with sixteen wins, six of them after turning pro, which caught the attention of one of the most successful owners, Lord Bicester, who asked him to ride regularly for him. Bicester, an eighty-one-year-old banker and Lord Lieutenant of Oxfordshire, needed a second jockey to ride his horses when his regular jockey, Martin Molony, was riding elsewhere. It was a wonderful break for Dick because Bicester's horses were among the best in the land and ran in all the most important races, and his string of steeplechasers, most of them trained by George Beeby at Compton, included three of the best jumpers in the country: Finnure, Roimond and Silver Fame. Dick felt guilty about abandoning George Owen after all he had done for him but Owen generously told him that he could not possibly pass up such a glittering opportunity. Dick was to ride for Bicester until Bicester's death eight years later at the age of eighty-nine. As for Owen's vital part in nurturing Dick's talent – and subsequently that of two other future champion jockeys, Tim Brookshaw and Stan Mellor – Dick reckoned that it was not that he was a brilliant teacher nor even particularly encouraging but that he gave his young jockeys a mass of experience on every kind of horse and then let them go when they were ready to spread their wings.

Dick's first race for Bicester was not until October, so in August he and Mary spent a few weeks on the Devon circuit again with Owen's horses. They stayed with Victor and Wenfra Dennis in an hotel in the south-coast resort of Torquay, which was crowded and jolly with bunting because the Olympic Games yacht races were being held there. Dennis, as full of beans as ever, clambered one night over his bedroom balcony, balanced precariously on the flimsy glass roof over the hotel entrance, and tied two chamberpots so that they dangled above the entrance beside the Olympic flags. An hilarious crowd gathered on the pavement beneath, the manager called the police, and eventually the pots were cut down by the hall porter. A few weeks later Dennis was dead. He had known he did not have long to live but had been determined to enjoy his last holiday with them. His death, just three months after that of Mary's father, reminded them that even when you are twenty-eight and twenty-four life is short and precious.

George Beeby's stables at Compton were 130 miles south of

Cholmondeley Castle and at first Dick spent many hours driving between them two or three times a week, but the situation was impossible and Dick and Mary decided that their future lay in the south and that they should move to Berkshire.

Dick became very fond of old Lord Bicester over the years that he rode for him and loved the way he doted on his horses, coming to see them daily, pockets bulging with sugar lumps and nuts, and always ensuring that they were given a summer holiday each year in the fields around his sumptuous home, Tusmore Park. Dick wore His Lordship's colours – black blouse, gold sleeves, red cap – for the first time on 26 October at Nottingham, where he rode his wonderfully reliable jumper Parthenon, but his career as Bicester's second jockey began badly. Parthenon came nowhere and four days later, when Dick was riding Silver Fame, the easy favourite in a race at Worcester, and was cantering down to the start, he noticed that the horse's nose was bleeding. Not knowing what to do, Dick nervously asked the starter if he could withdraw from the race and was relieved when Beeby congratulated him and said it could have been disastrous had he raced Silver Fame with a burst blood vessel. Soon afterwards he had his first ride at Aintree on Parthenon in the Grand Sefton Steeplechase. Dick was nervous as well as excited to be tackling the two-mile Liverpool course for the first time and to be jumping its huge fences, each with a frightening drop on the landing side. The ditch in front of the terrifying Chair jump, for instance, was six feet wide, the fence itself more than six feet high and a yard wide, and when Parthenon jumped the massive fence at Becher's Brook Dick felt as if he were flying again. But after the first few fences he started to enjoy the ride and they finished second. Later Dick considered Aintree to be the greatest steeplechase course in the world, and it became his favourite course – along with Hurst Park and Kempton – so long as he was riding a good jumper that had courage.

Silver Fame's nosebleed had cleared up by 13 November, when

Dick won on him at Stratford-upon-Avon, and at the end of his racing career Dick reckoned that the horse – a big pale chestnut with a white blaze on his face – was the greatest Bicester ever owned, a beast that was always determined to win, knew exactly what was necessary to do so, and never gave up. On 4 December Dick won again, this time at Kempton Park on Finnure, a big chestnut gelding that he came to love the best of all the hundreds of horses he rode because of Finnure's high intelligence, alertness, powerful jumping and exhilarating speed in a finish. But Dick never let himself become too fond of any horse. 'You mustn't become sentimentally attached to a horse,' he told the *Western Mail* in 1989. 'It's so easy for them to fall and break their neck or a leg and you find yourself going out to ride in the very next race.' In fact Finnure lived to a fine old age.

On 27 December Dick won again on Finnure at Kempton and came second on Roimond in one of the most important races of the year, the King George VI Chase. Roimond was a magnificent looking horse – a big, muscly dark chestnut – but quite different in character from Silver Fame and Finnure. Although he was a great jumper, Roimond was moody: when he wanted to win and made an effort he was superb; at other times he simply could not be bothered and there was nothing that Dick or any other jockey could do to get him going, so that riding him could be exhausting.

In December too Dick had a harrowing experience that was to haunt him for years. Owen went off to the bloodstock sales at Newmarket and left him in charge of the stables, and late that night, doing his final rounds, Dick noticed that Russian Hero was in serious pain, grunting, sweating and thrashing around. Dick called the vet, who told him that the horse had colic, an agonising, sometimes terminal affliction in which the bowel has become twisted. They hauled the horse to his feet and the vet told Dick that he and the stable lad should keep Russian Hero walking around the yard, all night if necessary, until the bowel untwisted itself. Dick and the lad stayed up until dawn, keeping Russian Hero on his feet for hours until he recovered at last. Dick had saved the horse's life, but later he was to claim he wished he hadn't.

At the end of March Dick realised at last his dream of riding in the Grand National when Bicester put him up on Roimond. Despite his eagerness to ride in the race, any jump-jockey will confess that the most harrowing hours of his whole career have been those on the morning and early afternoon before riding in his first National. It has been quite impossible to sleep the previous night and the changing room is stiff with tension and nervous excitement, the jockeys white-faced and apprehensive, sitting in silent rows, staring at their boots. Every one of them dreams of winning the race, yet none dares to believe it might happen. This is it: the Big One; thirty threatening fences, many of them five feet high, every one of them frighteningly lower on the landing side; and in 1949 they were even more daunting than they are now.

Dick always insisted that the National was not an especially dangerous race and said it was rare for a jockey to be badly hurt. He admitted that horses were sometimes killed but argued that just as many died on dangerous little country courses but nobody complained because such races were never reported widely. He swore that most horses loved Aintree and pointed out that many have tried to complete the race even after losing their jockeys. On the surface, at least, he seemed remarkably calm as he mounted Roimond in the parade ring and then – because Roimond was carrying the top handicap weight of 11st 12lbs – as they led the parade of forty-three runners past the stands towards the start amid a vast crowd of a quarter of a million blurred faces and the whirring of the cinema newsreel cameras.

Roimond started at odds of 22/1 – the favourites were Anthony Mildmay on Cromwell (6/1) and Bryan Marshall on Happy Home (10/1) – and as soon as the tapes shot up there was simply no more time to think and worry. In his autobiography Dick tried to explain the thrill – even ecstasy – of riding in the National but confessed that it was beyond his skill as a writer. There was only the sudden loneliness amid the thundering of hooves on every side, the rippling haunches, flashes of bright silk colours, wind whistling, the steaming smell of galloping horses, rasping breathing, the grunts of the jockeys, the sudden looming mountain of each alarming fence, the soaring take-off, a high view of the world and then the crunch of landing, fallers perhaps on every side, horses crashing, whinnying, jockeys curs-ing, diving smack into the mud, and then it's away again and the gallop towards the next, and on and on for four-and-a-half miles and nearly ten relentless, breathless minutes. Five fences first and then over Becher's Brook, named after the Colonel Becher who fell there twice during the 1839 Grand National and later remarked how disgusting water tasted without brandy in it. Then another fence and the sharp ninety-degree left at the Canal Turn, then it's Valentine's Brook. Three more fences alongside the Leeds and Liverpool Canal. Left again and unlucky fence number thirteen, then fourteen. Then oh God the sheer magnificent terror of The Chair. And past the stands. The Water Jump. The roar of the crowd a cyclone in your ears. And left again at the start and off again around the whole course for the second lap: Becher's again, the Canal Turn, Valentine's, and fallers all the way, in front and beside and behind you, fallers everywhere – but not you.

Of the forty-three horses that started that day, only eleven finished, among them Roimond. Dick rode brilliantly, Roimond jumped wonderfully well, and they kept up among the half-dozen leaders all the way. At one stage they led the field over several fences and as they entered the last mile Dick allowed him-self to dare to believe that he might be going to win the National at his first attempt. But then to his dismay he was overtaken by a horribly familiar horse whose jockey was wearing horribly familiar black-and-white quartered colours, colours that Dick had worn so often himself. He was going to be beaten by a 66/1 outsider, none other than his old partner Russian Hero. To the roars of the huge crowd they fought it out neck and neck towards the stands, but as they hit the final stretch and Russian Hero forged ahead, Dick knew with a sickness in his heart that he and Roimond were going to be beaten into second place by the horse whose life he had saved only three months earlier. And had he not left George Owen to ride for Lord Bicester he would probably have been riding Russian Hero himself that day and would have won the National at his first go.

Dick and Roimond came in eight lengths behind Russian Hero to collect the second prize of £1,158 (£23,400 in today's values) for Lord Bicester, who was delighted since no horse of his had ever done better than seventh in the National. Russian Hero's owner, Fearnie Williamson, hosted a wild dinner for a hundred people that night at the Blossoms Hotel in Chester to which both Dick and Mary were invited, and after Williamson, Owen and the jockey Leo McMorrow had all made speeches, Dick rose to his feet and said how delighted he was for them all but that if he had known three months previously that Russian Hero was going to beat him 'I'd have let the bugger die!' To add injury to insult, Russian Hero never won another race.

It was not much consolation for Dick when he won the Welsh Grand National at Chepstow in April on Fighting Line, which was trained by Ken Cundell in Compton. A week later he had his first treble when he rode three winners at Bangor-on-Dee, one of them Rompworthy, which was trained by his brother, Doug, and at Cartmel he notched up another two wins to reach a total of twenty-three winners in his first season as a pro.

Dick's parents were thrilled and relieved by his success, especially now that Vince had retired, aged sixty, and he and Molly had sold Chestnut Cottage and moved into a flat in a converted old house just outside Wokingham. Dick had become so successful that he was asked by yet another trainer to ride his horses, Gerald Balding, whose yard was twenty-five miles away at Weyhill, near Andover, and from 1949 Dick rode for Balding and Cundell as well as Beeby and Bicester.

So how good a jockey was he?

There was certainly no doubting his courage: he approached every fence with a fearless boldness, riding high with leathers much longer than is customary nowadays when jockeys prefer to ride in a much tighter style. Dick believed that riding with long stirrups made it easier for him to grip the horse with his legs, to urge it more effectively over a fence, and to feel at one with the horse, and in many photographs of him soaring exuberantly over a huge fence, legs stretched, it looks as if he is flying. According to the British racing commentator Peter O'Sullevan, Dick was 'one of the outstanding horsemen of his era', he wrote in a foreword to Bryony Fuller's book *Dick Francis: Steeplechase Jockey*. Sir Edward Cazalet, whose father, Peter Cazalet, employed Dick as his first jockey for three years in the 1950s, agreed. In a preface to Ms Fuller's book Sir Edward said Dick was a superb horseman whose horses were always well balanced and relaxed. Fred Winter, one of Dick's main rivals as a jockey, told Cazalet that Dick was 'very competitive but the best loser I ever rode against. He gave nothing away in a race but was always the first to come up afterwards and say "Well done" if you happened to come off best.' And Dick's brother, Doug, told Ms Fuller: 'I am very proud of him as he was a remarkable jockey. He had the most beautiful hands and you never caught him in the wrong position in a race. In my opinion, of all the top jockeys I saw ride, Dick was the finest horseman of them all.'

Les Foster, Frank Cundell's head lad in the late 1940s, told me that Dick had been one of the best ten jump jockeys of those years along with Fred Winter, Michael Scudamore and Bryan Marshall. 'He was a great jockey and a smashing bloke, really a gentleman,' said Mr Foster. 'As a jockey he was one of the best because he treated horses as though they were with him, not knocking them about. He rode them to his liking. He *made* Crudwell because he knew how to school him properly. He won fifty races on Crudwell but Crudwell couldn't jump at first till Dick took over.'

Kath Walwyn, the widow of the Lambourn trainer Fulke Walwyn, for whom Dick rode as stable jockey in 1954–55, told me that he was 'a wonderful horseman and horses always jumped very well for him. He wasn't a great finisher but he was always in the right place at the right time over the fences. He'd be in my Top Twenty jockeys of all time. He was a sort of gentleman rider, always beautifully turned out, a terribly nice person, quiet.' The ex-jockey and racing luminary Lord Oaksey agreed. 'He was a superb horseman but not a superb jockey,' he told me. 'He was wonderful at presenting a horse at a fence but not so good in the finish.'

The racing journalist Tom Forrest, who later worked with Dick for many years on the *Sunday Express*, told me that Dick was 'a very, very good horseman. His great strength was riding big horses.' But Forrest added:

I wouldn't put him amongst the top two or three of the jump jockeys that I have known, but what he *was* is one of the kindest men I've ever seen in delivering a horse to the last fence. He'd take a great big lumbering horse round three miles over fences and it would arrive at the last fence hardly knowing it was in the race, as fresh as it had been at the first. He was beautiful as far as that was concerned, one of the best. But he always had a big flaw in his jockeyship and that was the inability to ride a really vigorous finish. He was unable to do that because he had so many injuries and his shoulder kept dislocating. His arms would come out of their sockets. For that reason he wasn't one of the very, very greatest jockeys. But he was still a smashing jockey. If you had a good horse you couldn't have had a better man to keep it a good horse.

Less impressed was another Champion Jockey (in 1946–47) who rode against Dick hundreds of times, Jack Dowdeswell, who told me that Dick could ride badly, especially after he started riding for the Queen (later the Queen Mother) and her trainer Peter Cazalet. Mr Dowdeswell told me at his home in Lambourn:

Because he was the Queen's and Cazalet's jockey he thought he owned the course and owned the nearest way round. Sometimes he'd be a bit pugnacious – in fact quite worried about pushing his way in and riding a bit rough. I don't think he *meant* it, *intentionally*, but he would push his way through where another stylish jockey would do it quickly. Bryan Marshall, a great jockey, didn't like him at all and thought Dick thought he owned the racecourse. Dave Dick doesn't like him either, I know. Dick Francis was a good *chap* but he wasn't a mixer. He never made big friends, friends who would do anything for him. *'You paddle your own canoe'*, they'd say, *'we're not going to look after you!'* When he was in trouble there wouldn't be anyone to pull him back into place. Because he rode for Cazalet and the Queen you got that feeling that he thought he could rule the waves, as it were. He was inclined to be a bit too keen on the royal family.

Dowdeswell described Dick as 'a very dour sort of rider: he got every ounce out of a horse but he wasn't pretty' and he remembered Dick as being less than friendly towards his fellow jockeys:

There was a lot of camaraderie in jump racing. After a meeting – say at Kempton, Sandown or Windsor – we got back to The Swan at Shefford and we'd spend an hour there having a natter about the day and tomorrow, as pals do, but Dick was a bit stand-offish. I never heard of Dick going to a pub with other jockeys. He was an outsider. When Mary went racing she would sit in the car and knit all day and they'd go quietly home and have a meal. I never heard of him mixing. In some ways he was unpopular. He never had *great* great friends. He wasn't a chap to muck in.

Lord Oaksey told me:

I think that's true. Dick wasn't at all a Dave Dick-type jockey. At that time they whooped it up on a Saturday night and Dave was completely different from Dick and a wonderfully exciting character. The live-it-up part of the racing world despised Dick because they thought he was too prim and proper. I don't think he ever got drunk.

Kath Walwyn agreed:

Dick was a bit precious in that way. He didn't go off with the boys. Someone like Dave Dick was the complete opposite of him and they didn't get on at all. They were totally different characters. Dave was a swashbuckling jockey for whom life was wonderful and he lived it to the limit: he was an incredibly funny, wonderful personality and anything but quiet, and he would drink at weekends, and Dick didn't approve of that when you were riding. Dick very much gave the impression that he was more a member of the gentry. He always gave slightly the impression that he was an amateur and I'd describe him as that: a very good amateur.

One famous jockey who disliked Dick always called him 'Old Mother Francis' and another who rode against Dick many times confirmed that he 'wasn't one of the boys' and told me: 'I didn't have a lot to say to him.' He reckoned that Dick had been only a 'moderate' jockey. 'He was a good horseman,' he admitted, 'the sort of bloke I'd send out on a green horse to educate it for a good day's hunting, but if I wanted to have a bet on one I wouldn't put him up. I wouldn't call him a jockey: he was a horseman.'

Stan Mellor, another rider who raced against Dick and also became Champion Jockey, agreed. 'He was not a *jockey* jockey,' Mellor told me. 'He was a very good steeplechase rider, really good, and stylish too over the fences, really top-flight. His riding career was marred by his shoulders – that was the tragedy of Dick, really – but he was a good rider, no question of that.' Mellor remembered that Dick always used to turn up at the races wearing his blue RAF coat and highly polished shoes. 'He was always very dapper and dressed well, a little bit of a dandy,' he said. 'He always associated himself with the best and always made sure he was in the right places. If the Queen Mother was going anywhere she'd have to fall over him to get there! He was well connected and a little bit aloof, and a lot of jockeys didn't like him for that reason. He was a person apart.' Mellor's wife, Elaine, suggested that Dick's unsociability was because he was always a loner 'and basically all he needed was Mary.'

Since all three trainers for whom Dick was riding regularly in 1949 lived a long way south of Cholmondeley Castle it was obviously absurd for him to commute so far to work, especially since Mary became pregnant in July. They began to think that they ought to move south permanently, now, before the baby was born, but in October they were struck by a terrible tragedy: Mary contracted polio and had to be rushed to hospital.

Effective vaccines for polio were not invented until the 1950s and when Mary caught it in 1949 it was still extremely dangerous, a virus that usually caused a mild fever, headache, sore throat, diarrhoea and some vomiting, but that if it attacked the brain or spinal cord could paralyse its victim, waste limbs, seriously damage breathing and swallowing muscles, and even be fatal. When Mary contracted it she was staying with her mother in London while Dick was riding in Scotland and at Cheltenham. She was taken to Neasden Isolation Hospital and when Dick rushed to her side he was horrified to see how ill, grey and old she looked, and when he returned the next night he was terrified to find her in an iron lung with only her head sticking out of the grey box and electric bellows pumping air in and out of her lungs. She was by now totally paralysed from her neck to her knees. Suddenly he was very frightened. Was his beautiful, beloved twenty-five-year-old wife going to die? Be crippled for life? Confined to the box for the rest of her days? Would she, like some polio victims, have to undergo a tracheotomy, an operation to cut a hole in her neck to allow her to breathe more easily? And what about the baby, now a foetus three months old? Trembling with fear, he found a telephone kiosk and called his parents. When his mother answered he burst into tears.

Mary, too, for all her brave attempts to hide her fears from Dick, was also deeply apprehensive about the future, and her fears surfaced nearly twenty years later in the seventh Dick Francis novel, *Forfeit*, published in 1968, in which the hero's wife is so crippled by polio in her mid-twenties that she is completely helpless, confined for ever to a breathing machine, and utterly dependent on her husband for everything. She cannot breathe without an electrical pump and heavy respirator, has to be fed, washed and taken to the lavatory, and cannot be left alone for a moment in case of a power cut. *Forfeit* even discusses with remarkable candour the difficulty of sex when a wife has polio, and the hero and his wife eventually give it up. Years later Dick often remarked that he and Mary had always enjoyed a wonderful love life together and this passage in *Forfeit* was obviously based on their fears of how their physical closeness might have been destroyed had Mary's polio been worse.

Luckily Mary's disease was not terrible enough to condemn her to the iron lung for life. She spent three weeks in it and while she lay in hospital, slowly recovering, he broke his arm after a fall and then his collar-bone again, which put him out of action for two weeks so that he sat every day at her bedside while they solved crossword puzzles together.

The jinx that had struck them both was soon to be broken. That season of 1949–50 was to be one of Dick's best and on Boxing Day he rode Finnure in one of the most brilliant races of his life in the King George VI Chase at Kempton. The 4/6 easy favourite was Cottage Rake, ridden by Aubrey Brabazon, which had won the two previous Cheltenham Gold Cups, but Finnure and Cottage Rake were neck-and-neck as they went over the final fence before Dick and Finnure slowly inched ahead to win an incredibly exciting race by half a length. In another tense finish, at Cheltenham, Dick rode Tommy Thrush to win the Seven Springs Chase by a length, and in a third nail-biting climax, on Finnure in the Champion Chase at Liverpool, Dick just managed to beat Arthur Thompson on Coloured Schoolboy, again by a length, after the two horses had galloped and jumped side by side for two relentless miles.

And then Ken Cundell offered Dick and Mary a new home in Compton, Yew Tree House, an ancient seventeenth-century black-and-white gabled building close to his stables, and although Compton was a flat, dull, ugly village, and the house needed to be repaired and decorated, they were able to move down to Berkshire at last. In the meantime they stayed in London while Mary had a tendon transplant operation on her left hand and returned to the hospital every day for physiotherapy to prevent her weak muscles withering. In later years she was always to suffer from weakness in her hands, wrists and limbs, but she had been comparatively fortunate since nearly a quarter of all polio victims are left severely disabled. 'I am actually extremely lucky, a walking miracle,' she told me thirty years later. 'I still can't lift my left arm up and I have unexpectedly weak bits, and my breathing is a bit bad. My chest muscles were affected and I wheeze and can't run. I used to swim like a fish, and dive, but when I tried to swim after the polio I jumped into the water and just sank. It took me fourteen years to get back to playing tennis.' She chuckled. 'Still, one of the blessings of polio is that I can't do too much housework so we had to have help in the house. I'm not terribly domestic and not madly houseproud, but I'm a born optimist. Even when I was in the iron lung I never thought I might be there for ever. All our life the biggest disasters have turned out not to be disasters at all.'

In March 1950 they moved to Compton, excited to have a proper house at last after two-and-a-half years living in cramped little rooms and excited, too, because Dick was due to ride Roimond again in the Grand National on 25 March and this year they were 10/1 joint favourite with Jimmy Power on Freebooter. But it was not Dick's lucky day, despite the glorious spring weather: Roimond was having one of his moods, refused to jump properly, and he and Dick fell at the seventh fence, leaving Freebooter to win. Just before they crashed they cleared Becher's so magnificently that a Press photographer captured the massive leap in a dramatic photograph that was used for several years by Player's cigarettes in advertisements under the inaccurate slogan 'Well Ahead'. Still, Dick took his revenge when he and Silver Fame beat Jimmy Power and Freebooter in the Stanley Chase at Sandown, and he ended the season with twenty-nine winners, three in hugely important races. In just his second season as a pro he had established himself as a leading jump-jockey.

Because of Mary's semi-paralysis the doctors offered her an abortion. 'No, I want to have my baby,' she insisted. 'I may never have another', and on the evening of All Fools' Day, 1 April, she gave birth to their first son in the Radcliffe Maternity

Home in Oxford. 'It was a special birth, of course, with me being paralysed,' she told Lesley Garner of the *Mail on Sunday* in 1982, 'so everybody came rushing in to assist and observe and it turned out to be perfectly normal. It was one of the most thrilling evenings of my life. I remember lying in bed giggling because I was so happy.'

Dick drove south like a whirlwind from Bangor-on-Dee, where he had been riding in several races, but there was no need to worry: both Mary and the baby were fine. They christened him Merrick Ewen Douglas and the nightmare was over.

CHAPTER 9

Triumph and Disaster

(1950–56)

Dick, Mary and little Merrick settled happily into their new home in Compton, where Dick could now ride for two trainers in the village, George Beeby and Ken Cundell, without commuting hundreds of miles. Like all successful jockeys, however, he still had to drive long distances six days a week throughout the winter to ride at one of the forty-five National Hunt racecourses scattered all over the country. He averaged seven hundred miles a week but luckily he enjoyed driving and Compton, just eight miles north of Newbury in the beautiful heart of the Berkshire racing world, was central enough for him to reach most courses within two or three hours. He loved the freedom of being his own boss, of being out on the open road and arriving at a course to be greeted by the smell of jellied eels, the cries of the newspaper vendors Johnny, Fatty and Tishy, the whispering of the tipsters. He loved the whole afternoon atmosphere of the races: the bustle, the tension, the gossip.

Mary's arms were still too weak to lift or feed the baby or to change his nappies, so they hired a full-time live-in nanny, Elsie Leo, as well as a cleaning woman, which freed Mary to go to the races again with Dick nearly every day. In September they took five-month-old Merrick to the races for the first time, and although Mary still had no huge interest in racing – she much preferred books and reading – she went along 'to pick up the bits', as she put it. On one memorable occasion she was asked what colour Roimond was and replied: 'auburn'. There was a stunned silence. No one would *ever* call a horse auburn: the correct term is 'dark chestnut'. Nor did she and Dick discuss horses or racing much, and although Dick was obsessed by both he claimed that Mary's lack of interest helped him to retain a sense of proportion about his work.

His life riding several horses a day was exhausting as well as exhilarating. It takes a great deal of strength and stamina to ride a big, strong horse over jumps and sometimes, after a difficult race in which his arms felt as if they had almost been pulled out of their sockets, Dick would dismount trembling so much that his legs would wobble and his hands shake. He avoided rich food and alcohol and went to bed early, except on Tuesday nights when he and Mary always went to see the latest play at the New Theatre in Oxford: her love of the theatre was as strong as ever. Each new day started early, too. Swathed in sweaters and scarves, he would drive in his Land Rover up to the icy, windy Berkshire Downs before dawn to exercise Beeby's and Cundell's horses, cantering them through the mist across the rolling Downs into the rising sun, sometimes alongside the budding fifteen-year-old jockey Lester Piggott, who rode Cundell's Flat racehorses and of whom Ken Cundell said to Dick: 'That boy is going to be the greatest jockey who ever lived, mark my words.' Another of Dick's jobs was to school the horses, teaching the youngest to jump over logs and small hurdles, and after an hour or so he would drive home, snatch a wash, a change of clothes and a hurried breakfast and then drive with Mary to the races. There he would change into his racing colours, shun any lunch, be weighed on the chair-scales by the Clerk of the Scales, go out to the parade ring before the first race, discuss tactics with his first horse's trainer and owner, mount the horse and set off for the start in the hope of winning anything between one and seven races that afternoon. After each race he would return to the weighing room to go through the whole process again. After the last race he would grab a cup of tea, a sandwich, perhaps a piece of fruit cake, and drive back home again. Each night he would be shattered.

Despite all this gruelling and dangerous activity, few jump-jockeys earned a great deal in the 1950s. The fee for riding in each race was £7-7s – about £110 in modern values – but the prizes were minute by comparison with Flat races, where jockeys could become seriously rich, because Flat racing was so much faster, flashier and fashionable than National Hunt racing and had always attracted much richer owners and sponsors. Any jockey winning a race could also expect the owner to give him 10 or 11 per cent of the prize money, but some owners were incredibly stingy: one was so mean that when Dick rode a winner for him he was given just a glass of sherry out of the boot of a car in the car park. Most steeplechase jockeys rode for the sheer joy of it and no more than forty or so – out of four hundred – made even a basic living from racing fees alone, and to do that they would have to ride in 100 or more races a season. Dick earned better than most. As one of the top dozen jockeys, he might ride in two hundred races in a season, which would earn him £1,500 a year – the equivalent of £22,000 in 1999 – plus 'presents' and prize money, and on top of that he was paid a generous retainer not merely by one trainer but by two, all of which put him in the super-tax bracket. Yet he had high expenses: a percentage of each riding fee had to be paid into the jockeys' insurance fund; clothes and kit often had to be replaced after falls; and he had to pay racecourse valets' fees every day to the men who washed, mended, cleaned and looked after his kit. Even so, Dick was pretty well off: not many jump-jockeys could afford a cleaning woman and a full-time nanny, and he and Mary were able to begin to entertain by having old friends like Roy Palmer and Eric Ginger to stay for the odd weekend.

In the new season of 1950/51 he just topped his previous record of twenty-nine winners by riding thirty. His performance at Kempton just after Christmas was particularly stunning: he won a three-mile chase on Bluff King; came second on Silver Fame in the King George VI Chase; won the two-and-a-half-mile Chiswick Chase on Possible; and won the Christmas Handicap Hurdle on Coup d'Épée. But his ride in the Grand National in April was a dreadful disappointment. He was riding his favourite horse, Finnure, and although they started at 22/1, Dick was convinced he had a wonderful chance of winning. Unhappily the starter, Leslie Firth, pressed the starting lever too soon, when half of the thirty-six runners were still milling about, and the tapes suddenly went up so that many of the jockeys were taken completely unawares. 'One of the maddest scrambles ever witnessed on a racecourse began as jockeys tried desperately to make up lost ground,' wrote Reg Green in *A Race Apart: the History of the Grand National*. They charged from a standing start in a ragged, panicky pack across the Melling Road towards the first fence, where several fell. Finnure jumped the fence perfectly but landed in the middle of the mêlée and was brought down, twisting his hock so badly that it was a year-and-a-half before he was able to race again and even then he was never the same and had to be retired. Twelve horses fell at that first fence and there is a miserable photograph of eight fallen jockeys standing beside the fence in disbelief, Dick looking furious.

Family life in 1951 was more successful. Mary's mother and Dick's parents got on so well that in April the elder Francises left their flat in Wokingham, moved into Molly's brother's flat in London – at 48 Norfolk Square, near Paddington station – and bought a lodging house a couple of hundred yards away at 131 Sussex Gardens, next door to the boarding house where Netta Brenchley lived with Jean, until a few months later when

Jean married yet another Dick, Dick Yorke, and went to live in Glasgow. The Francis boarding house was registered in Molly's name and she and Vince ran it for seven years. Unlike Netta, she was never late in paying her rates.

But Dick's racing the next year was a great disappointment and brought him only twenty-eight winners, and he had only one notable race when he won the Oaklands Chase on Senlac Hill at the Kempton Boxing Day meeting. At Cheltenham he had another bad fall and once again on a cold, damp, misty day he fell at the seventh fence in the Grand National, this time on Skyreholme. His career perked up, however, the following season, 1952/53, when he beat his record by notching up thirty-eight winners. One mount that turned out to be important for the future was Lord Hornblower, a horse he rode in Devon in August: although it did not win its race, it was owned by the publisher Michael Joseph, whose company was later to publish all the Dick Francis books. Joseph invited Dick and Mary to his Devon hotel for a drink and that brief meeting was to result in a publishing marriage that was to last for more than forty years.

Also to last for more than half a century was Dick and Mary's affection for the seaside hotel in nearby Paignton, the Redcliffe, where they were staying when they met Michael Joseph. They stayed there for the first time that summer for ten days, while Dick was riding at Newton Abbot, Exeter and Buckfastleigh, and enjoyed it so much that they were to return every summer.

Foremost among Dick's winners that year was Dorothy Paget's great, graceful chestnut Mont Tremblant, which was trained by Fulke Walwyn at Lambourn and ridden by Dick after Dave Dick broke his leg at Cheltenham. On Mont Tremblant he won the Ewell Chase and the Stanley Chase at Sandown, they came second in the King George VI Chase at Kempton on Boxing Day, and later he said that Mont Tremblant was one of the six or seven best horses he had ever ridden. In December he also had his first win on another great horse, Crudwell, in the three-mile Henry VIII Novices Chase at Hurst Park. Dick and Crudwell – a light brown horse that looked more like a Flat racer than a jumper – were to forge a magnificent partnership over the next few years. Crudwell was one of Frank Cundell's horses at Aston Tirrold, not far from Compton, and when Dick rode him for the first time on the Berkshire Downs he had a premonition that he and this magnificent horse were destined to forge a special understanding, and so it turned out. In the Henry VIII Chase they had an immediate rapport and each seemed to know what the other was thinking. It was uncanny. Although it was Crudwell's very first steeplechase, he jumped without any trouble, keeping behind most of the other horses, and then in the final straight he accelerated smoothly through the entire field to win easily. In their next nine races they won eight, an astonishing record, and eventually Crudwell was to win more National Hunt races than any horse since the turn of the century.

Although Dick always insisted that the racing world was not nearly as corrupt as you might think after reading a few Dick Francis novels, he did as a jockey come up against others who were decidedly less than honest. Some would accept a bribe to lose a particular race, and those who refused lost out because a corrupt owner would not ask them to ride for him again. Dick was once offered a bribe of £50 (worth more than £800 today) to lose a race when he was riding one of Doug's horses at Bangor-on-Dee, but Doug told the briber to go to hell. The Lambourn trainer Tim Fitzgeorge-Parker, for whom Dick rode occasionally, told me that Dick was 'as straight as a die'.

Common too was the use of drugs, and Dick rode twice in races when he was convinced his horses had been doped to win. The first was so hyped up that its eyes were rolling, its mouth foaming and it was prancing around the paddock, and it was so steamed up that, when Dick fell off, the horse ran off in a frenzy, escaped from the course and was eventually found ten miles away. The second horse had always been lazy and hated racing but on this particular day it ran with remarkable vigour and won easily. The next time Dick rode the beast it was as sluggish as ever.

Jack Dowdeswell was approached several times in the 1940s and 1950s to 'stop' a horse and was once offered the modern equivalent of £20,000 to pull a favourite. 'When they couldn't get at me they then doped the horse and it only came third!' he told me. 'A lot of doping went on in those days. Another trainer I was riding for was warned off eventually for life for ringing a horse at Salisbury, and a Welsh bookmaker was murdered in the early Fifties.'

For three years Dick rode happily for Bicester and the Cundell cousins, and he and Mary relished their life together with their lively little son. They enjoyed living in Ken Cundell's 350-year-old house in Compton, despite the dampness that infiltrated the wattle and daub walls, the uneven floors and the old chimney that had to be taken down because it was unsafe. But all of that pleasure was nothing compared with what was about to happen in their lives. That year of 1953 was about to become their *annus mirabilis*. First, on 10 February, Mary gave birth to their second son at the Radcliffe Maternity Home in Oxford. They called him Felix Richard Roger. And then a month later Dick was asked to ride his first horse for the royal trainer Peter Cazalet, one of the most successful and fashionable trainers in the land. Without that lucky break Dick would have been forgotten today except by a few gnarled old stable lads and a handful of racing fans. He would never have become Champion Jockey. He would never have ridden the Queen Mother's horses. He would never have become internationally famous for riding Devon Loch in the 1956 Grand National. He would never have been asked to write his autobiography. And there would never have been any Dick Francis thrillers, for who would have bought a novel by an unknown, middle-ranking jump-jockey? The moment that Peter Cazalet asked Dick to ride Statecraft in the Cheltenham Gold Cup in March 1953 was Dick's moment of destiny. He was never to look back.

Queen Elizabeth the Queen Mother, whose husband George VI had died a year earlier, had developed a passion for National Hunt racing and owned several horses that were trained by Cazalet in his impeccably stylish stables at his lovely William and Mary home, Fairlawne, near Tonbridge in Kent. On the day before the Cheltenham Gold Cup in March – which Dick was resigned to watching as a spectator – one of Cazalet's regular jockeys, who was due to ride Statecraft, was injured and Cazalet asked Dick to ride it instead. Just before the race Cazalet introduced him to the Queen and Queen Mother in the parade ring, twenty years after he had first met the Queen when she had been a solemn six-year-old and had presented him with a riding crop. Today she was wearing a fur coat and a yellow scarf. He bowed, shook hands with both royal ladies and was typically embarrassed that he could not doff his crash helmet since it was firmly tied onto his head. It was the start of a connection between the Francises and the royal family that was to last for nearly fifty years.

Statecraft pulled a tendon during the race and Dick had to dismount, but the Queen Mother and Cazalet had noted him as a possible successor to their retained jockey Bryan Marshall, who had decided to become a trainer himself. A couple of weeks later at Aintree Dick won the Topham Trophy on Irish Lizard, and two days after that he managed to come fifth in the Grand National, though only because there were only five finishers: every other horse, twenty-six of them, fell, refused or was pulled up, and four were killed. Dick's mount that day was Senlac Hill, a nightmarish Bicester beast that was so amazingly stupid and careless that the bookies rated it as a 66/1 outsider, the longest odds in the entire field, and were offering 50/1 against the horse even completing the course. Yet astonishingly Senlac Hill jumped sedately around the whole course twice, soaring over everything as almost every rival tumbled around him in the thick muddy conditions, and, although he came in a long way behind the first four horses, he at least finished the course.

A month later, at Sandown, Cazalet asked Dick to ride for him and the Queen Mother the following season as their first jockey. He could hardly believe it. From the end of 1953 he would be riding some of the best horses in the land and wearing the colours of the best loved owner in racing: the Queen Mother's pale Strathmore blue with buff stripes, pale blue sleeves and black velvet cap with a gold tassel. Dick said he would have to get the permission of Bicester and Frank Cundell. Such decency and modesty were typical of him. Cazalet's son, Sir Edward Cazalet, who was himself a jockey as a young man and later became a High Court judge, liked to describe the first time that Dick and his father met: Cazalet, as the local squire, had the right to appoint his parish priest and was due to interview a potential new vicar on the same day, so when Dick arrived, all charm and modesty, Cazalet spent a quarter of an hour discussing hymns and sermons before Dick could bring himself to stop him.

Bicester and Cundell agreed that Dick should ride for Cazalet as well and from August Dick was the Queen Mother's top jockey. During those years he met the Queen, the Queen Mother and Princess Margaret many times, at Cazalet's stables as well as at the races. The two queens' enthusiasm for horses was legendary and often Dick would find them splashing around in the mud and rain so long as there were horses nearby. The Queen Mother 'would be up and out, head-scarved and gum-booted against the cold early mornings, to watch her horses at exercise on the gallops,' wrote Godfrey Talbot in *The Country Life Book of Queen Elizabeth the Queen Mother*. 'Afterwards . . . she would go wandering round the stables with a basket of carrots and sugar in her hand, talking to all the men and animals on the spot. Trainers, lads and jockeys regard her as the perfect owner.' At

Lingfield races, on an afternoon when it was pelting with rain, Dick went out to ride a horse of the Queen Mother's in a minor four-horse race and was amazed to find her waiting outside in the rain to see her horse and to wish him good luck. And every year he would be invited to her jolly annual party for the racing world at her London home, Clarence House – and every year, for the next forty-five years, she sent him a Christmas card.

With three regular trainers to ride for and some of the country's best horses to ride, Dick started to rattle out the winners like a one-armed bandit gone berserk. In the first four days of the season he rode five winners for Cazalet. In November, at Sandown, he had six races in two days and won three of them, came second twice and was third in the other. Before Christmas he won three consecutive races on the Queen Mother's M'as-Tu-Vu and at Kempton on Boxing Day he was placed yet again in the King George VI Chase, coming third on Legal Prince. By the end of the year he had already beaten his personal record of thirty wins in a season and there were five months of racing still to go.

He was earning so much money that he and Mary decided that they could afford their own house at last, somewhere with a bit of land so that Merrick and Felix could keep ponies when they were older. None of the houses on the market appealed to them so Mary simply designed one herself, sketching plans for her dream bungalow on pieces of graph paper. Most couples buy furniture to fit into a house; Mary measured their furniture first and then built the house around it. They bought fifty acres of land from a farmer just outside the Oxfordshire village of Blewbury, four miles across the Downs from Compton but ten miles by road, and the builders started work on it in December.

In the New Year of 1954 the winners still kept coming. On 2 January Dick was beaten at Newbury by eighteen-year-old Lester Piggott – who rode in several jump races early in his career before he settled for the Flat – but Dick took his revenge a fortnight later at Sandown when he beat Piggott on Deal Park and rode three winners in a day. In February he won the National Trial Handicap Chase at Leicester on his beloved Crudwell and then learned that Cazalet wanted him to go to New York at the end of April to ride in a new American invitation race, the International Steeplechase at Belmont Park, against runners from several countries including Ireland and France. America! And all expenses paid! Plus a riding fee! He would take Mary, have a holiday, stay for two or three weeks, visit friends on the other side of the pond. What a wonderful year it was turning out to be.

Only the Cheltenham Gold Cup and the Grand National were both again disappointing. In both great races he seemed to be constantly jinxed. For the Gold Cup he was due to ride Lord Bicester's Mariner's Log but in an earlier race that afternoon he fell yet again, dislocated his left shoulder this time, and Mary had to rush him off to Cheltenham hospital, where the nurse in charge of the casualty department greeted them with the forlorn cry: 'What? Not you again!' In the National he rode a 40/1 chance, Icy Calm, but had to pull the horse up after about three miles when it tired and began to jump raggedly. To his chagrin the race was won by Bryan Marshall for the second year running. How could Marshall win twice in a row and he couldn't do it even once?

A week later he had another double, this time on Pondapatarri and Trambeza at Bangor-on-Dee, which brought his total number of wins for the season to an awesome seventy-eight, and by now he was so far ahead in the table of winners that no other jockey was ever going to catch him. By the end of the season he had ridden in 331 races, more than any other jockey, and the second most successful rider, Rene Emery, had ridden only fifty-eight winners, which made Dick Champion Jockey by a huge margin. His total number of winners, seventy-eight, was less than is customary for a champion jockey nowadays, but it must be remembered that in 1954 there were many fewer race meetings than there are now, there were no evening meetings, and jockeys were not able to increase their number of rides by flying between racecourses. Equally it has to be remembered that Dick might never have been Champion Jockey had his great rival Fred Winter not broken his leg in his first ride of the season so that he was not able to ride at all that year. 'That was why Dick was champion,' Lord Oaksey told me. 'Fred couldn't ride at all.' Kath Walwyn told me that Dick had been lucky to have so many of Cazalet's great horses to ride that season and Jack Dowdeswell claimed that Dick 'wouldn't have been Champion Jockey if he hadn't been riding for Cazalet,' but added: 'it's the same for all of us, really. I mean, let's face it: horses make champions.'

Dick was Champion Jockey after just six seasons as a professional. He had realised the second of his two great ambitions. There was only one dream left to fulfil: to win the Grand National, one day, somehow, eventually.

A week later he took Mary and the children to the Beaufort Hunt races in Gloucestershire for a picnic lunch in the April sunshine, but he had a very nasty accident when Pondapatarri fell and brought down another horse which kicked Dick viciously in the back. He felt numb all over, sick and terrified. He lay on the ground, unable to move. Was this it? The end of it all? The final irony after his best season ever? Was it he, not Mary, who was going to be paralysed, perhaps in a wheelchair for the rest of his life? Gingerly a doctor examined him where he lay, testing his reflexes, and then Mary and two ambulancemen took him carefully off to hospital in Bristol while Bryan and Mary Marshall looked after Merrick and Felix. Luckily Dick's good fortune that season had not deserted him: the X-rays showed that, although one of his vertebrae had been smashed, it would heal before too long. Bill Tucker, the surgeon, even agreed that Dick could still ride in America three weeks later so long as he wore a plaster jacket for the next four days and then a special brace made of steel and leather. Like some medieval knight encased in armour,

Dick boarded the *Queen Elizabeth* with Mary at the end of April for a five-day journey across the Atlantic.

In Britain the huge postwar wave of immigration had not yet started, so when they reached New York and drove through Harlem they were amazed to see so many black people in their garish clothes selling watermelons beside home-made signs that read 'Have A Good Belly-Wash' and 'Flush Out Your Kidneys'. As they drove out along Long Island, where they were to spend most of their three weeks in America, they were awed by the vast amount of space by comparison with cramped little old England. They loved the racecourse at Belmont Park with its lakes, brightly coloured flowers and giant, complicated Tote machine. Further out they loved the remote, empty beaches that stretched for miles. Above all they were fascinated by the differences between British and American racing: the fact that American racing was concentrated for several weeks at a time at the same racecourse; that American steeplechase fences were flimsy enough for horses to brush through them; that trainers and jockeys were terrified of the vicious New York Press.

Most extraordinary of all was the American authorities' success in stamping out cheating and corruption. Dick was astonished to be locked into the changing room four hours before his race and kept prisoner until it was over. An American jockey was not even allowed to speak to his trainers or owners. Every race was filmed at close quarters and scrutinised immediately afterwards so that any jockey trying to 'stop' his horse or to nobble his rivals would be exposed straight away. At the end of a race a jockey was not allowed to dismount until given permission to do so and Dick was stunned to see American jockeys sitting on their horses with their hands raised to ask for permission to dismount. Yet they were allowed to bet on horses they were riding themselves – which gave them an extra incentive to win – and to prevent a trainer entering two horses in the same race and fixing it so that the better of the two was beaten by the worse, all horses entered by the same stable or owner were treated as one, so that if one of them won then so did bets placed on the other. Every winning horse was given a saliva test, so that doping was impossible, all betting was controlled by the Tote, and no bet could be placed before the day of a race. Thanks to all these restrictions Dick believed that racing in the USA was as honest as it could ever be. Had he and Mary lived in America they could never have set the Dick Francis novels there because crooks simply did not have a chance.

The International Steeplechase was in the end a disappointment to all the European jockeys who had come so far to ride in it. Their horses had arrived in America only three days previously after a thirty-two-hour air journey and were still jet-lagged, so the first four past the post were American, and although Dick was riding Cazalet's excellent English chaser Rose Park, they came nowhere.

Back home in England Dick and Mary were sufficiently well-off to go off on their own for a holiday when the National Hunt season ended, leaving the children with the nanny, and they would drive around Scotland or Europe or take a boating holiday on the Norfolk Broads. In July they took the boys off to the Redcliffe Hotel in Paignton again and in August the three-bedroom bungalow was finished at last and they moved with relief into the first home they had owned. They were to live there for thirty-one years.

'He called it Penny Chase because he always believed that if you watched the pennies, the pounds would look after themselves,' Stan Mellor told me. 'In those days he was probably a bit tight. The other saying he used to quote was that you want to keep yourself in the best company and your horses in the worst. They were the two things he lived by.' The Francises' home in Compton, Yew Tree House, was eventually replaced by an immaculate estate of modern houses in a cul-de-sac called Yew Tree Stables.

Blewbury was a pretty, sleepy old Oxfordshire village with six hundred inhabitants, a twelfth-century church, two aged mills, a manor house and five pubs: the Barley Mow, King William, Red Lion, Sawyers Arms and the Load of Mischief. There were also about two hundred other dwellings, some four hundred years old and built of timbers from Henry VIII's navy that had been broken up at Buckler's Hard and floated up the Thames. But the Francises' unpretentious bungalow was startlingly modern and stood on a flat, bleak, windy site just outside the village on the road to Didcot with barely a tree in sight and surrounded by bare fields. Yet Dick and Mary loved it: it was just a mile from Frank Cundell's yard at Aston Tirrold, so that Dick could ride there on a bicycle, and they relished their view of the huge Iron Age earthworks to the east, the range of hills to the south and the ancient track of the Ridgeway. Here they would consolidate their wonderfully happy marriage – now seven years old but still no Seven Year Itch – and here they would raise four-year-old Merrick and eighteen-month-old Felix and teach them to ride and to love life and the English countryside. Even when they took a bath together and got stuck in the tub it ended in helpless giggles when Mary discovered that her arms were too weak to haul herself out and Dick could not move because he had put his shoulder out again. In the end they extricated themselves by letting all the water out first.

When the new season started in August Mary was still able to go with Dick to the races because their nanny Elsie Leo moved to Blewbury with them. Dick began the new season at a gallop, winning almost immediately at Newton Abbot on Diego Rubio, but the highlight of that autumn was when he was the guest of honour in October at the annual Cheltenham dinner for the previous season's Champion Jockey and made a nervous speech to the National Hunt committee, stewards and the Press as well as trainers, owners and other jockeys. It was the pinnacle of his career. He was about to turn thirty-four and no matter what came later, despite all the huge literary adulation that was to swamp him in later years, this was the ultimate experience of his life. Nothing else would come close to this, not all the bestseller lists in the world. Nothing else at all – except winning the Grand National. The one goal left. *Please let me win the Grand National.* And it would have to be soon: in two or three years he was going to have to retire.

That autumn he won three times in a row on Lochroe, most notably in the Henry VIII Chase at Hurst Park in December. Despite having a small, narrow frame, Lochroe was to become one of his favourite horses and one with which he developed a special relationship. The animal seemed to relish racing with Dick on his back and won thirty out of fifty-eight races. At Kempton on Boxing Day Dick won the Chiswick Chase on Cintra and came third on Mariner's Log in the King George VI Chase, but in the Christmas Handicap Hurdle his dislocated left shoulder suddenly came apart again as he was riding a tough finish against Fred Winter. He dreaded the possibility of another painful operation but Bill Tucker, who had operated on his right shoulder, discovered that the left one dislocated only when he raised his arm straight above his head and would probably stay in its socket if Dick kept it strapped up with a band of webbing to be worn across the top of the shoulder. From then on he was held together like a patchwork doll.

Sadly the triumphs of 1953–54 were never to be repeated and from now on Dick's racing career plummeted. Although he rode ferociously all season, 283 rides in all, he could manage only thirty-three winners, fewer than half his total the previous year. At the Cheltenham Festival, despite having several rides, he was not even placed. In the waterlogged Grand National, which was nearly cancelled because of three days of heavy rain, he rode Mariner's Log for Lord Bicester but fell at the first fence. In the Welsh Grand National in April, riding Crudwell, he came tenth. It was not a memorable year.

But worse was to come the following season – much worse.

It began deceptively well. He opened his score quickly by winning twice at Newton Abbot and on 25 November he had his first win on the great horse with which his name will for ever be associated: the Queen Mother's big, intelligent, brave brown gelding Devon Loch, which Dick later reckoned was the greatest and most gallant steeplechaser she ever owned. Devon Loch had been out of racing for two years with recurrent leg troubles but as soon as Dick rode him for the first time that November he told Cazalet that he would love to ride the horse in the Grand National. He was convinced that Devon Loch was a future Aintree winner. Their first win together was in Devon Loch's first ever race over three miles, the Blindley Heath Chase at Lingfield, and they won again at Sandown in December, and at Cheltenham in the National Hunt Handicap Chase in March he ran with such grit and stamina that, although he and Dick trailed at the back of the field for the first half of the race, they forged ahead towards the end and came in third, even though they were carrying much more weight than the horses that came first and second. The race had been run incredibly fast and Dick was convinced that here was the wonder horse that would at last allow him to win the Grand National.

Fifteen days before the race he fell and cracked his collar-bone yet again – for the ninth time – and he could hear the broken bits of bone scraping against each other in his shoulder. He was in a terrible quandary. If he told Cazalet about the injury he would never let him ride in the National, yet if he did not tell him and lost the race he would never forgive himself. What to do? Could he really throw up his best chance yet, perhaps his last chance, of winning the great race?

He said nothing, and continued to ride with the shoulder strapped up and was reassured when the bone held even during a hard race at Lingfield when he managed to beat Fred Winter by a neck after a gruelling finish. In the final week before the

National Dick rode in several more races and had another winner without suffering any weakness from the broken collar-bone. There seemed to be no need to say anything to Cazalet. It was going to be all right. He was going to ride in the National, and he was going to win.

On the day of the great race, Saturday 24 March 1956, Dick, Mary, Vince and the boys were staying at the Buck Inn near Doug's house at Bangor-on-Dee, thirty-five miles south of Aintree, but Dick spent much of the morning alone, silently planning his campaign of attack. In his mind he rode and rerode the race time and again, matching Devon Loch's abilities to every obstacle, gauging each fence, calculating the likely tactics of his greatest rivals, imagining every possibility.

The huge crowd at Aintree included a party of officials from the Soviet Union, including the ex-Prime Minister Georgi Malenkov, and the atmosphere in the changing room that afternoon was as tense as ever. With a prize of £8,695 at stake for the winning owner – about £124,000 in modern terms – and at least 10 per cent of that for the winning rider, the twenty-nine nervous jockeys were as silent and white-faced as ever, each sitting alone with his hopes and fears. The favourite, at 7/1, was Bert Morrow on Must, followed by Fred Winter on Sundew at 8/1 and Bob Turnell at 10/1 on Carey's Cottage. Dick and Devon Loch were joint fourth favourite at 100/7 along with Dave Dick on E.S.B. and Jimmy Power on Pippykin. The Queen Mother's other entry in the race, M'as-Tu-Vu, had Arthur Freeman up and Dick's old partner Mariner's Log was being ridden that day by Rene Emery, though sadly Lord Bicester was not there to see his horse run: he had died not long before the race, aged eighty-eight. Other runners that day included Bryan Marshall on Early Mist and Stan Mellor on Martinique.

With heart pounding and mouth dry, Dick chatted with the Queen, Queen Mother and Princess Margaret in the parade ring and all agreed that the handicapper had been very fair by giving

Devon Loch only 11st 4lbs to carry. Then he mounted the great ten-year-old horse and the royals wished him God-speed and he rode down to the start with all the other runners. This was it. This was what he had been born for, raised for, trained for, ever since he had first thrown a chubby little leg across the back of Jessie the donkey in that field at Coedcanlas thirty years ago. This was his destiny.

They were off at a cracking pace as usual, the customary wild cavalry charge across the Melling Road led this time by Jack Dowdeswell on Armorial III, and as usual several horses fell at the first, this time four of them, including the favourite, Must, and Bryan Marshall on Early Mist, but Devon Loch galloped as if inspired, jumping like an angel. They soared over Becher's, and the seventh fence where Dick had come to grief twice in previous Nationals, and they took the dog-leg Canal Turn with ease, and floated over Valentine's Brook, and even when Domata stumbled and crashed just in front of them at the open ditch two fences later, and Dick was convinced that he would be brought down too, Devon Loch somehow swerved in mid-air, danced away from Domata like a four-legged ballerina, and galloped on.

For fence after fence it was a ride made in Heaven. Over the Chair they went as if it were only a footstool, and the Water Jump, and past the start and over the Melling Road again and off towards Becher's for the second circuit and out towards the Leeds and Liverpool canal, passing one horse after another along the way. Arthur Freeman and M'as-Tu-Vu fell at the nineteenth fence, Fred Winter on Sundew at Becher's, and when they reached the Canal Turn for the second time there was only one runner ahead of them, Jack Dowdeswell on Armorial III, and for the first time ever in a Grand National Dick was so confident that he held a horse back to calm him down and bide his time. Armorial III fell at the twenty-sixth fence and, although Alan Oughton caught up on Eagle Lodge for a moment, Devon Loch accelerated into the lead with just three fences to go. Oh God it was going to happen it was really going to happen. Devon Loch took the final fence as easily and unhurriedly as he had taken all the others and began the long gallop home in front of the packed and roaring stands, leaving E.S.B., Ontray and Gentle Moya stranded in his wake, with the vast crowd bellowing for the Queen Mother and Devon Loch and Dick Francis, and Devon Loch was still amazingly fresh after more than four miles and nothing was going to catch him now. Oh God what a glorious feeling, the best feeling of all his life, galloping in towards the finish in what would be the fastest Grand National in history – faster even than the great Golden Miller – with only a few yards to go to the post and no more fences to jump and the whole world yelling him on. 'From the stands and enclosures came the loudest cheering ever heard on a racecourse as the crowds gave vent to their joy at the first Royal Grand National winner for fifty-six years,' reported Reg Green in *A Race Apart: The History of the Grand National*. There was the post, just fifty yards ahead, just a dozen strides away. This was it. The greatest triumph of them all. The one after which you could die happy. The ultimate joy of being a jump-jockey. That magnificent surge of adrenalin. And it felt as wonderful as he had always known it would.

And then Devon Loch just fell down.

At one moment he was the certain winner, galloping smoothly along, just seconds from victory – at the next his hind legs suddenly stiffened, all four stretched out and he belly-flopped into the mud and slithered along the ground.

Dick sat for a moment in bewildered astonishment, glued to the saddle, as Devon Loch staggered to his feet. Dick tried to get him going again. *Come on, come on!* Even now they could still hobble across the finishing line and win. But Devon Loch seemed to be paralysed. He could barely move, his hind legs collapsed again, and Dick thought he might have broken a leg. Dave Dick came galloping past on E.S.B., amazed, to win the race by ten lengths from Gentle Moya and Royal Tan and Eagle Lodge. Dave Dick couldn't believe his luck. 'When he jumped the last he took off like a bloody lamplighter, like a sudden burst,' he told me, 'and I just dropped my hands. I thought "well, I won't beat him". Then he fell down and I nearly rammed him up the arse.'

Dick Francis dismounted, hurled his whip away in frustration, and numerous witnesses claimed that he was weeping although he always denied it afterwards. It would have been utterly reasonable had he wept: no other horse has ever come so close to winning. Dazed, he wandered across the course looking for his whip, catching his breath, trying to make sense of it all, dreading the moment that he would have to trudge all the way back to the changing room through all those silent crowds.

Devon Loch's stable lad, John Hole, led the horse away.

A St John's ambulance drove by. 'Hop in, mate,' called the driver. Dick climbed aboard, protected from all those eyes, and was driven to the first-aid room. He was numb. Five minutes ago it had been the greatest moment of his life and now he had never felt so miserable. How had it happened? What had gone wrong? A maelstrom of possibilities whirled through his mind. 'Tears streamed down his face as he walked away,' reported Graham Stanford in the *News of the World* the next day, 'and once inside the changing room he threw his whip in the corner and buried his head in his hands.'

'Afterwards I was with him in the weighing room,' the *Sunday Express* racing columnist Tom Forrest told *Wales on Sunday* in 1990:

> There were tears in his eyes – which is not to say that he was sobbing – and the words would not come to explain this sensation. All he could do was mutter. The only person totally composed was the Queen Mother. She stood there sympathising but looking exactly as poised as she is on platforms up and down the country . . . although

it must have been one of the worst disappointments of her life.

The young Duke of Devonshire and the Queen's private secretary, Michael Adeane, were both in the royal box when Devon Loch collapsed and three days later they sat on each side of the diarist Sir Harold Nicolson at a lunch in London and told him the full story. Nicolson wrote in his diary the next day:

> There was a complete hush. The Princess Royal panted, 'It can't be true! It can't be true!' The Queen Mother never turned a hair. 'I must go down,' she said, 'and comfort those poor people.' So down she went, dried the jockey's tears, patted Peter Cazalet on the shoulder and insisted on seeing the stable-lads who were also in tears. 'I hope the Russians saw it', said Devonshire. 'It was the most perfect display of dignity that I have ever witnessed.'

The *Daily Telegraph* racing correspondent reported the next day:

> This was the saddest and most dramatic event I have ever seen on a racecourse. I shall long remember the picture of the Queen Mother as E.S.B. was being led triumphantly in, going quietly towards the racecourse stables with a smile on her face to see if her horse was all right. A few minutes later the Queen and Queen Mother were congratulating the owners of E.S.B. just as if nothing untoward had happened.

As Dick was getting dressed an equally stunned Peter Cazalet stuck his head around the door of the changing room. Oh God, poor Peter: twenty years earlier, in 1936, his horse Davy Jones, ridden by Anthony Mildmay, had been just about to win the National when a rein had broken, and now the unthinkable had happened to him a second time. Poor Peter. Twice. How terrible. How dreadfully unfair.

'Come up to the royal box,' said Cazalet sadly. 'They want to see you.'

Oh God – and now the Queen Mother. What was he going to say to her? How was he going to explain it? The royal box was heavy with silent disappointment, the faces gloomy, but they greeted him – the two queens, a princess, Prince Philip – with a terrible sympathy that brought him again to the verge of tears. They told him how dreadfully unlucky he had been, how well he had ridden, how wonderfully Devon Loch had jumped, how beautifully he had timed his race. There was a lump in his throat but he struggled to apologise, even though it was not at all his fault.

'How did it happen?' asked the Queen Mother.

'I don't know,' said Dick.

The Queen Mother shrugged. 'That's racing, I suppose,' she said unhappily.

So what had happened? Some said that Devon Loch must have had a minor heart attack or tried to jump a non-existent fence, perhaps the Water Jump that he would have glimpsed on his left as he ran to the winning post. Dave Dick told me in 1999 that he was still convinced that the horse had suffered some sort of seizure. 'When I come upside of him his horse's tongue was hanging out and it was black, which is a sign of flux in his lungs,' Mr Dick said. 'I've told a lot of people that, but nobody's ever taken any notice.'

Dick Francis discounted all these theories right from the start. Four days later, after going to London with Mary and his parents to watch several slow-motion Movietone newsreel replays of the race, he told Jack Wood of the *Daily Mail*: 'I'm convinced it was cramp in the hind legs. I'm certain of it now. You can forget any ideas that he was frightened, either by the vast crowds or a man running towards him.' But later both he and the Queen Mother came to believe that Devon Loch had indeed been suddenly frightened by the huge roar of cheers from the stand as the vast crowd of 250,000 people realised that the Queen Mother's horse was going to win. One reason for Dick's certainty was that just before Devon Loch collapsed he pricked his ears as though he had hit a sudden terrifying wall of noise.

Dick and Cazalet left the royal box and went to the stables, where a vet examined Devon Loch but could find nothing wrong. The horse was chewing some hay. Cazalet checked his legs but they were fine. Dick patted the horse and leaned his head against his neck. *Oh, Devon Loch,* he thought, *what happened?* Still numb and devastated, Dick, Mary and Vince drove back to Doug's house in silence. What was there to say? When they arrived he was met by a barrage of questions from his and Doug's children. 'Jolly silly sort of thing to do, wasn't it?' said one brutally. 'Was the Queen cross, Daddy?' asked Merrick. And three-year-old Felix kept running along, falling flat on his stomach, and crying: 'I'm Devon Loch. Down I go, bump.'

To escape the continual telephone calls Dick and Mary went for a walk in the moonlight along a country lane towards the River Dee. 'Do you feel like jumping in?' she asked.

'It looks a bit too wet and cold,' said Dick, and they laughed, but they lay awake throughout the night, asking themselves over and over why it had happened. Why? *Why?*

Other theories have included the possibility that Devon Loch was suffering from a lack of oxygen, a surfeit of glucose, a weak hind leg, a blood clot or had slipped on a patch of soft ground. One trainer came up with a possible explanation so bizarre it was worthy of some future Dick Francis thriller: he suggested that the horse had been electrocuted by an underground cable that had shorted on Devon Loch's racing plates. Many racing people suspected that perhaps there was some basic flaw in the horse's make-up. Bryan Marshall rode him several times and, although he agreed that he was 'a lovely jumper', he told James Lawton of the *Daily Express* in 1979 that each time he had ridden Devon Loch 'there had been one crisis during the race. One minute everything would be right, the next everything was wrong. There was no explanation. It was as though something drained out of him. Each time the crisis passed, he got his legs again, but maybe at Aintree in 1956 it was simply that he had done too much and there was nothing left.' Marshall said something similar to Dave Dick. 'Bryan told me twice that he rode Devon Loch once at Sandown and he rolled about a bit with him,' Mr Dick told me. 'If a horse starts rolling about with you, even when he's walking, you want to get off quick because it's usually a sign of the heart.' The Newmarket trainer Sir Noel Murless, who rode the horse for several years afterwards as a hack, told Lawton that Devon Loch was quite simply 'stupid and the clumsiest horse I ever sat on. Even in his slow paces he would stumble walking over a twig.' This remark irritated Dick Francis, who pointed out that Devon Loch was old by the time Murless rode him and that the horse had jumped beautifully until the catastrophe.

The most extraordinary explanation of all was published in 1991 in the *People*, which reported that Cazalet's travelling head lad, Bill Braddon, always believed that Devon Loch had been brought down that day by a huge fart. The paper alleged that before Braddon's death in 1989 he had told two friends, Peter Jacob and Eric Bridgen, that he blamed himself for the horse's collapse because he had tightened his girth just before the off. 'What I didn't know until later,' said Braddon, 'was that Peter Cazalet had already done exactly the same thing in the saddling enclosure . . . up a notch and another for luck. It meant that the girth was two notches tighter than it should have been.' As soon as Devon Loch fell, Braddon claimed, he ran over to the horse and 'as soon as I loosened the girth there was an almighty *whoooosh* from the rear end. I'd never heard anything like it. I realised immediately what had happened. The poor animal had run over four miles with the wind building up inside its tummy because the girth was too tight. The wind must have finally started to force its way out on the run-in and the first explosion just forced its back legs to go.' Apparently Braddon kept his guilty secret for so long because 'Cazalet would have gone mad if he knew what really happened.'

Dick refused to accept the Braddon theory and stood by his own. On the Wednesday after the race he and the Queen Mother went down to Fairlawne to see Devon Loch, Dick rode him again and there was nothing wrong with him at all. His collapse was, and still is, a complete mystery. And like some terrible black joke there was at least one spectator who believed that Dick had been bribed to 'stop' Devon Loch – Dick of all people, who was later to become famous as the author of books about shiningly honest jockeys. Peter Lord, who was then a BBC radio sports producer in Bristol, watched the race in a pub in Wales and heard one local say of the horse: 'I reckon he was pulled.'

Ironically the tragedy ensured that the finish of the 1956 Grand National is now the most famous of all and Dick Francis better remembered than a dozen other jockeys who actually won the race.

Hundreds of sympathetic letters arrived, and when Dick went to Windsor Castle to see the Queen Mother she gave him an inscribed silver cigarette box as well as a generous cheque. And when the owner of Aintree, Mrs Mirabel Topham, eventually sold the course in 1974 she gave Dick a piece of wood from the finishing post and he had it made into a paper weight.

At the time Dick suspected glumly that in years to come he would be remembered not for winning 345 races nor for being Champion Jockey but as the man who *didn't* win the Grand National. Yet more than forty years later there are millions of people all over the world for whom the name Dick Francis means 'bestselling novelist' and who have no idea that he was ever a jockey. That's Fate, as usual, having her little joke.

The rest of his racing career was inevitably an anti-climax.

Three days later he won a novice chase at Sandown, and a week after that, at Chepstow, he rode two winners – one of them Crudwell, to win the Welsh Grand National – and he finished the season with a win on Lochroe at Cheltenham to notch up a total of forty-one winners. But nothing could make up for Devon Loch. Dick was inconsolable and haunted by disappointment the rest of his life. Yet his failure made him famous, a household name to millions who knew little about racing, and eventually it was to make him even more famous and richer than he could ever have dreamed. Had Dick won the race he would have been forgotten by now outside the racing world, for who else remembers all those other jockeys who won the National during the early 1950s – Jimmy Power, Johnny Bullock, Arthur Thompson, Bryan Marshall, Pat Taaffe? But because Dick *lost*, because of the poignancy of that tragedy, he was asked to write his autobiography, and then the novels, and his name became famous all over the world.

'He wanted all his life to win the Grand National,' Mary told me in 1980, 'but the ironic thing is that if he *had* won it there would have been no autobiography and no novels . . .'

CHAPTER 10

Scribbling

(1956–62)

A few weeks after that dreadful Grand National Dick's mother invited an old lady called Mrs Johnson to tea. Mrs Johnson's son John, a London literary agent, delivered her by car and noticed a framed photograph of Dick and Devon Loch jumping the last fence at Aintree. Molly told him that the jockey was her son. Johnson was intrigued. Would Dick like to write a book about the race? There was bound to be a market for such a poignant story, and Johnson could easily recommend a ghost writer.

Dick and Mary were interested and Johnson sent a ghost writer to Blewbury to discuss the project, but Mary was adamant that they had no need of a ghost writer. True, Dick had no idea how to write and his spelling was atrocious, but why should they share the royalties with someone else? Had she not been writing stories and essays for years and assessing books as a publisher's reader? Did she not have a degree in French and English? They decided to write the autobiography together.

'I'd never thought of writing a book,' he told me a few years later. 'I'd certainly never had any literary stirrings at school.' But Mary chivvied him through his memories, ironed out the wrinkles and polished the rough edges. 'I at least had a semi-literary education and he hadn't,' she told me. 'After all, he left school at fifteen, so I edited the book and put full-stops where there were commas. Right at the beginning one or two people knew I was helping him to write his autobiography.'

While they worked on the book he resumed his career as a jockey when the new season started in August, but something deep within him had collapsed along with Devon Loch and his riding career was almost over. Although he and Devon Loch won a two-and-a-half-mile hurdle at Nottingham at the end of October and then beat Early Mist at Sandown, they were themselves beaten at the end of November by Key Royal at Kempton and again at Kempton a month later by the horse that Dick had ridden unsuccessfully in America, Rose Park. Suddenly, at thirty-six, Dick's star was waning rapidly. He won three more races in December and on 7 January he won again at Leicester on his old favourite, Crudwell, to take his total for the season to twenty-two, but that was the final win of his career. It seemed especially appropriate that Dick should have had his last win on Crudwell: it was the fifteenth time they had won together and in all their twenty-two races they had been unplaced only three times. When Crudwell retired at the end of 1960 he had won forty-three National Hunt races, more than any other horse.

The end came with shocking suddenness. On Friday 11 January at Newbury Dick rode a horse called Prince Stephen, fell and was trampled by some of the other horses. He managed to walk to a Land Rover and even told the doctor that he would be all right to ride again the next day, but his injuries were much worse than he realised. He had been badly kicked in the stomach and as he drove home he felt terrible and started shaking. By the time he lay down on his bed he was racked by frightening spasms that were so bad that he could not even get undressed and continued all night. He had broken his wrist and was told he would have to be out of racing for at least a month. Eight days later Devon Loch's own career came to a sudden end when he was being ridden by Arthur Freeman at Sandown and was ahead of the rest of the field when his tendon suddenly gave way and he hobbled off the course. He never raced again.

Had Devon Loch not broken down as he did, Dick would have carried on riding if only to partner the horse yet again in that year's Grand National to have a final crack at it. But with Devon Loch put out to grass Dick also seemed past it. All the injuries were beginning to catch up with him and each time he fell he suffered worse than before and took longer to heal. Cazalet's owners were becoming wary of letting him ride their less reliable horses because they did not want him to injure himself again. One of the Queen Mother's friends, the forty-two-year-old Marquess of Abergavenny, a racing administrator who had himself been an amateur jockey, asked Dick to come to his flat in London one evening and told him it was time for him to make a graceful exit. 'Retire at the top,' he said. Most jockeys stayed on far too long and it was sad to see them having fewer and fewer rides and fading away until they became an embarrassment. It would be much more dignified, said Abergavenny, to go before being pushed.

Dick was stunned. He was being sacked by the Queen Mother. Obviously Abergavenny would not have said anything unless she had asked him to. Dick was distraught. Just two years after being Champion Jockey he was being fired. What else was he going to do? He was often asked to judge hunter classes at various shows but that was hardly a full-time job. He had no wish at all to become a trainer and take on all the exhausting stress, hard work, long hours, responsibility and financial worries that went with a trainer's life, not to mention all that daunting paperwork, bureaucracy and frustration. As he explained a few years later in a heartfelt column in the *Sunday Express*, 'many jockeys who are temperamentally well suited to the freedom and pace of their riding life do not take easily to being tied to one place or to a patient application to details' – skills that are as vital for a novelist as for a trainer. Dick was no more suited to the indoor disciplines necessary for being a trainer than he was for those required of an author.

When he left Abergavenny's flat that night he walked in a daze alone through the darkness of Hyde Park. 'I nearly flung myself into the Serpentine, I was so depressed,' he told Angela Lambert of the *Daily Mail* forty years later. He talked the problem over and over with Mary and took her along with him to see Lord Abergavenny again, but His Lordship was adamant: to all intents and purposes Dick was finished as a jockey; he really ought to bow out gracefully. But what should he do? How would he make a living? Don't worry, said Abergavenny: something will turn up.

Dick used an appearance on the TV programme *Sportsview* on 30 January to announce his retirement after nine years and eight months as a jockey – after 2,305 races and 345 winners – and was highly praised by the Press the next day. The *Daily Telegraph* commentator 'Hotspur' said that he had been 'one of the best steeplechase riders since the war – and one of the most courageous' and *The Times* racing correspondent wrote:

Francis will be much missed both as a rider and because of his personality. The part of his riding in races which was so admired was his quiet progress through the country. His long rein and lack of fuss gave his mounts confidence and they went well for him. His style . . . allowed horses to give their attention to the fences and to forget that they had someone in the saddle. Francis was, in fact, a rider of top quality and if he had a weakness it was that perhaps he did not finish in the run home in the most forceful flat racing style. His integrity and smiling frankness made him popular, and with his capable mind an early retirement from the saddle may not be a disadvantage for there is sure to be a demand for his services in other racing roles.

Dick told the *Telegraph* that he felt very sad at giving up racing – 'it was my life' – and that he had no idea what he was going to do next. 'I'm not sure,' he said. 'I have no hobbies and hate gardening. I hope to continue dealing with horses but nothing is definite yet.' He was offered three part-time jobs almost immediately: as an official race judge, as a race commentator, and as a racing journalist. He accepted all three but soon dropped out of commentating because he found it difficult to remember all the horses' names and colours and equally tricky to think of something to say about them. But the third job, to lend his name to a series of ghost-written articles for the *Sunday Express*, was to lead to his writing a weekly column for the next sixteen years.

In 1957 the *Sunday Express* was a resoundingly successful Fleet Street national broadsheet: a solid, middlebrow 'family paper' that sold three-and-a-half million copies each week and was to sell four-and-a-half million four years later. It had been edited for the past two-and-a-half years by a forceful, irascible, thirty-eight-year-old Scotsman, John Junor, who was to continue as editor for twenty-nine more years and to become a cur-mudgeonly, opinionated Fleet Street legend renowned for his bigoted, puritannical, right-wing views. Junor would announce stridently that you could never trust a man who wore a beard and that 'only poofs drink white wine', and when I joined the paper myself as a reporter in 1965 he exhorted me to 'avoid clichés like the plague'. Yet he had an uncanny knack of knowing precisely what his middlebrow public wanted to read and that included columns by famous sports stars. In 1956 the footballer Stanley Matthews was writing a regular soccer column for the paper, in 1957 the cricketer Jack Hobbs wrote one briefly, and the cricketer Denis Compton and footballer Danny Blanchflower also wrote weekly columns for the *Sunday Express* for many years. Junor knew nothing at all about racing but he knew that the name of Dick Francis would help circulation. It was indicative of Junor's egocentric character that he had little contact with Dick or any of the other big sporting names he hired and when he came to publish his autobiography, *Listening for a Midnight Tram*, in 1990 he made no mention of any of them. In Junor's beady eyes these sporting icons were mere circulation fodder.

At first Dick was extremely nervous about taking on the job. He couldn't write or spell, so how could he be a journalist? 'Dick said he couldn't do it,' Mary told me years later, 'but I told him I would help him write the columns and he got more and more confident. He learned to write by practice. He learned really by writing for the *Sunday Express*.'

On 24 February, less than a month after he retired as a jockey, the *Sunday Express* announced excitedly 'DICK FRANCIS joins our team' and promised: 'Starting next Sunday, he will give a weekly intimate, authoritative survey of the racing scene. He knows the trainers, the owners, the riders, and, from his unrivalled experience in the saddle, the HORSES – and the COURSES which suit them best.' His first article, about a thousand words long, appeared on 3 March across four columns beside a large photograph of him and under the headline: 'WHY I GAVE UP THE RIDING JOB I LOVED . . .'. It began poignantly:

> For the first time in 10 years I shall be watching at next week's Cheltenham National Hunt Festival instead of riding. Watching, I confess, with envy, for my heart (with a fine disregard for anatomical accuracy) is still in the saddle. I have found it hard to give up the job I love in order not to become bad at it as the years pass, but steeplechasing is a young man's sport, and I was already at 36 one of the oldest National Hunt jockeys riding. Perhaps it is better to put one's light out with a flick, than to struggle on while the current weakens and the filament grows dim.

Describing the joys of the Cheltenham Festival, he wrote that it

> is a three-day feast for enthusiasts. Impoverished squires
> save up for it, the Irish invade it, and amateur jockeys
> invent dead grandmothers to get the days off for it.

The article went on to assess the chances of various horses at
Cheltenham, Ludlow and Haydock during the coming week.

It was a highly professional start and one with Mary's stylish
fingerprints all over it. Les Vanter, who was then the deputy
sports editor of the *Sunday Express*, told me: 'When Dick came
into the office each week with his article there'd be marks on the
typewritten copy in his wife's handwriting.'

The second article, on 10 March, was again about Cheltenham
but only seven hundred words long, and this time assessed the
course as well as the horses, but the following week Junor gave
Dick a whole page to run a long, two-thousand-word 'inside
story' account of the Devon Loch Grand National fiasco. It was
in fact an extract from Dick's autobiography, which was nearly
finished and was at that stage called simply *The Dick Francis
Story*. At first John Johnson wanted to send the typescript to
the publishing firm of William Collins but Dick and Mary asked
him to try Michael Joseph first since they had met him and Dick
had ridden several of his horses. Johnson thought that a jockey's
memoirs weren't Michael Joseph's 'sort of thing' – but Joseph
accepted the book immediately and planned to publish it just
before Christmas.

The next week Dick's column – this time about the imminent
Grand National and the sort of horses that tend to win the
race – was back to about seven hundred words again, and
so it remained almost every week for the next sixteen years
except for the really big occasions like the Derby and the Grand
National, when Junor would allow him much more space. On
8 March Dick was granted licences to act as a starter and judge

during the rest of the National Hunt season, but for months he still ached for the loss of the life he had loved. In his *Sunday Express* column the day after the National he wrote: 'It would have been foolish of me to pretend, as I watched the horses parade before the National, that I did not envy those lucky 35 jockeys, or that I did not feel a pang as I looked towards the place where Devon Loch fell last year.' Mary suffered too. 'I wept for six months because he was so unhappy,' she told me in 1980. 'His body was getting too old before his mind.' The full extent of his anguish can be judged by the last three mournful sentences of the second edition of his autobiography, published in 1974, in which he wrote wistfully that, despite the huge success of the Dick Francis books, the best years of his life had been as a jockey.

Luckily his work for the *Sunday Express* kept him closely in touch with the racing world. Three mornings a week, in search of copy for his articles, Dick would rise earlier than usual and drive up to the Downs above Blewbury to ride, train and school racehorses for several local trainers – Frank Cundell, Helen Johnson Houghton, Fred Maxwell and Michael Pope – which meant that he was still able to ride great horses every week. Two or three times a week he would go to races all over the country and keep up with the latest gossip. In May he was interviewing the ex-jockey-turned-trainer Sir Gordon Richards and riding out with him on the Downs. He went to see Devon Loch, who was still recuperating from his fall. He went up to Newmarket to look round Cecil Boyd-Rochfort's stables and assess his horses. And there were some small compensations attached to his retirement. 'He always called me "major" or "sir" when he was riding,' Tim Fitzgeorge-Parker told me, 'but when he finally retired he said "if you don't mind, sir, may I call you Tim again?"'

In June Dick tipped Tempest to win the Derby but added nervously: 'do not put more than the buttons of your shirt on it, for jockeys are notoriously bad at picking winners!' It was wise advice: the Derby was in fact won by Crepello, which the *Sunday Express*'s senior racing writer, Tom Forrest, had made his nap selection, though Tempest did come in fourth. Forrest actually tipped correctly three of the first four horses in the Derby, which made Dick realise humbly that as a tipster he was not in Forrest's league.

Later that summer Dick went to Kingsclere to look round Peter Hastings-Bass's yard, to Newmarket to see Fred Armstrong's stables, to Goodwood to profile the leading Flat jockey Scobie Breasley, to Ogbourne to assess Gordon Richards's runners again, and to Fairlawne to ride out nostalgically with Peter Cazalet's string. In the autumn he rode out on the South Downs with Fred Winter, now Champion Jockey for the third time, and with Fred Rimell's string at Kinnersley, near Worcester, and on a magical early morning at the end of September he cantered out on Devon Loch again and was delighted to find how well his old friend and partner had recovered. And early in October he made a sentimental journey back to Cholmondeley Castle to ride out through the well-loved parkland with George Owen's string and his latest *protégé* stable jockey, twenty-year-old Stan Mellor.

At first Dick did not believe that he would be writing for the *Sunday Express* for very long. For several months he saw it merely as a stop-gap: he was a horseman, not a writer. The sports editor, Bill Smith, kept urging him to accept a permanent contract but he kept refusing until eventually he realised that there was nothing much else on offer, that at least the journalism paid the bills and that it gave him special access at racecourses if he was a member of the racing Press.

In November, after a trip to Ireland to look at Vincent O'Brien's and Tom Dreaper's horses, Dick signed at last a proper contract with the *Sunday Express*. Considering that he was famous and an ex-champion royal jockey, he was badly paid: just £20 a week, the equivalent of only £14,300 a year in 1999, less than any junior Fleet Street reporter would earn today, and for that he even had to sign away the copyright in all his articles. The parsimonious Junor, true to his Scottish ancestry, was notoriously thrifty when it came to his staff's salaries, and the fact that Dick was prepared to sign such an exploitative contract underlines how difficult it might be for him to earn a decent living now that his racing days were over. 'He came in to the office once a week, usually on a Friday,' I was told by Tom Forrest. 'He would wait until his stuff was read and then push off. As a journalist he was useful to have around because of his name. His columns probably increased circulation at the very beginning but what he did was to keep a readership. People who didn't care about Flat racing very much but were really keen jumping people would buy the *Sunday Express* for Dick's column.'

Stan Mellor agreed. 'It was the first thing everybody read,' he told me, 'and everybody talked about it all week. He always had right from the start with his writing that thing where he could grab people. Sometimes you'd say "oh, see what the silly bugger's saying this week!" but he grabbed you.'

Dick had rarely put a bet on a horse because he claimed he was no good at gambling, but as a racing tipster he was 'as good as most,' said Forrest. 'Personally Dick was not naturally a whizz-bang of a character,' admitted Forrest, 'but he was a nice man and I liked him thoroughly. He was very quiet, modest, and he's still exactly the same. He could liven up with a drink inside him, if you went out for a meal with him, but he was a naturally quiet bloke.'

Gus Hines, a *Sunday Express* sports sub-editor from 1961, told me: 'The thing I remember about him particularly was his modesty. I don't want this to sound boring because he's not a boring man at all, but he *was* a modest chap. Dick was a *nice* feller to work with.' It was Hines's job to edit Dick's articles. 'When he brought his copy in every Friday morning it was mostly publishable,' said Hines. 'We might make the odd query but he was always very amenable, he never quibbled at all.'

Leslie Vanter, who became sports editor in 1966, told me that Dick was 'very nice in a humble, naive way but he was never a man of authority, not a good conversationalist, and he wasn't very bright.' Vanter claimed that Dick was incapable of writing his column all by himself:

> Mary had an attack of some sort once and had to lie flat on a board for two or three weeks and couldn't move, and when Dick came into the office as usual that week, lo and behold – no copy. He and Gus sat down at a typewriter and Gus fired questions at him, and between them they produced his column – and they did so together for the next two weeks as well.

Hines has no memory of this:

> No, I don't remember that incident. It may well have happened but it was so long ago. I know Les has said this, but the only copy I ever saw came out of Dick's pocket and was put in front of me. If Mary did anything in the background, I don't know. I know he and Mary were devoted to each other. Dick is a very nice guy but I don't think he'd have the drive necessary without Mary behind him.

Alan Hoby, the paper's chief sports writer, said:

> People suspected his wife did a lot of the writing. She used to come on the telephone very knowledgeably and the secretary or Leslie would speak to her about the column. But I liked Dick very much. He was very quiet, the typical understated Englishman: unostentatious, courteous, quietly spoken.

Gus Hines remembered that Dick had no special friends at the *Sunday Express*:

> He used to just come into the office, talk to us and leave his copy. Sometimes we'd go over to the Devereux pub up Fleet Street and have a drink and a sandwich, but he never came to the parties. Apart from the odd drink, he was not one of us. He's the sort of bloke you didn't find anecdotes about. He was very much an outsider. He'd ring in later to see if John Junor had passed his article.

Working for Junor was indeed like sitting an examination in kindergarten. 'When you talk about nice guys they always sound boring,' said Hines, 'but I never found Dick boring at all.'

It was certainly Mary's literary skill that ensured that Dick's autobiography needed little alteration by the publishers, though it included an embarrassingly fulsome note thanking the Queen Mother 'for the great honour of her patronage, and for her gracious consent to the title of this book' without explaining why it should be necessary to obtain her consent for a book entitled *The Sport of Queens*. In a chapter which was added for the second edition of the book in 1974 Dick reported that writing was such hard work that he would never have written a second book if the first had been rejected.

At the end of November he was persuaded by the *Sunday Express* to stick his neck out and tip a dozen National Hunt horses – 'Twelve for the Jumps' – that he expected to win races in the next few months after seeing them on the gallops or riding them himself. Three of his tips were to do remarkably well: Noble Legend, trained by Frank Cundell, went on to win five of its nine races that year and to come second twice; Feluma, trained by Ryan Price, won four of its nine races and was second once; and Cazalet's Double Star won three of its seven races and was placed in three others. Dick's twelve choices eventually had eighty-nine races in all that season and won twenty-eight of them – a 31 per cent success rate – and were placed first, second or third in 72 per cent of their races. Not bad for a novice tipster.

The Sport of Queens – priced twenty-one shillings and dedicated to Merrick and Felix – was published on 2 December 1957. It was in some ways an odd book which glossed over several aspects of Dick's life, most notably two of the three schools he attended in Maidenhead and his RAF training in Rhodesia, and it says surprisingly little about Mary, who appears only briefly as a walk-on extra. Nor was there anything about his parents' later years, possibly because Vince was by now suffering the agonies of prostate cancer and he and Molly had fallen on hard times and had left their boarding house in Sussex Gardens and were living in the little flat at 48 Norfolk Square, in a seedy part of London just 100 yards from the noise and bustle of Paddington railway station. They did not even own the flat themselves: in the official records the occupier's name was given as being Mary. Typically Vince registered Molly on the voters' roll by again misspelling her name 'Catherine' as 'Katerine'. Sadly all three of Dick and Mary's surviving parents had come down in the world.

The *Daily Telegraph*'s 'Hotspur' reviewed *The Sport of Queens* on publication day and said it was 'delightfully written', 'enthralling' and 'probably the best racing autobiography since that of George Lambton.' The reviewer added that Dick had been 'one of the outstanding National Hunt jockeys of the last half-century' and 'a beautiful horseman.' The first edition sold out in a week and had to be reprinted, an American edition was published in New York by Penzler Books, and suddenly the Francises realised that there might actually be some money in writing books. *The Sport of Queens* sold five thousand hardback copies in Britain over the next two years – 'quite good in those days,' I was told by Leslie Cramphorn, a Michael Joseph rep who later became Sales Director – and eventually sold about fifty thousand copies. Admirers in the racing world raised £1,000 for Dick as a retirement present after a whip-round organised by Peter Cazalet and with the royalties from the book Dick was able to buy a new car (a Jaguar) and ponies called Joan of Arc and Smoky for Merrick and Felix.

Dick was disappointed that at first Merrick preferred ball games to horses, but consoled himself with the knowledge that both he and Felix were well behaved, polite and tidy. Their nanny, Elsie Knott, however, was less impressed and gave in her notice, saying she could no longer cope with them. 'Dad pretended to be furious and said "Go to your room",' Merrick told Jenny Knight of the *Sunday Times Magazine* thirty years later. 'After a while the forbidding figure of Dad appeared carrying his riding whip. We had never seen him looking quite so angry or incongruous so we both burst out laughing, at which point he burst out laughing and had to walk out of the room.'

By the beginning of 1958 Dick had settled into a new routine that was to change little over the next few years. He would ride out on the Downs most mornings with one of the local trainers, sometimes help them school their green young horses, and three or four days a week he would drive to a racecourse to watch the horses and pick up gossip and ideas for his column. Now and then he would visit some trainer's stables to do an interview and assess the horses there, on Thursdays he and Mary would put together an article and on Fridays he would take it up to London to the *Sunday Express* office in Fleet Street. Occasionally, instead of simply assessing and tipping horses, he would write an opinionated 'think piece' in which he castigated the racing establishment or suggested improvements in racing rules and conditions. In January 1958, for instance, he published an article describing the long, hard working conditions of stable lads, who were paid just £7-10s a week (the equivalent of £100 in 1999). The Francises started to have much more of a social life, often meeting friends like Fulke and Kath Walwyn for drinks or supper or having acquaintances like Stan Mellor to stay, and in June and

July each year, when National Hunt racing was suspended, Dick would take a holiday of four or five weeks and he, Mary and the boys would spend a couple of weeks at their favourite seaside hotel in south Devon, the Redcliffe in Paignton, which Dick had found to be handy for Newton Abbot races during his years as a jockey. Amazingly they were to return to the Redcliffe year after year for more than forty years, even after the huge success of the novels had made them millionaires.

The Redcliffe Hotel is a most unlikely haunt for a bestselling author: a vast, gaunt, grey, cement monstrosity overlooking a nasty beach of red mud. When I arrived there at 3 p.m. on a summer Saturday afternoon in 1998 the bar was closed and, even though I was staying as a resident, I was told that it was impossible to order even a beer or a sandwich until the restaurant opened at 6.30. I walked along the seafront, buffeted by a fierce wind, to marvel at the lines of flags cracking in the gale – flags boasting that this was 'The English Riviera' and depicting huge, proud palm trees, blue sky, turquoise sea and golden sand as though this were the Caribbean. The only living palm trees in sight were some miserable, forlorn little plants cowering against the gale and no more than two feet tall. The sea and sky were both grey. The wind was moaning. A woman and two small children in anoraks were huddled bravely on the red mud. Some Riviera. And this was 30 May.

It is true that there are some lovely spots in the surrounding area: the beautiful River Dart near Hexworthy; the ancient clapper bridge at Postbridge; the villages of Cockington and Widecombe in the Moor; Dartmoor; eleventh-century Buckfast Abbey. And as the family expanded Dick and Mary liked taking the children and later the grandchildren on a steam train trip to Kingswear, a fishing trip, a ferry ride to Brixham, to Paignton zoo or the model village at Babbacombe. But what makes Paignton such an odd choice for the Francises to return to every year is that it is such a downmarket holiday resort, mock genteel yet irretrievably inelegant, the sort of resort that attracts fat men wearing small vests and large tattoos. The Inn on the Green ('Torbay's Loveliest Inn') had a condom vending machine in the gents' lavatory adorned with pictures of grinning rubber contraceptives. And the pier was mainly a raucous, vulgar 'amusement arcade' offering one-armed bandits, gambling machines, video games and 'Super Bingo' played with the aid of electronic buttons.

Understandably the cosy, unsophisticated Redcliffe Hotel makes the most of its most famous customer and the large lounge on the first floor is called the Dick Francis Suite and decorated with photographs of Dick riding in races. 'The Francises are a lovely family, such a *solid* family,' one of the waiters told me. So are most of their other customers. At dinner that Saturday night an elderly lady pianist was playing requests – 'Land of Hope and Glory', 'Rule Britannia', 'There'll Always Be An England' – and when she started to tinkle the tune of 'The Teddy Bear's Picnic' dozens of diners sang along: 'If you go down to the woods today you're sure of a big surprise . . .' It was all pretty naff.

Back home in Blewbury Dick often rode his old chum Crudwell on the gallops and in September he went down to Kent for another sentimental ride with Peter Cazalet's string at Fairlawne. At the end of November he repeated what was to become an annual practice by picking 'Twelve to Follow Over the Jumps', but this time he was much less successful: his twelve tips won only a quarter of their races and were placed in little more than a third. Four of his chosen horses had thirty-eight races between them but won just twice.

In December he crossed the Irish Sea again to visit Dan Moore's stables in County Meath and to ride the champion American steeplechaser Neji, and among his more forceful articles that year was one in which he claimed that most National Hunt trainers could barely make ends meet and urged the authorities to boost prize money by accepting sponsorship from companies.

The Francises took their holiday as usual at the Redcliffe Hotel but at the end of July it became obvious that Dick's father, now tragically thin and wasted by prostate cancer, was dying and Dick raced up to London to be with him. He was at Vince's bedside in the London flat in Norfolk Square when he died on the 26th, aged seventy. Vince left everything to Molly but his estate was worth only £3,483-2s-0d, about £46,000 in today's values, which would not have given her a comfortable old age. She lived on alone in the flat for seven more unhappy years. 'His death broke my mother's heart,' Dick told Lynda Lee-Potter of the *Daily Mail* in 1998. 'She lived a few more years but she didn't recover. She was never at peace again.'

As for Mary's mother, Netta left London in 1959 and moved out to Oxfordshire to be nearer to Mary and Dick. She was now sixty-four and a grandmother five times over: Jean, who was living with her husband in Glasgow, now had two children; and Ewen had just become a father for the first time with the birth of his son Mark. Netta moved to Abingdon, ten miles from Blewbury. Dick's brother Doug, now the father of a son and daughter, was also on the move in 1959: he left Bangor-on-Dee and bought Carden Park in Cheshire, where he continued to train racehorses, most of them jumpers.

Dick's journalism had by now settled into a predictable groove: another report after riding out with Cazalet's string; another ride on Crudwell; an article demanding that National Hunt jockeys be given their first pay rise since 1947. As for his 'twelve to follow' that year, they were embarrassingly unsuccessful. Only one in five went on to win their races and three of Dick's tips had thirty races between them and won just one. It was not a good day at the office.

Dick entered the Swinging Sixties by writing a warm tribute to his old mentor George Owen, now fifty-two, in which he prophesied that Owen's latest stable jockey, twenty-two-year-old Stan Mellor, would one day become Champion Jockey – and five months later Mellor did just that. At the end of January Dick urged the National Hunt authorities to consult jockeys more often and advocated the formation of a Jockeys' Association. A month later he went to Ireland again to nose around a couple of stables there and tipped Kerstin, Team Spirit and Merryman II for the Grand National. The race was in fact eventually won by Merryman II. In September he was riding out yet again with Cazalet's string in Kent and Neville Crump's in Yorkshire, where he rode Merryman II himself, and he predicted that five young jump jockeys could go on to become stars: David Mould, Chris Stobbs, Ramon Atkinson, Dick Broadway and George Ramshaw. He was right about Mould but the others were to prove less successful.

In the first week of October Dick and Michael Scudamore took it in turns to ride Crudwell – who had now won more races than any horse in 100 years – in the ring during each performance of the five-day Horse of the Year Show at Wembley, and at the end of the month his annual *Sunday Express* list of 'twelve to follow' was more successful than the previous one: a quarter of his choices won their races and more than half were placed first, second or third, and Dick's reputation for picking winners was reinforced when he tipped a 100/7 outsider, Knucklecracker, to win the Hennessy Gold Cup at Newbury at the end of November and the horse romped in by fifteen lengths. And in December he stuck his neck out again and tipped a nineteen-year-old baronet, Sir William Pigott-Brown, to become top amateur jockey one day, which the lad duly did.

But most notable of all Dick's articles that year was one that appeared in the *Sunday Express* on Christmas Day 1960, for it gave a foretaste of the sort of skulduggery that was soon to inspire the plots of all the Dick Francis novels. In a long, top-of-the-page article Dick reported that Knucklecracker's trainer Derek Ancil was so worried about the possibility that crooks might try to nobble the horse before it ran in the King George VI Chase the next day that he had fitted a big new padlock to the door of the horse's box and was going to sleep beside it with three dogs in case any villains should try to break in. Was it this, maybe, that ignited the first spark for the first Dick Francis novel, *Dead Cert*? It was certainly about now that Dick and Mary started to write that first thriller together. Mary still loved going to the theatre and they still had their permanent Tuesday booking for seats at the Oxford Playhouse, where they went one night in 1960 to see a thriller and decided on the way home that they could do just as well themselves with a novel. In later years Dick always said that *Dead Cert* was written simply because he was not earning enough from journalism and needed to make a little money to replace a threadbare carpet and to fix a rattle in his car. 'Mary collaborated on the thrillers from the start,' he told William Foster of *In Britain* magazine in 1978. 'We both work out the plot and then I put pen to paper. She's a tremendous help when I'm looking for words. She has a university degree in English and French and takes more getting past than a sub-editor.' For advice about writing fiction they also consulted their Blewbury neighbour Geoffrey Boumphrey, a sixty-six-year-old writer who had written several books and had edited *The Shell Guide to Britain* as well as the *Oxford Junior Encyclopaedia*.

In May there was yet another news story that may well have helped to shape the first novel: three weeks before the Derby someone broke into Noel Murless's stable at Newmarket and nobbled one of the favourites, Pinturischio, by giving him a huge dose of a diarrhoeic drug. Murless improved security at his yard but the nobblers promptly did it again: the horse had to be withdrawn from the race and never raced again. A few years later it was discovered that the crime had been an inside job and that the villains had been helped by one of Murless's own stable lads. The Dick Francis novels may have been fiction but at first they were inspired by fact.

They were not by any means the first to be set in the racing world, nor even the first to be hugely successful. Numerous authors had written stories about racing: Leslie Charteris, Conan Doyle, Rudyard Kipling, Ellery Queen, Damon Runyon, Somerville and Ross, Edgar Wallace, John Welcome and many others. Sir John Squire had even written one entitled *The Dead Cert*. But most successful of all the predecessors was the Manchester-born journalist Nat Gould. In 1891 Gould, then thirty-three, had published his first horse racing novel, *The Double Event*, which became an immediate bestseller. With amazing productivity the genial, balding, bewhiskered Gould wrote another 131 horsey novels over the next twenty-eight years that sold an estimated twenty-five million copies and allowed him to be described by his publisher as 'the most popular living novelist' and 'The World's Favourite Author'. Five Gould books written between 1910 and 1919 were filmed.

After working for six years as a journalist in Newark and eleven years as a sports journalist in Australia, Gould returned to England to write scores of racing novels until his death in 1919, some with titles similar to those of the Dick Francis books. One, published in 1900, was called *A Dead Certainty*. Others were *Banker and Broker* (1893) and *Odds On* (1920), foreshadowing the later Dick Francis titles *Banker* and *Odds Against*. The ambience of the Gould books is decidedly similar to that of the Francis ones, crammed as they are with dodgy jockeys, corrupt stable lads, 'pulled' racehorses, dopers, rich owners, greedy gamblers, viciously violent crooks and all manner of racing skulduggery. *A Dead Certainty* tells a very Franciscan story about a jockey, a bent bookmaker and a couple of women who are tied up by villains. In *Banker and Broker*, which has a strong streak of romance and love interest, like so many of the Francis books, one jockey is killed by another during a race. So, too, in *The Head Lad*, in which a crooked jockey deliberately bumps the favourite's jockey at Tattenham Corner during the Derby and the victim is killed in the fall. In *The Dark Horse*, another tale of murder and violence, a racehorse called Black Diamond is kidnapped (like the stallions in the 1967 Francis novel *Blood Sport*). In *The Exploits of a Race-Course Detective* Gould's investigator Val Martyn solves the case of the kidnapped jockey who is held prisoner on a boat (like the hero of the Francis novel *Risk*); the bookie found dead in a clump of bushes on Newmarket Heath (like the villains in the Francis novel *Bonecrack*); the racing stable where the certs mysteriously start losing their races (as in the Francis novel *Whip Hand*). In one of the stories the villains try one night to dope the favourite for the Lincoln but nobble the wrong horse because the favourite has been moved to a different box; in the Francis novel *Bolt* the villain tries one night to kill a favourite but kills the wrong horse because the favourite has been moved to a different box. And Gould's 1901 novel *Warned Off* has a theme remarkably similar to that of the 1969 Dick Francis novel *Enquiry*: in both books a kind, utterly honest jockey is unfairly warned off by the stewards after another jockey has given biased evidence against him and vows to restore his good name.

Gould, however, churned out nearly five novels a year – some full-length, 300-page hardbacks, others little ninety-six-page 'yellowback' paperbacks with garishly coloured horsey jackets that sold for sixpence or a shilling each – and the standard of their writing was not nearly as high as that of the Dick Francis books. Their style was naive, crude and unpolished by comparison. Too often they rattled along with page after page of inconsequential dialogue, telling simple, shallow stories with thin plots, bad punctuation and little narrative power, description, subtlety or tension. Yet I must confess to a shiver down the spine when I read the 1918 Nat Gould novel *The Steeple-chaser* and found that it anticipated uncannily Dick Francis's Grand National fall on Devon Loch nearly forty years before it happened. The hero, Phil Riseley, is about to ride his hunter Topper in the Grand National and is warned by a gnarled old veteran jockey to be especially careful at the end of the race:

'Never relax till you're past the post. I've seen a horse win when he hadn't a dog's show, for the reason the leader came on to his knees at the last fence.' Sure enough, Topper nearly loses the race despite jumping the final fence ahead of all the other horses. 'Phil was jubilant. There was a clear run to the winning post, and the old horse was going so well defeat seemed impossible. He indulged in pleasant thoughts of winning . . . Then a strange thing happened.' Topper, like Devon Loch, seems to try to jump a non-existent obstacle a few yards before reaching the finishing post. 'Topper was sailing ahead towards the post when all of a sudden he jumped a foot track across the course. Phil was so surprised he almost lost his balance; it was so utterly unexpected. There was a shout from the crowd as Topper gave this remarkable performance; it might cost him the race.'

Topper recovers, of course, and wins the National, but it is spooky to think that Nat Gould foretold a Grand National collapse like that of Devon Loch two years before Dick was born.

Most first novels are at least partly autobiographical and the first Dick Francis, *Dead Cert*, was no exception. Its hero is Alan York, a twenty-four-year-old millionaire amateur National Hunt jockey who has come to England from Southern Rhodesia – from Induna, near Bulawayo, where Dick had started his RAF pilot training in 1943. York's jockey friend Bill Davidson seems a cert to win a particular race – at Maidenhead racecourse – but is killed during the race, thus becoming the dead cert of the title. York suspects that Davidson has been murdered, vows to track down the killers, is assaulted in Maidenhead Thicket near Dick's old school and is beaten up, knifed, deliberately brought down in a race, kicked in the head by a horse, booted in the ribs and face by a villain, knocked unconscious, hunted by a ruthless pack of murderous Brighton taxi drivers and breaks his collar-bone. York is not yet the archetypal wounded Dick Francis hero, but his girlfriend's aunt – like some of Mary's relatives – haughtily considers that she should not be consorting with a jockey, and one of the horses in the book, Admiral, is obviously based on Finnure or Crudwell.

Dead Cert is remarkably accomplished for a first novel, even though it is inevitably a little amateurish in parts and several characters behave in ways that are simply not credible: a couple of girl telephonists, a police sergeant, the chief villain, a crooked jockey, York himself. They also speak decidedly more like Mary than Dick, using words like 'presently' and 'elucidate' and sentences like this: 'Racecourses were not designed for the convenience of newly affianced lovers.' The sex scenes are gauche and naive and the sudden ending is disconcertingly abrupt. But otherwise the book is slick, crisp and authentic in its insider's view of the racing world. It starts with a gripping description of a steeplechase race on a winter afternoon that is pungent with the whiff of sweating horses and cold fog, and it ends with a tense, exciting description of what it is like to ride in a race when a rival jockey is trying to knock you off your horse.

Michael Joseph's widow, Anthea, who was now running the company, snapped *Dead Cert* up within ten days of its arrival in her office and planned to publish it in January 1962 – a good month to launch a new novelist because few new books were published in the January lull after Christmas and so a first novelist had a better chance of being reviewed. It also made commercial sense to publish *Dead Cert* as the work of Dick alone because of his fame as the royal jockey who failed to win the Grand National. 'Originally the first book was going to be published under the name of Dick and Mary Francis,' I was told by Raleigh Trevelyan, who was Editorial Director at Michael Joseph at the time, 'but it was felt to be much more saleable to just say Dick Francis. After all, he had been a jockey and she was quite happy that it should be like that.' Amazingly, even that first typescript needed no rewriting or editing. 'It just went straight into print,' said Trevelyan.

Peter Day, a young editor at Michael Joseph in the 1960s, was impressed by Mary's willingness to let Dick take all the glory. 'One wonders how difficult it must have been for her at first to see Dick taking all the praise,' Day told me. 'I felt that Mary had more of a personality – she's immensely strong. When the two of them came into a room Mary was quite obviously very dominant. You felt that nobody would get one over on her whereas he was always enormously polite, a gentleman.'

Michael Joseph was the perfect publisher for the Francis thrillers, determinedly middlebrow and middle-class, with a remarkable list of bestselling middle-market authors that included H. E. Bates, Roald Dahl, Monica Dickens, C. S. Forester, Paul Gallico, Richard Gordon, Arthur Hailey, Richard Llewellyn, Norah Lofts, John Masters, Gladys Mitchell, Miss Read, Keith Waterhouse and H. G. Wells. A few years later they were to be joined by James Herriot. Dick and Mary were in excellent company.

While the book was being edited, printed, bound, jacketed and marketed, Dick returned to the weekly *Sunday Express* treadmill, travelling to Ireland again at the end of February to cover the racing at Leopardstown, tipping O'Malley Point to win the National – it was in fact won by Nicolaus Silver – chatting with Lester Piggott on the gallops at Blewbury, judging the hunter awards at the British Timken Show in August, reporting on the amazingly indestructible twenty-one-year-old jumper Craggmore Boy in September. In November once again he chose his 'Twelve to Follow' for the season and his success rate was almost identical with that of the previous season: 26 per cent of his tips won their races and 57 per cent were placed, though once again a couple of horses managed to win nothing despite having thirteen outings between them. To make up for them one of Dick's tips, Anzio, trained by Fulke Walwyn, won four of its six races and came second and third in the other two; and Granville, trained by Ryan Price, won four of its five races and was third in the other.

Dead Cert was published quietly in January 1962, a slim volume of 206 small, closely printed pages, priced at fifteen shillings and with a striking jacket that showed a horse tumbling over a fence and falling upside down on top of a jockey. On publication day Dick received an advance of £300 – £3,600 in modern terms – which was not bad for a first novel. Mary, especially, with her love of books and all those years of scribbling away at stories and assessing other writers' manuscripts as a publisher's reader, was thrilled to see a Francis novel in print at last, in the bookshops, on the review pages of a couple of newspapers, on the shelves of the public library. The first print-run was a cautious three thousand copies. 'Peter Hebdon, our then Managing Director, said "we won't do anything rash",' Leslie Cramphorn told me, 'but I remember him saying to me: "You know, Leslie, this author is going to be the most valuable on our list." Even so, we thought Dick would reach no more than a modest ten or twenty thousand sales in hardback and we couldn't see other than the racing fraternity as the main market. But by the time I left the company in 1984 he was selling fifty thousand of each book in hardback.'

There were few reviews of *Dead Cert* but the *Daily Telegraph*'s 'Hotspur' called it 'probably the best racing thriller written since the war' and in the *Sunday Telegraph* the future Poet Laureate Cecil Day-Lewis, who wrote crime novels under the pseudonym Nicholas Blake, wrote:

> Master criminal implausible, but love interest and racing detail right in the groove. Tremendous finale – thugs in radio cabs versus hero on horseback. Author (ex-champion steeplechase jockey) takes fences beautifully in first ride over criminal course.

The fictional Dick Francis bandwagon had started rolling. A publishing phenomenon had been born.

CHAPTER 11

The Novelist

(1962–67)

For fifteen years Mary had put Dick and the children first but now she was about to spread her wings. Merrick was nearly twelve, Felix almost nine, and her many talents were about to blossom into vivid life. Over the next twenty years she was to become not only the mainspring that drove the writing of the novels but also a pilot, air-taxi proprietor, dress-shop owner, painter, accountant, wine merchant, professional photographer, computer programmer and worldwide traveller. In the summer of 1961 she started by opening a small dress shop with Frank Cundell's wife Barbara in St Peter's Square in Wallingford, a small town five miles from Blewbury, even though neither had any experience. 'It was an odd place to have a shop because it was out of the main thoroughfares but it got a name,' I was told by Keith Foster, the son of Cundell's head lad. 'Mary and Barbara worked very well as a partnership and it became a thriving little ladies' dress shop selling upmarket clothes, exclusive stuff.' They called the shop Francelle – part Francis, part Cundell, part 'she' in French.

Mary's new interest delayed production of the second novel and it was to be two years before it was written. At first there was no suggestion that *Dead Cert* might be just the first of a whole series of racing thrillers, but good hardback sales and the fact that it was also published in the United States by Holt Rinehart encouraged them to start researching a second.

In the meantime Dick soldiered on at the *Sunday Express* in a weekly routine that had become as predictable as the paper's endless articles about the Second World War. In January each year he would write an opinion piece: that year, an article urging that hard-up jockeys should be officially insured against loss of earnings during long spells of bad weather. Each February and March he would assess the chances of the runners at Cheltenham and in the Grand National as well as covering some of the lesser races. His forecasts were rarely successful: in 1962 he tipped Frenchman's Cove to win the National from Nicolaus Silver and Solfen but none of them came anywhere near. Even more embarrassing, Dick asserted in his column that the National was 'rarely, if ever' won by a horse over twelve years old or that had not won all season, only to be proved completely wrong when the first three horses (Kilmore, Wyndburgh and Mr What) were all aged over twelve and only Wyndburgh had previously won a race that season. Each April there would be more tips and think-pieces – in 1962 he criticised racecourse valets for increasing their charges to jockeys – and in May he would always write about the Derby. After the summer break of June and July it would be back to Devon and some of the smaller tracks, a trip to Ireland in September, his pick of the 'Twelve to Follow' in November and then the December meetings leading up to the exciting climax of the King George VI Chase at Kempton on Boxing Day. Now and then he would come up with a nice curiosity – in 1962 a profile of a seventy-four-year-old grandfather who was still riding in National Hunt races, Bobby Renton – or a trenchant lecture (in November it was a blast against owners who failed to pay their trainers). But in general each year was much the same as the one before.

Dick's personal routine had become predictable, too: riding out every morning, racing most afternoons, visiting trainers' stables to interview them and size up their horses, going up to the *Sunday Express* offices in London every Friday, taking the boys and their ponies to Saturday gymkhanas, and holidaying in Paignton every July.

Dick's skill as a tipster reached its nadir in November when his 'twelve to follow' for 1962–63 turned out to be the least successful of his career. The horse that he predicted would be 'the sensation of the jumping season' and would win the Gold Cup, Duke of York, won none of its five races. Five other horses failed to win anything either and not one of the twelve won more than one race that season, despite having fifty-eight outings between them. Overall that year Dick's tips won only one in ten of their races. Perhaps his forecasts were affected by the terrible icy weather that winter – the coldest in England since 1740 – but every other racehorse would have been affected, too. Sadly, Devon Loch, now seventeen and in retirement along with the Queen Mother at Sandringham, was too old to survive the stunning cold and had to be put down. It was, however, excellent weather to huddle indoors and get on with the second novel, *Nerve*, which may well have been inspired by Dick's old *Sunday Express* story about Derek Ancil's fears that villains might nobble Knucklecracker, since it describes how a villain might nobble racehorses by feeding them doctored sugar lumps. It starts with a wonderfully arresting first sentence in which a jockey shoots himself in the parade ring at the races and tells of an up-and-coming young jockey, Robb Finn, who suddenly starts to ride winners until one day the winning stops and every horse he rides fails to come anywhere. Are they all being nobbled? How? Why? By whom? Finn vows to find out and is soon being punched on the nose, attacked with a tyre lever, rendered unconscious, tied up, kidnapped, doused with icy water and held prisoner in a freezing stable. And as always the book is dusted with light autobiographical touches. Mary's asthma, for instance, a legacy of her polio, was worse than ever that dreadful winter and one of the characters in *Nerve* suffers terribly from it, too: the wheezing, gasping for air, the edge of panic.

In March Dick demonstrated yet again the difficulty of predicting the result of the Grand National when he tipped Dagmar Gittell to win followed by Springbok and Loving Record and the race was duly won by Ayula at 66/1 followed by Carrickbeg and Hawa's Song, though to be fair he had tipped Hawa's Song as a possible dark horse. His 'twelve to follow' for 1963–64 at the end of October were much more successful and turned out to be his best list so far: 34 per cent of his tips won their races and 60 per cent were placed, thanks particularly to Verly Bewicke's Snaigow (which won six of its ten races and was second in two more) and Tommy Robson's Magic Court (which won four of its nine outings). Dick ended the year with a provocative article in which he claimed that the Grand National was not nearly as hazardous as it had been when he had ridden in it since its fences had been rebuilt three years earlier. 'It is not any longer a serious challenge to a horse's courage,' he wrote, but agreed that the race was better for the spectators now that there were fewer fallers.

When Michael Joseph published *Nerve* in 1964 the *Daily Express* said it was 'superbly exciting' but otherwise there were few British reviews. British national newspapers tended to review thrillers in cramped little ghettoes where each author was lucky to be noticed in fifty words, and it has to be admitted that *Nerve*, like *Dead Cert*, was still pretty amateurish, particularly in the unlikely explanation at the end. But the basic idea was an excellent one, the love affair subtler and more convincing and the glimpses of racing from the inside were fascinating: the arrogance of some Jockey Club stewards, the humility of the jockeys and their continual struggle to lose weight and to recover from falls, the camaraderie of the changing room, the intricacies of betting and bookies. There is also a deep, almost painful love of the game, an affirmation of the mystical unity of horse and rider, and you can almost smell the despair of Dick's helpless love for his lost career. As for Mary's contribution to the book, it is surely there in the knowledge of oboe, *cor anglais* and how a great musician digs the composer's bones out of a piece of music and dresses the skeleton in his own interpretation. Above all there is an unexpected depth to the book, a hint here and there of a philosophical resonance that is rare in thrillers by unknown novelists. When *Nerve* was published in New York the crime novelist Ross Macdonald was highly impressed and Anthony Boucher wrote: 'One's reaction is not "how can a great jockey write such a good novel?" but rather "how can such an excellent novelist know so much about steeplechasing?"' In general, though, it was not until the third novel that the reviewers began to notice that here was a thriller writer of subtlety and style. As for sales, it was to be years before the books sold in large numbers. 'The success was a very gradual build-up,' I was told by Alan Brooke, Michael Joseph's managing director from 1980 to 1989. 'Even after seven or eight books they were selling only ten or eleven thousand copies. The first two were paperbacked by Penguin but didn't make much impact and the later ones were moved to Pan.' In the early days it was almost impossible to sell the books in Australia. 'The Australian distributors used to be contemptuous of Dick's books,' reported Brooke, 'and thought nobody in Australia was interested in books about English racing and thought the books would never succeed.'

While Dick was still producing his weekly column throughout 1964 – interviewing Fred Winter ('the greatest steeplechase jockey ever'), visiting stables and racecourses all over the country, travelling to Ireland – the Francis fiction factory managed amazingly to produce not just one but two new thrillers, *For Kicks* and *Odds Against*, for 1965, the only year in which two novels were published. By now Merrick and Felix were both away from home at Mill Hill public boarding school in North London, so while Dick was predicting wrongly that Acrophel was one of twelve horses to follow that season (it managed just one third in nine races) and that Mill House would easily beat Arkle in the Cheltenham Gold Cup (in fact Arkle won by five clear lengths in record time) and that the first three horses in the Grand National would be Flying Wild, Purple Silk and Kilmore (in fact Team Spirit won, followed by Purple Silk and Peacetown), the fevered rustling of paper and scratching of pen at Penny Chase were as loud as the early morning thudding of hooves of Dick's racehorses up on the gallops. Unhappily Dick's riding was interrupted in July when he was judging the hunter championship at the Royal Show at Stoneleigh Abbey in Warwickshire; his horse slipped on a muddy patch of ground and he fell and had to be taken to hospital with concussion and yet another broken collar-bone.

'Dick and Mary were very good neighbours,' I was told by Mrs Hazel Dexter, who moved with her husband and children into the house next door in Blewbury in 1964 and ran the kennels there for many years. 'I don't think they had any friends in the village though they did have racing friends. He was a very keen gardener and loved his roses.' Mrs Dexter's daughter Jane, who was then eight and now runs a riding centre nearby, remembered that Mary was often unwell and that, although Merrick and Felix's ponies were kept in a field beside the house, she did not remember the boys ever riding them. Merrick was in fact already riding racehorses at the age of fourteen but Felix was not horsey at all, so Dick was grateful that she, her sister and a couple of young girlfriends rode the ponies regularly:

A gang of us used to spend nearly all our time riding them in the paddock until we were in our early teens.

Dick always seemed so pleased that we were riding his ponies all day. I can imagine we were running around the fields being horrible and I'm surprised that he was so pleased to have us hanging around in his back garden. They were very good neighbours and you'd never get a complaint from them about anything.

Yet the Dexters were never invited to the big annual champagne party that Dick and Mary gave at Penny Chase for their friends every year and to which they invited the local farmers as well as actors such as Arthur Lowe, Dulcie Gray and Michael Dennison, publishers such as Anthea Joseph and her young managing director Edmund Fisher, writers like Gavin Lyall and his wife Katharine Whitehorn, and racing people such as George Beeby, Helen and Fulke Johnson Houghton, Michael Pope, Barbara and Frank Cundell, and Kath and Fulke Walwyn. 'They kept themselves to themselves,' explained Jane Dexter. 'They didn't meet many people in the village and never went to the pubs.'

Gavin Lyall and Katharine Whitehorn became close friends of the Francises after meeting them as fellow members of the Detection Club, and stayed with them regularly at Blewbury. 'They introduced us to the Thames,' Lyall told me. 'For a few years we used to have long weekends with the boats.' He remembered Dick as being

a very quiet sort of bloke, and dogged. You can't shift him. But it's difficult to think of them separately: they always seem to be together. Politically they're very right-wing. During a typical evening with them, after dinner, a political argument blows up and Kath and Mary are going hammer and tongs and Dick has just fallen asleep. But they're enormously kind, generous people and we were always delighted to go and stay with them. Dick used to take Kath off to the races on a Saturday afternoon and

Mary said she'd had enough of that and she and I used to adjourn to the pub and talk cooking or something. Mary quite clearly opted out of going to the races once his riding days were over.

Lyall was particularly struck by the way the Francises stuck to their oldest friends and routines:

> It's extraordinary the way they do cling to their roots and habits and old friends. That is a strong aspect of them. That and a somewhat deferential view of royalty, of course. We met the Queen Mother at some dinner Mary gave at some restaurant in London and I was very taken aback: there was some guy talking to the Queen Mother and *flattering* her to her face, and obviously sincere, and I thought 'this is ridiculous'. 'I do think you're wonderful, ma'am,' he was saying. It was quite incredible, and this bloke was going on. It left me completely tongue-tied. I didn't know what the hell to say.

For Kicks was the first novel to put Dick Francis firmly onto the literary map. The idea for the book came when Dick and Mary were watching dog trials before the races at Cartmel and wondered if horses as well as dogs could hear the high-pitched shepherd's whistles that are inaudible to humans. Dick bought one of the whistles, blew it in the paddock at Blewbury, and the ponies all pricked their ears, although he could hear nothing. This was the book for which the reviewers began to reach for their superlatives and it was to win the Crime Writers' Association's Silver Dagger Award for the second best crime novel of the year, being beaten only by Ross Macdonald's *The Far Side of the Dollar*, which won the Gold Dagger Award. The huge success of the book is puzzling because it is not nearly one of the best in the Francis *oeuvre*. It starts in a long, slow, dull fashion, proceeds in a desultory manner and is generally beyond credibility. There are too many improbable moments, too much unlikely dialogue, and the hero is so absurdly goody-goody and tolerant that he becomes seriously irritating. And at the end the book takes far too long to tie up the loose ends. Even so, the ultimate solution is brilliantly clever and unexpected, and it is illuminating to spot Mary's fingerprints all over the story in its references to several of the literary subjects that she had studied at university: Ancient Icelandic, Anglo-Saxon, Alfred the Great's *Chronicles*, Middle English, the Greek *Meditations* of the Roman emperor Marcus Aurelius Antoninus, the poems of John Betjeman.

The novel's protagonist, Daniel Roke, the rich young owner of a stud farm in Australia, is persuaded by the Earl of October to come to Britain to impersonate a cockney stable lad so that undercover he can investigate how ten mediocre but hyper-active racehorses – all obviously doped up to the eyeballs – have managed to win races they should never have won yet have shown no sign at all of being drugged when tested. Setting what was by now becoming the violent pattern for the Francis thrillers, Roke is beaten up more than once, accused of raping an eighteen-year-old girl, kills one of the villains during a sadistic battle that is lovingly described over several pages and is arrested for murder. There are as usual some fascinating snippets about the racing world and several real trainers appear under their own names – Owen, Cundell, Beeby, Cazalet – but in the end there are too many highly unconvincing passages. A Jockey Club steward conspires to stop the favourite in a race even though he is one of the good guys. One semi-literate stable lad says 'ye gods' while another remarks: 'I'm fed to the back molars'. A young petrol pump attendant in the north-east of England says 'blimey!' and 'I ask you!' when in fact he would say 'ach, away, ya booger!' In fact it seems utterly incredible that a rich middle-class fellow like Roke could possibly manage to masquerade as a scruffy stable lad for as long as he does; it is simply absurd when the police suddenly drop the murder charge; and the scene when he finally makes it up with the Earl of October, and the final couple of pages, are ludicrous.

Nevertheless, *For Kicks* was greeted with high praise when it was published in February. 'Absolutely first class,' said the *Sunday Times* and the *Daily Telegraph* was so excited that it reviewed the book twice, once on the literary page ('Mr Francis writes almost as well as he rides') and again on the racing page, which reported that 'Dick Francis knows racing backwards and he is deservedly making a great name for himself as a writer of racing thrillers.' The *New York Times*, too, went into raptures, calling the novel 'an absolute beauty' and adding: 'the detection is ingenious and detailed; the gimmick is a fine one; and the background of life among horses and trainers and stable lads (and criminals) is so real you can smell and taste it. As a puzzle, as a thriller, it's a winner.'

The success of the book meant that foreign publishers began to buy translation rights. In the United States, however, Holt Rinehart, which had published *Dead Cert* and *Nerve*, rejected *For Kicks*. Tom Wallace, a senior editor there in 1964, told me: 'Our mystery editor, Louise Waller, read it and turned it down because we hadn't done that well with his previous books – three or four thousand – and we decided we'd put our money elsewhere and start off with a new face. He was the fish that got away.'

For Dick and Mary that rejection was in fact a stroke of luck since the book was then taken on by the doyenne of New York mystery editors, Joan Kahn at Harper and Row. Wallace said:

> It was Joan Kahn who made Dick Francis. When she published him the bookshops didn't just think 'this is by Dick Francis' but 'this is by a Joan Kahn author'. She was elfin, very petite, aggressive but charming, six inches shorter than everyone else at a cocktail party but you'd make a

bee-line to her because you knew that she was going to be the most lively and interesting person there.

Kahn, barely five feet tall, was a legend in New York publishing, particularly keen on British crime writers and edited many of them, including John Creasey, Cecil Day-Lewis, Nicholas Freeling, Michael Gilbert, Patricia Highsmith and Julian Symons. I was told by her successor at Harper and Row, Larry Ashmead:

> She was a very wealthy eccentric: perky, dogmatic and outrageous. Joan was small and totally messy. Everything was piled up – old manuscripts, books, papers – and eventually her apartment was so filled with stuff that she had to move permanently into a second apartment. She never threw anything out. She was feisty, smart and bright: very Peggy Guggenheim looking; that middle-aged Jewish look.

'A Joan Kahn Novel of Suspense was about as high as you could go within the genre,' I was told by Mel Zerman, a Harper and Row sales executive throughout the 1960s and 1970s. But despite the success that Kahn was to make of the later books, Louise Waller's rejection of *For Kicks* was quite justified since it is not a good book. The other Francis novel published in 1965, *Odds Against*, is much better and easily the best of the Francis books so far. Published eight months after *For Kicks*, it starred the first of the classic damaged Dick Francis heroes: the injured jump-jockey Sid Halley, who has been forced to retire because of an injury to his hand and now works as a private detective in the racing section of an inquiry agency. There is a depth to the character of Halley that makes him easily the most memorable wounded Francis hero of them all. Born the illegitimate son of a Liverpool window cleaner and a nineteen-year-old girl, and orphaned as a teenager, Halley left school at fifteen, eventually became champion steeplechase jockey but was forced to retire at the age of twenty-nine after being terribly injured in a race when he fell and his arm was slashed to ribbons by the sharp horseshoe of a galloping rival. Now thirty-one and separated from his wife, Halley is torn by a terrible nostalgic yearning for the way of life he once loved but has lost.

'Sid Halley is me,' Dick told Sue Lawley on the BBC radio programme *Desert Island Discs* in 1998. 'I'm very tidy-minded and I suppose I am a bit of an outsider. A lot of the characters in my books are based on myself. They're very autobiographical.' There are, of course, also numerous differences between Dick and Halley and references in the book to words and subjects about which Dick would probably know nothing whatever – porphyry, for instance, a type of rock, and words like 'contrapuntally', and sentences such as this: 'informed opinion has as much chance of osmosing as mercury through rhyolite.'

The plot – inspired by the closure of Hurst Park racecourse, near Hampton Court, to build a housing estate – concerns Halley's investigation of a rich villain who is trying to take over 'Seabury' racecourse and to sell it for development, and an extra depth is added to Halley's humanity because he is not some impossibly noble hero but behaves often in an illegal, underhand fashion to make his investigations. The violence starts with the first sentence, when Halley is shot by a .38 at one o'clock in the morning, and continues relentlessly as he is beaten up, attacked by a gunman, his flat bombed. In a wonderfully tense scene he is hunted at night like a terrified stag, cornered in the labyrinth of rooms and corridors under the stands at Seabury racecourse, trapped in the boiler room as the boiler seems about to explode, captured, beaten up again and tortured horribly with a poker when his ruined arm is damaged even more, deliberately and brutally, in the most sadistic fashion, so that eventually his hand has to be amputated. This sadism is blatantly sexual and involves a beautiful married woman, Doria Kraye, who is voluptuously sado-masochistic even in front of her equally perverted husband. In one scene, while Halley is tied helplessly to a chair, she kisses him so hard that she draws blood and licks it with pleasure. It is only the first of many surprisingly explicit sexual episodes in the Dick Francis novels, and Doria Kraye could have come straight out of one of Ian Fleming's James Bond thrillers.

One of the book's small flaws is that several characters – like so many in the Francis novels – are given bizarre names (Doria, Chico, Zanna) even though they are apparently English. But otherwise it is a rollicking read: neat, clever, full of intimate glimpses of the racing world, peppered with nice lines and graced by a perfect ending. This was the novel that should have won the Silver Dagger Award for that year and it is not surprising that this is the one that was chosen as the basis for a TV series twelve years later. The critics were equally impressed – 'another of Dick Francis' superb racing thrillers,' said the *Daily Telegraph* – and the books were by now already so successful that Dick and Mary were able to afford to buy a cabin cruiser which they moored nearby on the Thames and used for weekends messing about on the river and for holidays in June. Euan Cameron, Michael Joseph's Publicity Manager between 1966 and 1968, told me that after just four novels

Dick was already a star author at Michael Joseph. Peter Hebdon, our Managing Director, would drill it into you as a publicist that here was an author who was going a long, long way and we were to take care of him. When Dick Francis came into the office there was great excitement because everyone, from every secretary to the tea lady, had been informed about it. Peter would say that Dick was coming in and we were not to ignore Mary but in fact to pay as much attention as possible to her and make sure she got everything she wanted. I have a vague recollection of tea being prepared and

Mary being charming, a little bit like the Queen Mother coming in. She was rather sweet, not daunting, but we were all made nervous because of what Peter Hebdon had told us beforehand. We had to pay equal attention to her. Mary would go round rather regally saying hello to all the secretaries.

Michael Joseph even employed Mary as a reader to assess unpublished thriller manuscripts. Shrewd judge though she was, Dick later claimed that one of the books she turned down went on to become a huge bestseller when it was eventually published in 1971: *The Day of the Jackal* by Frederick Forsyth.

Not everyone was delighted by the success of the books. 'I was slightly annoyed because I thought it gave racing a very bad name,' Kath Walwyn told me. 'There was a lot of doping, absolutely – my father's horse was doped before the Derby – but Dick's books made out that every part of racing was crooked. If you read his books you really thought there was no honest person in the game.' Dick was so alarmed by this sort of reaction that he asked the Jockey Club's Senior Steward, Lord Cadogan, if he was giving racing a bad name but Cadogan assured him that in fact the books were an excellent advertisement for racing.

So how exaggerated were they? 'There were times when people stopped horses, as there is now, and there was a lot of doping,' Les Foster told me, describing the day he discovered that three of Cundell's racehorses had been doped so heavily that two – both favourites due to run that day – never recovered properly and never raced again. The need for security at racehorse stables was so strong in the 1960s that Cundell installed an alarm that was switched on every night before he had a runner.

Inspired by the increasing success of the books, Dick's journalism in 1965 became noticeably more confident. In March he predicted that Jay Trump would just beat Freddie to win the

Grand National, and that was exactly what happened. Each week the *Sunday Express*, which prided itself on being a crusading newspaper, carried on its masthead a logo of a medieval crusader and Dick began to live up to the image. In August – after judging the hunter classes at the Great Yorkshire Show in Harrogate – he savaged the Jockey Club for withdrawing Tommy Robson's training licence because of an allegation that one of his horses had not been trying hard enough in a race. Dick lambasted the 'undemocratic' club for the 'antiquated procedure' of its 'small, secret inquiries' and compared its hearings to 'the secret political trials in Iron Curtain and African countries.' It was a bold article and doubtless earned him some enemies within the Jockey Club.

A week later he was at it again, this time lambasting the authorities for providing 'uncomfortable, dingy' racetracks, 'disgusting and unhealthy' lavatories, 'cheerless' bars and tea-rooms, 'expensive, stodgy and unimaginative' food and bad seating, and bemoaning the lack of *'gaiety'* at so many courses. Three weeks later he was campaigning for photo-finish cameras to be used at all jump-racing tracks. A fortnight after that he was saying it was absurd that Wales had so few racetracks that even the Welsh Grand National had to be run in England (at Chepstow) and demanding that a new racecourse should be built at Cardiff. In November he urged the authorities to follow the American custom of paying bonuses to jockeys who came second and third so as to encourage them to ride hard right to the end of a race. And in December he was insisting that novice hurdles – 'the dreariest races on the card' – could be improved if the authorities made all horses acquire minimum qualifications before being entered for them. All in all it was an impressive run of crusading. Even his 'twelve to follow over the jumps' for 1965/66 turned out to be more successful than usual with nearly a third winning their races and more than half being placed.

Now that the novels were doing so well Dick and Mary agreed with Michael Joseph that there should be a new thriller published every year in time to catch the Christmas market, and they decided that the next one should focus on one of the aerial horse transport businesses that flew racehorses all over the world. To research the subject they flew to Italy and back on a horse transport aeroplane, an unpressurized old DC4 run by LEP Transport. They left Gatwick airport at six a.m. with Dick helping to look after the eight horses on board and with Mary making copious notes all the way and taking photographs. In Milan she nipped into the city to rubberneck the Gothic cathedral, the royal palace and the opera house while Dick helped to unload the horses and to load eight more for the return journey. They took off again three hours later, Dick again helping to offload the Italian horses once they were back in England. It had been an exhausting day but in just a few hours they had accumulated enough information to assemble the skeleton of the new book, which they were to call *Flying Finish*. They also consulted an airline captain, Peter Palmer, the British Bloodstock Agency and went to Oxford airport to learn some basic details about light aircraft, and although Mary had never even been in a small plane before – and had only been airborne six times in her life, always in airliners – she became so fascinated that she started to take flying lessons at the Oxford Air Training School at Kidlington towards the end of 1965.

The idea at first was that she would take two or three lessons simply for some basic research for the new book but she came to love flying so much that she took many more and eventually flew solo and became a qualified pilot – an extraordinary achievement for a forty-one-year-old housewife who was still crippled and weakened by polio. She was to go on to buy her own light plane, a Piper Cherokee Arrow with the registration number G-AVXF – 'a very sophisticated aeroplane, like a sports car,' she told me – and to fly regularly for the next eleven years, taking annual examinations and having medicals, chest X-rays and electro-cardiograms so as to renew her licence every year.

Three years after getting her pilot's licence she even published an instruction book that was to be given by the British airline BOAC to all its potential professional pilots, *The Beginner's Guide to Flying*, which was to be reprinted three times. Mary was to buy two more aircraft and from the end of 1969 was to run her own air-taxi company for seven years. Her commitment and dedication to everything she tackled were phenomenal. She told me in 1980:

> I did it at first because Dick had flown only in the RAF when they had had the sky to themselves and there were very few civilians up there. They flew on beams and did night flying without lights and it was a totally different sort of flying. But by 1965 the sky was full of civilian planes and there were new regulations and methods of navigation. It was all so different and the instructors at Oxford couldn't possibly tell us everything in the bar in one evening. Dick was busy doing his job at the *Sunday Express* so they said – almost as a joke – 'send your wife, we'll tell her and she can tell you'. I didn't have any wish to learn to fly but I was quite happy to go up four or five times to learn the basics. Then I wanted to go solo so that I could at least say that I'd flown a plane. And so it went on. I do actually like learning things – and it was *there*.

It is odd that nobody asked why Dick should need Mary to do this daunting research for him when he had already flown for hundreds of hours in the RAF. After all, his job with the *Sunday Express* was only part-time and it was only twenty years since he had left the RAF, so it would surely have made more sense for him to have had a few refresher lessons to bring him up to date than for Mary to start flying right from scratch. Yet nobody ever asked Dick why he did not do this research himself.

The Air Training School at Kidlington was the largest for

airline pilots in Europe, with forty full-time and four part-time instructors. Only one in twenty of the pupils was a woman and after taking a medical test and being granted a Student Pilot's Licence, Mary started (at a fee of £9-5s an hour) with several hours learning on a Piper Colt before moving on to a Piper Cherokee. Luckily the asthma that was to plague her later in life was not yet always obvious, since no one suffering from asthma or high blood pressure was allowed to fly solo. Her teacher, John Mercer, was a good instructor, she told me wryly: 'He was supposed to be good with women, i.e. he thought that women are fools.' She had to learn an awesome amount about all the complex checks and details vital for safety in the air, from everything about engines and flying controls to navigation, map reading and wind direction, and then to fly for at least forty hours – ten of them solo – before getting her Private Pilot's Licence. She learned how to check everything before even thinking of turning the engine on: brakes, fuel gauges, anti-collision beacon, red and green navigation lights, fire extinguisher, rivets, screws, radio aerials, oil level, propeller blade, air intakes, tyres, flaps and tailplane. She learned about emergency drills, taxiing, climbing, descending, stalling, spinning, approaching, landing, forced landing, overshooting, crosswinds, sideslipping and steep turns. She learned how to keep checking everything during a flight: temperature and pressure gauges, altimeter, airspeed indicator, rate of climb and descent indicator. She learned that if you fly too fast – in a high-speed dive, say – you may tear the wings off your aircraft. She learned that landing is no more than a controlled crash. She learned about isogonals, Magnetic North, True North, gyros, Q Code, radio, VOR, ADF, ETAs and flight plans. She learned how to follow a railway or motorway without crashing into someone following the same landmark but coming the other way. She learned how to fly on the right, and to look out of the window as much as possible, and who has the right of way if two aircraft are landing at the same time. She learned to keep a meticulous log book and to record every detail of a flight. She studied aviation law. The work seemed to go on endlessly.

Yet, despite all the complexities, she claimed later that learning to fly was no more difficult than qualifying for a driving licence, though it was obviously expensive to buy and run your own plane. A new small aircraft then cost between £4,000 and £8,000 (£44,000 to £88,000 in today's terms) and about half that if it was five years old, but it had to be replaced after ten years. And running a small plane cost between £4 and £8 an hour (£44 to £88 in 1999).

Mary told me:

> In the end I did the Instrument Rating which was really like taking a degree of flying and which only about twenty women had done. When I went to take the written exam they looked me up and down and said '*I think you've come to the wrong place*', but I passed at the first attempt, which was rare for anyone. My instructor had tears in his eyes and said '*you don't know what you've done for me*'. Yes, I was anxious a couple of times. Once I was really frightened *on the ground*: I was going to the airfield in a car and I thought 'I'm stupid, here am I, a middle-aged housewife, and I'm going to take the Solo Cross-Country, the first big part of a pilot's exam.' That was the first long-distance flight you did on your own before you could get your licence and it was at least sixty miles and you had to find and land at two strange airfields before returning to base. I thought '*I'm a fool. I'm going to kill myself. I should turn back*'. That was the only time I was *really* frightened. But once I was up in the air I was all right

– even though she was lost for ten minutes at one stage during the flight when she flew right over an important landmark, a railway junction, but failed to see it because it was immediately beneath her and she had to turn back after five minutes to look for it. Astonishingly Mary was due to give a dinner party when she returned home that night.

One of her nastiest moments lasted ten terrifying minutes as she descended from 9,000ft with a temperature gauge showing that the oil was boiling, though luckily the reading was due to a faulty gauge. Nor was she keen on doing solo aerobatics, and she avoided stunts like the loop and the roll. 'I never felt secure enough,' she told me. 'My body didn't like it, my skin would sweat and I really didn't need to do it.' But like Dick she came to love the freedom and exhilaration of flying.

During 1966 Dick continued to write crusading columns as well as profiles and horse-tipping articles. In January he was castigating the bookies for being mean with the ante-post gambling odds they were offering the punters, in April he was urging Liverpool city council to save Aintree as a racecourse instead of succumbing to 'emotional blackmail' and 'materialism's greedy claws' by allowing thousands of houses to be built on the site. In January, too, he reported a story that might have come straight out of a Dick Francis thriller: the chairman of the Turf Board, Sir Randle Feilden, was urging all trainers, jockeys and stable lads to do everything possible to prevent doping. Trainers should stable their horses overnight before a race at the racecourse so as to prevent any skulduggery, he suggested, and he urged the racing world: 'Let's have more dogs, locks, patrols and warning systems.' Dick supported these suggestions. Most stable lads 'are strictly honest,' he asserted, 'though a few may stifle their consciences, take the offered 50 or 100 quid, and feed the loaded apple to the selected animal.'

In March Dick's dismal Grand National record continued when he tipped the 11/4 favourite Freddie to win the race but it was beaten by twenty lengths by a 50/1 outsider, Anglo. In May he judged the hunter classes at the Oxfordshire County Show and in June he and Mary went to the United States and spent three weeks crossing the continent from New York to Wyoming, Salt Lake City and San Francisco by Greyhound bus, stunned by the size and variety of each state and goggling at everything through its green glass windows in a heatwave with temperatures of 100 degrees or more as they travelled seven thousand miles by road. They were struck by the fierce, stark, lonely beauty of the Nevada desert with its parched dust, cacti and huge emptiness, and fascinated to discover that wherever they went in America it was just as you would expect it to be – just like the America of all those films. In the little desert town of Rock Springs in Wyoming the heat shimmered over a pile of rusting motor cars and an old man sat in a rocking chair on his front verandah. At dawn in the Yellowstone National Park they spotted a huge moose emerging from the mist. Jackson was a town straight out of a western movie, where everyone wore cowboy clothes, a stage coach stood in front of the drug store, the raised boardwalks had hitching rails all along the main street, and the hotels had names like The Rustlers' Hideout and The Covered Wagon. They visited the Piper aircraft factory and spent a weekend on a dude ranch in the Rockies, near Jackson Hole, where Dick rose at 5 a.m. each morning to ride into the hills, on one occasion along a narrow path with a sheer rock face on one side and a 300ft drop on the other. Mary also nervously rode a horse there for the first time in twenty years, reassured by the large western saddle which felt like an armchair. The ride took them up through woods high into the Teton mountains, where they reached an altitude of eleven thousand feet and a stunning view across a deep blue lake nestling at the bottom of a pine-clad valley. This was where the next novel had to be set. This was magical. The return home, however, was less idyllic: an airline strike forced them to return by bus again and they had to endure a marathon drive from Denver to New York in forty-two hours.

Back in England Mary won her Private Pilot's Licence in

September by passing five gruelling examinations: two flying tests (solo cross country and general flying); two written tests (on aviation law and navigation and meteorology); and an oral test about the Piper Cherokee. Her achievement was astonishing and the novel that emerged from all this incredibly serious research, *Flying Finish* – about a brilliantly clever fraud in the bloodstock and horse-transport businesses – made the very most of the excitement and dangers of flying. At the end of the book there is a wonderfully tense, vivid description of a pilot's solo escape from the Mediterranean to England in a DC4 – the horse-transport in which Dick and Mary had flown to Italy – with no map and dwindling fuel. The story is also full of fascinating glimpses into the cockpit and the climax is excellent, though the murderous violence is much more vicious than in any of the previous novels. The chief villain is utterly sadistic, callous and evil, and the chilling horror he wreaks is described with such lingering relish that the novel reads at times more like a book by Stephen King. It is also flawed by having a most unlikely hero: a young Old Etonian viscount, Lord Henry Grey, an impossibly decent ex-amateur jockey who is for some odd reason working as an air-transport groom. But the love scenes are the most moving in any Francis novel so far and there are moments when the book threatens to become something deeper and more serious than a thriller. Joan Kahn, however, complained that its plot was too far-fetched because no one could ever hijack an aircraft. Dick liked to claim later that her letter arrived on the very day that the first aeroplane was hijacked on a flight from the USA to Cuba.

The reviewers raved about the book when it was published in October 1966. 'Men of action are by no means invariably good writers,' pontificated the *Daily Telegraph*, 'but Dick Francis is an exception.' The book, said the *Telegraph*, was 'fiercely exciting'. Its sister paper, the *Sunday Telegraph*, agreed, and Dick's *Sunday Express* books columnist colleague Robert Pitman said that the book was 'superb' and added: 'Few action stories have ever had such a convincing hero . . . With this book Dick Francis takes his place at the head of the field as one of the most intelligent thriller writers in the business'. Even the usually snooty *Times Literary Supplement* announced that the book was 'excellent', and the *New York Times* declared it 'magnificent' with 'a rich atmosphere of horses, flying and high-octane evil'.

From now on every new Francis novel was to attract rave reviews, but sadly 1966 was not entirely a happy year: Dick's mother, now seventy-six, miserable without Vince and increasingly ill and senile, had to be moved out of her London flat to the Charlton Kings area of Cheltenham in Gloucestershire to be near her brother.

Dick's fame by now was such that in March he was interviewed by Roy Plomley on the BBC radio programme *Desert Island Discs*, for which he had to choose eight favourite records, a favourite book and a luxury. His musical selection was popular middlebrow: *Chattanooga Choo Choo*, Tony Bennett singing *I Left My Heart in San Francisco*, Howard Keel's *Oh What a Beautiful Morning*, *I Have Got Nothing But Time*, the Beatles' hit *I Wanna Hold Your Hand* played by the Boston Pops Orchestra, Acker Bilk's haunting clarinet melody *Stranger on the Shore*, the theme music from the TV programme *The Sky At Night*, and *David of the White Rock*. For his luxury he chose a mirror – he had always liked to look dapper and groomed – and his book was *The Spirit of St Louis*, Charles Lindbergh's account of how he made the first non-stop flight from America to Europe in 1927, a book dedicated with nice irony to Lindbergh's wife, Anne, 'Who will never realise how much of this book she has written.'

The Francises' trip to the USA inspired the next novel, *Blood Sport*, much of it set in America, and while it was being written Dick toiled on at the races, the gallops and the *Sunday Express*, advising northern trainers to stop whingeing that they were the poor relations of National Hunt racing and tipping three horses for the Grand National that came nowhere. In May he was castigating the National Hunt stewards for taking eleven weeks to investigate a case of suspected doping of Ryan Price's horse Hill House, which had won the Schweppes Trophy in February. Had the horse been got at? Or could its own digestive system somehow have manufactured the drug that had been found in its blood? When tests showed that Hill House *did* somehow manufacture cortisone himself, Dick wrote a furious article demanding an inquiry into the inquirers and attacked the secrecy and delay with which such inquiries were always conducted.

The hero of *Blood Sport*, English security adviser Gene Hawkins, travels to the USA to track down several highly valuable stallions that have been kidnapped and his trip is notably similar to that of the Francises. The ranch where they had stayed in the Rockies plays a central part in the plot, and there are numerous autobiographical echoes, including a boat like theirs moored on the Thames, a mention of the *Sunday Express*, and the first of many yearnings in the Francis novels for a home in a climate warmer than that of England.

Hawkins is so lonely, depressed and suicidal that he is almost a parody of the typical suffering Francis hero, but despite a couple of moments when he should simply have turned the case over to the police – and a decidedly grim, downbeat ending – the book is tense and exciting, with some nice stylistic touches. There is also a hint of authorial melancholy when Hawkins develops tender feelings for a pretty seventeen-year-old girl, the first of several similar relationships between Francis heroes and teenage girls that crop up later in *Enquiry*, *Banker*, *Decider* and *Wild Horses*. Although Hawkins is thirty-eight and the girl seventeen, he feels a fragile yearning for her that transcends physical lust: she represents something vital that has been lost in his own life. Could it be that Mary or Dick regretted not having a teenage daughter now that Felix was fourteen and Merrick seventeen, riding out regularly for both Cundells and Major

Verley Bewicke, and about to ride (and come third) in his first amateur race? Although Mary adored both her sons, perhaps she wished that she had a daughter as well. At seventeen Merrick had also passed his driving test, though the first time he borrowed Dick's car he drove it into the back of another and smashed the wing and headlights. Dick insisted that he should pay for the repairs until Mary persuaded him to let the boy off.

The reviewers were as warm as ever when *Blood Sport* was published in October, from the highbrow *Times Literary Supplement* to the middlebrow *Daily Telegraph*, for whom Violet Grant wrote: 'Thoroughgoing professionalism is always fascinating and Mr Francis's know-how is irresistible even to the unhorsy.' Mr Francis's know-how led him in November to choose his second most successful list of 'twelve to follow over the jumps' so far. A third of his tips won their races that season and nearly two-thirds were placed, thanks to classy horses like Sixty-Nine (trained by Denys Smith), The Laird (Bob Turnell), Different Class (Peter Cazalet), and Persian War (Brian Swift).

Unhappily the pleasure of getting such good reviews yet again and of making such satisfying racing forecasts was overshadowed when Dick's mother died that same week in Charlton Kings of heart failure and senility on 10 November 1967, aged seventy-seven. 'She died of a broken heart, really,' Dick told Graham Bridgstock of the *Evening Standard* in 1989, and in 1998 he told Lynda Lee-Potter of the *Daily Mail*: 'It's a terrible thing to say, but I think she was happy to die.' She died intestate and Dick had to apply to the High Court for Letters of Administration before he and Doug could inherit her estate of £7,306-9s-0d net (about £73,000 in modern values). The older generation was passing on – only Mary's mother was left – and Dick and Mary's generation was about to come into its own. For them the best years were just round the corner.

CHAPTER 12

The Bestseller

(1968–73)

The books were now so successful – each selling about 20,000 copies in hardback in Britain – that Lester Piggott asked Dick to write his biography and the newspapers began to mention him in the diary columns as well as the book pages. 'If I had my own way,' Dick told the *Evening Standard* diarist in January 1968, 'some of my books would be a bit quieter but people always seem to be crying out for more blood.' Whose way was it, then, if not his? Mary's? Perhaps there had been some disagreement about the increasing level of violence and sadism in the books.

After ten years on the *Sunday Express* his column had become lighter but also more indignant. In January he rode Foinavon, the 100/1 outsider that had won the 1967 Grand National, and reported that the horse's constant companion was a goat called Susie that accompanied Foinavon to the races and provided him with two pints of milk a day. In February Dick was demanding that the authorities should lift unfair racing restrictions on trainers in areas affected by foot and mouth disease and pay them compensation. In March he managed to tip two of the first four horses in the Grand National – Moldore's Token and Rutherford's – though it was Red Alligator that won the race rather than his forecast, San Angelo. In April he argued under the headline 'It's Time To End This Mid-Winter Racing Madness' that the traditional National Hunt calendar should be completely revised so as to have more jump racing in the early summer and less in the icy months when meetings often had to be cancelled. And in May, before going off to Exeter to judge the hunter classes at the Devon Show, he was urging reforms at Aintree to save the future of the Grand National.

In the meantime Merrick left Mill Hill school to become Ryan Price's assistant trainer at Findon in Sussex and to ride regularly as an amateur jockey, and Mary was working not only on the research for the next novel, *Forfeit*, but also on her A to Z instruction book *A Beginner's Guide to Flying*, which began with A for Aptitude, B for Bills and C for Checks and went on right through the alphabet – E for Engines, K for Keep Your Eyes Open, U for Upsadaisy – until Z for Zat's It! It was a cheery but serious 189-page handbook for learner pilots with numerous rather amateurish diagrams, many of them drawn by her flying instructor, John Mercer, and it was packed with detail, practical advice and jaunty common sense.

Forfeit was the most autobiographical of all the novels, easily the best so far, and went on to win the Mystery Writers' of America prize for the year's best crime story, the Edgar Allen Poe Award. The hero, James Tyrone, is a Sunday newspaper racing correspondent whose wife is crippled by polio, and there is about the book a strong sense that this is how Mary imagined their marriage would have been like had her polio been worse than it was and had she been confined to a breathing machine and completely dependent on Dick for everything. Tyrone writes a weekly, crusading racing column for the *Sunday Blaze* and is also ghosting the autobiography of a famous retired jockey with a name uncannily like Lester Piggott, Buster Figg, who is interested in nothing but money and has gambled in thousands of pounds even though jockeys are not allowed to gamble. Like

Dick, Tyrone goes into the Fleet Street office only on Fridays to hand his thousand-word column to the Sports Editor and to wait until the Editor himself has scrawled 'OK' across the top of the page, just as John Junor used to do. Like Dick, Tyrone sits wherever he can find an empty seat in the vast, open-plan office and opens his mail – sometimes vicious, anonymous letters – or mooches around while awaiting the Editor's verdict, arranging railway travel warrants to next week's racetracks, writing up his expenses claim forms, collecting the cash from the accounts department. Like Dick he sometimes goes out at lunchtime with the Sports Editor and a couple of colleagues for a drink and a sandwich at the Devereux pub in Devereux Court, just off Fleet Street. Tyrone even mentions one of Dick's real *Sunday Express* colleagues, Brendan Mulholland, the reporter who went to prison for four months in 1963 rather than reveal his sources to the Radcliffe Tribunal in the Vassall spy case. Journalistically, at least, James Tyrone is Dick Francis, which suggests that Dick had come to share his jaundiced views of British journalists, who are depicted as mean, ruthless swines who would cheat a blind man selling matches. Like Dick, Tyrone suffers pangs of conscience about the way he earns his living and knows that his friends are sometimes wary of him, never quite sure whether they can trust him not to publish their secrets, and he determines never to print anything private.

In the novel his wife Elizabeth's polio makes it difficult to make love and although Tyrone is a good, kind man he has an affair with a beautiful, mixed-race teacher which is described with unexpectedly explicit relish. Even so, he loves Elizabeth deeply and will never leave her, and although she finds out, she allows the affair to go on so long as it is conducted discreetly. One suspects that this is precisely how the wise Mary would have handled a similar situation in her own marriage if the polio had left her as helpless as the fictional Elizabeth.

Forfeit tells how Tyrone investigates a betting scandal in which a vicious South African bookmaker forces a drunken racing columnist to encourage gamblers to bet ante-post on horses that are then withdrawn from their races at the last minute, so that the punters lose their money. Surprisingly there are several careless errors about Fleet Street that no Fleet Street journalist would ever have made: to take just the most obvious, the nearest Underground station to Fleet Street is not Farringdon but Blackfriars. Perhaps it was Mary, not Dick, who did this particular piece of inaccurate research. It also has to be admitted that Tyrone is at times so noble and stiff-upper-lip that his unbelievable decency and self-control are decidedly annoying. When he is beaten up on a train he pretends to the guard for no obvious reason at all that he is drunk. When the villains are killed in a car crash Tyrone lies to the police for no obvious reason instead of saying that they were brutal criminals. And *Forfeit* offers the first account in a Dick Francis novel of a deep antagonism between a father and his two sons, a damaged relationship that is to resurface often in later Francis novels. All in all, though, *Forfeit* is a marvellous, mature thriller. The long, tense passage towards the end, as Tyrone tries to spirit his polio-stricken wife away to a nursing home to save her from the villains, is splendidly exciting and the book has depths of character as yet unusual in a Dick Francis novel, and it thoroughly deserved its Edgar Allen Poe Award.

A couple of weeks after the book was published Dick picked his 'twelve to follow over jumps' and came up with his best list yet when 35 per cent of his tips went on to win their races that season, most notably Excess, trained by Tom Jones, which ran in ten races, won six and came second in two. At the end of February there was a welcome variation to the routine when he and Mary crossed the Atlantic again to celebrate the joint publication in New York of *Forfeit* and *The Sport of Queens*, and there he told the *New Yorker*: 'Mary is very helpful to me. I always have to show her my racing copy and if I can get it past her I can usually get it past the sub-editors in Fleet Street. She also works out a lot of the crimes for the novels. My colleagues say she has a crooked mind.' Mary smiled enigmatically. 'I just put in the full-stops,' she said, 'and some of the semi-colons.'

From New York Dick wrote a column about American steeple-chasing and in May he had some fun interviewing the oldest jockey still riding regularly in National Hunt races, fifty-nine-year-old Major Joe Pidcock, but otherwise he was beginning to find the relentless demands of the *Sunday Express* job a trial. At the end of March he tipped Arcturus, Fort Sun and Game Purston to come first, second and third in the Grand National only to see them beaten by Highland Wedding, Steel Bridge and Rondetto, and he seemed increasingly to be repeating himself in his columns: arguing again that there should be more jump racing during the summer, that jump jockeys should be paid more, that something should be done to secure the future of Aintree. Even his twelve to follow at the end of 1969 included three horses that he had already recommended the previous year and this year only 29 per cent of them won their races.

He did not need to continue much longer at the *Sunday Express* for financial reasons because by now the books were making a great deal of money. David Frost had just bought a film option on the next, *Enquiry*, four had been serialised on the *Woman's Hour* BBC radio programme, the Piggott biography would obviously be highly lucrative, and even in America the name Dick Francis was now so well known that a Flat race was named after him at the Pimlico meeting in Maryland in March. Dick probably hoped, too, that the boys would soon be less dependent on him and Mary. Merrick, now nineteen, had given up his career as an amateur jockey – 'I wasn't actually good enough,' he told Jenny Knight of the *Sunday Times Magazine* in 1987 – and was concentrating on his job as Ryan Price's assistant trainer in Sussex, and Felix, now sixteen, was about to sit his A-level exams at Mill Hill in maths, physics and computers. Felix did suffer one setback when he spent three months in 1969 having an operation on his hip, which ended his hopes of becoming a pilot like his parents. Eventually he went to London University instead, took a physics degree and settled for teaching.

Every now and then there came another reminder that the thrillers were not always completely far-fetched – in 1969 a favourite in a handicap race at Epsom, Alloway Lad, was doped on Derby Day – and by now a new Dick Francis novel was published every September. The hero of the eighth novel, *Enquiry*, Kelly Hughes, was again at least partly based on Dick in that he is a leading steeplechase jockey, was born in Wales at Coedlant Farm rather than Coedcanlas Farm and went to the local village school. Like Dick's parents, Hughes' parents never wanted him to become a jockey but had hoped that he would get instead a safe, boring job in the town hall in Tenby. Unlike Dick, Hughes is a grieving widower and another Francis character who can't stand his father and whose father can't stand him.

Hughes is scrupulously honest but is accused of 'stopping' a favourite so that its trainer could collect a big win by betting on another horse. Hughes and the trainer, who lives near Lambourn, have been framed, but the evidence against them seems conclusive and they are stripped of their racing licences and 'warned off' so that they are banned from riding, from every racecourse and even from racing stables, and cannot continue to work at all. Hughes vows to find out who has framed them and to restore his job and reputation, and he finds himself on the receiving end of some serious violence, attempted murder and the vicious hatred of a homicidal madwoman. Blackmail is also involved as well as some surprisingly kinky sex in the form of an upper-class taste for flagellation and orgies.

The book is flawed by a slow, rather dreary start, an unlikely love affair between thirty-year-old Hughes and a nineteen-year-old girl, Roberta, and a slushy ending. There is also a decidedly unlikely denouement during which the villain confesses everything for no obvious reason and even admits to having tried to commit murder twice. In New York Harper and Row's initial reader was unimpressed and urged that the book should be heavily revised to make it more exciting and less predictable, contrived and corny, adding:

> The whole novel has an aura of femininity about it which put me off. Also the development of the affair with Roberta is rather too chaste. They need to do more hopping into bed and less chatting about social differences over the coffee cups. For that matter more solid masculine action [*on*] all scores is called for.

Dick always claimed in interviews that none of the novels ever needed any rewriting but the Harper and Row archives show that Joan Kahn often asked for changes to be made, especially to the early novels, and her sister Olivia told me: 'The books needed a *tremendous* amount of editing, a great, great deal. Joan did a lot of work on them.' Even so, *Enquiry* offers some interesting insights into Dick and Mary's views. Once again we have a hero who is disenchanted by the standards of Fleet Street and the lazy, stupid, incompetent or actually corrupt Stewards of the Jockey Club.

Once again the reviewers were enthusiastic. 'Highly ingenious,' said the *Times Literary Supplement*, which was by now a fervent Francis fan, and the *New York Times* found in the book 'all the elements that Dick Francis handles so superbly: horseracing so vibrantly portrayed that it fairly gallops from the pages . . . filled with suspense, high drama and the bristling hatred of revenge'.

The books were now so profitable that Dick and Mary bought fifty acres of land next to the house in Blewbury and three expensive light aircraft, two of which they leased out as an investment to the Oxford Air flying training school. The third was for Mary to fly herself – the fast little sporty Piper Cherokee

Arrow, which she kept at the Kidlington airfield – and before long she was flying friends like Lester Piggott to and from the races. 'It was very sunny above the clouds,' she told me in 1980, 'and Lester often used to travel with his shirt off to get some sun and he'd be smoking a cigar and reading the *Financial Times*.' Soon other jockeys – Pat Eddery, Joe Mercer, Jimmy Lindley – as well as trainers and owners started to ask her if she would fly them to the races, and business became so brisk that in November she set up a small air-taxi business called Merlix Air Ltd, a combination of Merrick and Felix's names. Although Mary had published only one book under her own name, she described herself in the official company records as an 'Authoress'. She hired six British Airways pilots to fly the air taxi in their spare time from the field behind the house in Blewbury and to ferry trainers, jockeys and owners to and from racecourses and sometimes across to Europe at a charge of £24 an hour (£226 in 1999 values). Although Mary did not pilot the taxi herself because she would have needed to take a 700-hour flying course to obtain a commercial pilot's licence, she continued to fly now and then and took the bookings, made all the arrangements, kept the books and oversaw the business. On one occasion she did fly Piggott herself from Oxford to Shoreham, much to the horror of her insurance company, which begged her never to do it again because Piggott was second only to the Queen as an expensive risk. They were right to be nervous: in June a small air taxi ferrying Joe Mercer and Bill Marshall to Newbury racecourse crashed, killing the pilot and severely injuring Marshall. To reassure her customers Mary told Brough Scott of the *Evening Standard*: 'All air taxi firms are hedged in by the most stringent regulations. We have to do just as much maintenance, checking and insurance as they do on the big jets, so that you are as safe in an air taxi as you are in a Jumbo.'

She did, however, experience a couple of hairy moments in the air herself. 'Once I was frightened when I was flying to

Scotland in cloud,' she told me in 1980, 'and there was a fifty-knot wind and ice on the propeller and wings' – a nasty little irony considering that she had been drawing de-icing equipment at De Havillands twenty years earlier. 'The ice was breaking off in bits here and there and hitting the windscreen and I was anxious that it would break the windscreen,' she said. 'Dick was fast asleep in the back and when he woke up he said *"I don't know what you were worrying about"*!' Dick was always imperturbable. 'She took me and my two boys up for a ride in her plane a couple of times,' Gavin Lyall told me, 'and did a touch-and-go landing outside their house in Blewbury and then we flew down to Littlehampton, had a picnic, and flew back. And Dick just dozed off in the back.'

Mary's energy in taking on all these new ventures was astonishing considering that she was still helping to run the Wallingford dress shop, though her mother enjoyed helping out in it, too, to such an extent that when Mary's old school friend Mary Youll visited them in 1970 she was convinced that Netta was the owner of the shop. In addition Mary's book *The Beginner's Guide to Flying* was published by a Michael Joseph subsidiary, Pelham Books, in July, and the first Dick Francis short story, *Carrot for a Chestnut*, in which a stable lad is bribed to use a doped carrot to nobble the favourite in a race, appeared in the USA in *Sports Illustrated* magazine just after Christmas. It was unhappily a leaden yarn with a decidedly weak 'surprise' ending, but such was the success of the Dick Francis name by now that the quality barely seemed to matter and the tale was republished three times over the next few years. The Francis short stories were never nearly as good as the novels and the disparity was underlined by the superior quality of the next book, *Rat Race*, which was inspired by Mary's day-to-day experiences running Merlix Air.

The hero, Matt Shore, is a thirty-four-year-old pilot who lives in a dingy caravan, flies small planes for Derrydown Sky Taxis and suffers from permanent depression and poverty. His life

is a mess thanks to a nasty divorce and a couple of flying
scandals for which he has been unfairly blamed, which has led
him like so many Francis heroes to hate the British Press. Shore
knows nothing about horses but often flies jockeys, trainers and
owners to and from racetracks, and someone blows up his air taxi
moments after he and his passengers have left it. Another plane
is sabotaged, a rival air-taxi company starts trying to destroy
Derrydown's business, an insurance scam is floated and Shore
is beaten up, stabbed and bombed again before finally getting
the girl. The book is packed with information about flying in
the 1970s and if the air-taxi business really was like this it is
remarkable that Dick and Mary stuck it out for seven years, for
judging by the book it was a snakepit of whingeing passengers,
sly informers and aggressive competitors who would do you
down at the first opportunity.

The book does suffer from several infelicities. One of the
characters is an irritatingly unconvincing and unnecessary hippy
called Chanter, and I kept wondering how any jockey could
afford to hire a private air taxi almost every day, though Lester
Piggott did use Merlix Air often after he and his wife, Susan,
became directors of the company in July 1970 and lent it the
baffling sum of £126.03 that year, the equivalent of £1,115.36
in 1999. Some of the descriptions, too, are truly dreadful: 'He
shut his mouth with a snap and gave me a hard stare'; 'Their
mouths tightened in chorus'; 'My jaw literally dropped'. Even
so, there are also some genuinely tense, exciting moments –
especially when the inexperienced heroine is lost while flying
a plane above low cloud without a radio – and there are as
always the usual nice Dick Francis touches. When, for instance,
the heroine asks Shore why she can say anything she likes to
him he knows it is because he is utterly bland and negative.

As usual the Press loved the book but Dick's touch at the
Sunday Express was not quite so sure. In March he bombed yet
again with his annual Grand National forecast when he tipped

Dozo to win, followed by his brother Doug's entry Ginger Nut and Pride of Kentucky, and instead the first three home were Gay Trip, Vulture and Miss Hunter. He did, however, manage to tip several future winners when his November list of twelve to follow turned out to be the most successful of them all: an amazing 53 per cent of his tips won their races and 71 per cent were placed first, second or third. Bula, trained by Fred Winter, won all seven of its races that season. Another Winter horse, Into View, won four of its six races and Royal Relief, trained by Edward Courage, not only won four of its six races but came second and third in the other two. And Titus Oates, trained by Gordon Richards, won four of its seven races and was placed in two others. It was a triumph of which any racing tipster would have been proud.

One issue that exercised Dick increasingly was that his beloved Grand National might be killed off because the Aintree racecourse was losing money every year. Its owner, Mrs Mirabel Topham, who was by now in her eighties, could not be expected to stand the losses for ever and negotiations for the track to be taken over by Liverpool Corporation seemed to be getting nowhere. Dick returned to the subject several times in his column and reported glumly in the first week of 1971 that that year's National, the 125th, could well be the last. Eventually all his campaigning – first as a journalist and later as a member of the Save Aintree committee – was to be effective and the race was saved that year when Tophams, the Levy Board and British Petroleum contributed £10,000 each to boost the prize money to more than £30,000. Despite all Dick's successful efforts to save the race, however, he was as unlucky as ever when it came to forecasting the winner. That year he tipped Charter Flight to win, followed by Cnoc Dubh, Gay Trip and Vulture, but it was Specify that was first past the post.

In February 1971 one of the *Sunday Express* racing page headlines could once again have come straight from a Dick Francis novel: 'Was Persian War doped in Schweppes?' it asked over an article by Tom Forrest reporting that the stewards at Newbury racecourse had ordered the champion hurdler to be tested for drugs after it had trailed in third last out of twenty-three runners after staggering all over the track and making no effort at all to race. Yet again it seemed that perhaps the thrillers were not always so far-fetched after all. By now they were being published in several languages as well as English – including Welsh, Japanese, Norwegian – and the Czech edition of *Rat Race* sold out its entire first print-run of 70,000 copies in two days. The books were being read on radio and republished for different markets in numerous digests and in shortened or simplified editions for people with learning difficulties. As Dick and Mary started to travel all over the world to promote the books and research the next one they were thrilled to see them piled high in airport bookstalls everywhere.

Yet their moments of triumph were tinged with unhappiness. In 1971 they were appalled to learn that Merrick – now twenty-one and working as Josh Gifford's assistant trainer – was planning to live with his girlfriend, Elaine Bidgood, a local butcher's daughter who was four years older than he. 'Dad absolutely hit the roof,' Merrick told Jenny Knight of the *Sunday Times Magazine* in 1987. 'There I was, an assistant trainer, living off my parents, because in those days if you wanted to ride you couldn't be paid. He said it was totally the wrong thing to do – I would never get on in racing and no one would ever respect me. He wrote me a very strong letter demanding: "please don't do it". So we got married.' The wedding took place in June in the parish church in the Sussex village of West Tarring. Elaine and Merrick, who resembled Dick so strongly that he could have been his twin at the same age, moved into a house in Findon which was bought for them by Dick and Mary and named Crudwell Cottage after the great horse that Dick had ridden so often. Yet it might have been better if Dick had not pushed Merrick into the marriage, which was to end six years later in divorce. 'There was a clash of personalities,' Merrick told Jenny Knight. 'It's difficult when you have parents who are blissfully in love. It comes as a shock when you marry thinking it will be marvellous.'

Generally Dick, Merrick and Felix always got on extremely well but the tenth novel, *Bonecrack*, published that year, was yet another that dealt with the tensions, rivalries, unhappiness and even blatant cruelty that can build up between fathers and sons, and it describes not just one horrible father but two. The narrator, Neil Griffon, a thirty-four-year-old businessman, is the son of a cold, unappreciative Newmarket racehorse trainer who expects him to sort out his problems for him when he is in hospital after a car crash but who has always been constantly critical, ungrateful and unloving. As a child Griffon had never been beaten but had often been given cruel mental punishments and had sometimes been locked in his bedroom for three or four days at a time. His description of his unhappy childhood is so deeply felt that it reads like autobiography, yet Dick always denied that the bad father-son relationships in the books were based on his own relationship with Vince. So could it perhaps have been *Mary*'s father who had inspired so many references to cold, heartless parents that keep appearing in the Francis novels? It certainly seems unlikely that any novelist would keep harping on about it unless there were some deep need to exorcise it. Perhaps it was William Brenchley who had been a less than satisfactory father. If so, that might explain why Mary's mother clung all her life to the memory of her happy schooldays and never cut the umbilical cord with Milton Mount, and it might even help to explain the sadistic relish with which so many of the violent scenes in the Francis novels seem to have been written.

The book's other bastard of a father, who is actually evil, is the vicious Italian multi-millionaire crook Enso Rivera, who is quite prepared to break horses' legs – or resort to torture, drugs, blackmail, even murder – if that will persuade Griffon to take his spoiled, arrogant, eighteen-year-old son Alessandro on as a jockey and to let him ride the favourite in the Derby.

Bonecrack seems at times to be just the same well-tried mixture as before: the sadistic violence starts on the first page; the explicit sex includes discussions of syphilis, sterility and the vaginal orgasm; the reader wonders long before the end why Griffon doesn't simply report Rivera to the police and have him locked up; and the gory ending has as many corpses as the final scene of *Hamlet*. Yet the book also has moments of genuinely high tension and excitement, some splendid lines and the final page is excellent. The examination of father/son antagonism, too, gives it a depth unusual in a crime novel as Griffon gradually tames the arrogant young Alessandro as he might break a wilful colt, and as the two men come to understand and respect each other and finally escape the looming shadows of their fathers. When the book was published in October the *Times Literary Supplement* reported that the Francis novels had 'a sweet, moral tone' and were 'as shapely as a classic fairy story', and *Time* magazine put Francis 'in the company of writers like John Buchan, who created a highly personal genre and then used it, beyond sheer entertainment, to express a lifetime's accumulation of knowledge and affection.' The nicest reaction of all came from the Queen Mother: 'more sordid than ever,' she said with glee.

In March Vince's old yard at Holyport, W. J. Smith's Hunting Stables, was closed by Horace Smith's daughter, Miss Sybil Dayer-Smith, and went out of business, but Dick's enthusiasm for horse shows lived on and he was invited to be a judge at the 1971 Johannesburg International Horse Show, which went on for two weeks. He and Mary flew to South Africa to join a couple of dozen other equestrian stars such as the Olympic show-jumpers Anneli Drummond Hay and Piero d'Inzeo and they stayed with the director of the show, Christopher Coldrey, and his wife, Jane, on their farm outside Johannesburg. While there they went to several race meetings and spent a long weekend in the Kruger

Game Reserve, where they slept for three nights in simple huts and were fascinated to be able to study at such close quarters a huge variety of wild animals and mesmerised by the hot, sweet, musty smell of the real *bundu* Africa – a smell that reminded Dick of his year in the RAF in Rhodesia. And they were delighted to stop at a remote petrol station in the Kruger Park and to find there a rack full of Dick Francis paperbacks. 'The chap who owned the store asked me to sign one for him,' Dick told me with childlike delight afterwards. 'It was most satisfying.'

He felt at home, too, at the racetracks at Germiston and Johannesburg's Newmarket, where the atmosphere was the same as it was at the Newmarket back home except for the fact that the stable lads were all black and the horses smaller and with upright fetlocks that made them look as if they were standing on tip-toe. But the highlight of their journey was a trip down a gold mine at Welkom, 160 miles south of Johannesburg, where they changed into white overalls, boots and miners' helmets, clipped heavy lighting power packs round their waists, climbed into a cage with open sides, and plummeted four thousand feet beneath the earth's surface at an alarming speed of 2,800 feet a minute. Underground they squeezed onto a railway truck that carried them two more miles into the deep intestines of the earth, where they disembarked and stumbled behind a guide through the darkness of long tunnels, with helmet lamps blazing, right up to the front-line African miners drilling blasting holes into the rock face. The Francises were hugely impressed by the size of the whole enterprise, the awesome organisation and efficiency, the roar of the air conditioning and drilling, and the astonishing facts and figures: that for every ounce of gold you had to blast and lift to the surface three tons of rock; that the gold-bearing reef was only a foot deep on average, so that removing the gold was like extracting a thin slice of meat from a huge sandwich; that in the early days of mining so much rock was dug out from under Jo'burg that the city sank by about a yard. All in all they relished their trip to South Africa except for one thing: Dick disliked all spirits but the whiskies were far too weak for Mary's taste because the locals tended to drown them with water. Back home they decided that the next novel, *Smokescreen*, should naturally be set in South Africa and that the hero should be a film star, so to complete their research they went along to Pinewood studios to watch a film being shot.

It was not only the novels that were increasingly successful in the bookshops: *The Beginner's Guide to Flying* sold so well that in August it was reprinted, and Mary often received letters from grateful student pilots thanking her for answering questions that they had never dared to ask their instructors. The air-taxi business, however, did not seem to be quite so profitable. In 1971, its second year of business, Merlix Air Ltd bought a Cherokee 140 for £2,000 but soon managed somehow to sell it again for a profit of £4,500, which gave the company a trading profit for the year of £3,717, although it still declared an accumulated loss of £1,524. The company did a little better in 1972: although it made a net loss of £106 it carried forward a profit of £2,388.

Meanwhile Dick's career at the *Sunday Express* was dwindling towards its close. In November 1971 his twelve to follow were much less successful than those of the previous year and only 23 per cent of his tips won that year and 45 per cent were placed. He still enjoyed some aspects of the job, like the jovial colour piece he wrote about a female blacksmith, and in January he took on bravely the formidable forces of feminism when he argued that women should not be allowed to ride in National Hunt races because few of them were strong enough to control big jumpers on professional racecourses and because 'I would deny them the equal right to cripple their limbs or disfigure their faces. Jump racing is as physically wrong for girls as is boxing.' He even went as far as to call women jockeys 'snakes in the grass' and admitted wrily: 'My life won't be worth living this week!' But otherwise the *Sunday Express* job was beginning to become a drag and to get in the way of the worldwide travelling that he and Mary were increasingly undertaking. In 1972, for instance, he went to the United States in May to join the *Sports Illustrated* team covering the Kentucky Derby at Lexington and to sniff the air for a Derby Day story that the magazine wanted him to write for its Kentucky Derby issue a year later. He and Mary also went to Norway to watch the Norsk Grand National at Øvrevoll in Oslo and to sign copies of the novels, which were by now highly popular there, and were amazed to discover at one meeting that the last race of the day was run in complete darkness, with floodlights shining on the finishing line, which seemed like an open invitation to commit all sorts of thrillerish skulduggery in the dark. The Oslo course was a small, charming one with a pretty pond in the middle of it: 'just the place to find a body,' said Dick, and of course that is precisely where the body is found in the next novel, *Slay-Ride*.

In South Africa Mary had been disconcerted by the weakness of the whiskies: in Norway she was taken aback by the high price of alcohol, the number of drunks and the discovery that the stern licensing laws were even barmier than Britain's: even in an hotel restaurant you could not order a brandy until after 3 p.m. and drinking was illegal altogether on Saturdays and Sundays. But the Francises were impressed by the leisurely Norwegian approach to life and the lack of queues, even in Oslo, and they discovered the joys of eating cured salmon, reindeer steaks and cloudberries, delicious caramel-flavoured berries so rare that their harvesting was restricted by law. They spent just two days in Norway but they were enough to provide the background for the next novel.

One notable journalistic success in 1972 was when Dick predicted that an unknown nineteen-year-old jump-jockey riding in his first season for Fred Winter, John Francome, would one day become Champion Jockey. Francome was to achieve the title four years later, eventually to win it seven times and to ride more

National Hunt winners (1,138) than anyone in history before he retired in 1985. Dick was, however, as unsuccessful as ever when it came to forecasting the result of that year's Grand National: he reckoned L'Escargot would win, followed by Astbury and Rough Silk, but the first four past the post were Well To Do, Gay Trip, Black Secret and General Symons.

As usual he was asked that summer to judge one of the major county hunter class championships, this time at the Essex County Show, and in August he bought himself a racehorse at Ascot sales: Fortition, a hurdler owned by the Labour politician and chairman of the Horserace Betting Levy Board, Lord Wigg, who was retiring and giving up owning racehorses. The books were now selling so well – and *Dead Cert* was about to be filmed – that Dick paid two thousand guineas for the horse, the equivalent of £16,588 today.

When *Smokescreen* was published in the autumn it turned out to be an absolute dud and the worst Francis novel yet: a dull, slow, unexciting and utterly unconvincing yarn about a thirty-three-year-old English film star, Edward Lincoln, who flies out to South Africa to investigate why a friend's racehorses keep failing to win races they ought to win, and finds himself doing all the things that the Francises did in South Africa but without any obvious reason for him to do them and without any connection at all to the plot. Most of the book is sheer travelogue, with long chunks of irrelevant information and endless dreary potted lectures about gold, gold mining, the Kruger Game Reserve and South African politics, and completely devoid of any tension or real narrative. Nothing much happens until the final fifth of the book. What does happen is quite ludicrous, and the villain is so obviously a baddie right from the start that he might just as well have worn a huge badge saying MURDERER.

Smokescreen is best forgotten except that beneath the dross it glints here and there with autobiographical reflections and some revealing insights into Mary's and Dick's increasing fame as literary stars. After Edward Lincoln has made a film in which he is shown hanging by one hand over a 'thousand-foot drop', for instance, he reveals that the scene has been trick-photographed with some very small boulders in the Valley of Rocks in North Devon, near Lynton, where Mary was at school during the war. Lincoln agonizes over the morality of coldly observing and using the misery of others to enhance his acting, just as writers do for their books, and like Dick and Mary, he too, has to put up with sycophants as well as those who make condescending remarks about his work. He comes to loathe all those 'personal appearances' that successful actors and writers have to make and that leave him feeling used and exhausted, and like so many other Francis heroes he sneers at the Press now that he no longer needs publicity as much as he did once. Fame was perhaps beginning to become a burden for the Francises as well as for Edward Lincoln.

Some reviewers were blind to *Smokescreen*'s huge flaws and the *Evening Standard* even claimed absurdly that it was 'certainly his best thriller' and 'truly exciting'. The books had become such successful bestsellers that by now it was a rare critic who dared to suggest that they were not always wonderful, though one was the American reviewer Martha Duffy, who noted in *Time* the 'wide streak of rather naive masochism' in the books, criticised their increasingly travelogue content, and pointed out that the real strength of the Francis novels lay in their chilly descriptions of English winter racetracks rather than the arid heat of the African bush. When James Fox of the *Sunday Times Magazine* asked about the sex and sadism in the book, Dick confessed: 'The publisher said sex and sadism sells. They didn't tell me to do it but they lapped it up.' Dick went on to claim unconvincingly that the world of racing was not at all class conscious, remarking: 'The Queen Mother gives a party every year for her racing friends who go and talk to her and to the Queen just as I'm talking to you. There's no class distinction there.' As for people possibly being envious of their wealth, Mary told Fox: 'There's an awful lot of jealousy. People only resent wealth because they haven't got it. Why should one resent what other people have?' Success obviously had its drawbacks.

Still, the Francises' disillusionment with the Press did not prevent Dick talking to a *Daily Telegraph* reporter at the launch party that Michael Joseph gave to mark publication of the new book. 'It always takes me a lot of time to write,' he claimed. 'I am constantly altering words, sentences and paragraphs whereas on a horse I feel completely at home,' and he went on to say that he made so many alterations to his manuscripts, with numerous arrows and deletions, that no one else could read them. Yet in the revised edition of his autobiography, published fifteen years later, he was to claim that he never rewrote more than a word or two. Dick also told the *Evening Standard* that he wrote the books 'after dinner with a cup of coffee or glass of wine and work late into the night', a claim that completely contradicted the many times he told interviewers that he usually went to bed early while Mary stayed up late. It also contradicted a remark in the second Dick Francis short story, *The Day of Wine and Roses*, which was being written that year, that no writer could drink and write at the same time. Equally strange, considering Dick and Mary's apparent aversion to the Press, was the claim by the Michael Joseph publicity department a few months later that Dick was the 'least known' of all the bestselling novelists and was 'yearning to be "discovered".'

That year of 1972 was to be Dick's last full year as a journalist and towards the end of it he wrote two trenchant columns jeering at the National Hunt authorities for trying to make jump-racing softer than it had been when he had been a jockey. From October jump-jockeys were forced to carry a medical passport to every racecourse and to be declared officially fit before each race, so that no jockey would ever again be able to ride with broken bones or hidden bandages, as Dick and his contemporaries had done so often. Sneering at 'the clammy hand of bureaucracy' and 'this punitive, fussy, meddling legislation' that was 'curtailing people's freedom', he argued that it was up to the jockeys themselves, as responsible, self-employed adults, to decide whether they were fit to ride or not, rather than having to submit to some 'over-cautious physician'. In December he was at it again, arguing under the headline 'DON'T MAKE JUMP RACING TOO SOFT!' against a Jockey Club plan to use plastic fences instead of birch, gorse or spruce. He wrote: 'Jump jockeys always did get maimed, or even killed. They accept the possibility; and anyone for whom total personal safety is of supreme importance is unlikely to take up the profession in the first place.' Dick had long accepted that risk, pain and jump-racing went together, and when he fell that very week and dislocated his shoulder yet again while out riding on the Downs near Blewbury he simply gritted his teeth and put up with the agony until the shoulder was put back into place.

In November he picked the last of his annual dozen horses to follow over the jumps, a list that turned out to be his second most successful, with 67 per cent of his tips being placed and 47 per cent of them winning their races. Heading his list was the phenomenal Killiney, trained by Fred Winter, which had nine races that season and won eight of them. It was a resounding finale that left Dick with a respectable overall career record as a tipster (apart from the Grand National) during which 30 per cent of his 'twelve to follow' tips had won their races and 56 per cent had been placed. But by now he had decided that it really was time to leave the *Sunday Express*. He had never enjoyed it much and when John C. Carr asked him for *The Craft of Crime* in 1982 how he had liked being a journalist Dick replied: 'I can't say I really liked it because I hated it – If you picked up a little bit of news that wasn't quite proper and if you could use it, editors, quite rightly so, expected you to use it, but I hated to print anything in the paper that would give the people I was writing about a black name, a dirty name.' As he told Jan Moir of the *Daily Telegraph* in 1997: 'I felt I was stepping on people's toes all the time, although I never wrote anything derogatory about anyone.' In the same year he told Rachelle Thackray of the *Independent on Sunday*: 'I didn't like asking people questions and fearing that they didn't want to be asked this and that. I wasn't a good newspaperman.'

Luckily he no longer needed his *Sunday Express* income. The books were now such huge bestsellers that his name appeared that year for the first time in the 1973 edition of *Who's Who* (recreations: boating, tennis) though he fibbed when he claimed in it that he had been educated solely at Maidenhead County Boys' School and had been an RAF pilot throughout the war from 1940 to 1945. Still, now that he and Mary were rich they could do a bit more than boating and tennis and started to travel a great deal, and Dick bought Mary a Triumph sports car and himself a new three-litre Rover with a vanity numberplate made up of his own initials, RSF 222.

In his last couple of months on the *Sunday Express* he went to Lambourn to interview two of his old champion-jockey rivals who had become trainers and now had yards there, Fred Winter and Stan Mellor, and to write generous articles about both. In March he was as usual completely unsuccessful in tipping the result of the Grand National, plumping this time for Ashville, Beggar's Way and Spanish Steps only to see them beaten by Red Rum, Crisp and L'Escargot, though Spanish Steps did come in fourth. It seemed cruelly appropriate that the day on which his last Grand National report appeared in the *Sunday Express* was All Fools' Day. All his life he had dreamed of winning the National and yet he seemed to be jinxed whenever he rode in it or wrote about it.

He wrote only one more proper column, a typically furious attack on the Jockey Club for refusing to grant 'my old mate' Fred Winter a licence to race his horses on the Flat because they feared that he might use Flat races simply to tune up his jumpers instead of trying to win. It was 'the most extraordinary decision of this racing year,' fumed Dick, 'simply unbelievable', and he added: 'Was there any situation more conducive to anger, more designed to arouse contempt for authority?' It was a splendidly noisy swansong and a fitting one with which to end his journalistic career.

On 29 April he wrote his 805th and final piece for the *Sunday Express* under the headline 'FAREWELL – AND THANKS FOR READING ME . . .' After sixteen years he had had enough. Politely he claimed in the article that they had been 'enjoyable, rewarding years' though the truth, as he was to write later in the second edition of his autobiography, was that he was delighted to escape from journalism at last. Dick was simply not a natural writer. His soul was lifted not by words but only by horses.

CHAPTER 13

The Phenomenon

(1973–79)

W hen Dick left the *Sunday Express* at the end of April 1973 the novels were published in fourteen languages and each was selling better than its predecessor. In Britain *Smokescreen* had sold 25,000 in hardback in five months and *Bonecrack* over 100,000 in paperback, so that the current British royalties alone amounted to at least £20,000 a year (£140,000 in modern terms), not including sales of the earlier novels, let alone those in the USA or other languages. Worldwide the books had sold nearly five million copies and their fans included not only the Queen Mother but also Kingsley Amis, Sir John Betjeman, Bing Crosby, Philip Larkin, Ray Milland and C. P. Snow (Lord Snow), who claimed to have read every one of the books. Snow wrote in the *Financial Times* in July of Dick's 'considerable inventiveness, both in plot and in technical devices . . . In many respects his books are deeper than so much work which we dignify . . . by the name of Art.' Dick, he said, had 'qualities and gifts which few novelists begin to possess', his books were 'wonderfully good' and his understanding of his protagonists 'raises his books a class above nearly anything of their kind. It gives them their dynamic, their flux of internal energy, and . . . their reassuring certainty that one is in the company of a wise and grown-up man.'

Snow's article 'was a great boost to my ego,' Dick told me four months later. Even people in the racing world were reading the novels, despite the fact that horsey types tended to restrict their reading to the *Sporting Life* and large cheques. 'The books have got to be larger than life,' Tom Forrest told me. 'Even so, loads of people in racing read him.' And the books were not impossibly over-dramatised: that summer the trainer Arthur Budgett felt it necessary to have his two Derby prospects protected by an armed guard.

The Francis books were also by now highly regarded by many other writers. 'I love the books: they're great,' I was told by Margaret Yorke, herself the author of forty-one crime novels and winner of the 1999 Crime Writers' Association's Diamond Dagger Award for a lifetime's achievement. The crime novelist and critic H. R. F. Keating agreed. 'I rate Dick Francis very high,' he told me. 'Like Conan Doyle he's not just a crime novelist, he's a very good writer. He's hugely popular *and* he writes good books, and there are only a handful of writers like that.' And P. D. James told me that she rated the early Francis novels 'quite high because they move very quickly, he's very good at dialogue, has a strong narrative line, and the horses, the special knowledge.' A mark of the high esteem in which the books were held was Dick's election as chairman of the Crime Writers' Association for 1973–74.

In May Pan Books advertised *Bonecrack* on the front of London's red double-decker buses – an astonishing expense for a publisher to undertake for a novel – and Dick and Mary stood delighted in Oxford Street and watched the buses rumbling by. They were so confident of their continuing success that they bought a flat in London, in Hans Place, near Harrods, which they used as their local corner shop even if they wanted a bottle of milk or a light bulb, and the flat allowed them to stay overnight in London after visits to the West End theatre. And when Dick was invited to appear on Michael Parkinson's influential TV chat show he declined because he did not want to upset some friends who had asked them to dinner that night. The filming of *Dead Cert* was scheduled to start in July, directed by Tony Richardson, whose movies had included *Look Back in Anger*, *Saturday Night and Sunday Morning*, *The Loneliness of the Long Distance Runner* and *The Charge of the Light Brigade*. The film was to star Scott Anthony and Judi Dench, with ex-jockey and *Daily Telegraph* racing correspondent (Lord) John Oaksey as co-screenwriter and technical adviser and Merrick in charge of the horses. Film options had also been sold on several of the other books and the Press was now beginning to interview Dick regularly.

One of the first interviewers, John Hall of the *Guardian*, reported that the bungalow at Blewbury contained a photograph of the Queen Mother (signed 'Elizabeth'), a lot of moquette furniture, and a plastic palm tree in a pot. Frankie McGowan of the *Evening News* thought it strange that during her interview Mary 'hovers protectively around him and gently corrects any impression he gives which she thinks is misleading.' Certainly some of Dick's remarks to Ms McGowan seemed rather gauche. He claimed not to write explicit sex scenes 'because I don't know enough. In fact Mary supplies all the information about the female anatomy that I need' and because 'quite young people read my books and so does the Queen Mother'. He also claimed that 'the first time he introduced a scene into the book which involved sex his first thought was how the Queen Mother would react', and he said he gave her an early copy of each book.

Alan Brooke, who became Editorial Director of Michael Joseph in 1974, told me 'Dick's an incredibly lovable and kind person' but 'he wasn't brilliant at remembering people's names and he'd call you by the wrong one. I'd been at Michael Joseph for four or five years before he got my name right.' The Francises had become favourites in the Michael Joseph stable. 'At our author parties they were so friendly to everyone,' Leslie Cramphorn told me. 'They were almost part of the company.'

Realising that Mary was just as interesting as Dick, the *Daily Telegraph* sent Jane McLoughlin to Blewbury in May to interview her and Mary told her that she and Dick had started Merlix Air partly because 'our accountant said we needed to start a new business.' If part of their motive was to show a tax loss, they were successful: Merlix declared another loss (of £352) at the end of 1973 (£2,432 in modern terms) and of £1,142.28 in 1974 (£6,796). 'The jockeys set us impossible tasks sometimes,' Mary told Jane McCloughlin:

> They say they want to ride in the 2 p.m. at Cheltenham and then the 3 p.m. at Ayr. Of course we have to turn that kind of impossibility down, but usually we'll have a go. We have to work to split-second timing sometimes. It can all depend on a local variation in the weather. Once when we had to get Lester to Shoreham a sea mist came in. We couldn't land and had to go back to Gatwick.

Mary still flew Dick to and from the races occasionally, taking off from the field behind the bungalow and sometimes landing on the course itself. 'Flying is so much safer than driving,' she said.

Despite all this gung-ho activity she remained a cerebral woman. 'She was not exactly scholarly, but she was learned,' I was told by her crime writer friend Gwen Butler. 'She's an intellectual – and *so* unassuming and gentle, such a warm, honest person.'

In May *Sports Illustrated* published the second Dick Francis story, *The Gift*, though they renamed it *The Day of Wine and Roses*. The tale of an American racing columnist covering the Kentucky Derby, it was a much better story than *Carrot for a Chestnut*, starting and finishing extremely well, though the characters are as always given some extraordinary names (Piper Boles, Harbourne Cressie, Clay Patrovitch) and the *Sports Illustrated* journalists who had let Dick follow them around the previous year may not have been too happy about the way the story's journalist protagonist, Fred Collyer, is depicted as a lazy drunk who fiddles his expenses outrageously. There is, however, also in Collyer a hint of Dick himself in that Collyer has become deeply bored with writing his racing column. When the story was republished in *Ellery Queen's Mystery Magazine* it was given yet another title, *The Big Story*. Sadly May was not all wine and roses for the Francises: at the end of the month Peter Cazalet died at the age of sixty-six after a long, painful illness.

The trip to Norway resulted in the next novel, *Slay-Ride*, and although the book was bright with local colour this time the travelogue was less obvious than in *Smokescreen*. The hero, David Cleveland, a Jockey Club investigator with a degree in psychology, is sent to Oslo to investigate the disappearance of an English jockey and several bags of cash from the racetrack at Øvrevoll. Rarely for a Francis hero, his life is pretty happy until he finds that he is investigating not just a theft but a murder, and in the process is nearly drowned, stabbed, almost blown up by a bomb and just about frozen to death. It is not one of the better Francis novels: it takes far too long to get going; the villains are obvious long before the end; and the icy mountaintop climax scene is absurdly unlikely. One asks yet again, even before the story is half told, why Cleveland does not simply bring in the police instead of indulging in ludicrous, dangerous lone heroics. There is yet another cold father-son relationship and a startlingly explicit sex scene when Cleveland lusts after his Norwegian friend's wife, who proceeds while they are dancing to help herself to an orgasm that is described in surprisingly graphic detail. So much for Dick's repeated claims that he disapproved of explicit sex in novels. Still, it is difficult to believe that the scene could have been written by any man, let alone a man like Dick: it has Mary's fingerprints all over it.

Most of the reviewers were again enthusiastic, though the *Daily*

Telegraph reckoned that 'there's not quite as much excitement as in the best of these books' and Francis Goff in the *Sunday Telegraph* wrote that 'the hero is a little too good to be true', which could be said about almost every Francis hero. One reader who was beginning to look askance at the violence in the books was the Queen Mother: when she met Felix at London University, where he was now an undergraduate and she was Chancellor, she told him that she enjoyed the books but hoped they would not become any more bloodthirsty.

In December I went to Blewbury to interview Dick for my books column in the *Sunday Express* and was struck by the unpretentious simplicity of the red-brick bungalow where they had lived happily for twenty years and showed no sign of leaving despite their wealth. Dick's study was very small with a tall antique chair of Molly's (with a tapestry cover that Netta had made) and a desk beneath a picture of a hunting scene captioned 'If there's a paradise on earth – this is it, this is it, this is it.' He was still riding out regularly with the Old Berkshire Hounds even though he was now fifty-three. 'It has a sporty pack and it's a delight to see them working in heavy country,' he told William Foster of *In Britain* five years later – except that Dick would have said 'workin'' because he always dropped the 'g' as so many horsey people did in those days. His favourite pursuits, he would have said, were ridin', huntin' and boatin'.

During our interview Dick kept dropping heavy hints that Mary contributed much more to the books than anyone suspected and claimed that he found writing utterly exhausting – 'it's much more wearin' on one's physique than ridin', and I mean *physically* exhaustin',' he said – and he confessed 'I still consider myself more a man of action than a man of words, more a horseman than a writer. If someone said quickly "what are you, Dick?" I'd say "a jockey".' And whenever he made some mistake about one of the books Mary would correct him quickly. It felt as if she were sitting in on the interview as a minder. He said:

She has a very retentive memory, much better than mine. She comes on all my research trips with me – it's good to have two pairs of ears and eyes. She does a lot of my research and corrects the proofs – she's much better at spellin' – and she's a great help if I get stuck with a bit of English. She reads every chapter as I finish it and we discuss a book a lot. She's got me out of several awkward spots and one book, *Odds Against*, was completely her idea. I couldn't think what the devil to write about.

Mary looked annoyed at this point and became embarrassed by his determination to make me understand her huge contribution to the books. 'You will give people the wrong impression,' she said with a touch of irritation, to which he replied firmly: 'I want you to have the credit.' I returned to London baffled, wondering how a man like Dick could possibly have written so many excellent novels. What decent novelist would ever say 'if I get stuck with a bit of English'? And Dick told me that he was still going to the races two or three times a week, yet these were the very months, from January to April, that the books were being written each year. Few authors can write a full-length novel in just four months, yet here was one who apparently did so every year despite having trouble with the English language, riding out on the Downs three mornings a week, going racing twice or thrice a week and who admitted watching television most nights. 'Quite a lot of midnight oil gets burned here and we don't entertain as much as usual,' Dick told me, yet he had always been an early-to-bed and early-to-rise man. In my column that Sunday I said that Dick 'seems such an unlikely novelist' and that the writing of the books was 'almost a partnership'.

Time and again during that interview Dick's answers chimed like a cracked bell. 'I feel awkward if people say "Oh, that's Dick Francis",' he said. 'I don't like bein' lauded in bookshops and made too much of.' Yet a minute later he told me that in Harrods recently a stranger had asked if he were Dick Francis and 'that was quite satisfyin'.' He admitted that the novels were written to a formula but explained that the publishers wanted it that way. On the question of all the violence in the books, he said: 'People like readin' about gore and I don't think it encourages violence, though seein' it on television might more than in a book. The sort of people who read books are not the sort to go into violence in real life and the others probably can't even read.' So was there as much skulduggery in racing as in the novels? 'Not nearly so much,' said Dick, 'but readers like to think that these things go on.' And what about all the sex in the novels? 'I don't bring in unusual sex,' he said. What about the explicit sado-masochism in *Odds Against*? The flagellation in *Enquiry*? The dance-floor orgasm in *Slay-Ride*? Had he forgotten all these books? Dick turned to Mary. 'My sex life isn't unusual, is it?' he asked. She shook her head.

As for the Lester Piggott biography, Dick had recently spent three days in Newmarket interviewing Piggott on tape. 'It's a good financial proposition and quite a challenge,' he said, 'but he's a very difficult fellow to pin down.' Michael Joseph's 'good financial proposition' was in fact an advance of £100,000, more than £600,000 in modern values, though Piggott would have kept at least half of that. Michael Joseph were also paying Dick royalties of 17½ per cent on the novels – 2½ per cent more than the usual top royalty rate – yet 'I don't make a fortune,' he fibbed, 'and we don't have any really extravagant luxuries, but we have made security for our boys when they grow up.' Merrick was now twenty-three, Felix twenty. It should be remembered that during the 1970s tax rates in Britain were incredibly high under the Labour government and at one stage high earners were paying tax at 83 per cent on earned income and 98 per cent on investment income.

I asked Mary about Dick's nature. 'He's not really shy but

perhaps he is diffident,' she said. 'He is very much in many respects like his heroes – quiet and controlled.'

After a dozen novels it was increasingly difficult to come up with a good new plot and as the January writing deadline approached he and Mary cast about desperately for an idea for the next novel. What about artificial insemination, perhaps? But no – better not. So many Francis fans had written to suggest such a plot that they might be accused of stealing someone else's idea. Then Dick remembered that when he had been staying with Piggott in Newmarket in October a woman at Tattersalls horse sales had been fuming about the dishonesty of bloodstock agents, whom she alleged were all crooks who resorted to price-fixing rings and blackmail to push up the cost of racehorses and therefore their own percentages. He and Mary picked her brains about the ways in which an agent might cheat his clients, and then to research the book they flew to America with twenty other racing people on a package tour to spend a week at the bloodstock sales at Hialeah in Florida.

They fell in love with Florida immediately, relishing the warmth and sunshine, spending long, hot days on the beach and balmy, floodlit nights at the sales. They could hardly believe that in January, after just an eight-hour flight from icy London, the temperature could be seventy-five degrees and they revelled in the clear skies, the glittering hotel pool, the palm trees, the bright colours, the warm blue Atlantic. They had expected Miami to be vulgarly garish and were surprised to find that there was a sort of nobility about the huge, monolithic hotels. They loved the cold fresh orange juice, the stone crabs, bluepoint oysters, barbecued baby ribs, sumptuous American canapés. They drove the long causeway highway to Key West, hopping from island to little island, marvelling at the sun-bleached wooden buildings, the sand dunes, sparkling water, little jetties, fishing boats, the vast skies, the endless sea. They met people who seemed to have got their priorities right in a way that few English people managed to do: Americans who put relaxation and pleasure as high as work on their daily agenda; people whose lives were not sacrificed to their jobs but resembled one long summer holiday punctuated by brief spells of labour. This was the way to live. This was to become their dream: one day they would live in Florida.

They went to the horse sales at Hialeah and were charmed by the pretty racecourse, perhaps the most beautiful in the world, with its 225-acre park, elegant clubhouse, royal palms, fountains, cascades of colourful flowers, bright cages full of rare birds, its little decorative railway, the small lakes dotted with flamingoes. They were also astonished by what they learned about corrupt bloodstock agents. The fiddles were legion. An agent might approach a breeder and offer to push up the bidding for a horse in exchange for a share of the profit: if the breeder refused, the agent would threaten to persuade his fellow agents not to bid for the horse at all so that it would be sold at a loss. An agent sending a racehorse abroad might charge the owner an air fare but send it cheaply by sea. Or he might charge the owner to insure the horse but merely pocket the premium: should the horse die on the journey the agent would return the premium and claim that he had been unable to arrange the insurance in time. Or an agent might insure an expensive thoroughbred for thousands of pounds but send a similar but inferior horse in its place: on the journey the inferior horse would conveniently die, allowing the agent to collect a fortune from the insurers for the 'death' of the expensive horse. It was all perfect material for a Dick Francis novel.

In February they returned reluctantly to the ice and snow of England, well after the time that the new book should have been started but at least they had a plot for it at last, and they had a title: *Knock Down*, a reference to the auctioneer 'knocking down' a horse. Despite the awful weather they had much to look forward to. In April *The Beginner's Guide to Flying* was reprinted for a second time, and *The Times*, which rarely published fiction, commissioned the third Dick Francis short story, *Nightmare*, a tale of horse-napping in America that had a clever ending and was a great improvement on the first two stories. Most exciting of all was the month of May: at the end of it Merrick's wife, Elaine, was due to have Dick and Mary's first grandchild, a girl called Jocelyn, but before that, on the night of 9 May, they attended the premiere of the film of *Dead Cert* at the London Pavilion, where the guests of honour were Princess Anne and Captain Mark Phillips.

It was hoped that *Dead Cert* would be the first of a series of films based on the Dick Francis books. The film options for all twelve had already been sold – 'the boys were educated on all the film options,' Dick told me – and he and Mary were also working on scripts for a seven-part Anglia TV series about a Jockey Club investigator, *The Dick Francis File*, to be co-produced by the broadcaster David Jacobs. '*Dead Cert* really is a super film,' Dick had told me during our interview and even five months later he told *Newsagent and Bookshop* magazine: 'I think they made a good job of it.' But five years later he had changed his mind completely. The film was 'a total disaster,' he told Brian James of the *Daily Mail* in 1979: 'The whole thing was meaningless. Princess Anne took it very politely, but I could hardly utter a civil word.' In 1986 he told Clive Hirschhorn of the *Sunday Express* that the film had been

> an utter disaster. I blame the director, Tony Richardson, for its failure. He chopped and changed it about so badly it was virtually unrecognisable. This was particularly embarrassing because Princess Anne sat next to me at the premiere. It was the first time I'd seen a completed version of the film and I was appalled. I'm sure the princess hated it, but, of course, she was very gracious.

Unhappily the critics agreed. The *Daily Telegraph* referred to the film's 'improbabilities [*and*] absurdities'. Margaret Hinxman said in the *Sunday Telegraph* that it was 'dated [*and*] old-fashioned'. David Robinson observed in *The Times* that 'the mechanics of pastiche show all too clearly.' Even the downmarket *News of the World* sneered 'it's a lame loser' and the *Daily Mirror* called it 'an also-ran . . . Only the horses emerge with any credibility.'

John (Lord) Oaksey, the *Daily Telegraph* racing correspondent who had been the film's technical adviser and had appeared in it as a riding double when it was shot at Fontwell and Aintree, agreed. He wrote in the *Telegraph* in 1997:

> I am still wondering, in vain, how we managed to make such a nonsense of it all. Films about horses are always full of pitfalls and the first problem was that the original crime on which *Dead Cert* was based involved stretching a wire across a steeplechase fence to trip up a famous horse! Try filming that live – with Equity and the RSPCA breathing together down your neck . . . we managed to turn Dick's first masterpiece into an expensive Turkey. Only Mary Gordon Watson's immortal Cornishman V (winner of two Olympic gold medals) never put a foot wrong.

Lord Oaksey also told me:

> The *Dead Cert* film was tremendous fun to make but a disaster as a film. It's bloody difficult making racing action films. The original crime was stretching a wire across a fence on a foggy day so that the favourite and the hero's best friend were given a disastrous fall: well, you cannot do that on film. We found it very difficult to have one horse fall in the right colours and at the right place. Equity sent us two or three stunt men but (a) they didn't look at all like jockeys and (b) they were

very brave, they could fall off while galloping flat out, but that wasn't the point. I was doubling for the hero, Scott Anthony, who couldn't ride, and I stood in for the vet when the actor didn't turn up: my first and only dramatic line was 'the urine sample's no good'. We also had the adorable Judi Dench, who was absolute heaven but totally miscast as a trainer's wife and was actually *terrified* of horses! Her husband, Michael Williams, was supposed to be the baddie jockey but he must have weighed about 13 stone then – and a short 13 stone, too – and he didn't look at all like a jockey, more like a pocket Sumo wrestler! The film lasted less than a week in London and I don't think it ran anywhere really.

In fact it ran for three weeks in London and later went on general release.

Tony Richardson admitted that the film was a disaster even though he had hoped it would be a big commercial hit. 'We found more and more that the story, which reads so smoothly, didn't have the underpinnings of character that alone can give a script life,' he confessed in his autobiography, *Long Distance Runner*. There were huge problems with Merrick's horses, too:

We could get only one or at the most two takes before they became exhausted. They were nervous and skittish. It was very hard to accustom them to helicopters, which I needed to get close to the action, and it was difficult to coordinate helicopter flights to the oval and irregular courses. We used cameras everywhere, even 8mm cameras concealed in jockeys' helmets and boots, and we trained professional jockeys to handle cameras while in the race. At the end of the first showing of the film to United Artists, one of the executives said, 'Well, the horses were great.' Which summed it all up.

Most producers who tried to film the Francis novels found them too difficult to adapt so that in the end *Dead Cert* was the only one to make it into the cinemas. Nor did the *Dick Francis File* TV series ever reach the screen: in 1975 Dick and David Jacobs did set up a company called Francis File Ltd 'to exploit the books of Dick Francis' but the company never traded and was dissolved in July 1982.

Still, when *Knock Down* was published in October – on the same day as the new edition of *The Sport of Queens* – the reviews were as fulsome as ever. Its hero was an unusually honest bloodstock agent, Jonah Dereham – a namesake of the book's Michael Joseph editor Jenny Dereham – who has been in typically Franciscan fashion orphaned at sixteen, left poverty stricken, and is now divorced and the only support of a horrible drunken brother. Dereham suffers even more when the villains bash him on the head, burn his stables down and try to murder him with a pitchfork as he soldiers doggedly on in his crusade to clean up corruption in the bloodstock business. Dereham, like Dick, is a famous ex-jockey who hated school, found complete happiness as a jockey and desperately misses his life as a jockey. He has also broken numerous bones and has three fused vertebrae and a shoulder that tends to dislocate and has to be kept strapped up with webbing to stop him raising his arm.

Knock Down is not in the top rank of Francis novels despite some excellent lines and some splendid dialogue. Parts of the plot are ludicrously unlikely, especially the behaviour of a fireman and the police, and some of the writing is pretty awful: three of the villains are 'as thick as thieves' and when six of them threaten Dereham, 'six upper lips curled in unison'. And the ending is quite embarrassingly sentimental.

Even so, Dick had by now become a sort of literary cult figure not only in Britain but even in Norway and Czechoslovakia. The publication of *Slay-Ride* in Norway took him and Mary to Oslo, where one of the races was called the Dick Francis

Handicap. They went on to Prague to do more publicity, to watch some racing and to spend some of their Czech royalties, which in those Cold War days were deep-frozen behind the Iron Curtain, and they enjoyed the trip so much that they returned for a proper holiday the following year. Their international success was such that by the end of November they were able to help Merrick to rent Alex Kerr's racing stables at Coldharbour near Dorking, in Surrey, and to set him up as one of the youngest racehorse trainers ever. Merrick, now twenty-four, had not had much success riding in fifty races as an amateur jockey and had decided that it was time to do something else, and within a couple of months he had attracted enough owners to have a string of fourteen horses in his yard and to saddle his first two runners at Newbury in February.

In December Dick went up to London to sign copies of *Knock Down* and tapped on a prearranged door only for it to be opened by the beaming *This Is Your Life* TV presenter Eamonn Andrews, who declared in his ringing Irish tones 'Dick Francis, THIS IS YER LOIFE!' and Dick found himself under the eyes of the TV cameras and a host of his nearest and dearest – Merrick, Felix, Doug, Elaine and little Jocelyn as well as old friends and acquaintances from his RAF days and the racing world. Dick glared at Andrews and brandished his autograph pen. 'I've a good mind to write this all over your bloody face!' he said before settling down to listen to the guests telling stories about him as Andrews read out snippets about his life, played a video-recorded tribute by Sir Gordon Richards, and introduced several jockeys and trainers: George Owen, Stan Mellor, John Gale, Tommy Cusack, Martin Moloney, Derek Ancil, Tim Brookshaw, George Slack. Other guests – Kingsley Amis, Gavin Lyall, Katharine Whitehorn – said how much they enjoyed the books, Anthea Joseph claimed she had realised how good the first book was as soon as she read the first page, and Eric Ginger and Roy Palmer recalled their days in the RAF. It was a nostalgic evening and the ultimate TV accolade.

Merlix Air was looking less successful. The Piper Cherokee was sold in November for £9,250 even though the company had valued it as being worth only £984 on the very same day, to produce an immediate profit of £8,266. The company bought a replacement, a Piper Seneca, for £28,240 and immediately depreciated its value by £5,648 to £22,592. In February one of the company's major customers, the racehorse owner and breeder Viscount Chelsea, became a director and in March both Lester and Susan Piggott resigned as directors. In September Dick and Mary sold 90 per cent of the shares to Lord Cadogan's company Cadogan Estates, which then lent £21,315 to Merlix, but despite all these rearrangements Merlix still showed a loss of £994 at the end of the year and for the next ten years it was to show huge losses which increased almost every year. In 1977 the loss was £8,798, in 1978 £11,104, in 1979 £25,916 after selling the Piper Seneca and buying another plane for £100,000. During the 1980s Merlix's losses rocketed – £34,606 in 1980, £66,832 in 1981, £95,518 in 1982, £104,856 in 1983, £130,528 in 1984, £115,154 in 1985 – a total over nine years of more than a million pounds in modern values. Yet when I interviewed Mary in 1980 she claimed that the air-taxi business, which was still being operated from the field at the back of Penny Chase, was 'profitable', and in his introduction to a paperback edition of *Rat Race* Dick also claimed that Merlix was a 'successful little business' when it was sold to Cadogan.

'We have one board meeting a year, a dinner party,' Mary told me, 'with Lord Chelsea, and Dick as chairman, and me as company secretary.' She gave up flying herself in 1976, after eleven years as a pilot,

> basically because it was becoming a bind; all the paper-
> work, etc., and the rising price of oil, and my eyesight
> was not so good, and you have to take exams every year.
> If there'd been *another* exam to do I might have gone on,
> but I'd done all there was to do, I'd been running the

air-taxi business for seven years, and I'd written a book on how to fly, so what else was there to do? In the end there was more hard work than actual satisfaction from flying. I have been nostalgic about flying many times since, and talking about it now makes me nostalgic, but I don't actually regret giving up. You can't afford to fly just for fun: it's very expensive.

Work on the next novel was interrupted in March 1975 when Felix, now twenty-two, married a twenty-three-year-old civil servant, Anne Hillesley, an accountant's daughter, in her parish church near Dartford in Kent, undeterred by the fact that Merrick's first marriage was heading for divorce and that their Uncle Ewen was also about to get married for the second time in the Isle of Wight, where he was working as the publicity director of the Isle of Wight Tourist Board. 'Felix and Merrick are very different,' Alan Brooke told me, 'but Felix is a nice guy too: a little bit pedantic, slightly schoolmasterish.'

Merrick's unhappy first marriage ended when he left Elaine to live for six months in a caravan with a twenty-year-old secretary and horsewoman, Barbara Joanes. 'Mum and Dad were totally and utterly appalled,' he told Jenny Knight of the *Sunday Times Magazine* in 1987. 'The fact I had gone from one situation into another upset him more than anything else. He attacked me at Ascot one day. He said: "What the hell do you think you are doing? You have a wife and child and you are living with someone else." I explained that my wife and I could not be happy together. I think he went home feeling bad about the way he attacked me.' Eventually Merrick and Elaine were to divorce and he and Barbara to marry.

The relationship between Dick and Merrick was not always easy and could seem stilted to outsiders. 'I was never short of love,' Merrick told Jenny Knight, but even though he was by then thirty-seven

there is still a sort of generation gap between us. We
have a very, very deep love for each other which we
never really express. If we haven't seen each other for
six months we shake hands. He is not demonstrative. I
suppose the reason we haven't been able to talk to him
is because there are no grey areas. Things are either right
or wrong. So often one grows to know what one's father
will not approve of. It is my one regret that we are close
to one another without being able to say it or show it.

In Britain in the mid-1970s it was fashionable for even vicious
criminals to be considered to be victims just as much as their
victims were and politically correct to remark 'we're all to
blame' or 'it's Society's fault.' One cynical joke of the time
told of the man who was mugged and left unconscious in the
street. He was found eventually by a couple of social workers,
one of whom shook his head sadly and remarked: 'whoever did
this needs help.' The joke inspired the next novel, *High Stakes*,
in which a rich racehorse owner, Steven Scott, is victimised by
the racing world when he sacks a popular young trainer, Jody
Leeds, who has been training his horses but also cheating him.
Although Scott is utterly justified in sacking Leeds, and Leeds
is even more of a crook than Scott suspects, it is the hero who
is ostracised by the racing world and the villain who is treated
like a martyr.

The book begins brilliantly, with a fast, exciting and baffling
start, although it has the usual unlikely names (Andy-Fred,
Ganser Mays) that were increasingly common in the Francis
books. There are also a couple of quite unbelievable moments.
When Leeds complains publicly that Scott has sacked him
unfairly, not one of the journalists who write about the row asks
Scott for his side of the story even though any half-competent
journalist would do so and his newspaper's lawyer would insist
on it. It is equally absurd that a very rich man like Scott should

be terrified of being sued for slander by a poor man like Leeds, especially when Scott could easily prove the accuracy of his slander. And when the love interest appears Scott treats her in such a restrained, unpassionate fashion that one wonders whether he might be homosexual. Even so, *High Stakes* is a much better novel than its three predecessors and exposes intriguingly some of the clever scams and betting coups that unscrupulous trainers can pull on their owners.

It is also full of autobiographical touches. Like Mary, Scott is wary of horses and when he travels to Florida for the bloodstock sales he revels in the warmth after the snow, ice and gloom of the English winter. Chapter Nine is almost entirely a hymn to the blue skies, sunshine and laid-back lifestyle of Florida and it is obvious that the Francises have already fallen in love with it. That year they also travelled to the South of France and the Balearic Islands to see if they might like to winter there.

When *High Stakes* was published in October the *Observer* judged it the 'best thriller of the year', which underlined the huge difference between the Francis novels and short stories, for when *The Times* published the fourth short story in October, *Raid at Kingdom Hill*, it turned out to be a perfunctory, unconvincing little yarn about a racetrack bomb-warning hoax with a particularly poor 'surprise' ending. This story, too, was later retitled *The Royal Rip-Off at Kingdom Hill* when it was reprinted elsewhere.

In September Mary and Dick returned to Czechoslovakia for a two-week holiday, explored the Bohemian mountains as well as Prague and met a painter, Josef Jira, who was to provide the spark for the next novel, *In the Frame*. They were introduced to him by their Czech translator, who took them to Jira's studio where they were seriously impressed by his passionate, vigorous paintings. Jira could not speak English, but he let Dick and Mary watch him work for a couple of hours and they were riveted by the way he attacked the canvas with astonishing power. The book was conceived then and born after they went on a book-promotion trip to Australia and New Zealand and met the Australian horse painter Michael Jeffrey, who also let them watch him paint in his studio and gave them advice about paints and painting.

They loved Australia, from the Sydney opera house to the wines. With its energy and openness it seemed to represent the future, and they were amused by the cultural differences, the drive-in alcohol shops, the restaurants with B.Y.O. on their doors (Bring Your Own booze). They were, however, amazed when they watched Australia's richest race, the Melbourne Cup, and found that the best seats in the stand were reserved for men only: their wives and girlfriends had to sit up on the roof and yet seemed not to think that there was anything odd about it. They flew into the ancient heart of the great continent, to the remote town of Alice Springs, and were awed by the fierce heat and the huge, red, empty spaces of the outback which was known locally as Gaba – the Great Australian Bugger All – and they laughed at the hotel sign that read: 'We don't swim in your toilet. Please don't pee in our pool.'

After flying on to New Zealand, which felt a strangely alien place with its hot springs, sulphur craters, gorges and weird un-European vegetation, they returned to England, read about paints and painting, consulted art gallery experts, set up easels in the sunroom at Blewbury and started to paint. Mary completed a picture of a horse but they both agreed that its neck was too long and that neither of them was ever likely to make it as an artist, but all that research resulted in a new novel in which a young horse painter, Charles Todd, flies to Australia and New Zealand to investigate a murderous gang of crooks who sell forged paintings of works by major artists like Sir Alfred Munnings, steal them back and sell them again and again. 'Over the years the racing content of the books declined and that was a deliberate strategy to appeal to a wider audience,' Alan Brooke told me.

The book is impressive in its minute details of painting, artistic techniques, colour, texture and famous painters, but the whole does not quite jell and is unconvincing. Todd seems unreal, perhaps because he has no proper emotional life, and once again the book reads at times more like a travelogue than a novel. Once again there are the customary swipes at the Press and some very graphic violence which is described with slightly too much relish: when the body of a murdered woman is found we are given a decidedly nasty description of her bright, half-open eyes, her slack jaw and the pool of urine between her legs. Nevertheless, the distinguished crime novelist and critic Edmund Crispin wrote in the *Sunday Times* that Dick was 'a beautiful writer, one of the few best-sellers who never resorts for his appeal to banality or to clichés.'

Certainly the next book, *Risk*, was superb and possibly the best novel yet. Mary already oversaw the family finances with her usual efficiency and to extend her research into the world of accountancy she picked the brains of her crippled, wheelchair-bound accountant Lionel Vick – an ex-jockey who had severed his spinal cord in a terrible fall – and his associate Michael Foote, who helped to provide the basis for a story about a scrupulously honest Newbury accountant, Roland Britten, who has a couple of hundred clients in the racing world, from jockeys and trainers to owners and bookies, and who also rides as an amateur jockey, which means that he has a unique financial overview of the entire racing business in and around Newbury, from Lambourn and Blewbury to Compton and West Ilsley. Britten is a typically damaged Francis hero in that his father was killed when he was nine and his mother committed suicide when he was thirteen, but against all the odds he wins the Cheltenham Gold Cup on a rank outsider and is kidnapped afterwards and held prisoner in the dark for a nightmare fortnight aboard a boat that takes him to Minorca. As Britten investigates the kidnappings he finds himself agonising over a tough moral question: if you discover that your friend is a crook, do you turn a blind eye or turn him in? In that question lay an uncanny premonition of the dilemma that Dick and Mary were to face themselves ten years later when Lester Piggott was sent to prison for fraudulent tax evasion amounting to more than £3 million. When Piggott was sentenced Dick defended him loyally but he and Mary must have asked themselves the same question: where should your loyalties really lie, with your friend or the law? When one of the fraudsters in the novel complains that prison is dehumanising and that he has been treated there worse than an animal, Britten replies brutally that he has only himself and his insatiable greed for money to blame. The same was to be said of Piggott.

Risk takes a hard look at tax-dodging and dissects the way in which a small initial dishonesty, fertilised by greed, can grow into a huge crime, and makes it plain that tax levels in 1977 under the British Labour government were so high that rich people like the Francises were left with little option but to emigrate. *Risk* also took a couple of serious risks of its own. Two of the crooks are described as having been officials on the local Newbury council, where they are said to have managed to steal a couple of million pounds before being found out, and the elected Newbury councillors are portrayed as lazy, inefficient or corrupt – accusations which gave the real officials and elected members of Newbury District Council a strong case for libel against Dick. Similarly the Newbury police are portrayed with astonishing contempt as being uncaring, incompetent buffoons and completely uninterested in the fact that Britten has been kidnapped. Dick was lucky to escape a couple of writs. The book also includes the weirdest, kinkiest and most unlikely sex scene to appear in any of the Francis novels, in which a tall, skinny, plain, dowdy, middle-aged headmistress with a big nose and grumpy mouth suddenly asks Britten to fornicate with her because she is still a virgin and curious about sex. They have only just met but he agrees because she has saved his life, and the encounter is described at surprising length and in remarkably explicit detail.

17. The good loser: Dick (second from right) smiling bravely at the Grand National Jockeys' Dinner in March 1950 after he and Roimond had fallen at the seventh fence despite being the 10/1 joint favourites. With him (left to right) are Tony Grantham, Dave Hanley and his long-term rival Dave Dick, who was to beat him six years later in the cruellest Grand National of all.

18. The winner: Dick and the Queen Mother's Devon Loch heading for the first of many wins together at Lingfield on 25 November 1955.

. The royal jockey: meeting the Queen at the races – and struggling to bow and doff his helmet – in 1956.

20. The tragedy frame by frame:
Devon Loch collapsing mysteriously
just fifty yards from the winning post
in the Grand National on 24 March 1956.

. Incredulous and inconsolable: Dick Francis, stunned and grief-stricken, with an Aintree official moments after Devon Loch's spectacular fall from grace. Later he wept.

22. Facing up to it: Dick and Mary at home – and waiting for the telephone to ng – after the events of 1956. His career as a jockey is almost over. What now?

23. The scribbler: Dick at the races in 1957, the year he became a racing columnist with the *Sunday Express* and published his autobiography, *The Sport of Queens*.

24. The photographer: Mary with the camera that inspired the 1980 Dick Francis novel *Reflex* and led her to become a professional photographer.

25. The celebrity: Dick dressed as Dick Turpin at a charity event in June 1983, the year that the Francis novel *The Danger* was published – appropriately, it was about a kidnapping for ransom.

26. Messing about on the river: the Francises drifting on the Thames in 1983 in their new two-cabin motor cruiser, *Tenpenny*.

27. Watching the runners: Dick at Newbury races in February 1984, during the writing of the Francis novel *Proof*.

28. Honoured: Dick with Mary, Merrick (left) and Felix outside Buckingham Palace after collecting the OBE from the Queen in 1984. 'She told me how much she enjoyed my books,' he told the *Evening Standard* proudly.

29. In exile, 1986: Dick on the beach outside the Francises' Sea Ranch Club apartment near Fort Lauderdale in Florida ...

30. ... and inside the apartment, with Mary, Felix, daughter-in-law Anne, and grandsons Matthew (aged seven) and William (three months).

31. The phenomenally successful
Francis partnership – literary,
marital and personal
– in August 1996.

32. Dick, aged seventy-six,
beginning to show his age
at last at a signing session in
Harrods for *To the Hilt* in 1997.

33. The Francises' million-pound apartment (ground floor, left) on Seven Mile Beach, Grand Cayman, in March 1999.

34. Dick's favourite morning walk: the beach outside the Grand Cayman apartment at dawn.

35. Their final resting place: the two grave plots (bottom right) – just a hundred yards from the Caribbean Sea – that Dick and Mary bought in Cayman's West Bay cemetery in 1993 to prove to US tax authorities that they intended to spend the rest of their lives on the island.

Even so, *Risk* is an excellent thriller. It starts fast with an exciting description of what it is like to ride in the Cheltenham Gold Cup, and is compulsively readable throughout and sizzles with real feeling and tension. The descriptions of how it feels to be a captive for day after day, alone in the silent dark, are vivid: you can almost feel Britten's fear and pain. And the solution of the mystery comes with a double-barrelled shock and a nice ending. The book, the sixteenth novel, rightly earned euphoric reviews, and as for the recurrent criticism that the novels were too far-fetched, Dick liked to tell the story about the night that he and Mary had dinner at a London restaurant and returned to their flat to find the telephone ringing: the caller was a complete stranger who thought she was telephoning the very restaurant that Dick and Mary had just left.

There was one major sadness for the Francises that year: Merrick, now twenty-seven, and Elaine were finally divorced in June after six years of marriage, and Dick and Mary, so happily married themselves for thirty years, were devastated, especially because of their three-year-old granddaughter, Jocelyn. 'The family are very important to Dick and Mary,' said Alan Brooke, 'and the ups and downs of Merrick's complicated marital life obviously caused them a lot of pain.' Merrick was to remarry seven months later, oddly enough again in church, despite being divorced.

The books were now increasingly reviewed not merely as crime stories but as general novels, and it is understandable that their author began to feel restless at being confined to the crime genre and to wonder whether Michael Joseph would publish a more literary Francis novel that had nothing to do with horses. Well . . . yes, they said reluctantly, but they would much rather not because millions of readers all over the world expected a Francis novel to have at least something to do with horses, so why risk losing them? Mary could of course have written a straight novel under her own name, and it would have attracted plenty of attention because she was Dick's wife, but reviewers might well compare the two styles and a Mary Francis novel would never sell a tenth as well as a new Dick Francis.

Just before *Risk* was published the Francises went to the Soviet Union to research the next novel, *Trial Run*, and to spend some of their rouble royalties that were locked away in Russia. They took with them their British literary agent, Andrew Hewson, who had taken over the John Johnson agency and who spoke Russian, and in Moscow discovered to their surprise that Russian TV had cheekily made a three-hour pirate film of *Dead Cert* that had been shown twice on the local network but for which they had paid Dick nothing. The Russians jovially invited them to watch some clips from the film, which Dick later reported was 'delightful' although he could not understand a word of it.

It was the year that John le Carré published his spy novel *The Honourable Schoolboy* and Moscow was still the gloomy, sinister city described in so many Cold War thrillers of the 1970s: an Orwellian Moscow dominated by the grim, grey Soviet president Leonid Brezhnev. Informers were everywhere: old women sternly guarding apartment blocks and hotel corridors; suspicious henchmen loitering even in bus shelters and stopping all foreign cars leaving town. The walls of the hotel rooms were bugged, though you could find out where the bug was by holding a live tape recorder up against the wall: whenever the recorder encountered a microphone it would emit a whine. Foreigners were watched and followed all the time and any contacts with Russians were treated with suspicion. Foreign diplomats and journalists were forced to live in segregated compounds. The city had no telephone directory: if you wanted to find out somebody's number you had to ring an operator who would demand to know why you wanted to speak to that particular person and who would withhold the number if your reason was not acceptable. And a telephone call to England could take more than a day to be connected. Over everything hung a heavy depression as melancholy and claustrophobic as the massive advertisements that shrieked 'Glory to the Communist Party'. People arrived at houses and left them in ones and twos: anything more would attract official attention. Most spooky of all were the wary, unlaughing faces of the Russians themselves: white, podgy, expressionless; in Brezhnev's Soviet Union it was dangerous to be seen to be thinking.

Mary and Dick did the usual touristy things, visiting the Kremlin with its deep red walls and golden towers and domes; snowblown Red Square; St Basil's Cathedral with its bright onion-shaped domes of blue, green and gold; the dreaded KGB prison, the Lubianka, resembling from the outside a genial office building; the Lenin museum; the pale yellow British Embassy, looking a bit like Buckingham Palace. In the GUM department store, which with its little stalls and alleyways was more like an indoor market than a proper shop, they were amazed to see hundreds of people patiently queueing to buy a new shipment of winter boots in a line that stretched out of sight, and the shortages of food were legendary: no eggs this week but onions for the first time in four months. They were told that there were only two decent restaurants in the whole city and they were indeed duly disgusted by the meat served up in their hotel, though they loved the ice-cream with blackcurrant jam. They were impressed by the vast underground stations of the Moscow metro but found the long escalators drab by comparison with the garish posters and advertisements of the London Underground. They were appalled to find that all traffic was forced to stop if even a minor politburo official was driving past in his official Chaika limousine. And they were stunned by the piercing icy cold that chilled the bones, ached the soul and brought on Mary's asthma.

Back in England they attended Merrick's wedding to Barbara Joanes at the United Reformed Church in Dorking on 7 January and Dick took charge of Merrick's stables while the newlyweds went off on honeymoon. But Mary developed bronchitis very badly again – and then her mother, who was now eighty-two and living in a tiny, one-bedroom, warden-supervised home on a modern housing association estate for the elderly in Blewbury, died of heart failure in bed five days after the wedding. Netta left her estate of £14,127 (£46,195 today) to be shared equally by Mary, Jean and Ewen, except for a special memento that went to her great-grand-daughter Jocelyn: a silver purse containing ten threepenny pieces.

Mary's own life was constantly threatened by dangerous chest complaints. Gwen Butler told me:

> She is fairly fragile and very valiant. She was very brave about her asthma and I sympathised with that because my husband had terrible asthma from which he eventually died. I remember saying to Dick that he ought to see Mary had someone with her most of the time because you can pop off just like that with asthma. You only need to stop breathing for less than a minute and you're gone. It's a killer, asthma.

By now the books had become an inevitable target for American academics and the first to break cover, an Associate Professor of English at the University of Puget Sound in Washington, Barry Bauska, published an assessment of the Francis *oeuvre* in the magazine *Armchair Detective* in 1978 in which he noted that many of the villains in the Francis books had hyphenated names (Ellery-Penn, Kemp-Lore, Rous-Wheeler, Carthy-Todd) whereas a list of the heroes 'sounds like a roll-call of Robin Hood's stalwart men': Alan York, Rob Finn, Sid Halley, Henry Grey, Gene Hawkins, James Tyrone, Kelly Hughes, Matt Shore, Neil Griffon, Edward Lincoln, David Cleveland, Jonah Dereham, Steven Scott, Charles Todd.

Dick was also by now a member of the Detection Club and its leading light, Julian Symons, invited him to write a short story for the club's new anthology *Verdict of Thirteen*. The result, *Twenty-One Good Men and True*, was built on a nice idea – a radio transmitter is used at the races to commit a clever betting fraud – but like most Francis short stories it is too diffused and never quite holds together, possibly because there are too many characters and different points of view, and it is spoilt by a ludicrous coincidence. Like Mary (and numerous Francis characters of this period) the protagonist dreams of abandoning damp old England to live in the tropics. Like most of the Francis short stories its title was later changed: it became *Blind Chance* when it was reprinted in *Woman's Own*.

Dick's view of the process of literary creation at this time was wonderfully off-hand. 'Writing a story is a bit like riding in a race,' he confided airily to William Foster of *In Britain* magazine in 1978. 'You've got to have a good start, drama and excitement. By the time the field – or, in this case, the characters – have settled down, the hero's got to be nicely placed, sailing over all the obstacles placed in his path. On the run-in, the last chapter, you let him take over and stay in the lead. It's as straightforward as that.' Easy, really. Nothing to it. You would never have guessed that he hated writing.

The Russian novel, *Trial Run*, which was partly inspired by the success of Princess Anne and her husband, Capt. Mark Phillips, as Olympic riders, tells how an English horseman, Randall Drew, goes to Moscow on behalf of the British Royal Family to see whether it would be safe for a royal brother-in-law to ride there in the Olympic Equestrian games. There Drew finds himself lost in a maze of murder, drugs, homosexual scandal and international terrorism, bashed on the head with a riot stick, and chucked into the numbingly freezing Moskva River, where he nearly dies.

Despite the James Bond background, *Trial Run* lacks the tension that would have made it exciting. There are, however, a couple of biographically revealing moments. Drew, like Mary, suffers from bronchitis and dreams of leaving England to live somewhere warm, and there is a depth of feeling in the description of his medicine box stuffed with Ventolin tablets, Intal spincaps and other drugs to help him breathe. Mary herself often coughed and gasped for breath and carried a pocket bronchidilator inhaler, and in the novel Drew carries a syringe to inject himself with adrenalin in an emergency. And yet again the British Press is described with contempt as being a ruthless, grubby persecutor of its victims and in the end the villains all turn out to be journalists. This regular sneering at newspapermen seems less than generous considering how kind the British Press had always been towards Dick and Mary.

In 1978 Yorkshire Television began to make a six-part series, *The Racing Game*, produced by Jacky Stoller, that was based on the 1965 Sid Halley novel *Odds Against* and five other stories scripted by other writers. The series was networked across Britain in November and December 1979 but the critics were not impressed – the *Daily Telegraph* complained that the characters were all absurdly blacker than black or whiter than white – even though the three-times Grand National winner Red Rum played the part of a kidnapped horse. Even so, the tortured, one-handed Halley was played by the Royal Shakespeare Company actor Mike Gwilym effectively enough that when the series was screened in the USA under the title *Mystery!* in 1980 and 1981 American sales of the Dick Francis books tripled the following year. Gwilym's performance so impressed Dick and Mary that it inspired a second novel about Halley, *Whip Hand*, which was dedicated to Stoller and Gwilym, who became such a good friend that he stayed several times at Blewbury: 'it was just like Sid Halley coming in and sitting down with us at home,' Dick told John C. Carr. Both Gwilym and Stoller were shareholders in the company that made the TV series, Dick Francis Films Ltd – along with Dick and Mary, who owned 22 per cent each – and it was the most successful of the three companies that were set up to exploit the film and TV possibilities of the novels, and even ten years later the company had a turnover of £306,000.

In November, as part of their research for *Whip Hand*, Mary and Dick went up in a hot air balloon and then she immersed herself in the scientific world of bacteria and equine medicine. She had learned of a strange bacterial pig disease, erysipelas, that was also found in Man but not in horses until 1944 when a mutant version of the bacteria had begun to infect horses, too. It was the perfect scenario for a Dick Francis novel: what if unscrupulous crooks were deliberately to infect racehorses with the bacteria? So there was the idea for *Whip Hand*, which many would argue is the best of all the Francis novels and which went on to win the Crime Writers' Association's Gold Dagger Award as well as the Mystery Writers of America's Edgar Allen Poe Award – a double achieved only by two other novelists, John Ball with *In the Heat of the Night* and John le Carré with *The Spy Who Came in From the Cold*.

Sid Halley's reappearance in *Whip Hand* – the only time a Francis hero appears in a second novel except for Kit Fielding later in *Break In* and *Bolt* – gives the book a rare depth and quality, for he is not just another impossibly noble, whiter-than-white hero but a real human being. Most Francis heroes are fearless but Halley is terrified, as most of us would be should we be threatened as frighteningly as he is, and he is also riven by guilt and self-doubt. At one stage he even submits to the villains' threats and blackmail and skulks away in a convincingly cowardly fashion, something that no other Francis hero would ever think of doing. It is true that during one alarming scene the reader asks why on earth Halley does not just run for it instead of submitting meekly to torture, and in another it is incredible that he does not simply call in the police, but otherwise the book is firmly rooted in reality. Halley is real and human, which is one of the main reasons why *Whip Hand* is such a good novel: its hero is not a god; at times he is decidedly unheroic; Sid Halley is simply an ordinary man. The novel is also beautifully paced and judged, the science is fascinating and cleverly woven into the story and there is a wonderfully vivid set-piece scene in which Halley escapes the baddies in (of course) a hot air balloon. *Whip Hand* is a very good thriller indeed.

It is sprinkled, too, with numerous autobiographical touches: Halley's aching nostalgia for his days as a jockey; the hankering for sunshine and warmth; the need for friendship and gentleness in sex rather than unbridled passion, a common theme in several of the Francis novels. The reviewers were rightly impressed and 1979 turned out to be a watershed in their lives. *Trial Run* had sold 45,000 in hardback in Britain alone, *Risk* 245,000 in paperback. The TV series and *Whip Hand* lifted the Dick Francis thrillers into the bestselling stratosphere: *Whip Hand* was the first Dick Francis book to reach the *New York Times* list and from then on each novel was to become an American as well as a British bestseller. As the new decade dawned Dick Francis had become an international phenomenon, with each book selling huge amounts in numerous languages and earning vast royalties. They were so rich now that they could afford to be even more generous to their sons than they had always been, and in February they helped twenty-eight-year-old Merrick to move his string of twenty racehorses from Dorking to the heart of National Hunt racing, Lambourn, where he bought George Peter-Hoblyn's Delamere Stables – with seven acres, five terraced cottages, thirty-three loose boxes and two paddocks – for about £150,000 (about £433,000 today). In April Felix's wife, Anne, gave birth to their first child, Matthew, in Cheltenham. And every year Dick's *Who's Who* entry ('*Recreations:* boating, tennis') grew longer and longer.

Even apparent setbacks turned into bonuses. In 1980 Joan Kahn retired from Harper and Row and Dick decided to leave, too. Phyllis Grann at Putnam had long been trying to seduce him away from Harpers and had offered not only a $50,000 advance for the next novel – twice Harpers' offer – but also a major promotion campaign that would sell the books as main-stream novels, not merely mysteries. For years Dick, Mary and their New York agent, Sterling Lord, had been increasingly disgruntled with Harper and Row and now was the time to leave. 'Harpers hadn't been publishing Dick very well,' I was told by Ed Burlingame, who had just become Harpers' new Editorial Director. 'I wanted to keep him and told him and Sterling Lord that the new management was going to make changes, and I offered to pay double what Harpers had paid him before, but Sterling said that the milk was spilt and Dick wanted to go.'

Money was not the only problem, but it was certainly important. When Harpers had published their first two Francis novels, *Nerve* and *For Kicks* in 1964 and 1965, they had paid advances of $1,000 and had printed first editions of 7,500 hardbacks. As sales had increased, each advance and print-run had gone up too, but slowly, and it was not until 1973 that Harpers paid an advance of $10,000 and printed a first edition of 20,000 copies (for *Slay-Ride*). Even as late as 1978 the advance for *Risk* was only $12,500 until Harpers grudgingly agreed to pay $15,000; in 1979 the advance for *Trial Run* was still only $16,000; and *Whip Hand* in 1980 earned an advance of only $20,000 and a first print-run of 25,000, even though it was to go on to become the first Francis bestseller in the States. More important, though, was the fact that Lord and the Francises were fed up with Harpers' comparative lack of effort when it came to promoting the books. Several of the novels had been given decidedly uninviting jackets and several had been allowed to go out of print.

'In sales conferences Joan would repeatedly say year after year after year: "You are crazy not to push Dick Francis, he is going to be a big, big seller",' I was told by her sister Olivia Kahn, who was by then a full-time reader for Harper and Row. At one time Joan said "Please at least take a small ad in the *New Yorker*", which they did not do. It was one of the reasons why she finally left Harpers in 1980.'

'Harper never poured the kind of money into advertising and promotion that Putnam did right from the start,' I was told by Mel Zerman, Harper's sales manager at the time. 'Putnam realised that they had a very hot property here and they were going to go all out to make these books big bestsellers.' Even so, said Zerman,

> there was no question that Dick Francis was a star of the Harper suspense novels. He was brought over to the United States at least twice to promote the books and in New York City he appeared on some shows. I remember most vividly the last visit, which coincided with the annual Mystery Writers of America award ceremony when he won for *Whip Hand* and I was at the table with Dick and Mary. At the end of the evening he said 'we'll give you a lift home'. I don't think I've ever had an author do that before.

To be fair to Harper, they were not alone in underrating the potential of the Francis books. Three or four years earlier, said Zerman, one of the most powerful booksellers' buyers in the USA had made a speech at a sales conference during which he had said: 'Dick Francis should drop this whole horse-racing bit. Let him write mystery stories with another background. Enough of the horses, already.' Even Larry Ashmead, Joan Kahn's replacement at Harper and later himself a legendary figure in New York publishing, had serious doubts about Phyllis Grann's judgement. He told me:

> I had never read Dick Francis until that point, but I sat down and read the one that was under consideration, *Reflex*, and I really liked it a lot but I thought to myself

'I don't think Phyllis knows what she's doing breaking this guy out!' He was doing fine here but he wasn't up to a $50,000 advance: the numbers didn't justify it. But she's very clever that way: she sees who's under-published. Phyllis saw the gold there and burnished it up and gave him a new jacket and bulked the book up so it looked more like a major novel rather than a small mystery, and she got his first *Reader's Digest* Book Club selection, which in those days was fifty thousand bucks, a lot of money in those days. They gave him a new look and the next book just took off.

Even though the American market for British novels collapsed in the 1990s the Francis novels were still selling huge numbers in the USA right to the end of the century. 'British novels generally don't sell very well here any more,' said Ashmead, 'but Phyllis was smart enough to make Dick Francis a brand name and all you need to get an American to buy a book is if it's a brand name. That's what they're going to buy. It was a clever piece of marketing but it had to be done at the right time. If you tried to establish a British writer today it's almost impossible.' Mrs Grann herself, who went on to become Putnam's president, told Edward Zuckerman of the *New York Times* in 1984: 'I always took Dick Francis as a serious writer. I never read him as a "category" writer. I always read him as a really excellent novelist who happened to use the thriller form.'

Sterling Lord auctioned *Reflex* and Phyllis Grann won the auction and proceeded to give the book star treatment, printing it on thick paper so that it looked solid and important, giving it a major advertising budget and sending Dick around the country on a big promotion tour. 'We treated it as if it was going to be a major bestseller,' said Mrs Grann. 'We sent it out to the reviewers with a note saying, in effect, "this is not a thriller."'

So now Mary and Dick were free to go anywhere they wished.

Dick Francis had become a household name all over the world and the money was pouring in. As the 1980s opened they could make their dream come true: they could escape the terrible English winters at last and go and live in the sun.

CHAPTER 14

Flirting With Florida

(1980–85)

In January 1980 Dick and Mary escaped the gloomy British winter and flew to Malaysia for a three-week holiday in Penang and Singapore with Lester and Susan Piggott, their teenage daughters Maureen and Tracy, and Susan Piggott's brother Robert Armstrong and his new wife Mary Ann. Dick was to tape several interviews with Piggott for the biography but there was also time to revel in the heat and sunshine. They swam, sunbathed, picnicked on beaches, rode speedboats, went fishing, drank from coconuts, and marvelled at the melodious chattering of tropical birds. Both Mary and Dick felt wonderfully well and swore that this year, definitely, they would buy a flat somewhere warm where they could escape the northern winters every year. Their vow was reinforced when they returned to Britain and both felt terribly ill for three or four months, Mary racked by non-stop attacks of bronchitis and Dick plagued by polymyalgia rheumatica, a rare but painful nerve disease that attacks elderly people, stiffening their muscles in hips, thighs, shoulders and neck so much that they can find it difficult even to get out of bed and leaving them deeply depressed. In Dick's case he could hardly walk at times and had to be treated with corticosteroid drugs. As for Mary, her old schoolfriend Alison Shrubsole was much impressed by her fortitude when they met again. 'My over-riding impression is of an enormously courageous woman in overcoming the handicap of her polio aftermath,' she told me. 'When we last met in Cambridge in about 1980 she seemed to think nothing of withdrawing for a spell to the portable "iron lung" installed in Dick's car, "to recharge her batteries" as she put it. I marvel at the way in which, over many years, she was able to help so much with the research for Dick's books.'

Dick was almost sixty now and Mary fifty-six. They thought of buying a flat somewhere in the Mediterranean but decided that even there the winters were too cold. They considered the Canary Isles but did not want to have to speak Spanish all the time. They contemplated Arizona, but in the end settled for Florida and in September they flew to Fort Lauderdale and bought an apartment right on the beach facing the rising sun. Never again would Mary have to suffer an English winter but the move was a great sacrifice for Dick. 'He would much rather never have gone to live in Florida because of being away from England in the jumping season,' Tim Fitzgeorge-Parker told me.

Throughout 1980 Penny Chase was more of a word factory than ever. Apart from the work on the Piggott biography, two new short stories were published during the year. In January *Woman's Own* ran *Two to One Against*, a tale about a plump, plain, fifty-two-year-old woman's infatuation for the young jockey who rides her horses, and the publishers Gollancz commissioned *The Day of the Losers*, the story of a crook laundering stolen money by betting on the Grand National, for a new anthology. Both stories are based on absurdities, though *Two to One Against* gave a convincing portrait of the cynical contempt with which some jockeys and trainers exploit their rich owners, and both were reprinted elsewhere, though *Two to One Against* was renamed *Spring Fever*. A revised edition of Mary's *Beginner's Guide to Flying*, with better diagrams, was also retitled *Flying Start* when it was published in August, and there was the next novel to be researched, *Reflex*, for which Mary excelled herself. With incredible dedication she studied how to become a serious photographer, a professional with all the complex equipment to allow her to process, develop, print, enlarge and alter her own pictures. As usual with Mary there was nothing half-hearted about her research: she became such a good photographer that she was offered several professional commissions, Dick's publishers in Britain and the US paid her to photograph several book jackets, and Putnam asked her to produce a poster of Dick with a horse. 'I think I could almost make a living as a photographer if I had to,' she told me in July 1980, 'but the books make a good living.' She was hoping to take the photograph for the jacket of the Lester Piggott biography and perhaps to produce an entire book of pictures of Piggott. 'On that holiday in Penang I took a lovely picture of Lester the Domestic Man,' she said. 'He was carrying the household junk and wearing a little sunhat with Snoopy on it.'

To complete the research she picked the brains of two professional photographers, Bernard Parkin and David Hastings, and spent £2,000 on photographic equipment – nearly £5,000 in modern terms – that she installed in the downstairs lavatory at Penny Chase, which became her darkroom. She even learned how to develop and print colour pictures, which most professionals still shied away from in those days, and became an expert on different types of films, paper, emulsions, exposure times and developers. She found out about the primary colours of light and discovered why colour negatives were always tinged with orange at the edges and how to turn yellow into blue. She even learned how to coax secret, hidden pictures from apparently blank strips of film by using a bottle of Ajax window cleaner.

The novel that grew out of all this research, *Reflex*, tells how jockey/photographer Philip Nore, who lives in Lambourn, investigates a mystery involving another photographer and some naughty blackmail photographs. It is one of the best of the Francis books, with a taut start, a riveting plot, some baffling photographic puzzles (invented for the book by Ron Massey) and good characters who change and develop as much as a photographic negative. Nore, for instance, seems at first to be the typical psychologically damaged Francis hero: an illegitimate, orphaned son of a heroin addict who has been raised by a couple of homosexuals. Yet he is in fact most unusual – and much more interesting than most – because he has often been corrupt and deliberately lost races on the instructions of his crooked owner and trainer. Like Sid Halley, he is not some impossible paragon of virtue but properly human, with failings and weaknesses. There is also a memorable shock and a splendid ending. Above all there is a special rich texture to *Reflex*, a stylish depth that marks it out as a four-star read. And finally there is a joke that demonstrates the Francises' broadminded sense of humour. It tells of two naked statues – male and female – that have been gazing at each other across a park for a hundred years. An angel takes pity on them, allows them to come to life for half an hour, and tells them to do what they've always wanted. The statues dart into the bushes where there is a lot of scuffling, giggling and rustling of leaves. After fifteen minutes they emerge looking hot but happy. The angel points out that they still have another fifteen minutes of life, so why not go and do it again? Eagerly they look at each other. Again? Yes! 'OK,' says the male statue, 'but this time I'll hold the ****ing pigeon down and you can shit on it.'

At the end of July, to coincide with the publication of *Flying Start*, I went to Blewbury to interview Mary for my *Sunday Express* column. As always it was moving to see how fond the Francises were of each other. They seemed to do almost everything together, even interviews, and were constantly looking at and touching each other. He was so proud of her. 'She's an amazing woman,' he said with his eyes shining. 'She's my number one editor. She helps me with words too.' Mary was so much more articulate than he – blonde, sharp, with shrewd blue eyes – but always kind and loving towards him and openly protective after thirty-three years of marriage.

Even though Dick was almost sixty he was still rising before dawn and driving over to Lambourn two or three times a week to ride out on the gallops for Merrick, who was now training racehorses for the actor Oliver Reed and had just become a father for the second time with the birth in Swindon of his and Barbara's daughter Bianca, soon to be nicknamed Binkie. Dick had also bought a racehorse and a half share in another, both of which were being trained by Merrick. Mary was still busy helping to run the dress shop in Wallingford and taking professional photographs, among them a photograph of the Queen Mother for the jacket of a book about her interest in National Hunt racing. 'Her Majesty was very kind to stand around while her photograph was taken,' Dick told Edwin McDowell of the *New York Times* a touch oleaginously a few months later.

'Dick does the gardening and I do the washing and ironing,' Mary told me, 'but I'm not madly houseproud and I don't do any housework. We have a girl who comes in to do that for two hours two mornings a week. I do cook to a certain extent but there's another girl nearby who is a superb cook.' It was good also to discover that there was at least something that Mary had not mastered: she admitted that she had never learned to type and that they had to hire a secretary to type each book out. 'My life is spread between the family and the promotion of Dick's books,' she claimed, but it was that night that she telephoned me at home to beg me not to speculate in my article that she might be the author of the books, as mentioned in the introduction to this book. My article that Sunday appeared under the headline 'THE AMAZING WOMAN DICK FRANCIS MARRIED' and began:

Dick Francis's wife Mary is the vital influence behind

his massively bestselling racing thrillers. Short of actually writing them for him, she could hardly contribute
more . . . Her vital part in the success of the books is
greater than most Francis fans suspect.

When *Reflex* was published in the autumn the reviews were
rightly enthusiastic and Michael Joseph decided to sponsor an
annual race, the Dick Francis Handicap, at Lingfield racecourse
early in December, and to invite a handful of booksellers and
journalists to join a boozy day out at the races. 'We went down
by train and had a very alcoholic lunch with a room and a box,
a very convivial day,' said Alan Brooke. 'He would sell at least
a hundred books on the day and it made Dick and Mary very
happy.'

Sadly the excellent reviews for *Reflex* were the last of a Dick
Francis book that Anthea Joseph, now chairman of Michael
Joseph, was to read. In January, still in her mid-fifties, she
died of cancer. At her memorial service Dick read a poem
and Mary was especially devastated by her death. 'She gets
very emotional about Anthea and sometimes cries at the mention
of her name,' a friend told me in 1998. Mrs Joseph's daughter,
Harriet Hastings, told me that her mother and the Francises had
been very close friends. 'We saw a lot of them when I was a
child,' she said. 'They would often come for Sunday lunch and
they got on very well.'

Dick suffered further when he was interviewed at the end
of January by Diana Cooper-Clark for a book she was writing
about detective novelists, *Designs of Darkness*, and she asked him
a series of profoundly literary and intellectual questions about
crime fiction that left him baffled. It was a cruel ordeal because
he was completely out of his depth. Ms Cooper-Clark kept
asking philosophical and technical questions about writing, and
quoting V. S. Naipaul, Julian Symons, Somerset Maugham, G. K.
Chesterton and André Gide, and using words like 'formalism'

and 'hermeneutics', and Dick kept giving gauche, inarticulate replies in clumsy language that few professional writers would ever use. 'I never liked the word "genre",' he said, 'because it means that you're so directed up a certain channel or along certain lines and I try not to follow those lines. I branch out into all different ideas and different lines really.' Explaining the popular appeal of crime novels, he remarked:

> They're enjoyable to read and you can read them if you go to work everyday. You can read them on the train or you come home in the evening and the television is terrible so you go to bed and read, or sit up and read. The good novelist writes such that the reader imagines himself doing it and that's what they like, they think, 'Ah, I could do that.'

When Ms Cooper-Clark asked him 'does the best detective novel subvert that logical structure? Should it be tied to feelings and the unconscious to make it a more esthetically satisfying experience?' Dick replied bravely: 'I suppose so, yes. I'm probably not one who paints my novels in that way.' Throughout the interview he referred weirdly to his 'painting' a novel, character or plot, and he added:

> I try to give my main characters a cross to bear because I don't consider myself first and foremost a novelist. I've written twenty books but I find that giving them a cross to bear and writing about this cross or their other handicaps does help me to fill up the pages. It gets me from page 1 to page 250 or 300, but if I had to write like some of the other novelists who don't write about crimes, I don't think I could fill the book up.

One cannot imagine any other professional novelist ever making such a naive confession.

Asked about fear, Dick replied: 'I'd hate to show fear myself for those things I write about. Mind you, I've got fear if a snake crawled into this room.' At one stage he had trouble understanding the word 'critically', and when Ms Cooper-Clark told him that his books improved all the time he replied:

> Mary often says to me (I worry a lot about the writing), 'Well, you've only got to write one like you wrote the last and it'll do.' 'Well,' I said, 'no, I don't want to write one like I wrote the last. I want to improve on the last, providing I can go on improving, that's all I want.'

Dick was also contradictory. 'I write because I enjoy writing,' he said, even though he had always told other interviewers that he disliked writing. He denied that his novels suggest that Good may triumph over Evil and then asserted that 'Right does triumph in the end' and added: 'I do try to write with a moral scene running through.' At one moment he said it was a pity that nowadays only jockeys, trainers and valets were allowed into jockeys' changing rooms at English racecourses, at the next he said 'it's probably better' that way.

It seems barely credible that Ms Cooper-Clark can have conducted this interview without it dawning on her that perhaps Dick was not quite the writer that she thought he was. When she asked him about the personal significance of the various crippling afflictions that torment so many Dick Francis heroes it must surely have begun to occur to her that perhaps all this physical suffering in the books derived not from *Dick*'s own aches and pains but from *Mary*'s constant battles with polio, muscular weakness, asthma and bronchitis. Towards the end of the interview Ms Cooper-Clark remarked, 'I'm astonished to hear you say that you don't think of yourself as a novelist,' and Dick replied: 'I still think of myself as a horseman.'

Neither Anthea Joseph's death nor Ms Cooper-Clark's grilling could diminish Mary and Dick's excitement when they migrated south that month to move into their new apartment near Fort Lauderdale, armed at first only with a sofa-bed and a table, to spend their first winter in the warmth of Florida, 'The Sunshine State'. The part they had chosen was not some vulgar amusement-park Florida of entertainment arcades and people dressed up as Donald Duck and Fred Flintstone but the elegant, tidy, restrained east coast of Broward, south of Boca Raton and Palm Beach, a dignified holiday and retirement colony with hundreds of luxury condominiums, smart shops and restaurants sprawling along the 300-mile beach that runs from Miami all the way north to Jacksonville. Parts of Fort Lauderdale are decidedly stylish and it has tidy streets, a concert hall, museums, art galleries and a twenty-three-screen cinema.

Florida had always appealed to the British – by the 1990s an estimated fifty thousand were living there – and it was a wonderfully appropriate place for a crime writer to settle since south Florida was notorious for its high crime and murder rate, especially in nearby Miami, was soon to give birth to the TV series *Miami Vice* and had already inspired the crime novels of John D. Macdonald, Elmore Leonard and Carl Hiaasen. As Matt Schudel wrote in the Fort Lauderdale *Sun-Sentinel* in 1994:

> This is the place where naked men walk down the street carrying severed heads, where animal sacrifice is a public issue, where the jails are filled with bank presidents and mayors, where politicians go to bed with hookers and become South Seas fugitives, where foreign dictators spend years in exile or in prison . . . Whatever the reason – the drug culture, grifters on the run, the broiling sun – things happen in South Florida that you never see anywhere else. Forget California and New York – South Florida is by far the weirdest place in the United States. Real life exceeds even the most fevered imagination.

Carl Hiaasen told Schudel:

> They don't believe a grown man would climb into a vat of creamed corn to wrestle a stripper but I have the original ad from the *Palm Beach Post*. There's so much material here that if you read the papers and have half a brain, the plots are sitting right there. You can get a good idea for a novel just by walking from one concourse to another in Miami International Airport.

No wonder so many crime and thriller writers came to live in the area – Thomas Harris, author of *The Silence of the Lambs*, Elmore Leonard, Robert Ludlum, Lawrence Sanders, Robin Cook – as well as authors like Marilyn French, James Michener and the Nobel Prizewinner Isaac B. Singer. Even the condominium where the Francises had chosen to live, the Sea Ranch Club, was shadowed by crime and mystery. Four years earlier a wealthy sixty-two-year-old widow who lived in an apartment there, Anne Sessa, who was said to keep $500,000-worth of jewellery in a bag, had suddenly disappeared and was never seen again. Her new yellow Lincoln Continental was found at Miami Airport but there was no record of her having taken a flight and her body was never found. It was only one of several criminal mysteries that were to haunt the Sea Ranch Club during the years that Dick and Mary lived there.

The three-bedroomed flat that they had bought for about $200,000 was apartment 310 on the second floor of the middle block of a vast, three-building, fourteen-storey condominium of 723 apartments right on a glorious, wide, white beach at 5000 North Ocean Boulevard – eight miles north of Fort Lauderdale, in Lauderdale by the Sea – and set back from the busy four-lane coast road to Palm Beach. The area surrounding Sea Ranch Club consisted mainly of low-rise ribbon development – small

hotels, motels, vacation apartments, condominiums, a Howard
Johnson restaurant – and each Sea Ranch building was protected
by squads of suspicious security guards dressed in ferocious
uniforms with shiny silver sheriff's badges that made them look
like the local cops. But beyond the Sea Ranch Club's imposing driveways, pillared entrances and security cordons it was
one of the most exclusive and luxurious havens on the coast.
Between each of the three towering buildings overlooking the
glittering, turqouise sea were lazy, laidback swimming pools,
neat paved paths, trees of palm and sea grape, immaculate
lawns and beautiful, tranquil landscaped gardens ablaze with
tropical shrubs, ferns and flowers: hibiscus, begonia, cryum
lily, ixora, impatiens. There were three hard tennis courts, an
all-weather putting green, two shuffleboard pitches, and each
building had its own gymnasium, billiard room, card room
and spacious lobbies that resembled those of plush hotels with
their security desks, sofas, easy chairs, lush plants, expensive
paintings, flower arrangements and piped music. The residents
were mainly elderly but right across the road was a large par-
king lot and shopping precinct with fountains and thirty-eight
shops: banks, boutiques, cafés, hairdressing salons, a supermarket, bakery, laundry, liquor store, travel agent and even a Chinese
restaurant and a dark pub with horsey pictures on the walls. The
precinct, the Sea Ranch Centre, even spelt 'centre' the English
way. Dick and Mary felt at home immediately.

When they arrived for their first winter they brought a vicious
British flu bug which felled them both for several days, but once
they started to sunbathe they began to glow with the certainty
that they had done the right thing. This was the life: blue skies,
warm skins and palm trees instead of grey clouds, ice, snow,
slush, constant drizzle, people sniffing. They made the mistake
that first year of staying in Florida for less than three months,
returning to England in time for the Grand National, where
it snowed and Mary was immediately laid low again with

bronchitis. They would not make the same mistake again: in future she was to spend much more time in Florida.

The change of American publisher was an immediate huge success. *Reflex* stayed in the *New York Times* bestseller list for four months and went on to sell 85,000 copies in hardback in the US – more than three times Harper's usual sale – to become a main Book of the Month Club selection as well as Detective Book Club and Mystery Book Club choices, and to attract a $440,000 paperback deal. The success was due not only to Putnam's massive promotion campaign and the screening of the *Mystery!* TV series but also to the fact that *Reflex* was such a good book. 'Horse racing is a big sport around here,' explained ex-Holt Rinehart editor Tom Wallace, 'and particularly on the east coast we're all Anglophiles: we call them Brit-sniffers.' As the *New York Times* critic John Leonard put it: 'Not to read Dick Francis because you don't like horses is like not reading Dostoyevsky because you don't like God.' Or as Michael N. Stanton suggested the following year in *Armchair Detective*:

> The satisfaction really comes not through [*the books'*] adherence to a formula but through their adherence to a sense of values: the price of learning to need, the value of being vulnerable, the inestimable worth of human love.

Unhappily the upheaval of the move to Florida probably explains why the next novel, *Twice Shy*, was so bad. It was delivered as always right on time – by the annual deadline of 8 May – but it was a great disappointment, one of the rare real duds. The idea for the book was born when Dick went to Gulfstream Park racecourse and spotted someone selling little computers that claimed to be able to forecast winners, but the book also owed a great deal to Felix, now twenty-eight and a physics teacher at Cheltenham Boys' Grammar School. Felix's hobbies were computers and shooting and he provided so much of the background research that the book was dedicated to him. In addition Mary bought a computer herself, did a great deal of research into programming, and as usual became such an expert that she seriously considered writing a beginners' guide to computers.

Despite all this careful research – or because of it – the book is often sluggish, weighed down as it is by detail about computers that often seems irrelevant. But what finally sinks the book is that it is broken in the middle so that the young physics teacher hero of the first part, Jonathan Derry – a character based on Felix – disappears almost completely and is replaced by his younger racehorse manager brother, William, based on Merrick, so that the bubble of tension in the first half is burst and it takes too long for tension to build up again. This is a particular pity because the basic idea is an excellent one in which a professional gambler produces a computer programme that can predict about three times out of ten which horse will win which race. Any owner of the programme stands to make a fortune, so of course a family of villains decides to acquire it even if that means murder. But the book never really gets going and at times is so poorly put together that it reads as if it were written by some incompetent ghost-writer. The story is forced, dogged and unconvincing – at least a dozen moments are ludicrously unlikely – and the whole thing curiously bloodless. The main baddie is so absurdly evil and over-the-top that he becomes a pantomime villain rather than a terrifying threat. There is yet again a sinister father/son relationship and unhappily lazy lines such as 'the three men stood there as if frozen' and 'all the mouths were open, like fish.' And after twenty novels some lines have been repeated so often that they seem like old friends: heroes in the Francis novels are always saying things 'mildly' and have a tendency to 'sketch a wave'.

There are of course some good lines as well and we learn that if you want to preserve fingerprints on a pistol you should never put it into a plastic bag because the prints will be obliterated by condensation. And the last few pages are marvellous. But none of this can compensate for the book's huge faults. I think that *Twice Shy* is a very bad novel indeed, but not all the critics agreed by any means. No matter how bad a new Dick Francis novel might be there were always two or three reviewers who would claim to have been enraptured by it, and by now the Francis juggernaut was unstoppable: whereas *Reflex*, a much better book, had sold 35,000 copies in hardback, Michael Joseph had already sold 45,000 of *Twice Shy* by Christmas and ordered a reprint. In America Putnam sold 100,000 in hardback and Harper and Row jumped on the bandwagon by republishing *Forfeit* and *Slay-Ride* in an omnibus edition and began to benefit from Putnam's success by selling so many copies of the earlier books that, whereas in 1982 they sent Dick royalties of only $13,000, in 1984 his royalties from Harper totalled nearly $73,000. And it was estimated that the books had by now sold at least eight million copies around the world in eighteen languages, the latest of them Turkish.

One reason for the success of the books was that, unlike most adventure stories, they appealed to women as well as men. Women swooned over the Francis heroes because they are 'brave, chivalrous and stoical,' suggested the novelist Jessica Mann in the *Daily Telegraph* in 1988. 'They are the modern version of the knight in shining armour galloping to the rescue on his charger.' Or as Lynda Lee-Potter put it when she interviewed Dick in June for the *Daily Mail*:

> His heroes are as intrepid, resourceful and brave as James Bond, but unlike the caddish Bond they are one day going to turn into loyal and passionate husbands. They are modest, sweet natured, intuitive, highly sexed but controlled with a puritan streak. They can't be bought, conned, bribed, intimidated or seduced. They are romantics with the eyes of a hawk, the mind of a razor, like a

rock in the face of adversity and, I suspect, literature's nearest approximation to most women's dream of a heart-lurching lover.

Miss Lee-Potter told Dick that women must find him very attractive. 'I don't have affairs, if that's what you mean,' he said sharply. He also remarked: 'If a stranger ever asked me what I did I wouldn't say "I'm a writer". I'd say "I'm a jockey".'

It was a glorious summer for Dick and Mary. *Whip Hand* won the Edgar Allan Poe Award. Dick had his first Merrick-trained runner at Royal Ascot, Kinniger. In August Merrick's wife, Barbara, gave birth to his third child, Timothy, in Swindon. The Crime Writers' Association gave its Gold Dagger prize to *Whip Hand* rather than to Colin Dexter's *Service of All the Dead*, which won the Silver Dagger. Michael Joseph sponsored not just one race but an entire Dick Francis Day at Plumpton races. And then there came the sudden miraculous appearance of Jeremy Thompson, a professor of pharmacology at the University of California, who turned up with every Dick Francis novel in hardback and asked Dick to sign them all. While Dick scribbled Thompson chattered about the effects of drugs on people and horses, and the Francises were riveted: what a great idea for the next book. They followed Thompson back to Los Angeles, soaked up everything they could learn from him about drugs, watched several operations and returned with sturdy foundations for the next book. Mary also did some research in December at a merchant bank in the City of London, where they met a young banker who seemed perfect for the main character, and just after Christmas they migrated to Florida again for the winter and the new book, *Banker*, began to be written.

Just before they left Dick gave a puzzling interview to Dudley Doust of the *Sunday Times* in which he revealed that the first draft of *Twice Shy* had had no fewer than three protagonists but 'I cut the main characters from three to two for length.'

Yet in the same interview he reiterated his regular boast that the novels never needed any rewriting: 'the first draft will be the last draft,' he said. How can you delete an entire character without some rewriting? Under the po-faced headline 'FRANCIS: THE PLOT THICKENS', Doust wrote: 'Dick Francis, a mild man in a grey cardigan, doesn't strike you as a millionaire thriller writer.'

They soon settled into a cosy daily routine in Florida. Dick would rise early and walk along the beach to the pier half a mile away and back. He would swim in the sea, and again with Mary in the freshwater pool, before they settled down to the day's work. Dick told the local paper that he wrote for six hours a day on the balcony overlooking the sea, where he watched the liners and tankers gliding past. In the afternoons there were all the local attractions to enjoy: the racetracks at Hialeah, Gulfstream Park, Pompano Park and Calder; the buzz of Miami and Palm Beach; the mysteries of the Everglades and Florida Keys; the glitzy shops of Las Olas Boulevard, and the theatres, museums and art galleries; the Sea Ranch tennis courts; the numerous country clubs; the boats on the nearby canals that ran the entire length of the coast and gave the area its tourist title 'the Venice of America'. Above all Mary and Dick revelled in the average temperature of 77° and the average eight hours of sunshine every day. In the evenings they ate out in their favourite restaurants: the popular, crowded beachside Sea Watch, just two hundred yards up the road; Charley's Crab for seafood; the swanky, expensive, exclusive Tower Club where 'they check your bank book before they let you through the door,' as my taxi-driver remarked in 1999. Dick soon became a local celebrity, signing books, making speeches, his birthday listed in the local paper, the *Sun-Sentinel*, and he and Mary quickly made several friends among the Sea Ranch residents, among them Harriet and Herb Gilbert, Diane and Lew Gaynor and Pete Johnson, and would often invite them out for dinner. 'But they weren't real social,' Pete Johnson told me, 'not big drinkers or party people. They weren't big in the social whirl of the condo, though Mary was more outgoing than Dick. He didn't jump into everything.'

Banker, the twenty-first novel, turned out to be one of the best of them all, a gripping yarn in which a young London merchant banker, Tim Ekaterin, lends a stud owner £3 million to buy a magnificent stallion for breeding only to discover that many of the horse's offspring turn out to be horribly deformed so that the horse is suddenly almost worthless. Skulduggery is afoot, and Ekaterin sets out to discover why, how and who. Thanks to all that research in Los Angeles, the intricate details of chemicals and herbs that play such a vital part in the book are utterly mesmerising and provide a brilliantly clever, complex but completely understandable scientific foundation for the plot. But the book is a triumph not only because it is a fascinating, deeply researched story but also because it is extremely well written – so much better than the previous novel that it seems unbelievable that the two were written by the same person. *Banker* was written by a real *novelist* with a proper feeling for words.

There are of course the usual small irritations. Two characters are given silly first names: Dissdale and Calder. Every twenty pages or so someone says something 'mildly', and of course we have a 'sketchy' wave, and people are regularly so surprised that their mouths hang open: in one case 'with his fillings showing' and in another the mouth 'formed an oval of apprehension and shock'. But there are also some splendid lines and observations, and the love interest is particularly well handled: Ekaterin yearns for his friend Gordon's wife but they resist temptation because Gordon is a good, kind man suffering from Parkinson's disease. Their repressed passion throbs so strongly that when the novelist John Mortimer interviewed Dick for the *Sunday Times* he asked why they had not consummated their love. 'We asked four friends about that, two married and two unmarried,' explained Mary, 'and they all agreed that Dick's characters shouldn't go to bed together while the husband was still alive, no matter how much they wanted to.'

Once again the hero develops a deep affection for a teen-age girl and, apart from the sentimental cop-out on the last page, *Banker* is an excellent novel and was praised lavishly by critics as respected as Marghanita Laski, the *Times Literary Supplement*, John Mortimer and Philip Larkin. 'Dick Francis can only be judged by his own high standards,' Larkin wrote in the *Observer*. 'The absolute sureness of his settings, the freshness of his characters, the terrifying climaxes of violence, the literate jauntiness of style, the unfailing intelligent compassion – all these make him one of the few writers who can be mentioned in the same breath as Fleming'. Larkin added: 'The temptation for Francis to become "a real novelist" must be very strong. Let us hope he resists it; he is always twenty times more readable than the average Booker [*Prize*] entry.'

Out in the real world fact was proving again to be just as thrillerish as Francis fiction: in the week *Banker* was published a valuable horse in a stables in Yorkshire was nearly killed by some mysterious thugs who slashed it with a knife.

When the book was finished Dick and Mary went to Canada, where he signed a thousand copies of *Twice Shy* and judged a horse show, and then to sign thousands more in three bookshops in New York, where the novel was at number three in the bestseller lists. In one Manhattan bookshop an awed woman whispered 'is it true the Queen reads your novels in manuscript?' and he had to tell her that it was in fact the Queen Mother who read an early copy of each book, 'though I understand they all read my books.' Another admirer asked for a tip for the Kentucky Derby. 'Royal Roberto,' said Dick. The horse did not win. They also went to Washington DC to watch the International race at Laurel, where one of the races had been named after Dick.

The books were now being published in nineteen languages, the latest being Icelandic, and another publicity trip took Dick alone to Scandinavia for three weeks, the longest he and Mary had been apart in thirty-five years. As usual they returned to England for the summer and bought a bigger motor cruiser, *Tenpenny*, to moor on the Thames six miles from Blewbury. It had two double cabins and a galley as well as a saloon, so that Merrick, Felix and their families could enjoy it, too. In an article in the *Sunday Express Magazine* under the headline 'THINGS I WISH I'D KNOWN AT 18' Dick confessed to several regrets in his life. He wished that he knew more about practical things like radio and television so that when they went wrong he could fix them himself, and he concluded, 'my biggest regret really in many ways is that I spent so little time at school.'

In January they fled to Florida again, this time for four months and armed with their first word processor, but on 8 February fact intruded shockingly on fiction yet again when the legendary 1981 Derby winner Shergar, which was worth about £10 million, was kidnapped in Ireland from the Aga Khan's Ballymany stud in County Kildare and held to ransom for £5 million – just like Chrysalis in *Blood Sport* sixteen years earlier. The syndicate that owned Shergar, which included the Aga Khan, Robert Sangster and Stavros Niarchos, refused to pay up and the five-year-old horse disappeared, never to be seen again. The mystery was not solved until 1998, when a convicted IRA murderer-turned-informer, Sean O'Callaghan, revealed in his memoirs, *The Informer*, that Shergar had been kidnapped by IRA terrorists who had been unable to handle the highly-strung thoroughbred when he went berserk in their horsebox and had had to kill him.

By spooky coincidence the next novel, *The Danger*, was also about kidnapping for ransom – not of horses but of people, which had become a common tactic of terrorists and criminals at the end of the 1970s. Mary and Dick had recently met a retired kidnap-recovery expert at a dinner party and had picked his brains about kidnappers and how to rescue their victims, and had persuaded him to introduce them to some of his ex-colleagues and security experts. The result was one of the best of all the Francis thrillers, with an intriguing subject, extremely well written and gripping, and an excellent finish. One recent kidnap victim, in 1978, had been the Italian Prime Minister, Aldo Moro, and others had been taken for ransom on the wild Italian bandit island of Sardinia as well as on the Italian mainland, so *The Danger* starts with a kidnap in Italy, this time of a brilliant young woman jockey, Alessia Cenci, the daughter of a multi-millionaire who is told that his daughter will be killed unless he pays a huge ransom. Signor Cenci turns for advice to an English kidnap specialist, Andrew Douglas, who flies out to Bologna and proceeds to pit his wits against the wily criminal behind the kidnapping and to advise the Italian police as to the best way of saving Alessia's life, ensuring her freedom and reducing the ransom demand as much as possible. The details of all the delicate negotiations with the kidnappers, and the psychological studies of all those involved, are utterly fascinating as Douglas and the unknown chief kidnapper joust with each other through the dramatic tensions of three more kidnaps. There is little horseracing in the book but my only quibble is that one very sadistic scene is too lovingly described: when the kidnappers seize a three-year-old boy they treat him horribly and threaten to castrate him, a nastiness that seems unnecessary. Autobiographically the book contains a heartfelt passage about how liberating it feels to live in the United States.

Quite rightly the critics raved about the book. 'His heroes are metaphors for England,' wrote John C. Carr in his book *The Craft of Crime*, which was published in Boston that year and explained why the books were so popular even in the United States. 'Francis's heroes now are less concerned with enduring pain and more concerned with becoming good and useful and loving men,' wrote Carr. 'But what's most important is that they show us how to overcome our fears, how to conquer ourselves.

This attitude, that one must first conquer oneself, is very English. Charm, courage, and competence are also very English, as the world knows. And that is probably the elusive factor in any analysis of Francis's success.' Carr managed to make four errors of fact in his first twelve lines but his literary assessments were sound and he noted perceptively that the author of the Francis books tended to suck up to royals and aristocrats, to sneer at the *nouveaux riches* and to overdo the sadistic scenes. He reported that Dick had told him that British aristocrats tended not to be criminals but that 'Latin characters come over here and some Mediterraneans can be very nasty.' During the interview Dick referred to Mary less than aristocratically as 'the wife', and he and she were in fact the ultimate example of a *nouveau riche* couple.

That summer they returned as usual to England to holiday with the family in Paignton and to potter about on the Thames in their new boat, with Mary steering and issuing orders on a new walkie-talkie and Dick jumping on and off to secure the boat on a bank or in one of the numerous locks. They loved sharing the pastoral peace and quiet of messing about on the river and relished the silence of drifting past fishermen and meadows, past boathouses and elegant mansions with lawns sweeping down to the water, the grazing cattle, the gliding swans and bustling ducks, the numerous excellent riverside restaurants. They loved the *suburbanness* of it all, for there was about Dick and Mary's pleasures something very English middle-class suburban. They were multi-millionaires now but had hardly changed at all. And Dick's good manners were still as boyishly impeccable as ever. Michael Joseph's Editorial Director during the early 1980s, Philippa Harrison, told me:

I know of almost no writers who don't start behaving badly once they've made it, but Dick always behaved like a perfect gentleman. Loyalty and thanking people is a rare experience for publishers these days. Dick was a quite exceptional author.

Ever since the publication of George Orwell's sinister novel *Nineteen Eighty-Four*, 1 January 1984 had threatened to be an ominous date, but for Dick it brought another accolade: in the British New Year honours list he was awarded the OBE, which made him an Officer of the Order of the British Empire. He and Mary immediately escaped the British Empire by flying off to Florida, where Edward Zuckerman interviewed him for the *New York Times* and noted that, although Dick was apparently writing a novel about wines (*Proof*), and had apparently already referred in it to Epernay champagne, he kept calling it 'Empernay' and Mary had to correct him twice. 'At least he's got it right in the book,' she said. This time they stayed in Florida for six months, though Dick returned to England briefly in February, and they both returned in March to go to Buckingham Palace with Merrick and Felix to collect Dick's OBE from the Queen, undeterred by the jovial old English jest that OBE stands for Other Buggers' Efforts. 'She told me how much she enjoyed my books,' Dick told the *Evening Standard* as he emerged from the Palace.

His trip to the Grand National that year had a special significance because after years of campaigning to save Aintree he had recently become a trustee of a group that had been set up to protect its future and to run it under a 999-year management agreement, Aintree Racecourse Ltd. In April Dick was off again, this time to New York, where one of his fans had persuaded him to present the city police with a horse called Halley, named after Sid Halley. Nobody asked how Dick could write such good books so fast yet still have time to spend weeks in England and gallivant about during the very months that he was supposed to be writing them.

Sheila Murphy, Michael Joseph's Publicity Manager from 1984

to 1987, told me she was also struck by Dick's inarticulacy when he gave interviews:

> The only time I ever heard him say anything interesting in an interview was when he was being interviewed by Brian Matthews of BBC Radio London. Dick said (really rather sadly, I thought) 'my life ended when I stopped racing', and Matthews never picked him up on it. There was also an incredibly funny interview with Dick in some very literary magazine in which the interviewer keeps asking about the semiotics of the racing novel and Dick gives a series of monosyllabic answers – *yes, no, yes, no* – throughout. On the whole he was like that quite a lot of the time in interviews: very obliging, very pleasant, but *nothing*. It became quite difficult to get people to interview Dick by the time I got there because most people said he'd got nothing to say.

Mary, on the other hand, was forcefully articulate. At a London dinner party during the miners' strike in 1984 she and Dick sat at a table with two left-wing authors, Stan Barstow and Barry Hines, who were furious when she said the miners were lazy and greedy and that her father's employees had done more work in a day than the miners did in a week. One of the guests told me:

> She then said something which was so vicious about the miners' strike that all the colour went from Stan Barstow's face and he said 'You've come closer to making me lose my temper than anybody in the last 30 years'. Somehow we got onto the issue of the women anti-nuclear protesters at Greenham Common and Mary said that every woman who went to Greenham should be made to clean lavatories with toothbrushes. The whole table was in a state of absolute tension because it was broadly

a left-wing table. I had never experienced the feeling that there was then at that table. Then Dick said – perfectly! – 'have you heard the one about the Irishman, the Scotsman and the Englishman?' . . .

The crime novelist and critic H. R. F. Keating remembered an occasion after a Detection Club dinner at the Garrick Club when Mary 'had a real upper and downer with Katharine Lyall [*Whitehorn*] over some tiny thing that came up between them. I don't remember what it was but I remember it was nearly to the point of blows being almost exchanged. They were shouting at each other, red-faced. Mary's very right wing.'

The long campaign by British authors to be paid a penny or two each time their books were borrowed from Britain's public libraries had finally been won, and in February the first of these Public Lending Right payments were made to hundreds of authors: in Dick's case the maximum amount of £5,000 because more Dick Francis books were borrowed than those of any author except Catherine Cookson.

The next book, *Proof*, was set in the world of wines and spirits and racing was only marginal, but it was again one of the best of the Francis thrillers – the third superb novel in a row. Mary spent hours picking the brains of a couple of wineshippers, Barry Mackaness and her Scottish wineshipper brother-in-law, Dick Yorke, and she spent hours questioning her local wine merchant, Margaret Giles of Pangbourne Wines, who ran a little off-licence in a village ten miles from Blewbury. She discovered exactly what it was like to run a booze shop and how much hard physical labour it involves; how malt and grain whiskies differ; that if you want a cheap wine to drink with Chinese food you should go for Bergerac, Soave or Côtes du Ventoux; that Sauternes are just right with curry, ham or anything sweet; that there is only one food that is completely incompatible with wine, and that's grapefruit. In her usual dedicated fashion she became such an expert that eight years later she and Dick were to go into business with Miss Giles and to invest in Pangbourne Wines themselves. It seemed impossible for Mary to research any subject without becoming professionally involved in it.

Proof's hero is a young wine merchant, Tony Beach, who was left fatherless at the age of eleven, is now grief-stricken and lonely after the death of his beloved wife, Emma, and is burdened with guilt: he feels he is a coward because his father and grandfather were both immensely brave soldiers and horsemen, and he believes that Emma's death was his fault because she developed high blood pressure after he made her pregnant. Tony Beach is the classic Dick Francis hero: lonely, unhappy, self-doubting, wounded. He discovers that several cheap wines and whiskies are being sold fraudulently under expensive labels and sets out to track down the criminals responsible. The result is an excellent thriller that starts with a vivid crash and is very well written throughout. The book has some small flaws and repetitions. There is, for instance, yet another bad father/son relationship, and a couple of the jokes have already been used in previous novels. It is also startling to read that a middle-aged woman who drinks a bottle of gin a day isn't 'quite' an alcoholic. Still, when *Proof* was published in September the *Times Literary Supplement* said rightly that it was 'put together as brilliantly as ever' and in the USA *Publishers Weekly* reported that it was 'the best of Francis's bestsellers so far . . . it's a corker'.

The status of the books in America was now so high that even the feminist literary critics were praising them. Carolyn Heilbrun, the feminist Professor of Literature at Columbia University and a mystery writer herself, had become a fan, and another feminist academic, Marty S. Knepper, wrote a long, serious chapter lauding the Francis *oeuvre* in a book entitled *Twelve Englishmen of Mystery*. Ms Knepper, an Adjunct Assistant Professor of English at Augustana College and author of an article with the alluring title *Agatha Christie – Feminist?*, raved about the Francis books, especially because their heroes were not macho brutes like the heroes of most mystery stories by male authors such as Mickey Spillane, Dashiell Hammett, Raymond Chandler and Ross Macdonald. She wrote:

> The message in one hard-boiled mystery after another is that women cannot be trusted. Women in hard-boiled mysteries are not allowed to be three-dimensional human beings. They are portrayed as flat and emotionless. Francis's treatment of women characters is a notable contrast . . . [*he*] develops his women as human beings as they exist in the real world, not nightmarish specters that haunt men's dreams or helpless, clutching, dependent creatures . . . Francis' heroes, unlike most hard-boiled heroes, prefer women with lively minds with whom they can have long-term relationships rather than women with beautiful bodies with whom they can have one-night stands.

Ms Knepper would have been less surprised by the attitude of the author towards women had she realised how much Mary contributed to the writing of the books.

A month after *Proof* was published the Sea Ranch Club was devastated by the first of a series of scandals that was to hit it over the next few years. In October the sixty-four-year-old Vice-President of the residents' association, John R. Rhodes, resigned after he was arrested for grand theft following an alleged bank robbery. Nine months later he was also charged with conspiracy to import and distribute heroin. And in between those dates, on 4 March 1985, came the biggest scandal of all when another Sea Ranch director, seventy-five-year-old Roswell Gilbert, murdered his seventy-three-year-old wife in their apartment on the tenth floor of the building next to Dick and Mary's after fifty-one years of marriage. Gilbert, a retired electronics engineer, shot his wife, Emily, twice in the head with a 9mm Luger pistol as she lay on the sofa in their living room because he could no longer bear to watch her suffering after years of Alzheimer's Disease and osteoporosis, he told the police. But two months later he was found guilty of first-degree murder and sentenced to life in prison, where his seventy-sixth birthday present from his daughter was a copy of *Banker* by Dick Francis. Eventually Gilbert served five-and-a-half years and was released in 1990, at the age of eighty-one, and he lived on for many more years. While he was in prison hundreds of sympathisers – including Dick and Mary – wrote to the Governor of Florida to ask for clemency, but more than a dozen of Gilbert's Sea Ranch neighbours formed a letter-writing pressure group to oppose his release. His daughter, Martha Moran, told the *Sun-Sentinel* that she thought their opposition was 'based on petty condo politics because my father was a director of the condo, and they might have disagreed with certain attitudes my father had.' The manager of the building, Gene Hudack, agreed. 'Condo politics,' he said. 'Gilbert had opposed them so they got even.' A former member of the Sea Ranch directors' board, Sue Shaffer, who was later to become a friend of the Francises, added that some of the residents 'had an ax to grind with Roswell. They were never happy with the way the building was run.' The rows and rivalries between the directors of the three Sea Ranch buildings became so blatant and vociferous that four different legal firms became involved, huge legal costs were run up and the *Sun-Sentinel* later described the situation as 'a civil war'. This poisonous atmosphere of intrigue and antagonism at Sea Ranch was to grow even worse over the next few years and eventually to affect Dick and Mary so badly that in the end they went to live elsewhere.

It was five years since a Francis novel had been firmly set in the racing world and many Francis fans cheered when the next book, *Break In*, plunged deep back into the colourful equine world of racecourses, bookmakers and trainers' yards in Lambourn and Newmarket, and turned out to have a hero who was a champion jump-jockey. Just as Felix had helped greatly with the research for *Twice Shy*, so did Merrick with this one. He had been a trainer for ten years now and because he was not very successful he knew only too well the constant worries and problems of trying to make a living training racehorses. The book, which was dedicated to him, showed how easily a young trainer like Merrick could have his business ruined by tabloid journalists printing lies about him and suggesting that he cannot pay his bills and that his hugely rich father is refusing to help him out.

It is a highly readable story at the start and some of the descriptions of amoral Fleet Street characters are devastatingly accurate, especially the striking portrait of a tough but beringed and braceletted 'tiger-lily' of a woman journalist who was surely based on the famously bitchy *Daily Express* columnist Jean Rook. Several paragraphs in the book about the Press and its cynical, sleazy, inaccurate, spiteful ways are written with such passion that Mary and Dick were obviously thoroughly disgusted with journalists even though they always seemed eager to give yet another Press interview if it would help sell more books. The cuttings files of British newspaper libraries bulge with more interviews with Dick Francis than with any other novelist. *Break In* is also fascinating in its graphic description of the precarious life of a small, struggling trainer: the huge permanent overdraft, the difficult owners, the endless worries about horses and how to pay the stable lads. There are illuminating glimpses, too, of the life of a jockey trying to keep his weight down by eating little but lobster and fruit and realising that even if he becomes Champion Jockey his fame will be gossamer thin and forgotten in a few years.

Unhappily, though, the book quickly goes flabby. Its hero, Kit Fielding, is so noble and self-sacrificing that you want to smack him. The main villain is so ridiculously villainous, full of hatred and two-dimensional that he seems not human at all but just a pantomime joke, and the others are quite unbelievable.

The book is simply incredibile. Even the names are sillier than usual – Maynard Allardeck, Nestor Pollgate, Princess Casilia, Wykeham Harlow, Christmas Fielding – and time and again (in my case fifteen times) you shake your head in utter disbelief. People just don't *behave* like this. And the book contains not just one but two bad father/son relationships, and the ending is quite absurd.

Equally incredible, there was barely a squeak of protest from the reviewers. 'His best so far,' said the distinguished novelist Susan Hill. The *Financial Times* agreed and so did *The Times*, *Daily Telegraph* and *New York Times*. Re-reading *Break In* in 1998 it seemed impossible that they could have been reading the same book. Of all the critics only Marilyn Stasio, in her syndicated American book review column, reported that the story was 'clumsily told' and referred to the author's 'simplistic moral code' and sadism, the villains' 'preposterous proportions of wickedness', and the hero's 'dumb risks' and stupidity in not going to the police. But by now even the tiniest criticism of a Dick Francis novel had become almost pointless. *Break In* quickly sold 70,000 copies in hardback in Britain, more than any previous Francis novel, and many more in the States. For me it is best forgotten except for the fact that in retrospect it seems to have been telepathic. It was published just six months before the Lester Piggott biography at a time when Piggott was being considered for a knighthood and just a year before he was charged with tax dodging, and with uncanny prediction it describes how a racing man who is up for a knighthood loses it because of rumours about him circulating in Fleet Street.

The Piggott book may explain why *Break In* was so bad and its ending so hurried, because early in 1985 Piggott telephoned Dick to say that he was going to retire in October, which meant that the Francises faced a frantic rush to finish the biography even though they had already spent a dozen years tinkering with it. Dick hurriedly returned to England in May to watch a special two-horse 'superstars' Flat race at Warwick that had been arranged between Piggott and the recently retired National Hunt Champion Jockey John Francome – Piggott won, of course – and in November Dick flew to New York to watch one of Piggott's last races in America on the Breeders' Cup day at Aqueduct. 'Lester's helpful but not terribly communicative,' Dick told the *Sunday Telegraph* diarist ominously in September, 'but then he's never been very communicative with anyone.' A few years later he told the *Western Mail*: 'I knew it would be tough. Nobody who'd ridden so many horses could possibly remember names, dates and places, and . . . what further complicated things was that Lester couldn't communicate . . . He's very deaf and it's not easy to pick up what he says.'

Despite the rush to finish the Piggott book, Dick returned to London in September for the publication of *Break In*, to be a guest of honour at one of the famous Foyle's literary lunches at the Dorchester Hotel, and to enjoy the Dick Francis Day at Plumpton racecourse before returning to Florida in a frantic hurry to finish the biography and deliver it to Michael Joseph in time for them to edit, illustrate, print and publish it in four months.

For Dick and Mary, exhausted after completing two books in one year, there was a breathing space of a couple of months before work had to start on the next novel. They used it to move into a bigger apartment at the Sea Ranch Club because their application for American residents' visas had finally been granted and they would no longer have to spend half the year in Britain. From now on their permanent home was in Florida. They had cut the umbilical cord.

CHAPTER 15

Exile

(1986–92)

They say that if you move to Florida you add ten years to your life and it worked for Mary and Dick. They sold their second-floor apartment in B building at the Sea Ranch Club and bought a bigger, south-east facing flat on the sixth floor of A building with three bedrooms, three bathrooms and superb views over the Atlantic from every room. After thirty-one years in the Blewbury bungalow they put it up for sale, but kept the boat on the Thames so that Merrick, Felix and their families could enjoy it.

'Dick sold the landing strip at the back of the house,' his neighbour Hazel Dexter told me. 'He said he was selling it because he needed the money to buy the place in Florida.' Her daughter Jane added: 'The land got sold nearly immediately but the house was empty for a couple of years because it was right on the main road.'

The new Sea Ranch apartment, number 609, resembled a set for some glossy American TV series with its huge living room, glass walls overlooking the beach, large mirrors, white furniture, white carpets and photographs everywhere of Merrick, Felix and the grandchildren, whose nickname for their grandfather was

'Grandick'. The study had a big computer, a cramped desk, the Gold Dagger award, a signed photograph of the Queen Mother with Devon Loch, a huge photograph of Dick himself, and on the wall there hung a sign that said: 'I've been reading so much about the bad effects of smoking, drinking, over-eating and sex that I've decided to give up reading.'

Dick denied that they had moved abroad for tax reasons but they did not return to Britain for a year, which made them eligible to become tax exiles so long as they did not return to Britain for more than ninety days in any subsequent tax year. He missed even his beloved Grand National that year and instead of the usual family holiday in Paignton they flew the boys and their families out to Florida, the first of many visits. Dick and Mary blossomed in the sub-tropical warmth and developed an idyllic daily routine. He was still very fit and at 5ft 8ins he weighed 11 stone – just a stone more than when he had been at his peak as a jockey. He would be up at 6.30, make telephone calls to Britain because the cheap rate lasted until 7 a.m., watch the *Good Morning America* breakfast TV show, walk a couple of miles along the beach, swim for half an hour in the sea, rinse off with a quick dip in the pool, dry off in the sun, and then spend the morning doing any work that had to be done. John Keller, the garden maintenance manager at Sea Ranch, told me: 'If we were making a noise sometimes Mary would come out on their balcony just up there and put her finger on her lips and point inside to say that Dick was writing.' After a light lunch Dick would swim again, slop around in shorts, listen to the surf breaking on the sand six floors below, watch from the balcony as the huge cruise ships and tankers sailed in and out of Port Everglade, or replay video recordings of his old races or his *This is Your Life* programme. He bought a new Mercedes and enjoyed driving out and about. Each evening there would be a drink and the TV news at six o'clock, a cheroot, a bottle of wine, the moonlight gleaming on the ocean, and they ate out in restaurants at least twice a week.

Dick would always be in bed by eleven o'clock, though Mary liked to stay up at least until midnight. 'Mary hates going to bed,' Dick told Mary Kemp of the *Daily Express* in 1992, adding somewhat unfortunately: 'Ladies are made for the night.'

Bravely he told friends that he missed nothing about England except his favourite Panatella Castellas cheroots, Yorkshire pudding, pork crackling and old-fashioned ginger beer in stone jars, but he followed the daily runners and racing results eagerly in the English newspapers, which arrived about a week late, and he had the *Horse and Hound* delivered. 'I love it here,' he told the *Telegraph Weekend Magazine* in 1990. 'I feel perfectly at home . . . It is a wonderful way of life, and England is not all that far away, particularly by Concorde, which I prefer.' He was especially impressed by American hospitality: 'When I first arrived I was overwhelmed by their generosity. It took a while to accept that they were genuine, but they are.'

Now that they were living permanently in America they retired at last as directors of Merlix Air in March, giving their hundred shares – 10 per cent of the total – to Viscount Chelsea and Cadogan Estates, but Merlix continued to declare huge annual losses until it finally stopped trading at the end of 1993 with accumulated losses of a whacking £642,165.

By now the Francis books had sold an estimated twenty million copies around the world and were such certain bestsellers that the publishers had agreed amazingly not to change one word. Equally remarkable, they promised to keep every one of the books in print so long as a new one was written each year. 'I'm sure Mary must have negotiated that!' chuckled Gavin Lyall. The novels had by now become a target not only for academic theses but also for full-length books, the first of which – *Dick Francis* by Melvyn Barnes, a detailed, in-depth 'biocritical study' – was published in New York in 1986. Barnes, the Director of Libraries and Art Galleries for the City of London, was a Francis fan but not uncritical. He thought the romantic element in the books was weak and often irrelevant, but defended the sadism and violence and reckoned that their author was an enthralling plotter, a shrewd judge of character and a writer of 'uncommon wisdom and compassion' who had made 'an outstanding contribution to popular literature.' In particular, he wrote: 'Francis is the complete master of pace, as any successful jockey must be. Knowing when to hold back and when to surge forward is a vital element in a well-run and well-planned race, and his novels display this knack admirably.' It would be fun to see Mr Barnes's expression should he ever hear that the books were co-written by a woman who did not especially like horses.

Lester – The Official Biography was published at last in March and went straight to number one in the bestseller list. 'I'd been working on his book for all of eighteen years,' Dick told the *Western Mail* inaccurately in 1989: in fact it was only thirteen years. 'The book, though, was very well received,' he added – a claim that was utterly untrue. The biography was in fact so biased in Piggott's favour that it was condemned by the reviewers because every one of Piggott's less pleasant character traits were airily dismissed as though they were quite normal and acceptable. Piggott's legendary meanness and greed? Ah, well, that wasn't his fault at all, according to Dick: his mother had always warned him to be careful with money, and anyway he was jolly generous to his two daughters. What about his notoriously cold, monosyllabic rudeness, then? Well, he didn't mean to be rude: it was just that poor Lester was a bit deaf and had this speech impediment. What about his selfish 'jocking off' of other jockeys who had already been engaged to ride better horses than his? Well, it was only natural that Lester would want to ride the best horse in any race, and anyway it was the owner's fault, not Lester's. So what about his ruthless riding, which sometimes endangered other jockeys? Well, Lester just wanted to win for the owners and punters and the ferocious riding was often the fault of his rival jockeys, who would try to squeeze him out. What about his numerous suspensions? Well, people always had it in for Lester and he was always being victimised by the stewards.

The gist of the book was that Piggott was a genius who had been much misunderstood. Its bitty little chapters were decidedly short of anecdotes, narrative or any real insights into Piggott's character, and he had refused to be quoted on anything remotely personal, especially money, so that the end result was little more than a catalogue of his brilliant racing career, padded out at the end with ninety-five large pages – a third of the book – listing every one of his winners over thirty-seven years. To be fair, it had been a difficult book to write. 'Dick told me afterwards "I'll never never never never never write another biography",' said Tim Fitzgeorge-Parker. 'It was an appalling book. It was *dreadful*. Dick said, "Mary and I have hundreds of tapes of Lester that are completely unintelligible. All of us in racing know a lot of Piggott stories, but every time they put one in, the Piggotts took it out."'

There were several poor reviews. David Hadert said in the *Guardian* that the book was sycophantic and lacked objectivity. In the *Observer* Hugh McIlvanney wrote that there was 'something slightly disturbing' about the book and its 'blandness of tone': 'the reader is left with an uneasy conviction that the prime sources did not extend far enough beyond Piggott and his immediate family and two or three trainers.' McIlvanney added: 'there is an element of convenient rationalisation in the treatment of his attitudes to money and the usurping of rides assumed by other jockeys to be theirs.'

The full extent of the shabbiness of the Piggott biography was revealed eleven years later, in 1997, when TV's Channel 4 broadcast a devastating profile of Piggott in its *Secret Lives* series that painted a very unattractive portrait indeed. The powerful, hour-long programme, produced by Dominic Prince for Diverse Productions, included revealing, disillusioned interviews with the racehorse owner Robert Sangster, the ex-Champion Jockey Willie Carson and the racing journalist Charles Benson and accused Piggott of being an 'obsessive miser', an 'incorrigibly ruthless rider', and of betting on races even though jockeys were not allowed to bet. 'Money is his god,' said Benson during the programme, and he called Piggott 'avaricious', and Carson claimed that Piggott would delight in 'cheating someone out of sixpence' and admitted that being 'jocked off' by Piggott was 'very hurtful'. The programme included an hilarious clip from a 1981 TV programme in which Piggott had asserted that it was 'impossible to save much money' because of taxes, yet the *Secret Lives* programme reported an 'obvious tax fiddle' when the trainer Henry Cecil had sent letters to several of his owners asking them to pay Piggott in cash and to destroy the letter – a letter that led the Inland Revenue to raid Piggott's home. Even when Piggott agreed to pay a huge amount of back tax, the programme claimed, he wrote the cheque on a secret, undeclared bank account, which led inevitably to his arrest.

In the end the book was a disgraceful, mealy-mouthed white-wash that described Piggott as 'an ambassador . . . for what's best in sport'. Dick and Mary should have been ashamed of them-selves and certainly none of the upright heroes of the Francis nov-els would ever have written such a misplaced book, especially at a time when the Inland Revenue had already announced that it was making a major investigation into Piggott's tax affairs. Dick's 'adoration of Lester verges on worship,' wrote Brian Vine in the *Daily Mail* after an interview at the end of 1985. Hero-worship is not the best stance for a biographer. To take just a single example of how the biography glossed over the truth, one accusation against Piggott was that when he lost his whip during a race in 1979 he had snatched the whip of a French jockey, Alain Lequeux. The biography denied the story, claiming that Piggott had merely 'reached over and put his hand enquiringly on Lequeux's whip, more or less asking for the loan, and Lequeux, after a second or two, let him take it.' The *Secret Lives* researchers were having none of such a ludicrous explanation: they spoke to Lequeux himself, who insisted that Piggott had indeed snatched his whip. Told that Piggott claimed he had only asked to borrow the whip, Lequeux enquired: 'How? I don't speak English and he doesn't speak French.' The biography even had the gall to claim that Piggott wanted Dick to write the truth about him, and that the public's perception of him was 'always unerringly accurate . . . They expected honesty . . .'

Nine months after the biography was published Piggott was arrested on ten charges of tax evasion involving £3 million, and eventually sentenced to three years in prison in October 1987. During the trial his own counsel told the court that Piggott's 'miserliness' was 'a lifelong habit'. When the scandal broke, the media from all over the world besieged Dick in Fort Lauderdale, begging for interviews and insights, 'but I couldn't help,' he told Pauline Peters of the *Evening Standard* five years later. 'I knew nothing. Lester had made it plain that he didn't want to talk about money – that was his most sensitive subject.' Dick stayed publicly loyal to Piggott, but after Piggott served a year in jail and had been stripped of his OBE by the Queen, Dick confessed to the *Western Mail* in 1989: 'Frankly, I wouldn't have done the biography had the court case come up first, but I still think Piggott was badly used and that they made an example of him.' Or as he told Lynn Barber of the *Sunday Express*:

> I feel very sorry for Lester, I'm afraid he's been made an example of . . . Most jockeys, you know, hate paying tax and if they can get cash as presents, they much prefer it. I know that every time you get a present you *should* declare it, but if someone gives you £100 in cash – well, it's human nature – you don't declare every penny, do you?

Don't you? A Dick Francis hero would.

In May Felix's wife, Anne, gave birth to their second son, William, in Banbury – they were living now in nearby Bloxham, where Felix was teaching mathematics at Bloxham College – and Dick and Mary went on yet another promotion tour of Australia, crossing the entire continent by rail, one of their favourite types of travel, and watching the greatest of all Australian races, the Melbourne Cup, where Dick was a guest of honour of the Royal Victoria Racing Club.

Because of the last-minute rush to produce the Piggott biography, Michael Joseph did not expect a new novel as well in 1986 but *Bolt* was delivered only a few weeks late, much to their delight. Because the book had to be written in a hurry it had the same characters as *Break In*, from the Champion-Jockey hero Kit Fielding and his fiancée Danielle de Brescou to the ridiculous pantomime villain Maynard Allardeck. This time Fielding defends Princess Casilia's husband against the vicious threats of his absurdly unlikely French business partner, Henri Nanterre, investigates the murders of several of the princess's racehorses by someone who kills them with a bolt, and suffers lovesick agonies because he thinks that Danielle has fallen for another man. Once again the plot and characters are utterly unbelievable and sometimes seriously silly, particularly the stilted, ludicrous relationship between Fielding and Danielle. When Dick and Mary moved to Florida permanently they were warned that it would be difficult to write decently so far from their roots, and so it seemed. *Bolt* was another stinker. In *The Times* Marcel Berlins wrote that 'Parts of the plot verge on the preposterous. Francis's villains have always been on the exaggerated side of villainy, but *Bolt*'s Henri Nanterre is altogether too incredible, reminding one of Peter Sellers playing Inspector Clouseau.' Yet once again, inexplicably, some of the reviewers raved and Susan Hill was again impressed. 'This is the sequel to *Break In* which I said was his best so far,' she wrote in *Good Housekeeping*. '*Bolt* is even better'. Michael Joseph printed 75,000 hardbacks, the book was serialised in the *Sunday Express* and Pan ordered a first paperback print-run of half a million copies.

Once their first year of exile was over, Dick and Mary resumed their regular trips back to Britain, he alone for Cheltenham and the Grand National, both of them for Paignton, the annual book-launch party in London and the Dick Francis racing days, which were held nowadays at Stratford or Uttoxeter racecourses. There were also regular trips to New York and other cities for book-signing sessions and to the Kentucky Derby to watch the racing, and like many elderly American couples they started going regularly on cruises, which they adored.

In 1987 they added a brief chapter to *The Sport of Queens* to bring the autobiography up to date – it covered the thirty years since the first edition in little more than a dozen unrevealing pages – and it was republished in a new edition, and during the summer Wendy Leigh interviewed Dick in Fort Lauderdale for the *Mail on Sunday*. Finding him in Florida, she said, 'the home of shopping malls populated by blue-rinsed Americans, all reeking of too much money and too few manners, is rather like visiting Father Christmas in Hawaii. It just doesn't seem quite right.' Dick, however, insisted that he loved living in America. 'England isn't what it used to be,' he said. 'If an American sees someone driving along in a Rolls, they say, "Gee, I must get one of those". But an English person says, "Why should they have that?" I much prefer the American attitude. There is too much jealousy in England.'

Strangely he could not remember when he had won the OBE even though it had been no more than two years earlier, but he told Ms Leigh that he and Mary 'love each other very much and hate sleeping in different beds. We are also very good friends.' No buttoned-up, stiff-upper-lip Dick Francis hero would ever say anything so emotional to a stranger. He told her, too, that they never argued. 'Dick refuses to argue with me,' Mary told her. 'He listens to me going on and on till I run out of steam.' In

June they celebrated their fortieth wedding anniversary with a party on the beach and were delighted when Merrick and Felix turned up unexpectedly, flying by Concorde. 'Mary and I are very much in love and always have been,' Dick told Jenny Knight of the *Sunday Times Magazine* a few months later.

They were now so rich that they had become interested in the intricacies of shares, investments and the gold market – subjects that were to provide the background for the next novel, *Hot Money*, which has as its pivotal character a multi-millionaire who has just made £30 million on a huge gold-investment coup, and which turned out to be as excellent as the previous one had been terrible. Yet again it seems barely credible that both books could have been written by the same person, for *Hot Money* is as witty, sparkling, sharp and penetrating as *Bolt* is dogged and dull. Despite the fact that its hero is yet another Francis protagonist who has had a dreadful relationship with his father, the father in question, sixty-eight-year-old Malcolm Pembroke, is such a wonderfully vivid character – an outrageous, extravagant, five-times-married, father-of-nine, multi-millionaire – that he casts a glow over the whole book. When Pembroke's fifth wife is murdered and it seems someone is trying to murder him, too, one of his sons, Ian Pembroke, finds himself acting as a buffer between his father and his numerous siblings, all of whom are greedy to get their hands on their father's millions before he spends them all. There are too many characters, but most of them are also vividly realised and the novel depicts sharply the nightmare tensions in a family stained by sons' and daughters' greed and ingratitude. The book was dedicated to Merrick and Felix – perhaps to assure them that it was not about *them* – the reviewers were rightly enthusiastic, and that year's PLR figures showed that twelve of the most popular hundred books borrowed from British public libraries were Dick Francises: fewer than the phenomenal Catherine Cookson, who had twenty-eight in the list, but more than Wilbur Smith, Danielle Steel, Jeffrey

Archer or Jack Higgins. And worldwide sales now totalled more than twenty-five million in twenty-two languages.

In October Dick hosted a five-day train journey across Canada with a party of tourists who each paid $2,500 Canadian to experience 'Murder on the Transcontinental Train'. As he and Mary boarded the train in Toronto an actor disguised as a blood-stained horseman approached them to claim that his horse had been stolen, and throughout the journey they and the passengers were regaled by a cast of actors playing out a series of grisly murders. Theatre-mad Mary especially enjoyed the thespian side of the journey, which took them three thousand miles across the continent to Vancouver, clattering along beside Lake Huron, teetering high above Lake Superior and passing through Winnipeg, Regina, Moose Jaw, Medicine Hat, Calgary and up and over the Rocky Mountains before plunging down towards the Pacific coast. They relished the constantly changing scenery and atmosphere of the trip as well as the actors' mystery: the bold, exciting architecture of modern Toronto with its skyscrapers of black glass and gold; the huge, empty, autumn landscapes of Ontario and Manitoba; the endless prairies; vast forests of pine; the brilliance of the Northern Lights at night. The massive wilds of Canada would provide a stunning backdrop for the next novel, *The Edge*.

Despite their emigration to America, Dick and Mary remained staunchly British and in June 1988, after making another book-promotion trip to Australasia, they joined two hundred other Britons at a soirée in Florida to celebrate the Queen's birthday, before joining a cruise to Alaska and returning to Britain for the summer and publication of *The Edge*. In Paignton in July with a family party of twelve that included all five grandchildren (now aged from two to fourteen), Dick was grilled for the *Sunday Express Magazine* by Lynn Barber, who reported: 'You'd never guess that he was an author. He himself is extraordinarily modest about his writing – even reluctant to talk about it. When

I asked what passage in *The Edge* he was proudest of, he gave an embarrassed laugh and said, "I can't think of any – sorry. I'm proud of all the *help* I was given with the research".' When she asked him why so many Dick Francis heroes have some physical handicap he gave her an extraordinarily unliterary reply. 'Well,' he said, 'it's only sort of to fill the book up. I mean I didn't think just the plot could get me through three hundred pages.' Miss Barber also noticed that when discussing the novels with Dick he 'never seems to be able to remember the names of his characters' and she added: 'It is striking that, even after all these years, Dick Francis still prefers talking about racing to talking about writing. "I was a champion jockey; I'm not a champion writer," he says bluntly.'

Back home in Florida in September he was interviewed for the *Daily Telegraph* by Jessica Mann, who noticed that when talking about the books he often used the word 'we'. 'I wish that Mary would let me put on the books "by Dick and Mary Francis",' he said. 'I couldn't do it without her. Dick Francis is a joint effort.' He added: 'I would *love* to live my life again. I have had a most enjoyable life. I am a very happy man.'

He told Fionnuala McHugh the same thing when she interviewed them for the *Daily Mail*'s magazine *Male & Femail*. 'All our friends are envious of the life we lead because it's so lovely,' he said, and Mary agreed. 'There hasn't been a great deal of change in forty-one years,' she said. 'He was always enormous fun and he still is.' Dick told Ms McHugh that because Mary's right arm had been so badly crippled by her polio he still had to do up the back of her dresses for her. Her arm was so weak that if she wanted to brush her hair she had to rest her elbow on something, but as always she was indomitable. 'She has a mind of her own,' he admitted. 'Character-wise I think she's the stronger.' Mary, too, made a poignant confession:

It would be wrong to say I've never thought of writing

a novel, but I don't think I'm going to do it really. I don't have the time and I've got accustomed to his success so I would expect to have good sales which probably wouldn't happen. I have no feeling of missing out on anything. I only say that because people always ask me. I feel fulfilled with what we've done together. We have the most terrific fun. I'm absolutely happy just to be with him.

Theirs was surely one of the greatest love affairs.

When *The Edge* – a story of blackmail and murder aboard the Canadian Transcontinental Mystery Race Train – was published in September not every reviewer was as flattering as usual. 'An edge is what it lacks,' sniffed Sue Montgomery in *Today*, adding that the book 'strains credibility to its limits . . . if the whole train-load had gone over a precipice half-way through it would have been a blessed relief.' In *The Times* Marcel Berlins noted that recent Francis novels had 'hinted at declining mastery' and had 'demonstrated thinness of plot, poverty of characterisation, and carelessness of writing.' The book was indeed not one of the best. It opens with a waffly, pedestrian beginning, with far too much scene-setting and unnecessary detail, and becomes bogged down with too many confusing characters, some real, some actors pretending to be real. Mary's enthusiasm for the theatre led not only to quotes from *Hamlet*, *Othello* and Dylan Thomas but also to a convoluted story-within-the-story – as performed on the train by the actors – which is often gauche or plain silly. Both hero and villain are unbelievable characters and most of their fellow travellers have ridiculous names: Torquil Kelsey, Julius Apollo Filmer, Daffodil Quentin and Cumber Young, not to mention Mercer, Bambi and Xanthe Lorrimore. And it simply beggars belief that a cast of professional actors would allow an amateur outsider to keep rewriting their script only minutes before each performance.

After the trip across Canada, Dick and Mary had developed a taste for mystery train travel and they joined another long 'whodunit' train journey – this time from New York to Los Angeles, stopping at Washington, Atlanta and New Orleans – for which the passengers paid $2,495 each and Dick was the special guest. Then it was off to Toronto, where he addressed the Canadian Thoroughbred Horse Association, and then across the Pacific to publicise the books in Japan, their best foreign language market. It seems odd that the Japanese should have been so keen on such English stories, though I was once given an explanation by another thriller writer, Brian Freemantle, whose own books also sold well in Japan. Freemantle pointed out that in a Japanese office it is the humblest, most burnt-out or least influential employee who is given a desk by the window because high-flyers are considered too busy to look at a view. Consequently millions of Japanese Window Men would identify with Window Man characters in novels, such as Freemantle's own hero, Charlie Muffin, and all those humble Dick Francis heroes, especially since they were always being beaten up, which would undoubtedly appeal to the Japanese taste for sadistic TV programmes and cruel game shows.

The Francises were fascinated by the otherness of Japan: the tiny houses; the workaholic, male chauvinist culture; the lack of emotion; the worship of golf; the way the Japanese were constantly bowing to each other and apologising for things that were not their fault; the custom that Japanese hosts give presents to their guests rather than vice-versa. They slept on the floor, ate raw fish, and were highly impressed by Tokyo racecourse with its huge bicycle park and baby crêche, and by the way that everything possible was made out of recyclable wood or paper, even the little wooden boxes out of which they drank saké. They were less enthusiastic about the non-Western lavatories – just a hole in the floor – and refused to eat fugu, the puffer fish delicacy that can kill you in seconds if the chef fails to remove all the poisonous bits. And of course the trip gave them the background for the next book but one, *Comeback*.

Back in Fort Lauderdale the Sea Ranch Club was riven as usual by scandal and infighting. In April 1988 a seventy-four-year-old Latvian who owned two of the apartments had been accused of collaborating with the Nazis and killing thousands of Jews during the Second World War and threatened with deportation. And early one morning in January 1989 the bullet-riddled body of a fifty-two-year-old homosexual taxi-driver was found on the beach outside the Sea Ranch: he had been murdered by another homosexual who had picked him up in a bar the previous night. Undeterred by such omens – or by the constant bickering and infighting among the elected residents who ran the club – Mary was persuaded by the manager of A building, Gene Hudack, who had by now become a friend, to stand for election as one of the three directors of A building's board of management, and was duly elected to serve for three years. 'She didn't need to campaign,' Hudack told me. 'Both she and Dick had such a wonderful reputation, everybody loved them. They had tremendous warmth and compassion and were so friendly. I never heard them say anything wrong about anybody.' But her time on the board – and especially in her last year, when she was President of the entire three-building condo – was eventually to become a nightmare and to drive her and Dick away from Florida all together.

Another unhappiness was the ending of Merrick's second marriage. Merrick and Barbara were finally divorced in July and Dick and Mary had to pick up some of the financial pieces. Their friend Elaine Mellor told me:

> Dick takes on board a lot of the financial responsibility for the family. He didn't mind doing it, but initially he didn't feel it was the *right* thing to do because he did feel was it setting a pattern? Was it *really* helping them? He

was really agonising about this one day when I met him at the races – about the time Merrick's second marriage was going wrong – and I said 'oh, *come* on, Dick, they're family, you love them, they love you, you've got the money to help them sort it – DO it, and don't *worry* about it! What makes it work is that his family are all genuinely nice people. If they were conmen you'd have a different scenario.

That year's novel, *Straight*, turned out once again to be an excellent thriller with a splendid opening and a nice puzzle. It was so well written, slick and readable that it gave the odd impression that while an excellent novelist was writing the books in the years with odd numbers – 1987, 1989 – some much inferior writer was churning them out in the even years. The story, which was set in the worlds of semi-precious stones and modern electronic gadgets, was researched as thoroughly as ever thanks to the help of a couple of Dick and Mary's neighbours, Joseph and Danielle Zerger, whose company Zarlene Imports dealt in semi-precious stones. But unlike some of the previous tales it was not overwhelmed by too much research, despite an erudite quotation from Wordsworth and some French dialogue. It told of a jockey, Derek Franklin, whose brother dies suddenly and leaves him his gem business, a pile of modern gadgets, more than a million pounds-worth of missing diamonds and a whole load of trouble, and it is genuinely gripping throughout despite a highly unlikely confession by one of the baddies and rather too many occasions when characters are so surprised that their mouths hang open. The reviews were excellent, but even better was the accolade that Dick was awarded by the Crime Writers' Association, which gave him one of its rare Cartier Diamond Daggers in recognition of a lifetime's work. He insisted that Mary should be given a brooch replica of the dagger. By now even the most academic critics were taking the novels seriously, and a second major study of the *oeuvre* was published in America, this time by J. Madison Davis, an associate professor of English at Pennsylvania State University. His book was generally intelligent, informed and perceptive, though some of its little errors are embarrassing, like the claim that when Dick was given the OBE he was 'Knighted'. There is also the occasional pretentious sentence like this: 'As Red Riding Hood's clothing has been associated by Freudians with the onset of womanhood, so also in *Risk* the giving of a red cloak to Hilary Pinlock is a psychological symbol of her loss of virginity and new-found freedom.'

But Davis's criticisms were powerful and valid. He argued that often the research was too detailed and tended to overpower the narrative; that sometimes a Francis character was too unbelievable; that parts of the novels are too far-fetched; that most of the heroes are a bit priggish, 'too fastidiously romantic' and too good to be true; that each heroine is too predictably virginal; that the villains are too often of Italianate origin and are merely unsubtle caricatures of evil. On the whole, however, Davis was a great admirer of the Francis books, impressed because 'Francis shows a respect for women that many other writers do not', and noted perceptively the similarity between the typical Francis hero and Raymond Chandler's Philip Marlowe. As Chandler himself wrote of Marlowe in his 1950 essay *The Simple Art of Murder*: 'Down these mean streets a man must go who is not himself mean, who is neither tarnished nor afraid . . . He must be . . . a man of honor – by instinct, by inevitability, without thought of it, and certainly without saying it. He must be the best man in his world and a good enough man for any world.' You could hardly find a sharper description of the typical Dick Francis hero. 'In a sense, each novel is a morality play,' wrote Davis, 'and in each case, Everyman does battle with evil. He cannot defeat it – it is always just over the horizon – but he can resist it, defeat its minions, and do the best an ordinary man can do in the circumstances.' And Davis concluded: 'No one is a worse person for having read Dick Francis, and I sincerely suspect we are all made a bit more determined to do better against adversity.'

In November 1989 Mary's old school friend Nesta Coleman and her sister Nansi came to stay in Fort Lauderdale but Mary had to abandon them to fly back to Britain when her sister Jean's husband, Dick Yorke, died. When she returned her own Dick still went racing often and they both still attended horsey functions like the Derby Ball at Gulfstream Park. Dick still signed books in local bookshops and made speeches at literary and charity lunches, and Mary continued to hide even from her friends how busy she was behind the scenes. 'No one ever figured out Mary's routine,' her friend Sue Shaffer told me. 'I think she did a lot of research for Dick. I'm not sure that Mary cooks, so every single evening of every week they went out to dinner – and we went with them quite frequently, sometimes just the four of us, sometimes in large groups – and it was always some place very nice and very expensive like the Tower Club.'

'It was always the very best, the best wine,' said her husband, Lee. 'We went to Charley's Crab once and after dessert Mary said "let's have an after dinner drink. I think this would be nice" and pointed at the Remy Martin. It was $125 for a little glass! I couldn't, but she had one! Dick didn't.'

'He's not as heavy a drinker as she is,' said Mrs Shaffer. 'Dick is a great dinner companion but it's almost like you have to interview him. He doesn't mind listening to someone next to him as long as you don't need him to participate a lot in the conversation. Oh yes, Mary is the dominant partner. Absolutely.'

In February 1990 there was yet another reminder that the Francis novels were not impossibly far-fetched when an American dentist was arrested at Calder racecourse in Florida and charged with killing thoroughbred horses with lethal injections so that their owners could collect the insurance.

Back in England that summer Felix pretended to take his parents to see an old friend in Lincolnshire but drove instead to the RAF station at Coningsby, where he had arranged for them to have a half-hour spin in a four-engine Lancaster bomber just like the one that Dick had flown at the end of the war. Both Dick and Mary took turns to sit in the co-pilot's seat and to fly the giant plane. It was a nostalgic interlude yet Dick was utterly unsentimental about his days in the RAF. 'Some people look back to the war with affection,' said Felix afterwards. 'Not dad. It got in the way of his riding.'

That year's novel, *Longshot*, was another excellent thriller and told of a struggling young novelist, John Kendall, who is so short of money that he accepts a commission to write the biography of a Berkshire racehorse trainer and finds himself knee-deep in violence and murder. In a couple of revealing, heartfelt passages Kendall describes just what it is like to be a novelist: the daunting prospect of all those empty pages; the way you do all sorts of chores rather than begin writing; and yet the mysterious compulsion to start again and again. The book contains the usual small irritations: people constantly talking *mildly* and characters with silly first names such as Tremayne, Perkin and Mackie, but despite a couple of extremely unlikely scenes – would any murder detective really confide quite so much in a young novelist? – *Longshot* has some fascinating details about survival techniques in the wild and it is a splendid read with a solid feel to it.

Most of the reviewers agreed. The literary critic Hilary Spurling rated the Francis books highly and compared them with the highbrow novels of Iris Murdoch in a long, serious article in the *Daily Telegraph*:

> Both have a talent, amounting at times to genius, for taking imaginative possession of places or settings, for divining exotic possibilities in intrinsically unpromising material, for putting conventional machinery – hoists, cranes, planes, tractors, cars – to new and unfamiliar use. Both delight in bizarre ordeals, feats, risks and traps

– the more freakish and prodigiously contrived the better
– that drive their characters to the limit of endurance
and beyond . . . there is the same macabre and exuberant inventiveness about, say, the Jacobean scenes in the
deserted boiler-room in *Enquiry*, or the weird denouement at the wine-bottling plant in *Proof*.

Ms Spurling also made the intriguing observation that Franciscan
heroes

suffer all the traditional pangs of saints and martyrs
(as well as some beyond even medieval torturers to
devise) with the same exemplary patience, resolution
and composure. Kendall in *Longshot* is transfixed, like
Saint Sebastian, by arrows. Roland Britten in *Risk* is
literally crucified.

And just as *Longshot* was published in September there was yet
another reminder that the books were not all that exaggerated:
at Doncaster races two horses, Bravefoot and Norwich, were
nobbled in the racecourse stables when they were injected with
acetylpromazine, ACP, a fast-acting sedative that was used illegally in six out of the seven doping cases to be uncovered over the
next eight years. Three weeks later Flying Diva was also doped
with ACP at Yarmouth races.

In October Felix flew out to Florida with his two children,
who persuaded their grandparents to take them for the first
time to Disney World, and Dick marked his seventieth birthday
by giving up riding for good, which must have come close to
breaking his heart, but he put a bold face on it. 'We never sleep
apart,' he told the *Telegraph Weekend Magazine*. 'Yes, we are very
happy here, very happy indeed.'

But not for much longer. Mary was elected President of the
full board of the entire Sea Ranch condominium, with its 723

apartments, three huge buildings, nine directors, and budget of nearly $10 million a year, and the pressures of the job were to become horrendous. 'She was a wonderful President,' I was told by Harriet Gilbert, a fellow board member, and Sue Shaffer, who was also a director, said: 'Mary reminded me very much of Margaret Thatcher. She was very strong, but with a velvet glove. She spoke very succinctly but very softly, very pleasantly, and would never take shit.' That, however, was precisely what Mary was offered during her year as President. In Britain it was widely assumed that the Francises were living a blissful, carefree life in paradise but the truth was very different: 1991 was to be one of the unhappiest years of Dick and Mary's lives.

'It was almost a full-time job for Mary,' I was told by Gene Hudack, who was then the manager of 'A' building. 'She'd be in my office for business six days a week.' As President she had to oversee everything from labour contracts, building maintenance and landscaping to beach cleaning, the tennis courts and the purchase of chemicals for the swimming pools, and to make the job impossible each of the three Sea Ranch buildings had a separate board of three directors that guarded their own interests with vicious jealousy. Hudack told me:

> There were tremendous problems. We spent probably a million dollars in six years just on legal affairs. If 'C' building did something wrong and was being sued, we had to hire an attorney for 'A' building to protect us from that lawsuit, so we not only had our own private attorney for 'A' building, we had to join the attorney for the association to fight that case. It was bad. It really wasn't a happy place. There was a small group of people that would do nothing but harass and cause dissension.

Sue Shaffer, speaking of 'the friction that always existed among the three buildings', told me:

Every time 'A' would need something done in their particular pool or beach house area, the other two buildings would get together and block it: they didn't want the money spent there, so that was why there was all this fuss. Then the major blow-up was when we found that there was structural damage caused by the deterioration of concrete in building 'A', a little in 'B', very little in 'C'. There was a huge fight and everyone agreed they would pay for it – but then the work was to be done at building 'A' first but it began at building 'C' instead, and they started adding other things into the project, and started saying 'well, we don't think we need to do quite this much for building A' and it ended up in a lawsuit again.

Feelings ran so high that Dick and Mary bought a second apartment, number 605, on the same floor as their own, for hundreds of thousands of dollars, simply to buy some peace and quiet. The apartment was owned by one of Mary's most vociferous critics and to get rid of him 'Mary made him an offer he couldn't refuse, and he moved,' said Mrs Shaffer. The second apartment was kept for Merrick, Felix and their families to use whenever they came to stay.

Mrs Shaffer said:

Mary got a lot of hassle. A piece of concrete broke off of either Dick and Mary's balcony or the one up above, and she proceeded – as was her right as president – to take the steps necessary for an emergency measure. She arranged for the repair not only of that balcony but also to have all the balconies checked and it cost a lot of money and a lot of people felt they could have had just that one balcony checked. It was something like $150,000 or $250,000 and I remember Mary saying, 'you know, I thought I was doing right for the building but if they're so upset about it I'll just *pay* for the whole thing'.

Mary's enemies even accused her of accepting a bribe when new carpets were bought for the lobby, according to Mrs Shaffer:

> There was a lot of discussion for years afterwards that someone had to have made a lot of money in the form of a kickback. First they accused the manager, Gene Hudack, but then it spread from the manager to Mary, myself and Pete Johnson. I got accused of it, and so did Mary. Dick, Mary and Pete could buy every apartment in this place, and they're going to be interested in making a few thousand dollars in a kickback? It blighted her year as president. She really did do a good job but she just got tired of it. The phone would never stop ringing and it was constant interruptions and she felt that both she and Dick had paid a very high price and there was no appreciation.

'Mary was a strong woman,' said Gene Hudack, 'very strong-willed, and she never broke down and sobbed or cried in front of me, but I knew she could get to that point probably when she went home. She took a lot of flak and I think she cried in private. Yet even though there was trouble there was always a pleasant smile, pleasant soft words. People *loved* them, especially me. You'll never see nicer people than them. But that's con-dominiums.'

In the end the Francises, Shaffers and Johnsons all left the Sea Ranch Club because of the terrible atmosphere there, and Gene Hudack was eventually forced out as manager in 1995 when his enemies managed to take control of the board of directors, locked him out of his office, accused him of fraud and forced him to resign, which led to yet another court case when Hudack sued

'A' building for harassment. 'Gene did a good job and I never saw anything that would give credence to their claims,' Johnson told me.

It was not all misery that year. In May the Queen and Prince Philip visited Florida and the Francises joined 350 guests at a reception on board the royal yacht *Britannia*, and Dick received yet another accolade when he was awarded an honorary Doctorate in Humane Letters by Tufts University in Boston. But sadly the golden writing days were over. Nine more books were to be published before the end of the century but only one was to be much good. The engine was running down.

The next novel, *Comeback*, was received with increasing unease by the critics. Inspired by Dick and Mary's trip to Japan, its hero is a youngish diplomat, Peter Darwin, who has spent two years at the British embassy in Tokyo and tells of a brilliant vet who suddenly finds that almost every time he operates on a horse it dies and his career is threatened by the rumours. The details about veterinary practice and animal surgery are riveting – did you know, for instance, that horses cannot vomit? – and the solution is intriguing, but once again there are too many ridiculous names, too many mouths that hang open in surprise, and the reviewers were no longer prepared to praise without question. Several were openly rude. In the *Sunday Times* Paul Golding called the book a 'potboiler', 'butch-shlock' and 'lowly bedroom farce'; the hero 'insipid, smug' and 'cardboard'; the plot one of 'tedious improbability'; and the characterisation and prose style non-existent. In the *Sunday Telegraph* Anthony Daniels claimed that *Comeback* had little literary merit and was aimed too obviously at the American market: 'The narrator "bonks" another female character mainly, one feels, because "bonking" is one of the list of ingredients of any bestseller, and it can subsequently be ticked off the list . . . As for the plot, it relies on coincidence to a degree that would make a Victorian melodrama blush.' There was a bad notice even in the *Daily Telegraph*, which had usually given the novels rave reviews. 'The plot is more than usually embarrassing,' wrote T. J. Binyon, 'with a heroine who has stepped out of a 1970s film about Swinging London.' In the London literary jungle the natives were getting restless.

Dick and Mary returned to Britain to publicise the book and he told Pauline Peters of the *Evening Standard* that he and Mary 'have a very happy love life; always have had' and that the nearest they ever got to having a row was when they went out together since he liked always to be ten minutes early and she was always ten minutes late. 'I think she'd quite like a good row,' he mused, 'but I'm not that way inclined.' Revealing that Mary looked after the finances and that he had just bought his first new item of clothing for seven years – a pair of checked trousers – he claimed that 'as a writer you don't really make much money, no matter how many millions of books you sell.' Ms Peters noticed that in old age Dick had 'a slight, ramrod-straight figure with an oddly Buddha-like face, outwardly imperturbable to the nth degree' – caused, perhaps, by all those years of keeping a straight face while fibbing about not making much money.

By the end of 1991 Dick and Mary had had enough of the endless feuding at Sea Ranch and they slipped away in December for a fortnight's holiday on the West Indian island of Grand Cayman, and they fell in love with it immediately. They found the Britishness of the place especially attractive after Florida, and they were struck by the colour-blind friendliness of all the mixed races there. Back at the Sea Ranch the surrounding area was becoming increasingly commercialised. The beach there was often crowded and noisy, with a clattering of helicopters and light aircraft, some of them trailing long advertisements. Grand Cayman was suddenly where they wanted to live. Just along the beach next to their hotel a small condominium was being built – not a monster with 723 apartments but a place of human size with just thirty-six – and on an impulse they bought one straight away and planned to move in a year later.

Back in Fort Lauderdale Dick was interviewed in January by a young *Daily Express* journalist, Mary Kemp, who reported that 'he moves slowly but with great determination like a small, energetic tortoise'. He also told Graham Bridgstock of *Today* that he and Mary now had four TV sets in the flat, that his favourite programmes were two American quiz shows, *Jeopardy* and *The Wheel of Fortune*, and that it drove him mad when Mary sat up watching TV late every night because he was always in bed by ten o'clock and asleep when she came to bed.

By now it was obvious that Merrick, who was forty-one, was never going to be a huge success as a trainer, and at the end of January he gave it up and with Dick and Mary's help bought a company called Lambourn Racehorse Transport and soon owned a fleet of eleven horseboxes that ferried horses all over Britain, Ireland and Europe. 'He was probably never hungry enough,' one eminent racing journalist told me. 'Most of the best trainers like Paul Cole and Barry Hills had to win to progress. That basic need was not the case with Merrick.' It is not always a benefit being the son of rich parents, but Lambourn Racehorse Transport was to inspire the next novel, *Driving Force*.

Felix also changed the direction of his life in 1992 and gave up teaching to become Dick and Mary's business manager, though he still lived in England. One unhappy business venture in which they were involved from 1992 to 1994 was Pangbourne Wines Ltd, the little off-licence company run by their fifty-eight-year-old friend, Margaret Giles, who had taught Mary about the booze business for the 1984 novel *Proof*. When the company was started in February 1992 Dick and Mary owned 51 per cent of the shares and Miss Giles 49, and Miss Giles and Felix were also directors. 'It was just friendship,' Miss Giles told me. 'They came in just to help me out.' But although the company had a turnover of £190,000 and also borrowed £11,449 from Dick, it declared a trading loss of £8,500 and went out of business little more than two years later, in April 1994. Dick and Mary had not only to write off their entire investment in the company but also to satisfy the creditors, and a report by the auditors, Sinnett and Tayley of Reading, was a damning indictment of the way that the company had been run:

> In our opinion, the system of accounting during the period was unsatisfactory and certain records in support of gross profit, necessary for the purpose of our audit, were not maintained by the company. In our opinion, in this respect, proper accounting records have not been kept and we have been unable to obtain all the information and explanations that we consider necessary.

It was not a happy start for Felix as his parents' business manager.

Driving Force, the last of the good Dick Francis novels, told a clever, intriguing tale of how horseboxes like Merrick's could be used to smuggle live contraband into Britain from France. The hero, Freddie Croft, the ex-jockey owner of the horsebox company, bears a passing resemblance to Merrick himself and the book is dedicated to him. There is a splendidly tense scene when Croft struggles not to drown in icy water, some riveting biological details about ticks, rabbits and horses, and the useful information that King Alfred the Great was plagued by agonising haemorrhoids, which may explain why he burnt the cakes. On the debit side there is a surprisingly strong anti-police tone, as there is in many of the Francis novels, and one wonders what the Queen Mother thought of all the four-letter words in Chapter Twelve. All in all, though, the book deserved the reviewers' plaudits, although Max Davidson of the *Sunday Telegraph* complained that the characterisation of the hero was unacceptably shallow and pointed out the glaring inconsistency of having a protagonist who was remarkably stupid for the first two hundred pages and then suddenly incredibly clever.

But who cared? Every year the PLR figures confirmed that more Dick Francis books were still being borrowed from British public libraries than those of any writer except Catherine Cookson. Each new novel was selling 100,000 copies in hardback in Britain, another 100,000 in book club editions and half a million in paperback. No other author had ever had so many novels published by *Reader's Digest* Condensed Books. And total worldwide sales now were nudging fifty million copies in thirty different languages. There was only one cloud: Dick's arthritic hip had become so painful that he could no longer walk on the beach and in November he had an operation to give him a metal hip – and a medical certificate to persuade airport security guards to allow him through their metal detectors. The operation was so successful that ten days later he was driving his car again. 'Dick is almost impervious to pain,' Sue Shaffer told me. 'When he came out of hospital we went out to dinner the next night and he insisted on driving.'

But by now they had had enough of Florida and the endless hassles at the Sea Ranch Club. In June the condo had become involved in yet another legal wrangle, this time with the builder, but it was no longer Mary's problem. She was not President any more and had passed the poisoned chalice on to an unfortunate fellow called Donald Homer. She was free. At the end of 1992 she and Dick gave two farewell parties at the Tower Club in Fort Lauderdale and then flew south to Cayman to live beside the Caribbean Sea.

CHAPTER 16

A Shady Place for Sunny People

(1993–99)

G rand Cayman, 'the Monte Carlo of the Caribbean', is the most notorious of all the rich island tax havens. A tiny, jagged blob of coral, sand and palms 150 miles south of Cuba and 189 north-west of Jamaica, it is only twenty miles long, four to seven miles wide, 60ft high at its dizziest point, and it has no more than 35,000 residents – about 12,000 of them expatriates – and no industry at all, depending entirely on banking and tourism. Yet it is the world's fifth largest banking centre (after New York, London, Tokyo and Hong Kong) and is crammed with expensive hotels, smart restaurants, and duty-free jewellery and souvenir shops. It has nearly six hundred banks and the dinky little capital, George Town, welcomes two or three mountainous cruise ships every morning and proceeds to fillet the passengers' wallets all day before sending them off again into the sunset. As a result, Cayman's inhabitants enjoy full employment, little crime, 98 per cent adult literacy, a relaxed lifestyle and the highest per capita income in the western hemisphere, more than £18,000 a year tax-free. And the climate is glorious: temperatures average 75° in winter and 85°F in summer and help to provide some of the best fishing, scuba-diving and snorkelling in the world.

Cayman is still a British Crown colony where English accents are common, cars drive on the left, postboxes carry the royal insignia EⅡR and physical homosexuality is illegal. It still has a British Governor who lives in Government House behind a guardhouse and who wears on ceremonial occasions the traditional white uniform, gold epaulettes, gold tassels and tall, white ostrich-feathered helmet that once adorned the consuls of the British Empire. Yet Cayman boasts that it has no taxes at all, neither income tax nor capital gains, property nor inheritance, and it has strict confidentiality laws to deter the curiosity of taxmen from other countries. It does, however, levy massive import duties on everything, so that the cost of living is ferocious. A standard room at the Hyatt or Marriott hotels costs £194 a night in winter. Import a car and you have to pay duty of up to 40 per cent. A light lunch at Rum Point in 1999 – two hot dogs, two small beers and two choc ices – cost me £28. A small bottle of even the cheapest local Stingray beer in a beach bar cost £4, an ordinary supermarket 75cl bottle of Smirnoff vodka £24. A meal for two, with just one course and a half-bottle of wine each, cost £75. You can pay as much as £5 million for a house on the only decent white beach, Seven Mile Beach, £2 million for a three-bedroom beachfront apartment or £9,000 a month to rent it. Even a two-bedroom flat in an unfashionable area costs £1,875 a month to rent.

And yet to become a resident you only have to buy a house or apartment for at least £113,000, pay a residence fee of £12,000 and produce three written references, a police certificate of previous good behaviour, a letter from your bank manager attesting that you will not need to take a job on the island, and you have to pass an HIV test and declare whether you have ever visited a Communist country, and why. Such gentle restrictions, tax advantages and financial secrecy mean that Cayman is widely alleged to be a shady place where billions of criminal dollars are neatly laundered every year, a crooks' paradise just as hospitable to modern corporate buccaneers as it was centuries ago when Sir Francis Drake, Blackbeard and Sir Henry Morgan passed through with their own booty. As one character remarks in John Grisham's 1991 Mafia money-laundering novel *The Firm*, much of which is set on Grand Cayman: 'This place has always attracted pirates. Once it was Blackbeard, now it's modern-day pirates who form corporations and hide their money here.' A few months after Dick and Mary arrived, Gene Hackman turned up, too, to film *The Firm* on the island, which it depicted as a place of inordinate greed and corruption.

It is certainly greedy and a visitor constantly feels that his pocket is being picked, albeit legally. US dollars are accepted everywhere but it is not until you pay the bill that you realise that prices are in Cayman dollars, and the Cayman dollar is worth 25 per cent more than the American one, so that everything you buy turns out to cost a quarter more than you expected. Every restaurant adds a compulsory 'tip' of 15 per cent and then presents you with a credit card slip suggesting an additional tip of 15 per cent or 20 per cent, so that it is easy to end up paying £150 for a meal that according to the menu should have cost £100. 'That's how we make money, man,' grinned one Caymanian when I questioned the system. It came as no surprise to learn that Seven Mile Beach is in fact not even six miles long when you actually measure it. Even the barmen expect a 'tip' just for opening a bottle. And so it goes on, everywhere you turn. Greed rules. Grand Cayman is a culture with its hand out. Here the palms are mostly face upwards. And everywhere you go, even along the beaches, unfriendly notices snarl 'KEEP OUT: PRIVATE PROPERTY'.

Yet beneath the glitz and high living 'there is real poverty among the poor immigrant underclass that is propping up our lifestyle,' I was told by one senior Cayman official. 'There are lots of poor Jamaicans and Hondurans here who are paid no more than £125 a week to work five days a week cooking, cleaning and helping in the house, maybe until 10 p.m. every night, and they have to pay half of that for a room in a house with other immigrants. How do they survive with the cost of living as high as it is?' A live-in cleaning woman earns just £62 a week, not even enough to buy a couple of sheets for her bed. 'That's the dark side of life here,' he said. 'There's a much bigger gap between the rich and poor than there was.'

Perhaps the greed and exploitation were less obvious when Dick and Mary moved in to their first home on Cayman in December 1992: a luxurious, three-bedroom, three-bathroom, ground-floor corner apartment with a screened terrace at number 1 Coralstone Club. The Club was a stylish, pale blue condominium of three small, two-storey blocks two miles north of George Town and right on Seven Mile Beach with only a few palms and a thatched hut between them and the Caribbean Sea. The condo sat amid colourful gardens, wrapped in quiet and cleanliness, and was much cosier than the Sea Ranch Club and without the constant oppressive presence of uniformed security guards. It had two small swimming pools, two whirlpool spas, two tennis courts, cable TV, and an on-site laundry and housekeeping facilities to cater to Mary's lifelong distaste for housework. To rent one of the Coralstone Club apartments in 1999 cost a minimum of £388 a day in winter, to buy one at least £780,000.

'Dick and Mary were exceptional residents,' I was told by Alan Scott, who was then the Governor of Cayman and became friendly with the Francises after his wife met Dick when she was riding her horse along Seven Mile Beach one morning and he told her what a nice animal it was. 'You don't get celebrities of that type very much on Cayman. Most people who end up residing permanently tend to be retired bankers, usually Americans and Canadians.' Government House was half a mile along the beach from the Francises' apartment and soon Mary and Dick were dining regularly with the Scotts. 'They had no real close circle of friends,' said Scott. 'Their best friends were ourselves and the then-Attorney General. They preferred to be quiet and he keeps a low profile.'

Apart from an annual signing session in one of the local bookshops, The Book Nook, where a green parrot sits in a cage by the door, Dick and Mary lived a notably quiet and private life in Cayman and he resisted all invitations to make speeches and public appearances. Even the local newspaper, the *Caymanian Compass*, published just two articles about him in six years. 'Our policy is not to harass people who retire here or come on holiday,' I was told by *Caymanian Compass* reporter John Redman. 'They've come here for peace and quiet.' Strangely, though, Dick's address and telephone number were published openly in the local directory under 'FRANCIS, RICHARD (Dick)' as if to ensure that everyone knew precisely who he was.

The Francises sold their second Sea Ranch apartment but kept the main one in case the move had been a mistake, and they returned regularly to Fort Lauderdale on brief trips over the next couple of years, but they had not made a mistake. 'It's so peaceful,' Dick told Gene Hudack, 'and now I can walk right out on the beach with no one to bother me.' Eventually they sold the Sea Ranch apartment in 1995. 'It is one of the best of all the apartments,' Gene Hudack told me in 1999, 'and it must easily be worth $700,000 (£437,000) now.'

It seems that Dick and Mary did not move to Cayman simply to escape the unpleasant atmosphere at the Sea Ranch Club. 'It was also tax reasons,' Sue Shaffer told me.

'We were taxed quite heavily in the US,' Dick told Lynda Lee-Potter of the *Daily Mail* in 1998, 'and when we moved to the Caymans we had to prove that we were getting out of the US altogether. The people in the Caymans said: "If you get yourself a plot at the cemetery that will prove that you are going to stay here until you die". So we went to the town hall to book the plots.' There a woman official apologised because there were no plots left with sea views. 'Mary and I couldn't stop laughing, but we've now got two plots side-by-side, without a sea view.'

They paid £937.50 for the two graves just off Boggy Sand Road, two pre-fabricated, cement-lined, six-feet-deep boxes numbered U18 and U20 in the sandy West Bay cemetery on the edge of Seven Mile Beach just 100 yards from the sea. In March 1999 the graves were so neglected – one of them an open eyesore full of rubbish, bits of wood, scummy water and old flowers from nearby graves – that they seemed unlikely final resting places for a couple of multi-millionaires, though Dick insisted in another updated edition of *The Sport of Queens*, published in 1995, that Cayman was going to be their last home.

One of his few regrets about the move was that there was no racecourse on the island, but he still followed racing avidly through the British newspapers, which in Cayman arrived only a day late, and he and Mary took to their new home as enthusiastically as they had at first to Florida and continued to follow their Florida routine with Dick rising early as always and heading along the comparatively deserted beach for a walk and a swim. But sadly his walking was becoming slower: after suffering so many racing accidents his bones were beginning to ache badly with arthritis, especially his toes, and he was often in pain. He also had very high blood pressure. But neither he nor Mary were ones to complain and they still enjoyed their glasses of wine each evening and eating out often in the local restaurants. To show how content they were, and despite their apparent contempt for the British Press, they invited the gossip magazine *Hello!* to photograph them in their new flat and on the beach for a four-page picture spread, and then allowed *Hello!*'s rival *OK!* to photograph the whole family on the beach at Paignton for an article that was splashed across five pages. It was an odd thing to do since they hardly needed the publicity any longer and many people considered both magazines to be decidedly naff but Dick told Ian Woodward of *Hello!* that he was deliriously happy: 'We just open the door and we're on the beach. It's absolute bliss. Heaven on earth.' He admitted that he did not expect there to be more than three more books because 'as far as new plots are concerned, I have to scrape the proverbial barrel somewhat.'

The *OK!* interview was conducted in mid-July, a week after Merrick, now forty-three, married his third wife, thirty-six-year-old Alex Brown, who was Lambourn Racehorse Transport's sales manager, had also been divorced twice and had two young children. When they married at Newbury registry office Dick signed the certificate, reconciled at last to his son's chequered love life, which had recently included a long relationship with the TV presenter Sally Taylor. 'I think he was a little bit worried whether he should take on a third wife,' Dick told Lynda Lee-Potter, 'but we are delighted he has. We haven't had the unhappiness of having a child marry someone we didn't like. They were all nice girls but, somehow, they just didn't click.' He and Mary had been 'a bit upset at first' about Merrick's divorces, he told Angela Lambert in yet another *Daily Mail* interview in 1996, 'but we've got used to it. We are still very friendly with his first two wives, Elaine and Barbara. We see them often – we're not at daggers drawn. Merrick's first two marriages broke up not because either was going off after anyone else but because they just rather got on each other's nerves. I think that's reason enough for ending a marriage. You've got to live sweetly.' Merrick gave his new bride a racehorse as a wedding present and bought himself a speedboat.

In August the Francises set up yet another company in Britain to exploit the film potential of the books and named it after the Coralstone Club: Coralstone Films, which had a thousand shares divided equally between Merrick and Felix. There was also a third director, their London literary agent Andrew Hewson, and as their first project they planned to make a film themselves of *Decider*. Unhappily the book was decidedly below par: a waffly, pedestrian, unconvincing tale about yet another dysfunctional family at war over the family inheritance, in this case the family-owned racecourse. Once again the villains are absurdly melodramatic and the style embarrassingly bad, with sentences like this: 'Marjorie levelled a limpid gaze on the discomfited personage who'd made the error of condescension.' And this: 'Rebecca's eyes slitted narrowly under lowered eyelids, her face rigid.' The only notable aspect of the book is that the thirty-five-year-old hero is not only gooey about a teenage girl, like many Francis heroes, but is this time consumed by lust for her. And although the publishers had agreed never to change a line of a Francis book it was inevitable that one day one would come up against the rising tide of political correctness in American publishing that had already engulfed British writers such as Kingsley Amis, Maeve Haran and Jilly Cooper, and it happened with *Decider* because it described a tough, bossy female jockey as strutting about in a feline fashion like a lesbian. It was a graphic, accurate description of a type of woman we have all met, but Putnam insisted that the reference to lesbianism was 'very un-American', and eventually it was censored, even though Dick and Mary thought the objection extremely silly. Nor could anyone at Michael Joseph see what the fuss was about, so the sentence remained in the British edition.

This time Dick was interviewed – yet again for the tabloid *Daily Mail*, which was beginning to look like their favourite newspaper – by Corinna Honan. 'Find out who writes his books for him,' one of her colleagues begged her, and she reported that 'Dick's extraordinary lack of pretension has gained him a reputation in some quarters for being dull, the implication being this inoffensive little man who left school at fifteen could not possibly produce all that spare, imaginative prose. But of course he does, albeit with a little help from Mary.'

Ms Honan described him as 'a small, straight-backed gentleman in neat beige check trousers and brown blazer. His feet are clad in purple socks and dinky white boots that curve at the top. He looks like a benevolent elf.' She told him that in one English A-level set-book students were required to compare passages from Dickens, Trollope and Dick Francis. 'He blushed. He sheepishly examined the carpet. He said: "Ooh, I say. Made my day, that has".' Later he told Ms Honan that he wished Mary would agree to being named as co-author of the books and added: 'After I've written a book, it's often difficult to picture what is her idea and what is mine.' When Ms Honan asked him why there was so little sex in the books he replied: 'The Queen Mother reads my books, you know, and I'd hate her to read them from my pen.' Dick also remarked: 'Our marriage has remained a romance. We talk about everything. We sleep back to back but always have a cuddle every night first' – a curious claim considering that a few months previously he had been complaining to Mary Kemp of the *Daily Express* that he always went to bed by eleven o'clock, alone, and that Mary stayed up at least until midnight. He also had the nerve to claim yet again that writing was 'not all that lucrative', even though he and Mary regularly flew first class or by Concorde, were paying for private education not only for all five grandchildren but also for a nephew and a niece and had twice helped Merrick pay off his ex-wives.

Back on Cayman there was a flurry of excitement at the end of February when the royal yacht *Britannia* arrived at George Town and the Queen and Prince Philip came ashore for a two-day visit, and then – after Dick's usual trip back to England for the Grand National in April – he and Mary were off again to Australia on yet another promotion tour. Their constant globe-trotting was remarkably brave considering the continual deterioration in their health. Mary's old school friend Mary Youll and her husband Bill had lunch with them on Cayman in 1994 and Mrs Youll was distressed by Mary's physical condition. 'Mary's breathing had become quite laboured,' she told me. 'She had artificial breathing equipment that she carried around with her. She made very little of her disability but she obviously had deteriorated quite a bit.'

In September Dick was off on his travels again, this time to sign books in Seattle and to return to England for yet another two-week promotion tour, during which an article in the *Daily Express* remarked about Mary: 'She does not, contrary to rumour, write his books for him.' Simultaneously that month Bryony Fuller's picture book about his racing career, *Dick Francis: Steeplechase Jockey*, was published with a preface by Peter Cazalet's son, Sir Edward Cazalet, now a High Court judge, in which he praised Dick for being so modest and unpretentious despite his huge success. Few people had anything unpleasant to say about Dick and Mary except that they were both 'a bit silly' in their groupie-like worship of the Royal Family, and one acquaintance told me: 'They both insist on being given the red-carpet treatment when in London, and he only ever drinks Chateauneuf du Pape with everything, no matter what's being eaten. And he asks people like car park attendants if they enjoy reading and then hands out signed copies!' On the other hand, she said, 'those are all pretty harmless faults. He isn't greedy, he isn't profligate, and he's immensely loyal.' The same friend told me that Dick was 'pretty terrified of Mary', hated having to 'trot round the shops with her in those god-awful places they live in' and would much prefer to live in England were it not for her bad health.

The 1994 novel, *Wild Horses* – partly inspired by the recent death of the British MP Stephen Milligan during an auto-erotic sex game – was sadly no better than the previous one, and the books to come during the rest of the decade were to be just as bad. It was time to retire gracefully, just as Dick had retired as a jockey before he started embarrassing everyone. *Wild Horses* tells of a film director, Thomas Lyon, who is making a movie in Newmarket based on the tragic hanging of a trainer's wife many years earlier, and who finds himself uncovering unsavoury secrets from the past and becoming the target of a murderer who is determined to stop him making the film. Unhappily the story is overwhelmed by Mary's lifelong fascination with all things theatrical, so that much of the book is a schoolmarmish lecture about the techniques and problems of film making and packed with details about script changes, camera angles, screen lighting, camera crews and retakes. Mary's fingerprints are all over the book, from the obscure epigraph at the beginning (a verse by a nineteenth-century poet called Christopher Pearse Cranch) to the references to the joys of learning Latin, the philosophy of film making, Iago, and Henry V's speech before the battle of Agincourt. Much of the dialogue is so unbelievable that when one character asks 'why the *hell* am I telling you this?' the reader would like to know, too. As usual the characters have absurd names – Silva Shawn, Ziggy Keene, Rodbury Visborough – and as usual there is a ludicrous villain, a hatefully disfunctional family, and a clean, fresh-faced, freckly teenage girl. In fact the ingredients of a Francis novel had become so predictable and clichéd that the books were becoming parodies of themselves. The blatant sadism, too, was becoming positively unpleasant: the story is concerned with explicit sexual orgies and perversions and a brutal attack on an old lady is described with gruesome relish, even down to her aged, sagging breasts and glistening intestines.

'*Wild Horses* is an also-ran among Dick Francis's thrillers,' wrote the ex-Francis fan Charles Spencer in the *Daily Telegraph*. 'There is a weary sense of effort in the writing, and the saintly Dick often seems out of his depth as he wades through the murky waters of sexual perversion.' Helena de Bertodano reported in the *Sunday Telegraph* that the book was disjointed and undisciplined, the ending illogical and untidy and the female auto-eroticism quite unconvincing, though Dick insisted that women do indulge in such unusual practices. 'Mary did a lot of research into it,' he told Ms Bertodano, 'but I didn't want to dwell on it because the Queen Mother reads my books.' Dick's lifelong compulsive tidiness and punctuality would doubtless have interested a psychiatrist, but Ms Bertodano was taken aback to discover that although Christmas was still three months away he had already written and sealed all his Christmas cards which he had brought to England for Felix to post more cheaply in Britain in December: the envelopes were arranged in alphabetical order so that should one of the recipients die Felix could remove it from the pile. Most disconcerting of all, Dick kept forgetting the names of the books' heroes and even had trouble remembering the title of the new book, so that Mary had to be summoned for the information.

Despite the bad reviews, *Wild Horses* sold more than 100,000 in hardback in Britain, more than any other 1994 novel. In the USA it sold 295,000 and it was published in thirty-five languages. By now the reviewers' opinions were of no commercial significance at all. And once again, just as the critics were complaining that the books were far-fetched, real life proved to be just as melodramatic. At the end of September the Newmarket trainer Alex Scott, who trained dozens of horses for one of racing's richest owners, Sheikh Maktoum al-Maktoum, including the winner of that year's Derby, was murdered by his head stud groom, Clem O'Brien, who shot him in the back with a twelve-bore shotgun during a row over a yearling and was sentenced ten months later to life imprisonment.

Back on Cayman a new friend of the Francises, the crime novelist P. D. James (Baroness James), spent Christmas with them. Lady James told me:

> They're an amazing couple. She's astonishing, particularly. They have qualities I admire: courage, hard work. I could never start writing a book on January 1st and deliver it in May. And there's their general kindness, generosity of spirit, and lack of malice. They're such restful people to be with.

To research the next book, *Come to Grief*, Mary visited leukaemia

sufferers and an artificial limbs centre, but the book turned out
to be one of the worst of all the novels. As if to confirm that
inspiration was dwindling, it resurrected Sid Halley – the only
Francis character to appear in three novels – but even he could
not prevent the book being truly dreadful. Halley exposes a
popular ex-Champion Jockey as being the villain behind a series
of vicious crimes in which horses are found with their feet cut
off, but the plot is ludicrous, the motivation unbelievable and the
dialogue utterly incredible, with complete strangers suddenly
unburdening themselves to Halley and spilling the beans for no
obvious reason whatever. 'Why am I telling you all this?' asks yet
another Francis character. Good question. Even the characters'
names – Davis Tatum, Ellis Quint, Verney Tilepit, Willy Parrot –
pale beside the garish nonsense of the rest of the book. The book
describes a vicious anti-Halley campaign by the British Press, for
instance – especially a woman columnist called India Cathcart
– that is so shrill, immoral, libellous and impossibly guilty of
contempt of court that it could never happen. Saddest of all, the
style is quite dreadful. How could the stylish author of *Risk*, *Whip
Hand*, *Reflex* and *Banker* possibly have written a sentence like
this?: 'Blind-eye country, I thought, like the private back-stairs
of the great before the India Cathcarts of the world floodlit the
secretive comings and goings, and rewarded promiscuity with
taint.' But by now it made no difference whether a new Dick
Francis novel was any good and *Come to Grief* somehow won
the Mystery Writers of America award for the best crime novel
of the year, and the American hardback sold 303,000 copies.

Another revised edition of *The Sport of Queens* was published
that year with a very brief new chapter covering the past eight
years in just four pages, but the years were beginning to tell on
them both. When the *Daily Express* writer Tobyn Andreae interviewed Dick in August he reported that, at nearly seventy-five,
Dick was deeply tanned but frail, paunchy and wearing white
cloth boots to ease his aching feet. 'The reality is a pensioner who

takes small steps and small breaths,' he wrote, '. . . and who has a tendency to tell long, rambling anecdotes while forgetting the original point of a story'. He added: 'Dick became muddled about which book he was supposed to be promoting. He later admitted he gets confused with which character features in which plot.' He told Andreae he wished there were no need to keep churning out a book every year but the publishers were insisting on their agreement to publish one every year.

In October, not surprisingly, Mary had a heart attack and had to spend two weeks in hospital and then a couple of months of rest and recuperation. More than ever now she depended on Dick and he had to help her dress every morning. 'Who's going to do this after I've gone?' Dick asked her.

'I'm going first,' Mary replied firmly.

'We haven't talked about how either of us would cope on our own,' he told Lynda Lee-Potter. 'I just hope we die together.'

At seventy-two Mary was often exhausted and had to sleep every afternoon, but typically she used even her own heart attack as material for the next novel, *To the Hilt*, in which one of the main characters has a heart attack, too, and since the new book was about acrylic painting she ordered a pile of books about the subject and read them in bed. Dick, too, despite his frailty, was indomitable and tottered off on yet another promotion trip, this time to Slovakia, where he visited two riding clubs, a colt farm, the state race track at Petrzalka, and was surprised to find how many fans queued up in Bratislava to collect his autograph.

But there was a desperately tired lack of inventiveness about *To the Hilt*, which recounted yet another utterly unbelievable story, this time about a young painter, Alexander Kinloch, who manages to save his stepfather's multi-million-pound brewery business after the disappearance of its embezzling finance director despite the fact that he lives in a simple shack on a remote Scottish mountainside and turns out to be incredibly stupid more than once. Yet again there is little about horses and far too much about painting, acrylics, antique artifacts, jewellery and the rows and rivalries of yet another dysfunctional family. The characters' names are as extraordinary as ever – Jed Parlane, Tobias Tollright, Norman Quorn, Surtees and Xenia Benchmark – and the baddies are ridiculously unlikely. The vicious sadism – burning, this time – is described lovingly more than once and the sex is much more explicit than usual, despite Dick's continual insistence over the years that he disapproved deeply of graphic sexual descriptions in novels. In *To the Hilt* Kinloch exhibits a decidedly kinky interest in an eighty-year-old woman and hires a private eye who dresses up in women's frilly clothes, high heels, rouge and mascara. One villain is a closet homosexual, another a masochist who pays a prostitute to spank him, and a third is kicked so hard and often in the genitals that he has to be gelded. The book is sprinkled liberally with swear words: not only 'damn' and 'bastard' but even 'fuck', 'arse', 'buggery', 'bugger' and 'shit' (seven times). *To the Hilt* is the most foul-mouthed of all the books, which is odd when you consider that Dick and Mary were well into their seventies. When a young *Daily Express* reporter asked Mary about the sex scenes she replied: 'After thirty-four books we decided it was time to spice them up.' When he asked whether this might not offend the Queen Mother, as Dick had always claimed, Mary 'barked': 'Oh, for goodness sake, young man, the Queen Mother's had two children.'

To the Hilt is also one of the most blatantly Marian novels of them all, for time and again there are references that must have come from Mary rather than Dick. The epigraph at the beginning, printed in old Anglo-Saxon, is the ancient *Death Song* poem of the Venerable Bede that Mary studied at university, and there is a learned discussion of Anglo-Saxon poetry and history that betrays a deep knowledge and love of the subject. The book is spattered, too, with obscure words such as revenant, diminuendoed, nimbostratus, and piobaireachd and there is throughout a deep vein of philosophy about the spirituality of painting. There is also a diatribe about the unfairness of the British tax system, which taxes your son heavily if you give him cash but not if he wins the same amount in a casino. And three characters spend several days hiding out at the Redcliffe Hotel in Paignton. *To the Hilt* was embarrassingly bad yet many reviews were as bafflingly enthusiastic as ever and from across the Atlantic came the most welcome accolade of all: Dick was made a Mystery Writers of America Grand Master 'for a lifetime's achievement'. And as if to endorse the veracity of the books, the police began to investigate in September a case of suspected arson after four horses died when a barn at Jim Old's Barbary Castle racing stables near Lambourn burned down in the middle of the night and the winner of the Cheltenham Champion Hurdle, Collier Bay, was nearly burned to death.

Dick was in England at the time and took the opportunity to tell Angela Lambert of the *Daily Mail* that he and Mary had always had 'a very physical marriage':

> We had a good sexual life, and I think that's important. We've neither of us ever had an affair – at least, I haven't, and I don't think she has – and we don't want it. I've had a very happy life and I think the secret of a happy marriage is to stay together, to live your lives side by side. Mary and I like each other's company. We always have. That's all.

Sadly, however, the arthritis in Dick's feet was now so bad that he walked with a painful shuffle and had increasingly to use his brown Mercedes to go even short distances, and when one old friend met them again in London in the summer of 1996 he told me: 'I'm shocked by how ill Mary looks. It's the early stages of some degenerative disease. She turns round in stages. It's really serious. There is talk of this being the last novel.' Gavin Lyall agreed. 'Mary's got so many things wrong with her,' he told me in 1998, and 'I know Dick had a very close brush about 18 months ago, the side effects of some drug he was taking for arthritis. He started bleeding in the stomach and had to be rushed by plane from the Caymans to Miami.'

Dick announced that the next novel, *10-lb Penalty*, would be the last. It was conceived when he and Mary met the British Prime Minister, John Major, at a Test Match at Lord's cricket ground and he said he had read every Dick Francis book and invited them to look around 10 Downing Street. When they were ushered into the Cabinet Room they took it in turns, like awestruck children, to sit in the Premier's chair.

They celebrated their Golden Wedding anniversary, which fell on 21 June 1997, with parties before and after the date in Cayman, the Rainbow Room in New York, and Paignton, where they had a thrash at the Redcliffe Hotel with sixty guests in evening dress dancing in the ballroom, among them friends like P. D. James, Gavin Lyall and Katharine Whitehorn as well as all the family, including Doug and his wife and children. Dick wore a white tuxedo and gave Mary a diamond necklace, and in July they joined the Queen's own Golden Wedding garden party at Buckingham Palace, where four thousand couples who had married in 1947, the same year as she and Prince Philip, were served with tea, sandwiches, cake scones and fruit tartlets.

Less happily the shadow of Death was lengthening over their lives. Doug developed terminal cancer and the Princess of Wales was killed in a car crash in Paris on the night of 30 August, so that Dick and Mary cancelled the Dick Francis Steeplechase that was due to be raced at Stratford-upon-Avon the following Saturday – the day of her funeral. They went ahead, however, with the usual launch party at the Ritz 'because I know that Diana would not have wanted everyone to be miserable all the time,' Dick explained to Jan Moir of the *Daily Telegraph*. Even though he told her that he wished Mary would agree to being named on the books as co-author, he was in an unusually boastful mood. 'I wouldn't say that I am at the *top* of the authors,' he preened, 'but there are quite a few who would like to be in my position . . . maybe I haven't sold the same number of books as Tom Clancy, but *he* doesn't come out every year.' Mary gave him an old-fashioned look. 'What about Catherine Cookson?' she asked wickedly. Ms Moir was a bit naughty herself when she said in her article with brutal accuracy that Dick and Mary 'look like the kind of cherry-cheeked couple who might reply to a "Cook/Handyman Wanted" advertisement in a genteel magazine.'

That same week Dick and Mary resigned as directors of Dick Francis Films Ltd and handed the company over to Merrick and Felix, who became the sole directors, though there still seemed little chance that any more of the books would be filmed. Merrick and Felix were also joint owners of yet another company with the punning family name of Son Francisco Ltd, but by the end of 1998 it had never traded.

The Francises' visit to 10 Downing Street inspired a four-page description of the house in *10-lb Penalty*, which was dedicated to John Major as well as to their seventeen-year-old grandson, Matthew. Also seventeen was the book's hero, amateur jockey Benedict Juliard, the youngest of all the Francis heroes, who helps his father win a parliamentary by-election and later to become Prime Minister, but despite all the research details – and the inevitable Francis travelogue lecture about the inside of 10 Downing Street – the book is utterly unbelievable from start to finish. Almost every tired page exhibits yet another incredible incident or ridiculous line of dialogue. The characters are all as unlikely as their names – Orinda Nagle, Alderney Wyvern, Usher Rudd, Foster Fordham, Jill Vinicheck – and the murderous villains are merely absurd. There is far too much about the dull minutiae of politics and *10-lb Penalty* is so bad that it reads as if it were written by some semi-literate amateur trying to cobble together a desperately poor parody of a Dick Francis novel. It was the fifth book in a row to be seriously below par and T. J. Binyon gave it a savage review in the *Evening Standard*, the worst that any Dick Francis novel had ever had:

> With *10-lb Penalty*, it's sad to say, he has reached a nadir. This is undoubtedly by far the weakest of the entire *oeuvre*. It's not just that the book has less plot than the back of a cornflakes packet, villains whose villainousness could not be more obvious if they were to wear masks and striped jerseys, a device for connecting the two halves of the book so unbelievable that even Baron Munchhausen would have raised an eyebrow at it, and a portrayal of the upper echelons of political life – specifically a party at 10 Downing Street – which is not only devoid of all verisimilitude, but also hilariously and farcically ridiculous . . . Were it not for the occasional equine passage and one or two turns of phrase, it might be thought that someone had palmed off a ringer on the publisher. Fans should give this book a wide berth if they wish to retain their admiration for the author.

Mary and Dick were devastated by this brutal review and perhaps it made them decide not to write a new novel at all for 1998 but to settle for a collection of eight old and five new short stories, *Field of Thirteen*. Real life, however, was still as extraordinary as any Francis fiction. In 1997 a Newmarket trainer, Kamil Mahdi, and his fiancée were tied up and threatened by two gunmen who pretended to be racehorse owners and robbed them of jewellery and £2,000 in cash. Another Newmarket trainer, Roger Harris, and two other men were arrested after customs officials raided a horsebox and seized cannabis resin that was said to be worth more than £3 million. In October a third trainer, Luca Cumani, suffered two fires when an arsonist set the lofts of both his

Newmarket stables ablaze at night. In 1998 several British jockeys were arrested on charges involving the doping of racehorses and in London the police obtained a search warrant to raid the business premises of the leading bookmaker Victor Chandler before the warrant was quashed and Mr Chandler cleared of any involvement in doping horses. In June an American fraud and perjury case involving the mysterious death of a heavily-insured Kentucky stud-farm thoroughbred stallion opened in Texas, and in July a Press Association racing reporter, Neil Wilkins, was arrested at dawn – on suspicion of conspiracy to defraud – just a mile from Dick's childhood home at Holyport.

Back on Cayman, Dick and Mary decided to leave the Coralstone Club, where a Ritz-Carlton resort was about to be built right next door, and bought an even larger ground-floor, corner apartment, still right on Seven Mile Beach but three-quarters of a mile closer to George Town, that cost more than £1 million. Their new home was at 4 The Sovereign, a plush condominium of large, white two-storey buildings with towering white pillars, white roofs, a small swimming pool, tennis courts set amid palm trees and pretty, shady gardens with colourful shrubs and flowers, all dominated by a huge TV aerial. The Sovereign – an appropriate address for a couple who were so keen on royalty – was protected by big wrought-iron gates but there were no uniformed guards, so to deter inquisitive fans they installed huge, smoky, one-way picture windows around the verandah facing the beach and stuck up a computer-printed note on their front door that read 'PLEASE DO NOT DISTURB. Visitors for Mr and Mrs Dick Francis please see the Manager'. Inside there were fat armchairs, photographs of all the family, a large oil painting of themselves and a painting by a new friend, Carol Owen, the wife of the latest Governor of Cayman. Outside, on the other side of the main road, there was an Esso petrol station, a Burger King restaurant, and a smart parade of shops, the Galleria Plaza, that was so remarkably British that it included a small branch of Marks and Spencer, a Body Shop, the Book Nook bookshop, a dark English pub called the Pirate's Den which served Guinness and Tennants lager, and the Dickens Literary Café, where customers could read British novels and newspapers. Conveniently the liquor store sold Dick's favourite tipple, Chateauneuf du Pape, at £17 a bottle in 1999 – cheap by comparison with the huge nearby stack of bottles of Chateau Haut Brion at £286 each.

Despite the colossal prices, Cayman was becoming less and less attractive as the years went past. By 1999 the area was becoming badly over-commercialised. Too many condos and holiday apartments were being built and West Bay Road itself was constantly busy, even at 5 a.m., and often jammed with traffic in both directions. 'There are more cars here than people,' I was told by one disgruntled taxi driver. Parts of the island were filthy with litter and dumped garbage, and many pessimistic locals told me that Cayman had priced itself out of the holiday market. 'They've gone too far already,' said one senior official. 'They've killed the golden goose.' John Jefferson, a Member of the Cayman Legislative Assembly, warned the authorities during a debate in March 1999 that the growing 'concrete jungle' along Seven Mile Beach was deterring tourists and that business in some restaurants had fallen by 50 per cent in a year. Yet in the same week plans were announced for a five-storey, 231-room Holiday Inn on Seven Mile Beach to add to six other beachfront sites that had already been earmarked for large new developments. The greed of Grand Cayman became so blind and blatant that when the British TV interviewer Alan Whicker arrived in January 1999 with a camera crew to spend a week filming a documentary about Dick, the authorities made him buy six temporary work permits and charged him £2,000 even though the programme would be shown all over the world and would be an excellent advertisement for the island. Whicker's director swore that he would never shoot another film in Cayman. If Dick and Mary had been younger they too might have started to think about leaving. Grand Cayman was no longer paradise.

In July Dick telephoned Doug to arrange to see him in England the following Tuesday. 'I don't think I'll be here,' Doug said, and two days later he was dead. He was eighty-two. 'I'm not sad for him because he wanted to die,' Dick told Lynda Lee-Potter of the *Daily Mail* a few weeks later. 'He was in great pain. Just before he died he said to me: "Oh gosh, I wish they'd take me." It's brought death a little closer.' The *Daily Telegraph* published a long, affectionate obituary, describing Doug as a popular and 'distinguished figure in the racing world in his own right'. It also reported that he had once admitted that, although Dick always sent him a copy of each new novel, 'so far I haven't read a line of any of them.' He had always said quite openly that Dick had never been able to write, so why read the books?

Despite Doug's death, that summer's family gathering at the Redcliffe Hotel in Paignton needed fifteen rooms – on one evening twenty-two of them sat down to dinner – and Dick told Lynda Lee-Potter: 'I have to keep writing to pay for them all.' He said yet again that he and Mary were 'very much in love. We always kiss before we go to sleep and in the morning, too. In the Caymans we've got a water bed, which is lovely. If you're energetic in bed you can hear the water moving.' It was strange that he made such crass, intimate remarks to almost every interviewer when he claimed at the same time that he liked to protect his privacy.

Doug was only the latest of Dick and Mary's circle to be stricken by the years. In July Michael Dennison also died at the age of eighty-two, just months after he and his wife, Dulcie Gray, had holidayed with the Francises in Cayman, and in September Dick visited Fred Winter, now sadly laid low by a stroke, in Lambourn. For the first time in thirty-four years there was no new Francis novel in the shops for Christmas and when the *Field of Thirteen* collection of short stories was published in September the reviewers were not impressed. In the *Sunday Times* Stephen

Amidon described them as 'bland' and 'naggingly perfunctory' and David Meilton in *The Times* asked:

> Is it time that Dick Francis was put out to pasture? . . . The stamina certainly appears to be running out. Some of these tales sport characters and plots which are scarcely more than perfunctory and use the sort of descriptive wordiness which would not have been tolerated in the halcyon years.

Meilton's predecessor as *The Times*'s crime fiction reviewer, H. R. F. Keating, agreed that it was time to stop writing. 'The stories were *appalling*,' he told me. Most brutal of all was T. J. Binyon – again – in the *Evening Standard*:

> All thirteen stories are horrendously, woefully bad. They manage to break every single rule governing the writing of the short story – often all of them simultaneously. The settings are unrealistic, the characters unbelievable, the narration is either simplistic or incoherent, the story usually pointless, the approach often cloyingly sentimental, and the sting in the tail either absent or bathetically obvious . . . The real mystery is why these stories, written between 1970 and the present – a period during which Dick Francis produced some outstanding novels – should be so bad.

Sadly the critics were right. Most of the stories were indeed thin and atrociously written, and they read as if they were composed by someone utterly unused to writing fiction. It was undoubtedly time to retire, and someone at Michael Joseph or Putnam should have insisted on it if they cared about their author's reputation, but the Francis fiction factory clanked wearily on, churning out dud after golden dud. In 1998 Cayman narrowly missed being devastated by Hurricane Mitch. The waves outside their apartment on Seven Mile Beach were a terrifying 30ft high and inspired the thirty-seventh novel, *Second Wind*. Its hero, Perry Stuart, who was based on the British TV weatherman John Kettley, is a famous British TV meteorologist whose calm life is turned upside down when he finds himself chasing a Caribbean hurricane in a small aeroplane and landing on a remote Caribbean island that was based on a real island, Swan Island, a tiny speck of land about two hundred miles south-west of Cayman and a hundred miles off the coast of Honduras. Genuine Dick Francis fans prayed that the book would be the last.

Despite the dreadful reviews, *Field of Thirteen* went as usual to the top of the fiction bestseller lists and a first edition of *Dead Cert* was sold for £1,955 at the Bloomsbury Book Auctions in London, but in an interview with Rodney Masters of the *Racing Post* Dick admitted that it was time to quit. Mary was now very fat – 'asthma does constrict the chest,' Gwen Butler told me – and having to trundle around in a red electric golf buggy, and Dick's arthritis was so bad that he had become decidedly doddery and was using a walking stick. He was also increasingly deaf and muddled. In November he embarrassed his audience when he made a speech at a *Reader's Digest* Condensed Books lunch in London and told the same story – about an adulterous vicar – that he had told at a similar occasion two years previously. There was another awkward moment at Newbury races at the end of November when Dick was due to present the Hennessy Gold Cup but was upstaged at the last minute by the Queen Mother, who turned up unexpectedly and announced that she would present the cup herself. In the end they did it together and Dick was mollified by being invited to watch the race with her in the royal box.

But another unusual accolade came in December when the BBC's *Desert Island Discs* broadcast a second radio interview with Dick, a rare honour previously granted only to the actor

Sir Donald Sinden and the comedian Arthur Askey. This time he was interviewed by Sue Lawley and chose three of the same tunes that he had picked thirty-one years earlier (*Chattanooga Choo Choo*, *Oh What a Beautiful Morning* and *I Left My Heart in San Francisco*) as well as five new ones, among them Gershwin's *Rhapsody in Blue* (because he had loved listening to it on the radio as a child), Jeremiah Clarke's *Trumpet Voluntary* (because it reminded him of his trumpet-playing twelve-year-old grandson William), the overture from the film *Lawrence of Arabia*, and Kathleen Battle singing *Summertime*. But the song that stole the show was a poignant rendering of *Angel*, the haunting title track from the film *City of Angels*, which was beautifully sung by Dick's eighteen-year-old granddaughter Bianca, who had recently left school, hoped to become a singer, and had recorded the song at the Redcliffe Hotel that summer.

'If I had to choose only one song,' Dick told Sue Lawley, 'I'd take *Chattanooga Choo Choo*. I do enjoy that. It's always called my signature tune,' and he confessed yet again that he derived little pleasure from writing: 'I'd rather be a jockey any day. Writing to me is hard mental work. I've been a physical character all my life rather than a mental character.' Is it really possible to say such a thing after writing forty books? As for his luxury, he picked his water bed, and the book he chose was *Men and Horses I Have Known* by the Hon. George Lambton, published in 1924. Lambton, a jockey who had set up as a trainer in Newmarket in 1892, reminisced in his book about great Victorian and Edwardian racing men such as Fred Archer, Lord Rosebery, Lord Derby and King Edward VII and devoted four pages to a subject close to the heart of so many Dick Francis thrillers: doping. Lambton reported that doping horses with cocaine had started in America and that by 1900 'this horrible practice' had become 'a serious menace to horse-racing' and by 1903 'it had become a scandal'. He wrote: 'One constantly saw horses who were notorious rogues running and winning as if they were possessed of the devil, with eyes starting out of their heads and the sweat pouring off them.' Eventually doping was made a criminal offence, but even so, Lambton reported in 1924, 'some people think there is a great deal going on now.'

So who said the Dick Francis books are far-fetched? Right up to the end of the century the racing scandals continued. In January 1998 the jockeys Leighton Aspell, Dean Gallagher and Jamie Osborne were arrested in connection with alleged doping and race-fixing. Soon afterwards four regular racing punters were arrested, followed over a few months by six more. In January 1999 the jockeys Graham Bradley and Ray Cochrane and the ex-trainer Charlie Brooks were also arrested on similar charges, bringing the total number of suspects fingered in a year to sixteen. Several of them, including Aspell, Osborne and Brooks, were soon exonerated but Bradley appeared in the dock at Bow Street magistrates court in April charged with deliberately losing a two-horse race at Warwick, before he too was completely exonerated in June and the case against him was dropped. Five other men were also charged with doping horses. Nothing much had changed in a hundred years and the Hon. George Lambton would not have been at all surprised.

Weighed In

Dick's fame in 1999 was greater than ever. By now the novels had sold more than sixty million copies in thirty-five languages, including Basque and Korean, and in a debate in the House of Lords about the extent of corruption in racing Lord Rowallan suggested that fraud investigators had 'been reading too many Dick Francis novels.'

But how good were the books? Eleven were very good indeed: *Odds Against*, *Forfeit*, *Risk*, *Whip Hand*, *Reflex*, *Banker*, *The Danger*, *Proof*, *Hot Money*, *Straight*, *Longshot*; subtle, sinewy thrillers that stand comparison with those of any other writer of twentieth-century adventure stories and that justify the amount of attention that literary scholars were giving them. In 1998 yet another American academic, Rachel Schaffer, Professor of English and Philosophy at Montana State University, wrote a long study of the Francis *oeuvre* in the first volume of an encyclopaedia entitled *Mystery and Suspense Writers*, and her assessment is particularly relevant because Dick had admitted so often that most of the Dick Francis heroes were based on himself. She noted that most Francis heroes

> are loners . . . with serious doubts about their ability
> to resolve the problems they face . . . They are often
> emotionally reserved, keeping the depth of their feelings

to themselves to such an extent that others often consider them cold. They are also modest to a fault and cultivate their underestimation by others.

Professor Schaffer went on: 'The vast majority of Francis' protagonists also bear a variety of emotional or physical burdens of some kind, private fears and tragedies.' And she added:

> His style, tone, wit, humor, and phrasing skills show an innate talent for writing that is all the more surprising in a man who left school at age fifteen . . . Francis is the first to give credit to his wife for her editing help, but it is his unique voice that emerges from the process.

Oddly, though, despite such widespread praise, few of Dick and Mary's friends enjoyed reading the books, not even the writers. 'They've been doing virtually the same thing for forty years,' I was told by Gavin Lyall, who rated the author of the books as no more than 'a good, middle-ranking writer who's found a niche and developed it. It's not really my cup of tea,' he said. 'I get restless.' Gwen Butler was another author friend who did not enjoy the books. 'I didn't read them because it's just not my sort of thing at all,' she said. Mary Youll agreed: 'I must confess that had I not known Mary and Dick it is not really the type of book I would ever read,' she said.

As for the philosophy behind the books, Lyall quoted his wife Katharine Whitehorn: 'There's something that Kath said about them which I think is true: that they postulate a happy, contented world into which crime is an intrusion, a Land of Lost Content, whereas so many crime writers – myself included – take a much more cynical view of the world.' He concluded with a bizarre summing-up that could only be made by a professional novelist. Even though he had known them for years, he said, 'if I were putting Dick and Mary into a book I'd want to know a lot more about them. With a fictional character I'd have to give them something, some extra thing, to make them credible. You feel that there's a dimension missing.'

Others were prepared simply to accept Dick and Mary at face value. 'They're just two very nice people with two very nice sons,' Kath Walwyn told me. 'Dick's just a lovely person, always fair, and would never say anything nasty about anyone. They're completely bound up in themselves.' Alan Brooke agreed: 'One was always struck by the intensity of their marriage.' And Margaret Yorke told me: 'They're a marvellous couple because they are such a couple.' So what has made it such a solid marriage for more than half a century? 'I think there is this inter-dependence,' Elaine Mellor suggested, 'because Mary had polio and has been a semi-invalid all her life.'

'When you get something like that it tends to bind people,' Stan Mellor said. 'And Dick's a carer, really.'

Mrs Mellor said:

> The overall picture of Dick is that he's definitely a gentleman, a loner. He has his principles and he's a great family man: he cares desperately about each and every one of his family, which is very expensive now. If I say that Dick is a gentleman, a great family man, not a drinker, it makes him sound very dull in a way, but he's not dull at all. You can talk to him about anything and everything. After all this research he's done for his books it's made him progressively more interesting – an educated person, if you like. He's definitely someone whose character has built up.

Stan Mellor nodded. 'He's definitely ten times the man now as he was when he was riding, as a person. He's a man of the world.'

'He's definitely got a certain charm,' added his wife. 'He's a ladies' man. My mum, who would be about Dick's age, always found him very attractive. And sexy. I heard that many years ago from Sue, his niece. That's exactly what she said: sexy. Maybe that's why Mary's had to sit down all day!'

She roared with laughter.

In the end almost everyone who ever knew Dick and Mary agreed how nice, kind and loving they both are. 'I met him in the late fifties and have admired and adored him ever since,' Lord Oaksey told me. 'The thing I most admire is that he is exactly the same now as he was when I first met him. He is the most unchanged by success man that I have ever known.' One admirable trait is that the Francises are scrupulous about keeping up with old friends, even those whose lives are humble by comparison. Mary Youll and Les Foster are still receiving Christmas cards from them in 1998 and Mr Foster told me at his little house in Aston Tirrold: 'Dick calls every year when he's over. He keeps up with his old friends. He calls on an old friend in the village too, Mrs Morgan, who always came to his parties, and he sends us both a signed copy of each new novel every year.'

'Dick's charm consists in effacing himself in a way,' Gwen Butler told me. 'He's not dull: he's gentle. And Mary's not personally ambitious, which is reflected in the way she's worked with Dick. Perhaps she's spread herself too far, but they love each other. It's as simple as that.'

Towards the end of his life Dick is haunted still by the Devon Loch fiasco and at the end of the third edition of his autobiography he wrote wistfully that he still mourned that he never won the Grand National. And then, almost as a throwaway afterthought, the book concluded with a whimsical question wondering what it might have been like to be Shakespeare.

Shakespeare? Dick would never have had any wish at all to be Shakespeare: he hated writing. But Mary would: Mary, the Dark Lady of the Secrets, would have loved to be an acclaimed writer, perhaps a playwright. So maybe that is her own last regret, not Dick's. That she never wrote a series of books under her own name. That she, who loved the theatre so much, never heard the applause of an audience for her work, never made all those speeches, or signed all those books for admiring fans, or gave all those interviews, or won the OBE herself or the Cartier Diamond Dagger or became a Mystery Writers Grand Master. Regrets, she must have a few, for a woman of all her talents, energy and industry. At times she must have wondered at the cruel irony of it all, that Dick, who loathed writing, should have become so famous for it, and that she, who loved it, should be unknown.

But then people said that Shakespeare's writing was all the work of somebody else: the Earl of Oxford or Francis Bacon or Christopher Marlowe. But could Shakespeare, Oxford, Bacon or Marlowe ever have jumped all thirty Grand National fences at Aintree? Not just once, but three times, as Dick had done? Could any of them have ridden 345 winners, or become Champion Jockey? So in the end why should either Dick or Mary have any regrets at all? For Dick Francis was a great horseman, and 'Dick Francis' at best a brilliant writer of thrillers – and that should be quite enough for at least two lifetimes.

ACKNOWLEDGEMENTS

For their generosity in giving me interviews, photographs or guidance I am especially grateful to Frankie Arkle, Flo and Percy Arrowsmith, Larry Ashmead, Martin Benson, Maureen Bolden, Christopher (*né* Geoffrey) Bond, Peter Brenchley, Alan Brooke, Ed Burlingame, Gwen Butler, Beryl Caink, Euan Cameron, Frank Clark, Kitty Cole, Mabel Coppins, Leslie Cramphorn, Jack Crawshaw, Colin Cutler, Margaret Davies, Peter Day, Frank Delaney, Hazel and Jane Dexter, Paula Diamond, Dave Dick, Dick Douglas-Boyd, Jack Dowdeswell, Andrew Edwards, Elizabeth Ellett, Tim Fitzgeorge-Parker, Tom Forrest, Keith and Les Foster, Kathleen Gale, Karen Geary, Margaret Giles, Joan Ginger, Elizabeth Gossage, Phyllis Grace, Eddie and Joyce Greenslade, Terry Hall, Philippa Harrison, Harriet Hastings, Tim Heald, Joan Hearne, Jean Heath, Vernon Heaver, Geoffrey Hebdon, Joan Hewitt, Susan Hill, Gus Hines, Alan Hoby, John Hodges, Roy Hole, Gene Hudack, P. D. James, Pete Johnson, Olivia Kahn, H. R. F. Keating, John Keller, Jim Kinlay, John Kirby, Peggy Kirby, Margaret Lindsay, Jonathan Lloyd, Peter Lord, Mel Lucas, Gavin Lyall, Avril May, Elaine and Stan Mellor, David Merriman, Gwendoline Morley-Mower, Michael Morris, Peggy Munday, Mike Murphy, Sheila Murphy, Edith Nicol, Lord Oaksey, Luke Over, Edie Owen, Jane Owen, Roy Palmer, Jane Paoli, Philip Pedley, Jonathan Powell, Nancy Powell, Honor Preston, Sheila Read, John Redman, Jane Richards, Peter Samuel, Jean Saynor, Alan Scott, Lee and Sue Shaffer, Alison Shrubsole, Margaret Spencer, John Stephen, Steve Taylor, Evelyn Thomas,

Raleigh Trevelyan, Brian Uzzell, Les Vanter, Ursula Walker, Tom Wallace, Kath Walwyn, Ruth Williams, Richard Woolmer, Margaret Yorke, Mary Youll and Mel Zerman.

For help with specialist research I am deeply grateful to Sophie Badham of the Royal Holloway College Archives, where letters from former Holloway students Lucy Ben-Levi, Gillian Harris and Charmian Humphreys were particularly useful; Maurice Baird-Smith, DFC; the Bank of England Press Office; Margaret Clark of the Miltonian Guild; Margaret Davies of Sutton Girls' High School; Brian MacArthur; John McEntee; Henry Macrory; Fred McMillan of the RAF Aircrew Association; Steve Pickles of Royal Holloway College; Dominic Prince and Diverse Productions; Mike Toner; and Joe Wojak of HarperCollins in New York.

I am especially indebted to the following libraries and archives centres: the magnificent British Library at St Pancras in London; the New York public libraries; *The Times*, *Express*, *Daily Mail*, Press Association, and *Time* magazine cuttings libraries; Kate Fassett of the *Daily Telegraph* library; Tony Beard of the *New York Times* library; Bob Isaacs of the *Sun-Sentinel* Editorial Research Department in Fort Lauderdale; Diana Uzzell and the staff of the *Caymanian Compass* in Grand Cayman; the Congregational Library at Gordon Square in London; the Kingston Heritage Centre; the Berkshire, Cheshire, Devon, Hereford, Pembrokeshire and Surrey Record Offices; the City of Westminster Archives Centre; the public libraries of Haverfordwest, Maidenhead and Wokingham; Barnstaple Local Studies library; and Kathleen Shawcross of the Heritage Service at Sutton Central library.

I found a great deal of useful information in many newspapers, particularly the *Sunday Express* and *Daily Express* as well as *The Times*, *Sunday Times*, *Daily Telegraph*, *Sunday Telegraph*, *Evening Standard*, *Evening News*, *Guardian*, *Daily Mail*, *Mail on Sunday*, *Daily Mirror*, *News of the World*, *Independent*, *Independent on Sunday*, *Today*, the *People*, and the *Racing Post*. Other valuable sources were the *Armchair Detective*, the BBC, the *Caymanian Compass*, *Cayman Executive*, *Crawley Observer*, *Country Life*, *Evening News*, *Evening Standard*, *Maidenhead Advertiser*, *Miami Herald*, *Hereford Citizen and Bulletin*, *Hereford Times*, the *Sun*, the Fort Lauderdale *Sun-Sentinel*, the *Observer*, *Washington Post*, *Western Telegraph* and *Wales on Sunday* and the magazines *You*, *Sunday Express Magazine*, *Sunday Times Magazine*, *Telegraph Weekend Magazine*, *Country Life*, *Erinna Magazine*, *Hello!*, *In Britain*, *The Miltonian*, *The Miltonian Guild 100 Centenary Issue*, *Miltonian News Sheet*, the *New Yorker*, *Newsagent and Bookshop*, *Newsweek*, *OK!*, *Pembrokeshire Life*, *The Pembrokeshire Magazine*, *People*, *Sports Illustrated*, *Sutton High School Magazine*, *Times Literary Supplement*, *TV Times*, *Wentworth Milton Mount Magazine* and *Woman and Home*.

I read of course all the Dick Francis books: *The Sport of Queens* (Michael Joseph, 1957; Pan Books, 1995), *Lester: The Official Biography* (Michael Joseph, 1986); the short story collection *Field of Thirteen* (Michael Joseph, 1998); *Great Racing Stories* edited by Dick Francis and John Welcome (Bellew Publishing, 1989); *Classic Lines: More Great Racing Stories* edited by Dick Francis and John Welcome (Bellew Publishing, 1991); and the thirty-six Francis novels published before 1999, all by Michael Joseph: *Dead Cert* (1962), *Nerve* (1964), *For Kicks* (1965), *Odds Against* (1965), *Flying Finish* (1966), *Blood Sport* (1967), *Forfeit* (1968), *Enquiry* (1969), *Rat Race* (1970), *Bonecrack* (1971), *Smoke Screen* (1972), *Slay-Ride* (1973), *Knock Down* (1974), *High Stakes* (1975), *In the Frame* (1976), *Risk* (1977), *Trial Run* (1978), *Whip Hand* (1979), *Reflex* (1980), *Twice Shy* (1981), *Banker* (1982), *The Danger* (1983), *Proof* (1984), *Break In* (1985), *Bolt* (1986), *Hot Money* (1987), *The Edge* (1988), *Straight* (1989), *Longshot* (1990), *Comeback* (1991), *Driving Force* (1992), *Decider* (1993), *Wild Horses* (1994), *Come to Grief* (1995), *To the Hilt* (1996), *10-lb Penalty* (1997).

And finally the following books were invaluable:

Hendrik Baker, *Stage Management and Theatrecraft: A Stage Manager's Handbook* (J. Garnett Miller, 1968)

Earl F. Bargainnier (ed.) *Twelve Englishmen of Mystery* (Bowling Green University Popular Press, 1984)

Melvyn Barnes, *Dick Francis* (Ungar, 1986)

Trevor Barrett and Miles Cowsill, *Pembrokeshire* (Lily Publications, 1998)

Beacham's Popular Fiction (Beacham Publishing Inc., 1991)

Tony Benn, *Years of Hope: Diaries, Letters and Papers 1940–1962*, edited by Ruth Winstone (Hutchinson, 1994)

H. Bergel, *Flying Wartime Aircraft* (David and Charles, 1972)

Cyril Bertram Mills, *Bertram Mills Circus* (Hutchinson, 1967)

Caroline Bingham, *The History of Royal Holloway College 1886–1986* (Constable, 1987)

Martin Bowman, *Wellington: The Geodetic Giant* (Airlife, 1989)

Chaz Bowyer, *The Wellington Bomber* (William Kimber, 1986)

Chaz Bowyer, *Wellington at War* (Ian Allan, 1982)

Sarah Bradford, *Elizabeth: A Biography of Her Majesty the Queen* (Heinemann, 1996)

Shaan Butters, *The Book of Kingston* (Baron, 1995)

CADW: Welsh Historic Monuments: Martletwy (1997)

Teresa Carlysle, *Wentworth College: A History* (Wentworth College, 1997)

John C. Carr, *The Craft of Crime* (Houghton Mifflin, 1983)

Diana Cooper-Clark, *Designs of Darkness* (Bowling Green State University Popular Press, 1983)

Mabel Coppins, *Beyond the Village Green* (New Horizon, 1983)

J. Madison Davis, *Dick Francis* (Twayne, 1989)

John Elliott, *Palaces, Patronage and Pills* (Royal Holloway, 1996)

David M. Evans, *One Hundred Not Out: A History of Desborough School* (Desborough School, 1994)

Frank Foster, *Pink Coat, Spangles and Sawdust* (Stanley Paul, 1948)

Mary Francis, *The Beginner's Guide to Flying* (Pelham, 1969)

Mary Francis, *Flying Start: A Guide to Flying Light Aircraft* (Pelham, 1980)

Bryony Fuller, *Dick Francis: Steeplechase Jockey* (Michael Joseph, 1994)

Nat Gould, *Banker and Broker* (John Long, 1893)

Nat Gould, *A Dead Certainty* (John Long, 1900)

Nat Gould, *Warned Off* (John Long, 1901)

Nat Gould, *A Bird in Hand* (Readers' Library Publishing, 1908)

Nat Gould, *The Magic of Sport* (John Long, 1909)

Nat Gould, *The Stolen Racer* (John Long, 1909)

Nat Gould, *The Head Lad* (John Long, 1913)

Nat Gould, *The Steeplechaser* (John Long, 1918)

Nat Gould, *A Turf Conspiracy* (John Long, 1919)

Nat Gould, *At Starting Price* (John Long, 1920)

Nat Gould, *The Racing Adventures of Barry Bromley* (John Long, 1926)

Nat Gould, *The Exploits of a Racecourse Detective* (John Long, 1927)

Reg Green, *A Race Apart: The History of the Grand National* (Hodder and Stoughton, 1988)

John Grisham, *The Firm* (Century, 1991)

Hilda Harwood, *The History of Milton Mount College* (Independent Press Ltd, 1959)

Sir Geoffrey de Havilland, *Sky Fever* (Airlife, 1979)

Myra Hayles and Beryl Hedges, *Around Maidenhead in Old Photographs* (Alan Sutton, 1994)

Myra Hayles and David Hedges, *Maidenhead in Old Photographs* (Alan Sutton, 1992)

Hereford: City of the Marches (Hereford City Council Leisure Services, 1997)

Anne Holland, *Grand National: An Official Celebration* (Queen Anne Press, 1991)

Michael Joseph Ltd, *At the Sign of the Mermaid* (Michael Joseph, 1986)

Kelly's Directories of Berkshire 1928 and 1931; Maidenhead and Taplow 1929–1930; Berkshire, Buckinghamshire and Oxfordshire

1935; Bayswater and Paddington 1939; Devon and Cornwall 1939

Hon. George Lambton, *Men and Horses I Have Known* (Eyre and Spottiswoode, 1924)

Margaret Lane, *Edgar Wallace* (Hamish Hamilton, 1964)

Lawrenny National School Attendance Register

Lawrenny School Log Book

John and Rosemary Lee, *Wokingham: A Pictorial History* (Phillimore, 1990)

Charles A. Lindbergh, *The Spirit of St Louis* (John Murray, 1953)

Living in the Cayman Islands (Cayman Islands Government Information Services, 1998)

Elizabeth Longford, *The Queen Mother* (Weidenfeld and Nicolson, 1981)

Stephen Lowe, *Arthur Lowe: A Life* (Nick Hern Books, 1996)

Pat Lucas, *Fifty Years of Racing at Chepstow* (H. G. Walters, 1976)

Lyn Publicity Association, *A Guide to Lynton and Lynmouth* (Lyn Publicity Association)

Maidenhead County Boys' School Minutes, 1926–1933

Milton Mount Board of Management Minutes, 1931–1941

Milton Mount Board of Management Annual Reports, 1930–1941

Hugh Morgan, *By the Seat of Your Pants* (Newton, 1990)

Harold Nicolson, *Diaries and Letters 1945–62*, edited by Nigel Nicolson (Collins, 1968)

Peter Northeast, *This Venerable Village* (Blewbury Local History Group, 1981)

Luke Over and Chris Tyrrell, *The Royal Hundred of Bray* (Cliveden Press, 1993)

Ben Pimlott, *The Queen: A Biography of Elizabeth II* (HarperCollins, 1996)

George Plumptre, *Back Page Racing: A Century of Newspaper Coverage* (MacDonald Queen Anne Press, 1989)

Tony Richardson, *Long Distance Runner* (Faber & Faber, 1993)

Royal Holloway College Letter (November 1943 and November 1944)

Derek Salberg, *A Mixed Bag* (Cortney Publications, 1983)

Derek Salberg, *My Love Affair With a Theatre* (Cortney Publications, 1978)

C. Martin Sharp, *D.H.: A History of de Havilland* (Airlife, 1982)

Edward Sims, *The Fighter Pilots* (Cassell, 1967)

Horace Smith, *A Horseman Through Six Reigns: Reminiscences of a Royal Riding Master* (Odhams Press, 1955)

Fleur Speakman, *Chester* (Jarrold, 1995)

Julian Symons, *Bloody Murder: From the Detective Story to the Crime Novel: A History* (Faber & Faber, 1972)

Godfrey Talbot, *The Country Life Book of Queen Elizabeth the Queen Mother* (Country Life, 1978)

H. A. Taylor, *Test Pilot at War* (Ian Allan, 1970)

The 1999 Rates and Facts Guide to the Cayman Islands (Cayman Islands Department of Tourism, 1999)

John Travis, *Lynton and Lynmouth: Glimpses of the Past* (Breedon Books, 1997)

D. B. Tubbs, *The Lancaster Bomber* (Pan/Ballantine, 1972)

J. Wesley Walker, *A History of Maidenhead* (Thames Valley Press, 1971)

Gerald Wasley, *Devon at War 1939–1945* (Devon Books, 1994)

Richard Williams, *Royal Holloway College: A Pictorial History* (Royal Holloway College, 1993)

Robin W. Winks (ed.), *Mystery and Suspense Writers, Vol 1* (Charles Scribner's Sons, 1998)

Wokingham: A Chronology (The Wokingham Society, 1987)

Your Guide to the Tax-Free Cayman Islands (Century 21, 1999)

Philip Ziegler, *King Edward VIII* (Collins, 1990)

INDEX

DF = Dick Francis; MF = Mary Francis.